HERITAGE FINDINGS FROM ATLANTIS

BOOK III of the
GALACTIC SALESMAN TRILOGY

written by
Robert S. Sanders, Jr.

illustrations by
Mark J. Volzer

color cover art created by
Martin A. Enticknap

proofread and edited by
Paul Wulfsberg

illustrations by
Mark J. Volzer

color cover art created by
Martin A. Enticknap
copyright © May 2000 Martin A. Enticknap

cover design, typography and text production:
Parris Graphics and Printing
Murfreesboro, TN

Library of Congress Catalog Card Number: 00-91013

ISBN: 1-928798-01-2

type: young adult, science fiction adventure

Armstrong Valley Publishing Company
P.O. Box 1275
Murfreesboro, TN 37133-1275
Phone: 615-895-5445
Fax: 615-893-2688

printed in the United States of America

Table of Contents

The galactic station as originally conceived by Martin A. Enticknap
copyright © May 2000 Martin A. Enticknap

This novel is dedicated to Chispo, Rinto and Fraxino from Zotola on the planet around the star Al Nitak in the Orion star system. For their existence in their reality, I write this story for them. I wish I knew them in real life.

Introduction and Character Sketch

This novel is the continuation of *Mission Beyond the Ice Cave: Atlantis-Mexico-Zotola,* and is the third novel of the Galactic Salesman trilogy. Having completed their mission of eliminating the mysterious communications block in the mountains of northern Mexico, the teenagers return to Al Nitak in the Orion star system with their lively friends: Rinto, Fraxino, and Chispo in their Velosa cruiser craft. They examine more holographic plates, revisit the ancient galactic dump site, and find another bronze crate filled with . . .

Rinto, Fraxino, and Chispo are descendants of the people of Atlantis, and they live in a city called Zantaayer, Zotola, a beautiful clean city nestled within the Ciruclar Mountains. Their society is on the same level of technological advancement as their cousins on Earth. However, the air is crisp and clear because there are no fossil fuels used, since they never had a coal age.

Rinto and Fraxino Zapatero are wizards, to say the least, and they have an uncanny ability to interpret crystals, grow them, and harness their knowledge and intelligence to operate their Velosa cruiser craft and their crystal base computer system. They also have a secret lab in a cave deep within the Ciruclar Mountains.

Chispo Colancha is a lively character, always full of spark and enthusiasm, as his name suggests. He is Rinto and Fraxino's nearby neighbor and good friend, and he is involved in Rinto and Fraxino's projects, as well.

Tom, the galactic salesman, comes forth with another mission, this one the grandest of them all. He sends the teenagers to the high mountain reaches of northern Alaska where the Galactic Federation is overseeing a major 15-year galactic station project, to involve literally millions of Earth's telephone numbers, and to be built deep within Mt. Isto. By chance, they unearth five bronze crates, each containing a time frozen body . . . from Atlantis! Can they revive them?

Find out the true reasons for the galactic dump site and why the holographic plates were dumped there. Discover more revelations about trees and plants, from sacred stories, holographic plates, and the Atlanteans. Venture with them as they help Tom and his crew in building the galactic station in Alaska, what it features, from adventures, to time travel, and how it . . .

EXCERPT

"We came across what looked like the corner of a bronze crate."

"Really? A bronze crate?" Rinto now asked in disbelief.

"That's right," Tom replied, "and when we removed the dirt away from it with our ice picks that we had with us, we pried the lid off of it."

"I'll bet you found another box of holographic plates from Atlantis," Steven guessed.

"No, they weren't holographic plates, like you fellows found here," Tom informed them. "What we found when we removed the lid was a frozen body . . . time frozen, that is."

"Is that *right*?" Steven responded, no doubt surprised.

"You're kidding!" Robert responded.

Everyone showed surprise, and feelings of excitement ran through them.

"I take it the body is from Atlantis?" Morris asked Tom.

"Caymar and I believe it is, but we know of no means to revive the body nor how to unlock the time freeze. That's why we haven't told the Galactic Federation about it. We don't know how many more of these bodies there are. Caymar and I hid the crate and re-covered it with dirt right away. That's why I've come to you all about this. Maybe one or more of you have or know of some techniques to unlock the time freeze and revive this body or bodies, depending on how many more you all might find.

"I feel like it's very important to revive them, and I feel sure there must be several of these time frozen bodies buried among those mountain slopes. There's no telling what vital information they may have and what they can tell us about the region, why they were placed there, and what they can tell us about soul travel and galactic communication, in addition to their knowledge of their past culture, and possible knowledge about time travel."

"Time travel," Chispo responded. "That is far out!"

"That's right," Tom confirmed. "If you fellows can find and revive......

PROLOGUE

It was a bright sunny day in the remote high mountains of northeastern Alaska. Though it was mid summer, the climate was still somewhat cold, sometimes with strong biting winds. The rugged terrain was treeless, and arctic tundra covered much of the land that wasn't still occupied by snow and glaciers.

The time was late July, 1985, and at this time of year, there was continuous daylight since they were north of the Arctic Circle at a latitude of 69° north.

Tom, the galactic salesman from Sirius B, and his close friend Caymar were here on assignment from the Galactic Federation. The location of the assignment was in a remote valley tucked between three high, snow-covered and jagged peaks: Mt. Chamberlin, Mt. Michelson, and Mt. Isto, two of which towered at more than 9,000 feet. The continental divide lay only a few miles to the south, and the Arctic Ocean was only 50 miles to the north.

At this time of year, some of the snow had melted, and there were plenty of streams and alpine lakes in the valley. Reindeer, Caribou, and other wildlife could be seen at times grazing on the tundra. Mosquitos had been rampant earlier this summer, having hatched by the millions from the melting snow, but their rampage had nearly passed, and they would know the rest of the summer without those annoying pests.

Tom had yet to break the news of his sudden and recent assignment to Robert Joslin and his friends, who had just completed helping him and the Galactic Federation clear a communication block to the Orion star system. He had plans of first telling Morris who he knew had recently accompanied Robert and his friends to Zotola on planet Artenia around the star Al Nitak.

Tom and Caymar had been sent to investigate the remote, rugged terrain of northeastern Alaska's mountains as a possible site for a 15-year major project of building a secret intergalactic switching station to be hidden deep within the mountains. It would be the equivalent of literally millions of telephone lines.

Over the next fifteen years, secret plans would be made and agreements made with top government officials of planet Earth. Undercover accommodations would be made underground for protection and security purposes. In subtle and unrecognized ways, millions of Earth's telephone numbers would be made available, all in preparation for the switching station's grand opening at the turn of the millennium. Numerous star systems across the galaxy would be connected to the grand switching station, and many of Earth's residents would realize means and ways of communication that they would never have dreamed of. Funds would also be generated by "Universal Service Funds" and hidden charges such as "Universal Connectivity Charges" and "Carrier Line Charges."

This was to be one of the Galactic Federation's largest communication projects ever, and Tom and his crew were looking forward to soon getting started.

For the moment, Tom's crew was still on Sirius B. He and Caymar were walking the western slopes of Mt. Isto and were talking over the possibilities as to where to locate the entrances and exits for the underground tunnels.

As they came to a stream, Tom pointed upwards. "Caymar, take a look at that ridge on the slopes of the mountain above us," he told his friend in the native Sirian language.

"Yes, I see where you're referring to," Caymar responded in Sirian.

"That would be a grand location for one of the tunnels," Tom suggested.

"Yes, I agree. All of the switching equipment could reside within the mountain." Caymar pointed to the left. "Down there on that flat section of plateau, we could install the receiver/transmitter towers. It's above the valley floor, and snow and glaciers won't affect them there."

"That's a good point, Caymar," Tom agreed.

As they continued walking the mountain slopes which were wet from snow melt, they talked over the locations of the other tunnels. They looked to their west. The views of Mt. Michelson with Mt. Chamberlin further off were magnificent.

Caymar pointed to Mt. Michelson. "It's going to take years to excavate the necessary tunnels to accommodate the switching equipment."

"It's all in good time, anyway," Tom calmly responded. "We have fifteen years until the turn of the millennium."

"That point is true," Caymar acknowledged.

"Let's walk down to that flat area," Tom suggested, "and see how feasible it is for the receiver/transmitter towers."

The two of them descended the wet slopes of the mountain, sometimes crossing snowfields and small glaciers. They came across a small ridge that was above the snow.

Suddenly, Caymar stopped.

"What . . . What is it?" Tom asked him.

"I suddenly received a strange feeling." Then Caymar saw something sticking out of the ground. He walked over to it, followed by Tom.

"What have we here?" Tom expressed with enthusiasm rising. "It's a metal object."

"It looks like the corner of a large box," Caymar commented. He reached for it. "This is really unique!"

"Dig the dirt away from it," Tom directed. "This has really got my curiosity up."

The two of them raked the loose, wet dirt away with their hands, and they used surrounding rocks and also their ice picks to help them. It wasn't long before they had unearthed what appeared to be a coffin or crate made of bronze metal. Feelings of excitement and enthusiasm ran through both of them as they wondered what the crate contained inside.

Tom pried open the crate with the blade end of his ice pick, and he removed the lid.

"Cabernicolas!" he exclaimed. "It's a frozen human body. What a surprise!"

"To say the least!" Caymar responded. He inspected it. "It appears to be alive, but it's time frozen."

"I wonder what time period it's from?" Tom asked. "How do we revive it?"

"I don't know," Caymar replied.

"I certainly don't know any techniques to do so," Tom admitted. "Quick, put the lid back on it. Let's get this thing buried again, and let's NOT tell the Galactic Federation about out secret find."

"Good point," Caymar agreed.

They replaced the lid and covered the bronze crate with dirt until it was hidden from sight.

"Do you think there are any more of these in this region?" Caymar asked Tom.

"There's no telling. Probably so."

"Then let's search the region," Caymar suggested.

"Indeed we will," said Tom. As they searched the surrounding landscape for more clues, Tom brought up, "Caymar, I think we need to contact Morris about our find."

"That's a good idea. Morris, with his special abilities, might know how to and be able to unlock the time freeze and revive the person."

"There's no telling what information he might have to offer us," said Tom.

Suddenly, Caymar received another strange feeling.......

CHAPTER 1

THE HOLOGRAPHIC PLATES

July 23, 1985, 4 p.m.

"Peace and friendship will now prevail over northern Mexico," Robert stated.

"Right on!" Fraxino agreed.

"We still have over a month of summer vacation left," said Steven.

"Man, let's go see the Placatera Mountains above the town of Efforestow," Chispo suggested.

"Are there any more interesting movies to see?" Chris asked.

"Oh yeah, man," Chispo answered. "There's another one just being released called *Vision from the Ciruclar*, and it's really cool. It's about a native from Zantaayer who . . ."

"Zotola, here we come!" Rinto suddenly shouted.

As they were now cruising well above the central Mexican highlands of Zacatecas, Rinto sent his telepathic command to their craft's controls crystal. The forcefield accompanied by a green glow overtook them for a brief moment. They felt as if they were dematerializing, and then they were suddenly fine. They now found themselves flying over a desert valley in the region of Zotola on planet Artenia, and they were heading north toward the Ciruclar Mountains.

It was early in the morning, and the star Al Nitak had been up for an hour. Here the skies were more of a turquoise color with a slight tinge of green in comparison to Earth's skies.

"It's like I was telling you, dudes," Chispo continued. "It's about a native from Zantaayer who likes to go up into the Ciruclar Mountains and explore around. He finds some really neat artifacts from ancient times, including a Vegan sacred story stone. One night, he leads an archaeological investigation team up there and . . . well, I'll let you see the rest in the movie."

Chispo, by the way, had a lively, vibrant personality, and he was the most energetic and enthusiastic one among them. He was known to tell some exciting stories at times.

"What's the sacred story stone about?" Chris asked Chispo.

"I don't know," he admitted. "I haven't been to see it yet. I've just read the previews."

"Doesn't the native of Zantaayer have a vision atop the Ciruclar Mountains of some of the first Atlantean settlers, Chispo?" Fraxino asked.

"That's right," he replied. "That's how the movie gets its name: *Vision from the Ciruclar*."

Rinto continued flying the craft to the north toward the Ciruclar Mountains. Clouds covered some of their peaks, and the scenery was most attractive.

Fraxino took a holographic disk out of a box and inserted it into their on-board player. Everyone knew what to expect next, but Morris was quite surprised when music began to play, music that was not too different from the normal pop music of Earth. It was a very moving piece, and the beat was so invigorating that Morris' emotions were gripped with an uncanny sense of familiarity, even though he knew he had never heard the song before. Robert and his friends had felt the same way several weeks ago when Fraxino had first played the song for them, during their first arrival to Zotola.

"What's that song about?" Morris asked with considerable curiosity.

"Welcome to planet Artenia's Zotola!" Fraxino enthusiastically told Morris.

"That song's about taking charge of your life and living it to the fullest," Rinto replied, "to best explain it in English."

"So familiar! I feel like surely I must have heard it before," said Morris.

"It's one of our favorites," Rinto answered.

"It's really cool!" Fraxino added. "It's from a recent holodisk album by a group of young pop artists called *The Hydragyros*. They're from Zantaayer."

"*The Hydragyros*," Morris repeated. "I like that name. Really an impressive melody."

"I really like it, too," Robert told Morris.

They continued to let the holodisk play as it went through the album's songs.

Rinto now steered the craft toward the northwest, passing by the southwestern portion of the Ciruclar Mountains surrounding the city of Zantaayer, Zotola. He now turned toward the north again, lowered the craft's altitude, and approached the western side of the mountains. A few minutes later, he brought it in for a thrilling and perilous landing on the same narrow winding gravel backroad running along the forested ridge top. Trees and scenery whizzed by as he lined the vehicle-craft up with the direction of the road and touched down at a speed of nearly 100 km/h. Quickly, Rinto slowed down its speed, started the engine, placed the transmission in second gear, engaged the clutch, and proceeded north on the gravel road.

Soon, he turned right and made the half-hour descent to Zantaayer along the winding gravel road with hairpin curves. The city could be seen way below them through the trees of the forested mountain slopes. Most of the trees were Southern Beeches (*Nothofagus*), having been brought from Earth by the Atlanteans when they settled this world.

It never ceased to amaze them how much cleaner and clearer the air was here in Zotola than it was back on Earth. Such was life in Zotola on planet Artenia, the third planet out from their star, Al Nitak, thanks to the fact that they used hydrogen fuel instead of fossil fuels.

For Andrew, Chris, Robert, and Steven, who were natives of Tennessee on planet Earth, this was now their third time to visit Artenia. For Rudy, their Mexican friend from Bustamante, Nuevo León, it was his second visit. He still felt an eery sense of familiarity with the whole place, and he was still wondering whether his soul might be from here. For Chispo Colancha and Rinto and Fraxino Zapatero, this was home, as they were natives of Zantaayer, Zotola.

For Morris, however, this was his first time ever, and he was most impressed by the clean, crisp atmosphere. He was very glad the communication block that had been placed by the Atlanteans over 12,000 years ago had been cleared with the recent elimination of the crystal transmitters in northern Mexico's mountains.

"What a beautiful world you live on here," Morris told Rinto, Fraxino, and Chispo.

"Yes, we like it here on Artenia," Chispo agreed.

"It's strange really," Morris now told them, "but I feel more energized here than I do on Earth."

"That's right, man," Chispo confirmed. "We're at 98% Earth's gravity here on our world."

"Oh, really?" Morris responded. "Tell me more about your world. What size is it? How much of it is covered by land, water, ice, and . . .Well, you know what I mean?"

"Right," Rinto began. "Our world, Artenia, as you can see, is very similar to Earth, nearly a duplicate as far as temperature, vegetation, and climate is concerned. We have 250 million inhabitants. Nearly 50% of Artenia is covered by water. 15% is covered by ice at the poles, and the remaining 35% is land. We live in a city called Zantaayer. You can see it down there below us through the trees. It's the largest city on the planet with a population of 120,000. It sits at a latitude or 40° north and is situated on the northern coast of a region we call Zotola. We have warm summers, and our winters are mostly mild, since we live near the sea which we call the Elizabeth Ocean, as it would best be called in your English language. Our city of Zantaayer is nestled within a range of mountains on its other three sides, and they are called the Ciruclar Mountains."

"And what about the technical data?" Robert now asked, wanting to make sure Rinto also told Morris what he had earlier told the others the first time they had come to Artenia.

"Right, I was about to get to that," Rinto responded. "As far as the data on our star Al Nitak is concerned, it is somewhat larger and brighter than your Earth's sun. Artenia is located 260 million kilometers from Al Nitak, and its diameter is 11,500 kilometers. It takes 423 of our days for our planet to orbit Al Nitak, and our days are 25 $1/2$ of your hours long. That comes to 449.4375 of Earth's 24-hour days. Right, Fraxino?"

"That's right," his brother confirmed. "Also, our star, Al Nitak, is the bottom star of the three stars of the Orion Belt, and as we now know, it is 76.3 light years away from your Earth."

"Indeed it is," Rinto agreed, "once we discovered the true information from those holographic plates compiled by Atlantis' historical society."

"And to think we used to believe that we were 1,132 light years from Earth," Chispo commented.

"Yep, that's our government, covering up the truth," Rinto modestly stated.

"At least we know what the truth is," Robert mentioned.

"You mean the government here on this world has lied about the true distance between Al Nitak and Earth's Sol System?" Morris asked, showing a little surprise.

"That they have indeed," Fraxino answered.

"How weird!" Morris remarked.

"It's the truth, man," Chispo added, and he proceeded to explain to Morris the reason behind the government coverup. "It all started when this world didn't want your Earth's people to know and possibly realize that the Atlanteans came here. It was a government cover-up scheme designed to sweep the truth under the rug, man. Look at the size of Al Nitak. It's 1.6 times larger than Earth's sun, and at 1,132 light years from Earth, it would be a tiny speck in the sky, hardly visible, but you know how well it shows up in Earth's night skies. Man, it's 76.3 light years away, and not a bit further! And no, it's not any super giant nor 1,100 to 1,400 light years away, like your Earth's astronomy books have it listed."

"Chispo's right," Fraxino told Morris. "Rinto and I went to Zantaayer's central library several weeks ago to see if we could verify the data we read from the holographic plates."

"That's right," Rinto now said, "and we found some ancient books that did indeed have the original distance listed as 75 to 80 light years away."

"Really?" Morris responded. "It's just amazing how governments are sometimes afraid of the public knowing the truth. I mean, what's it going to hurt for the Earthlings to know that the Atlanteans came here, anyway?"

"Yeah, really," Chris agreed.

"So," said Morris, "with Al Nitak being listed as a supergiant and the distance being listed as 1,132 light years, Earth's residents would never suspect that the Atlanteans came here."

"That's right," Chispo enthusiastically agreed.

"It might come from an ancient wish of the Atlanteans to have been left in peace once they came here," said Andrew, "after their devastating disaster on Earth over 12,000 years ago."

"Over 65,000 residents of Atlantis came here 10,130 of our years ago," Rinto explained to Morris. "We base our calender on their arrival, and we are in the year 10130. A man named Cresma, who was a leader in his day, was very helpful in having them brought here to our world on a fleet of transport ships from Earth's Atlantis right after the devastating crustal displacement. On the first day of each year, we have a festive celebration in honor of who he was. We call it the day of Cresma. We also have a book called *The Book of Cresma* which relates a lot of ancient stories and legends, having been orally handed down over many generations . . ."

They continued talking. Finally, they reached the bottom of the mountain, and the pavement began. Rinto now shifted the transmission to a higher gear. They entered the edge of the city, and the houses began. They were not very different from houses back on Earth, and in some ways, this area could have passed for Tennessee. Rinto drove them to their house a few kilometers away. Soon, they were pulling into the Zapatero's driveway again.

"Yep, Dad's home," Rinto commented upon seeing his father's car parked in the driveway. Rinto and Fraxino's father drove an antique classic, a turquoise colored Tolejo sedan with a straight 6 engine and a 3-speed on the column. It very much resembled a late 1950's Ford Edsel, and Mr. Zapatero kept it in immaculate condition.

Rinto parked the vehicle-craft at the end of the driveway, and as everyone was stepping outside, Rinto and Fraxino's parents, Glecko and Sosta Zapatero, came outside to greet them.

"Dad, we had radical success!" Fraxino proudly exclaimed to Glecko.

"Nice going, sons!" Glecko told them. "I knew you guys would pull it off."

"It was quite a spectacle," Rinto added. "The explosions were more severe than we anticipated when we eliminated the transmitter device."

"Dude, severe isn't the word for it," Chispo reminded Rinto. "Outright dangerous would better describe it." Chispo went on to enthusiastically explain to Glecko and Sosta in detail how rays of light shot across the valley and bounced all over the mountains and how one ray came back and temporarily killed Chris. Chispo also explained how they had miraculously revived Chris and healed him by use of their on-board crystal first aid kit.

"Whew! That was close, guys," Glecko told them. "You never know what surprises you might get from eliminating crystal devices like that. There's so much energy packed in them."

"Yes, we found that out," Rinto agreed, "especially after their having been there for more than 12,000 Earth years."

"It surprised us," Fraxino added. "We weren't expecting it."

"Oh . . . would you look at those chairs," Glecko commented as he saw them in the back of the vehicle-craft.

"It's a wooden rocking chair with Palm leaf weaving," Rinto said to his father.

"We couldn't resist bringing some of them back with us from Mexico," Fraxino added.

"I brought one back, too," said Chispo.

"They're fine looking chairs," Glecko commented.

They began unloading the vehicle-craft. Rinto revealed the various types of baked bread and gave them to his mother. "It's bread baked by some of the natives of the town of Bustamante, and most of it is good," he told his mother in Artenian.

"Thank you. I'm sure we'll enjoy this with our breakfast," she commented in Artenian.

As they were bringing their backpacks inside, they continued telling Glecko and Sosta all about their adventures in Mexico.

They had just completed a mission there by having located and eliminated two twin dodecahedron crystal transmitters hidden in the mountains above Bustamante, Nuevo León. The device had been causing numerous conflicts among the natives. Morris, and then Tom, the galactic salesman, had come forth with the mission to eliminate the transmitters because they had been placed by the Atlanteans with the full intent of blocking spiritual and astral travel, mental telepathy, and also telephone communication via gravity waves with the Orion Belt and the star Al Nitak, the place to where the Atlanteans had fled more than

12,000 Earth years ago.

"Anyway, set your packs down inside, and Sosta and I will fix some breakfast for everyone," Glecko kindly offered. He now spoke to his wife in Artenian, and they went into the kitchen.

Meanwhile, Rinto and Fraxino were eager to view more of the holographic plates. Several weeks ago, they had visited an ancient galactic dump site in a remote region 100 kilometers south of Zantaayer. It was there that they had discovered and unearthed a large bronze metal crate containing 144 holographic metal plates. They had viewed several of the plates before having travelled to Mexico. While Glecko and Sosta were preparing breakfast, Rinto and Fraxino took everyone into the next room where they had their crystal base computer setup.

Morris found the setup very interesting indeed. To use crystals as the intelligence base and central processor was a most fascinating concept to him.

"This is ringing true of being more along the lines of how things are done on the world of the dolphins," Morris commented.

"Is that right?" Robert asked. "You mean dolphins have computers after all?"

"Well, not exactly that," Morris clarified, and he laughed a little, "but they do use crystals throughout their culture on Delikadove."

Rinto was switching on the controls as they continued talking about the setup. The Ulexite crystal base and crystal pack or array, which was connected to a keyboard and view screen, was all part of the computer system that Rinto and Fraxino had modified to be capable of handling matters more related to Earth. He even had translator programs telepathically imbedded within the crystal array, and the computer was capable of reading the Atlantean hieroglyphic script of the holographic data from the bronze metal plates and translating them to English for everyone to read. The crystal array stored information in the mental ether around it, in other words, the energy field, and it worked on somewhat the same principle as the human brain works. It was a most impressive display, and it served its purpose very well.

These holographic plates were a secret among them, and they had not told others in Zantaayer about them, let alone Zotola's news media, who would likely have confiscated them and used them in undesired ways, in addition to the inundation and interrogation by the news media that would have occurred as a result.

Chispo reached into the large bronze box, took out the index plate, and handed it to Rinto who placed it on the tray that read the data. Text soon started showing up on the screen, and all of them started looking at the listings which showed up in English.

"Look at that one," Robert commented. *"Friendships and Their Own Life Force."*

"Yeah, that looks like an interesting one," said Morris.

"Chispo, take plate number 84 out of the box," Rinto requested. Chispo did so, and everyone soon started viewing the literature on the screen, first in hieroglyphic script, followed by the English translation. *"Friendships and Their Own Life Force,"* said Rinto, and he began to narrate.

"Over the course of numerous studies throughout Atlantean society, it has been theorized and recently proven that friendships have their own life force, that is, they have a life of their own, as in a quantum energy system. For some people and the friendships they have, there is, in actual fact, a living energy system established that lives on its own and keeps the friendship going without much effort from the two people involved. For the fortunate ones blessed with this type of friendship life force, they, with the greatest of ease become very close friends, and they find that they are compatible with each other.

"Most people on the other hand have to work, sometimes very hard at a relationship to keep the friendship alive. They keep having to feed energy into it because the friendship won't live on its own. These people are not blessed with a friendship life force. Most people of Atlantis have determined that the best thing to do with the hard-to-make-live friendships is to abandon them.

"For friends with whom there is a self-living friendship quantum energy system which keeps itself alive, things go more smoothly, and friends like that can enjoy each other. They also feel free to be straightforward with each other. It is just easy and enjoyable, and the level of stress between good friends like that is much less than for the more difficult friendships. There is a sense of peace and trust between good friends, and that occurs very easily and naturally because of the existence of the living friendship energy system.

"These energy systems are thought to come from other levels of reality and from higher levels of thought, which, by definition, would be destiny, as it may appear that way. The subconscious minds between any two close friends set up these energy systems at the time they meet or even before they meet each other. Once they meet, they feel an immediate connection of friendship with each other, and they find each other instinctively familiar. In some ways they feel like they already know each other and have known each other for their whole life.

"For those who are not blessed with friendship quantum energy systems between them, they usually find themselves incompatible with each other. They have to have a lot of truth buried between them so that they can be "friends" and keep the relationship going.

"Atlantean psychoanalysts have discovered that people can actually communicate telepathically with the friendship quantum energy systems and cause them to work in their favor. They can be tapped into to cause changes for the better, and the two friends involved may also react according to the way the energy system is programmed, in ways consciously and/or subconsciously in their sleep. They can literally cause favorable conditions to replace what were obstacles or can even eliminate the obstacles which might have blocked or prevented the friendship from continuing."

"There is a whole lot of truth to what that plate says," Morris commented. "Friendships really do have a life of their own."

"No kidding?" Steven responded.

"Is that right?" Robert responded. "For me, that's a whole new way of looking at it. I never thought of it that way before."

"Me neither," admitted Chris, even though his area of interest was philosophy.

"I agree with what that plate says 100%, man," Chispo told everyone.

"True friends do things with each other to make each other feel better," Fraxino commented.

"¿Rudy, qué piensas de esta placa holográfica?" said Robert, asking Rudy what he thought of the holographic plate. He had just previously translated to Spanish and had told Rudy what the plate was about.

"Sí, sí, es cierto. Las amistades tienen su propia fuerza de vida," said Rudy, commenting that it's for certain that friendships have their own life force. In fact, Rudy went on to comment that he had always instinctively viewed friendships as being alive.

"I do agree that true friends do things with each other to make each other feel better," Morris informed everyone. "I can also tell you that most people have to keep a lot of truth buried between them to keep any friendship going at all."

"I think most of us here have just what that plate says," said Chispo. "Self living friendship quantum energy systems. We've been friends since we've met, maybe even before we met."

"It's always been amazing to me," Steven added comment, "how two strangers meet up for the first time, and they strike up a friendship immediately."

"I know," Chris agreed. "It happens a lot."

"That's just what this plate is about," said Morris. "Their friendship life forces were set into motion by their subconscious higher selves before they even physically met. Those who can telepathically communicate with their friendships are the ones who are most successful in having them . . . friends, that is."

Andrew placed the index plate back on the tray. "Let's look at the next plate," he said as he called everyone's attention to it."

"Oh, yeah," Chris commented as he saw one of the titles. "There's one that talks about meeting people for the first time."

"Hmm . . . *Meeting Familiar People and Acquired Nervousness*, plate number 85," Rinto commented. "That's odd. Let's have a look at that." He swapped plate number 84 for number 85. Text soon showed up on the screen, and Rinto began narrating.

"It has been an observed fact that when certain people of the right vibrational frequencies first meet each other, they immediately sense a strong connection of friendship, causing them to easily relate to each other, as if they have known each other all their lives. Now, for some of these individuals, it is true that their souls and life forces are instinctively familiar with each other, having known each other in previous lifetimes.

"A most curious aspect has been observed since over 2,500 years ago . . . the time of the disappearance of the Fluorite peace keeping crystal. At times, when two individuals connect very well with synchronous energy fields and immediately sense a good friendship, they sometimes get excited and feel energized with good feelings. As it turns out, one of the individuals, never both, is caused to acquire second thoughts about the friendship while the other person is caused to feel nervous for no sufficient reason. Once nervousness sets in, it can cause the friendship to be squelched and quite possibly blocked. The nervous feelings cause the person to feel awkward and uneasy, and he sometimes cannot concentrate properly.

"There are intelligent quantum energy systems having been set up by devious scientists during their mood control experiments that are still circulating, and those systems are specifically designed to detect true potentially good friendships and sabotage them, causing one of the two to acquire second thoughts and resentment and the other one to suffer confusing alienation and grief. This is done because these self-living quantum energy systems need to have energy fed into them to maintain their energy status (life), and resentment, grief, and suffering vibrate most closely with those particular energy systems cleverly designed by those who did the mood control experiments.

"The appropriate energy systems plant thoughts and feelings into the two individuals involved, and by this being done, the energy of the true friendship is corrupted, hindered, and cannot do its work properly. The friendship, as a result, fails."

"Golly!" Steven declared. "What a grim outlook on friendships."

"I know," Chris agreed. "Those energy systems wreaked havoc on more than we thought."

"I mean, sometimes I've watched friendships fail, but usually they work out," Steven added.

"I know what they're talking about concerning nervousness," Robert said to everyone. "I've actually felt that nervousness soon after meeting and making certain friends."

"Is that right?" Andrew responded. "I have too."

"And you know, sometimes a person will have dreams of *intimacy* of being close to someone," Chris added.

"I know what you mean," said Andrew, "and it can bring on feelings of embarrassment to one or both of the individuals involved."

"Dudes, I actually know of some people in Tennessee who have had dreams like that," Chispo informed everyone. "Usually the person dreamed about mysteriously becomes unsure about the other one."

"I know," Chris stated. "Feelings of uncertainty come about, and the friendship really suffers."

"It's like they lose their capacity to relate to each other," Chispo added.

"It's a shame that so many friendships have been lost on planet Earth due to such sabotage," Morris commented.

"Sabotage?" Rinto asked. "What do you mean, sabotage?"

"Those holographic plates speak the truth," Morris told them. "What I mean is that those intelligent quantum energy systems are capable of causing certain subconscious thoughts to enter one or both persons involved in the friendship, and the result can be embarrassing to them. Intelligent higher subconscious thoughts are known to sabotage friendships on Earth quite regularly."

"How can that be?" Robert wanted to know.

"Well, it's like Chris was saying," Morris went on. "Dreams of intimacy are known to be telepathically planted in one or both individuals with the intent of bringing on nervousness and embarrassment. The result, I'm afraid, is grief and resentment with loss of friendship."

"And all of this has come about because of Atlantean mood controlling experiments over 12,000 years ago?" Steven asked Morris.

"That's right," Morris calmly answered. "It's a shame, really."

Rinto placed the index plate back on the tray.

"Hmm . . ." said Robert as he looked at the index. "There's another holographic plate with nearly the same sort of theme."

"Plate number 86: *Sincere Appreciation and Loss of Friendship*," said Rinto as he looked at it. Let's have a look at that one." Chispo swapped plate 85 for plate 86, and Rinto began to narrate.

"One of the most outrageous human characteristics involves being seemingly mysteriously rejected by a very good and close friend who has been sincerely appreciated. Atlantean top psychoanalysts in their field have observed this unpleasant phenomenon and have mathematically determined that the severity of loss of friendship is directly proportional to the level of appreciation.

"Only certain individuals are affected by this most annoying and unfortunate phenomenon, and top scientists in their field have determined that the individuals are affected by one of numerous specifically designed quantum energy systems, this one specifically designed to cause the above mentioned outrageous reality to occur.

"The first known cases occurred shortly after the disappearance of the Fluorite peace keeping crystal more than 2,500 years ago, after which the devious reality controlling experiments began.

"It is extremely strange how the deviously designed system works, latching onto the etherical energy field of certain chosen individuals (people of Atlantean society) and causing the appreciated friend to mysteriously gather resentment and / or jealousy toward the other person. These energy systems are still circulating, and since Atlantean society team experts have been unsuccessful at terminating those systems, it is predicted that they will continue to circulate through Earth's population of people for many thousands of years into the future."

"Huh! That's really weird," Chris remarked. "It's almost as if the energy systems are jealous."

"That plate rings true, as well," Morris confirmed for everyone. "I have wondered why there were so many bad energy systems circulating around in the ether on Earth, and now I've had their origins confirmed, that they came from devious Atlantean mood control experiments."

"How terrible!" Robert remarked.

"You're not joking," Morris agreed. "That's one of the worst ones. It's as if the living thinking energy systems just cannot stand a truly good friendship, and they are programmed to seek those best friendships and destroy them by planting thoughts of resentment in the appreciated individuals. The thoughts of appreciation are like a key calling card and are detected by the energy systems floating around in the ether. It really is a shame how many excellent friendships were destroyed and lost over the ages due to that type of quantum energy system and the programming forces carried with it."

Everyone pondered for a few moments on Morris' comments. They knew he was right. Robert and his friends could all recall times in their lives when they had sincerely appreciated some friends of theirs and soon afterwards experienced their rejection and loss of friendship. They had been some of the worst feelings they had ever known. At least now they had a reasonable answer as to why it occurred. They were feeling sad.

"Probably one of the main reasons why the Atlanteans blocked Earth from their new world, here on Artenia," Chispo commented.

"So that nonsense of that sort would never occur on this world?" Robert asked.

"Exactly, man," Chispo answered.

Rinto had placed the index plate on the tray. "Here, let's change the subject and look at a different plate."

"*Memories Stored on Location*, plate number 75," Fraxino commented. He reached into the box and handed Rinto the appropriate plate.

Rinto placed it on the tray, and when text came up on the screen, he started narrating.

"Atlantean residents have taken note of a curious fact that many memories are triggered in people when they visit certain places. While some people think all memories are stored inside the brain, the fact discovered by top Atlantean science researchers is that most memories are actually stored in the ethereal energy field of each individual while very little of it is in the brain, which is merely a central processor and communication connector center for associating and recognizing the memories as they are thought. Many memories are stored on location, and when a person visits the same place again later in his life, he or she can remember more exact details of the place and can even remember what he or she was thinking about the last time he or she had been there.

"All thoughts that a person thinks are literally recorded within the matter of the material items of any location, such as rocks, soil, trees, or even buildings. The information of the thoughts are stored there indefinitely until the person returns to that site and triggers the appropriate recorded memories and thoughts to come forth and run through the mind of the visitor.

"Matter is mostly bound up energy, and since it is mostly holographic in nature, there is literally a phenomenal amount of storage capability within the energy matrix of matter itself of any location."

"It's like I was telling you all earlier," Fraxino reminded them. "Telepathic information and thoughts are recorded in the rocks and the ether around them."

"Like in Mexico where we saw those ancient paintings on the mesa sidewalls," Robert recalled.

"Exactly," Fraxino responded. "Crystals store telepathic information on the same sort of principle."

"You'd really be amazed at how holographic matter is," Morris pointed out. "In fact, reality itself is very pliable and can be altered."

"I've heard that matter is mostly empty space," Steven mentioned.

"That's right," Morris confirmed, "and it is there that memories can be stored by anyone and tapped into later."

"Interesting," Robert commented.

"Psychics actually use that method to read information from knives and other weapons that have been used to kill someone," Chispo pointed out.

"That's right," Morris agreed. "They can literally tap into and read the information that was recorded in the matter of the weapon itself. They can also read other peoples' thoughts by visiting the site of the crime, for example. People with those abilities can read and gather all kinds of historical information at old archaeological sites. In fact, some of Earth's archaeological teams actually hire and take psychic readers with them."

"Really? How interesting," Robert commented.

"It is, isn't it," Morris agreed. "Though they won't admit it on the public level, archaeologists make a regular practice of carrying those special people along so they can compare what they can see and say with the artifacts and physical buildings and structures of the locations they are studying."

"Do they really?" Andrew asked. "I didn't realize that."

"That is really strange that they would use people with psychic abilities," Chris commented.

"Where else do they use them?" Steven wanted to know.

"Oh, they can use them to read information from tombs and historical sites, like I was saying. They can use them to help find gold and treasures in mines, water dousing, and so on . . ."

As Morris explained his reasoning, Robert and Andrew were sometimes translating to Spanish for Rudy so he would understand.

Rudy had a brother, Roel, who was one year older. Roel had recently decided to stay in Pinos, Zacatecas, and they had recently visited him shortly before returning to Zotola. Though Rudy hadn't yet told the others, he was missing his brother Roel and wished that he had also come along. He would see what he could do. Maybe he could return and talk Roel into joining them.

Rudy still had some underlying feeling of familiarity with the place, like his soul might be from here. He had still not figured out nor pinpointed what it was, but he liked Zotola well enough. On his previous visit, he had enjoyed the road trip to Caloma when Chispo drove them there in his car, a futuristic looking Velva Dibe model.

As everyone was making comments on *Memories Stored on Location*, Rinto placed the index plate back on the tray.

"There's an interesting one," said Robert as he looked at the index list when it appeared on the screen. "*Energy Field Absorption and Character Repetitions*, plate number 89."

"Yeah, let's see it," Rinto agreed. He reached for plate number 89, took it out of the box, and placed it on the tray. When text showed up on the screen, he began to narrate.

"Over the course of time and through various observed traits of human character, it has been realized by most Atlanteans that when two or more people spend time together, their energy fields and character traits become absorbed into each other. Once they separate from each other, for hours or sometimes days, each person will have a strong sense of feeling like he is the other person. Characteristic traits and mannerisms of the other person ring out in the individual, especially when he talks.

"This occurs because the energy fields of the two people become recorded into each other and absorbed by each other, up to 20%, and sometimes last for days before wearing off and dissipating, allowing the two people to revert to being their unique personalities again.

"As the energy fields become impressed upon each other, and as their characteristics are repeated into each other's energy fields, the two friends establish a better level of communication with one another. They literally become more similar to each other during their time together because, quite literally, their energy fields become synchronized as they interact with each other, taking on each other's mannerisms.

"This phenomenon is actually a result of positive quantum energy systems circulating throughout the ether, and its purpose is to cause people to achieve better friendships with each other."

"Now *that's* more like it," Fraxino approved. "A positive outlook on friendships."

"You know, I've noticed that several times in my life," Chris declared.

"I have too," said Robert. "I notice it now, and also back when I was a child. After I would have a friend come over and visit, I would actually hear his voice ring out in my mind every time I spoke, up to hours after he had already gone home."

"I know what you're talking about," said Chispo. "The same thing happens to me, man."

"This collection of holographic plates certainly does cover the philosophical standpoint of the Atlantean society," Steven declared.

"I'll say," Andrew agreed.

At this point in time, Glecko entered the room. "There's breakfast ready if you want it," he offered to everyone.

"Thanks, Dad," Rinto responded. "We're coming." He switched off the crystal base computer and placed the holographic plates back in their crate. All of them walked into the Zapatero's kitchen.

As they were eating, Glecko brought up, "You know, guys, there's a really great movie that's just been released called *Vision from the Ciruclar*."

"Yeah, Chispo was telling us about it," Steven acknowledged.

"You guys might want to go see it," Glecko urged them.

"Yeah, we're going to, possibly tonight," said Rinto.

"I understand they find some artifacts including a sacred story stone," Glecko went on. "I think you'd find that interesting, seeing how you all actually found one in that ancient galactic dump site south of here."

"I wonder what sacred story it will reveal in the movie?" Robert asked everyone.

"I guess we'll find out when we see it," Andrew responded.

"What else do we want to do today?" Steven asked everyone.

"I don't know," said Fraxino. "Rinto, do you think there's anything else in that galactic dump site?"

"I'm sure there probably is," Rinto calmly replied to his brother.

"Then let's go there," Fraxino proposed to his brother. "We might find something else very interesting. After all, Rudy hasn't been there yet."

"Fraxino, I don't know about you, but I'm feeling really exhausted," Rinto admitted. "That was a lot of hard work we did this past week, growing those crystals, telepathically feeding intelligence into them, and adding the right combination of impurities in the growing process, building the Kaolinite device, and all. It's just taken it out of me, if you know what I mean, and I want to get some sleep."

Last week, Rinto and Fraxino had worked very hard and put a lot of effort into building the crystal device in their secret cave up in the Ciruclar Mountains. It was made of Kaolinite with phantom red crystals and Ruby crystals, as well. For several days, they had worked day and night, attending to the growing process. Meanwhile, Chispo had taken the others in his car up north to Caloma to visit his relatives. They had taken the crystal device to Mexico and had used it in the mountains above Bustamante, Nuevo León to switch off the two Atlantean crystal transmitters by tricking them into thinking they hadn't been tampered with in the first place.

"Fraxino, I don't know where you get your energy," Rinto admitted, "but you always have been a little more on the enthusiastic side."

"Yeah, I will admit you were pretty intense on it," Fraxino told his brother. "Why don't you stay here and get some sleep today, and Chispo and I will take the guys around."

"Sounds good," Rinto approved. He got up from the breakfast table and took a seat in the rocking chair they had just brought back from Mexico. "Oh, what a comfortable chair."

"Dudes, I'm coming with you guys today," said Chispo. "Rinto, is it okay if I leave my rocking chair over here for now? If I take it home next door, Mom's going to notice I'm back, and she might saddle me with work and chores to do."

"You mean like weeding more of her flower garden?" Andrew asked with a smile.

"Exactly, man," Chispo answered.

"No problem, Chispo," Rinto consented. "Just set the chair in the same room with all the backpacks."

"Thanks, man." Chispo walked outside and brought his rocking chair inside and placed it where Rinto had said.

Chispo Colancha was Rinto and Fraxino's long time friend and nearby neighbor. Their properties touched at their backyards, and a row of tall bushes ran the property line. There was a small path through the bushes, and Rinto, Fraxino, and Chispo regularly crossed under the bushes to visit each other and work on projects together.

"Ready to go, everyone?" Fraxino asked them all.

"Yes, as far as I'm concerned," Robert answered. "Thanks for the breakfast, Glecko."

"Not a problem, guys. That bread you all brought was wonderful . . . just out of this world."

They laughed at his clever comment. They got up from the table, walked into the next room, gathered some things from their backpacks, and they all boarded the vehicle-craft.

Fraxino did the driving and backed them out of the driveway.

Rinto and Fraxino's vehicle-craft was a hybrid landcraft-spacecraft. It was unique indeed because they had installed a home-grown crystal array plus a large Ulexite cube, their main controls crystal, and had telepathically instilled the crystals with the intelligence to counter gravity and make the craft fly.

Their model was known as a Velosa cruiser craft, and it was built by a Zotolan company called the Velosa Cruiser Craft Company located in the southern part of the city of Zantaayer. It had the shape of a modern large van, and the craft's body was made out of a mixture of various metals, including Vanadium, and mixed with a silicon base. The body was grown over a period of several months, and the craft's color was mostly green, tinged with yellow and brown.

Inside, the vehicle-craft looked not too different from a normal van. It had a steering wheel, seats, and a windshield. For land driving, the vehicle was powered by a Richmond in-line 6-cylinder motor, and it utilized a 5-speed manual gearbox. The engine ran on hydrogen fuel.

It was a most impressive vehicle-craft indeed, and Rinto and Fraxino, when it came to engineering feats involving intelligence with crystals, were geniuses to say the least. They had been teleporting themselves to and from Earth for well over a year now, and they had been taking Chispo with them. Chispo had recently completed a homestay with a family in Tennessee, and he attended school while he was there.

It had been one month ago that Rinto and Fraxino had, by chance or destiny, met Robert and his friends on the icy plains of Antarctica. Rinto and Fraxino had made a trip there to research their Atlantean ancestral heritage, and they located and explored an ice cave together. They had been very lucky because one of the cave's walls contained numerous hieroglyphic writings with crystals placed and interspersed throughout the text. The text had related a story of the devastating event of the Earth crustal displacement which had shifted Atlantis to the South Pole over 12,000 years ago.

"Fraxino, check out the fuel level, man," Chispo said to him.

"It's nearly empty," Fraxino commented as he looked at the gauge. "That trip we made to Pinos, Zacatecas used up more hydrogen fuel than we thought it would."

Fraxino drove them to the highway not too far away, and they pulled up to an Exxoll fuel station.

"Oh, golly man! Again?" Fraxino declared when he pulled up to the pumps.

"Price has gone up again!" Rinto remarked.

"Man, it was only at 11.7 for a couple of weeks," Chispo complained.

The attendant came to the vehicle-craft and filled its tank with hydrogen. Exxoll fuel company had a monopoly on all fuel stations throughout planet Artenia. Glecko had told them the story behind the name Exxoll and why the name appeared in Earth's alphabet instead of the normal Artenian script, which utilized a hieroglyphic type of text, somewhat similar to India's Sanskrit.

Some 15 years ago, the intergalactic fuel company called Exxoll had bought a monopoly on all of Artenia's fuel companies. It was an Earth based fuel company, known on Earth as *Esso* or *Exxon*, and it had expanded to a galactic level to test out the market on selling hydrogen fuel so that they could use those studies to soon begin selling hydrogen fuel on Earth. After all, they secretly knew that it would not be many years before Earth's conventional fossil fuels would be entirely used up.

"We were explaining to the others earlier," Fraxino told Morris. "Here in Zotola, we have a unit of currency called the Zotolan zúbola. Its value is the equivalent of just over 6 of your U.S. dollars. There are 144 duocibols to the zúbola, and hydrogen fuel right now costs 11.8 duocibols per liter."

"Recently, they've been raising the price every month or so," Rinto added.

"We're on base 12 here, dudes," Chispo reminded everyone.

"But what about the liter?" Morris pointed out. "That's not base 12."

"That's true," Chispo admitted, "but that's a mandate from the intergalactic fuel company Exxoll, who monopolized all the independent companies we used to have on this world."

Fraxino paid the fuel attendant 8 zúbolas for the fuel. He started the engine, pulled out onto the highway, and he drove them into Zantaayer's central district.

"There it is," Chispo suddenly announced with enthusiasm as they passed by a sign written in Artenian script. "It's already out, dudes."

"What, you mean the movie?" Chris asked.

"That's right," Chispo confirmed. *"Vision from the Ciruclar."*

"Good, then let's go see it tonight," said Robert.

Chispo then told Rudy in Spanish that the movie was already showing at the theaters.

Once at the city center, Fraxino took the highway south leading out of town. It was narrow, as most streets in Zantaayer were, and the road passed between mostly square shaped twelve story buildings along the way. Soon, they left the central district and were passing stores and commercial establishments, after which they passed several factories, including the Velosa Cruiser Craft Company.

The narrow two-lane concrete highway was busy with traffic as they reached the foot of the forested Ciruclar Mountains. Artenia didn't waste space with wide superhighways like Earth did. Chispo had explained to them that here on Artenia, the people believed in minimal impact. The highway, which to Earth's standards was a dangerous, narrow winding road, ascended the mountain slopes with hairpin curves. The forest sometimes made a canopy over the road which made it seem as if they were passing through a tunnel.

The trees consisted of Southern Beeches, Hemlocks, Black Locusts, Oaks, Poplars, Acacias, and Eucalyptus trees. Higher up there were Pine trees.

Fraxino whizzed along, making the ascent and taking the curves with the greatest of ease. Though the highway was narrow, it was a major thoroughfare with transport trucks going and coming, carrying supplies and goods to neighboring cities and towns south of Zantaayer.

Near the crest of the Ciruclar Mountains, the dense forest opened up and was dominated by Pine trees. Fraxino pulled over and parked.

"Take a look behind you, dudes," Fraxino told everyone. "Views are excellent from up here."

"It really is amazing how crystal clear the views are without Earth's air pollution," Morris commented.

"I know," Chris agreed. "Why can't Earth use cleaner fuels like hydrogen?"

"It won't be long," Morris assured them.

Fraxino was right. The view of Zantaayer, free of air pollution, was indeed crystal clear and spectacular, as well. To the city's north the Elizabeth Ocean stretched to the horizon. To their south, in the direction they were heading, the land was drier. They could see the desert valley stretching out beyond them to the distant Placatera mountain range. It was just this side of those distant mountains where the ancient galactic dump site was located. Rudy was looking forward to the adventure, as he had not yet visited there.

Rudy, more than the rest of them, recognized that this desert valley could have passed for one in Mexico. There were shrubs resembling Mesquites and various types of Cactus plants dotting the otherwise desolate landscape.

In an hour they arrived, having made a right turn to leave the highway. They were now at the ancient galactic dump site. It was basically a huge boulder field not too distant from the Placatera Mountains to the southwest. Though it appeared desolate, it had plenty of artifacts to offer to those who searched. Most people in Zotola knew nothing of the site, and it was therefore of little or no interest to the government nor to archaeological teams and explorers. This was a place that Rinto and Fraxino had discovered during past rock and crystal hunting adventures, as collecting rocks and minerals was one of their hobbies.

"We're here, dudes," Fraxino announced as he parked the vehicle-craft.

Everyone stepped outside and waited while Fraxino took some digging tools out of the back of the vehicle-craft.

"Here, take this pick with you," Fraxino said to Chispo as he handed him the tool. "I'll carry the prybar."

They made their way west across the boulder laden terrain, sometimes hopping over the boulders, and sometimes walking between them. More and more broken pieces of crystals could be seen scattered across the ground.

"This is a bit of a desolate site, isn't it?" Morris remarked with a smile.

"Yes, it's definitely away from the mainstream," Fraxino agreed.

"What do you think we'll find this time?" Robert asked everyone.

"Maybe another crateload of holographic plates," Chris speculated.

"Or sacred story stones," Steven added.

"Chispo," Robert suggested, "let's go back over to where we found those egg-shaped crystals that had tree cone images within them."

"All right, man," Chispo agreed. "Here, Fraxino. Take this pick with you all." He handed it to him. Chispo and Robert began to walk over there while the others went a different direction.

"Rudy, ven," Robert called out to him, inviting him to come with him and Chispo.

"Allí voy," he responded, saying that he was coming.

Meanwhile, Andrew, Chris, Steven, Morris, and Fraxino headed toward the site where they had dug up the crateload of holographic plates several weeks ago.

In ten minutes, Robert, Rudy, and Chispo reached the site of the strange tree cone crystals. Robert had earlier found one with an image of a Tulip Poplar cone within. These egg-shaped crystals were thought to have been grown by an ancient intelligent civilization from Earth over 100,000 years ago. They knew a lot about crystals and lived in what would later become Atlantis.

Chispo, Robert, and Rudy started looking around, turning over rocks, hoping to find one.

"Chispo, Robert, ven," Rudy suddenly said, calling them over.

"¿Qué . . . qué fue?" Robert responded, asking him what happened.

Both Robert and Chispo walked over to him. Rudy pointed to and showed them what he found. It was partially buried.

"Oh wow, man!" Chispo declared enthusiastically. "He already found one." He reached down and started raking the dirt away from it and carefully pried it out of the ground. As he wiped the dirt off of it, he started to look within it. Slowly, he turned it until the light from Al Nitak struck it at the right angle and revealed the ghostly image within.

"Far out! It's another tree cone!" Chispo declared. "Sure enough, man . . . the Buttonball Tree, another tree of extraterrestrial origin."

"Let's see it," Robert requested.

Chispo handed it to him. "Here's another tree that grows in your state."

Robert looked within the crystal. "Huh! What do you know! It's an image of a Sycamore seed ball cluster. You all call it the Buttonball Tree?"

"That's right, man," Chispo replied.

"This is another one of planet Earth's oddball trees," Robert commented. "I wonder what it all means?" Robert handed the piece to Rudy who took a look within it.

"Quien sabe lo que será," said Rudy, telling them he didn't know what the image might be.

Though Sycamore trees (*Platanus* genus) did grow in selected areas near Bustamante, it would have been asking a lot for Rudy to have recognized the seed ball cluster as having been from the Sycamore tree. In Spanish, the tree was known as Alamo.

"You know, Chispo," Robert brought up. "I believe Morris told me that this type of tree, in addition to the Eucalyptus, came from the world of the dolphins."

"That could be true, man, but there is an ancient legend here on Artenia . . . I don't know if it was handed down from Atlantean stories or not . . . but it says that the Buttonball Tree has a much more ancient origin, being extraterrestrial, and it's also of sacred value to several common intelligent races such as humans and other related species. Legend has it that it comes from the planet Alíonux, way off in another star system . . . The star is called Saidd."

"Where's that?" Robert wanted to know.

"It's a distant star nearly 3,000 light years away from here, barely visible and situated under the Pleiades."

"Under the Pleiades?" Robert asked.

"That's right, man," Chispo verified, "only much further away. There's an ancient word, *Nothgierc*, meaning global cluster of seeds, and the seed ball cluster has importance for keeping peace and harmony among the races, the way the seeds are all bunched together around each buttonball. The word has its origin from the land where the Buttonball Tree came from."

"Strange name . . . Nothgierc," Robert remarked. "It sounds alien enough."

"I agree, man."

Robert asked Rudy if he was going to keep the egg-shaped crystal.

"No, aquí está. Ten," said Rudy, giving it to Robert and telling him to keep it.

"Gracias," said Robert, telling Rudy thanks. He took his daypack off his back and placed the crystal inside of it.

"Let's go see what the others have located, if they've found anything," Chispo suggested.

"Yeah, okay. Let's go."

"Fraxino!" Chispo shouted to find out where the others were.

"Yeah!" he called back from a distance.

"We're coming over!" Chispo shouted back.

"Find anything?!"

"Yeah, Rudy found another egg-shaped crystal!"

"Cool!" Fraxino shouted in response.

They made their way over and reached the others in five minutes.

As Chispo reached them, he said, "Robert, show them what we found."

Robert took off his daypack, unzipped it, and pulled out what Rudy had found.

"Check it out, man," Chispo said to Fraxino as Robert handed it to him.

"Oh, cool!" Fraxino enthusiastically remarked. "It's from the Buttonball Tree. Take a look at this, Morris," Fraxino said to him as he handed him the piece.

Morris carefully looked at it and turned it at different angles in the light, soon revealing the ghostly image of the Sycamore seed ball cluster. "Really an interesting piece, indeed. This has very ancient origins. I can literally feel it. The civilization that grew this was very aware of the trees."

"I agree they must have had quite an interest in them," said Robert.

"Cygnus . . . for some reason that word comes to me," Morris added.

Chispo noticed that no one had unearthed any artifacts. "You all haven't found anything yet?" he asked them with a surprised look.

"No, not yet," Steven responded for everyone.

"You lazy bums," Chispo teased with a smile on his face.

"Oh, neat!" Chris suddenly called out. He was over in a rock crevice around 20 meters away.

"What? What did you find?" Robert responded.

"It looks like another box," he answered back.

"Really?" Robert asked with enthusiasm.

"No kidding!" Steven responded.

In seconds, everyone including Rudy was rushing over to where Chris was. There in a narrow crevice was an exposed corner of a bronze metal box. It looked very similar to the box they had earlier found with the 144 holographic plates.

"Far out, man!" Chispo shouted.

"We've done it again!" Andrew declared.

"Oh my goodness," Steven commented. "I'm not believing this."

"Come on," Robert urged. "Let's start digging."

Fraxino went for his pick and prybar which were lying on the ground nearby. He got down in the crevice and immediately started digging the dirt away on all sides of the box while the others watched. Chispo joined in and in minutes, they had the box unearthed. Chispo placed the prybar under the bottom of the box and successfully pried it out of the ground. The others joined in and with a lot of might, they heaved the heavy box out of the crevice and onto one of the rocks above. The box measured one meter in length, 50 centimeters wide, and 30 centimeters deep, a little bit smaller than the box of holographic plates they had found several weeks ago. Next, they carried the box to a more open area nearby, and Chispo pried the lid off of it.

"¡Caray! Que raro," said Rudy, commenting on what a rare thing they had found.

"Well, I will say!" Robert remarked.

"A treasure chest sure enough," Andrew declared.

Others made comments, as well. Inside the box were numerous bronze plates. Some of them had hieroglyphic writing casted into them. Other plates had small square pieces of crystals impregnated into them, some of them being of holographic crystal material.

In addition to that, there were various crystals stored in one corner compartment of the box. Most of them were greenish-yellow in color. A few of them were turquoise in color. One of them was orange, and Rudy reached into the box and picked that one up. Suddenly, he experienced a rush of thoughts, as if volumes full of information were suddenly being given to him. At the same time, Morris felt a rush of thoughts telepathically leaving him.

"Whew! What was that?" Rudy suddenly exclaimed. He placed the crystal back into the box, somewhat stunned.

"What was that weird rush of thoughts?" Morris asked everyone.

"Are you two all right?" Andrew asked them.

"Yes, I'm fine," Morris answered. "Just a bit dazed. That's all."

"I don't know what's just come over me," Rudy stated.

"Rudy, did I hear you speak in English?" Robert asked him.

"No, of course you didn't," Rudy quickly answered. Then he showed a look of surprise at himself. "Wait . . . Since when . . . You mean I know English?"

"You mean you just picked up the English language, too?" Fraxino asked Rudy.

"No . . . I mean . . . Well, it seems like I just did," Rudy answered, still dazed by what had just happened.

"Another one," Robert commented.

"First it's Glecko picking up English off of our minds," Andrew remarked. "Next it's Chispo being telepathically given Spanish by Rudy, and now Rudy suddenly knows English."

"I don't want to believe it," said Rudy, "but I've got all these English phrases running through my mind. It's overwhelming. Suddenly, I just know how to speak English. It's almost unreal."

"No kidding!" Steven responded.

"No joke," Rudy verified. "I can finally talk with all of you without translators." He walked over to Steven and shook hands with him. Then Rudy walked over to Morris. "It looks like we can talk directly to each other now."

"Yes, we certainly can," Morris calmly agreed. "This was probably meant to happen."

"How can that be?" Rudy wanted to know.

"I mean, as soon as you picked up that orange crystal, it must have served as a catalyst to facilitate the telepathic thought transference of the English language from my mind to yours. My knowledge of the English language got repeated into your energy field, and now your brain is processing the information and incorporating it into your being."

Rudy instinctively understood Morris' explanation. At the same time, Morris had always had a remarkable capacity for understanding how things worked, especially concerning telepathy and energy systems. With this thought transference from Morris that occurred, Rudy automatically picked up more understanding from Morris.

"Are those plaques throwaways from the days of Atlantis?" Rudy asked everyone.

"We think they are, man," Chispo answered, "seeing how that box of holographic plates we found here a few weeks ago is also from Atlantis."

"Really? Is that true?" Rudy responded.

"That's right. Man, I can't believe they just tossed this crate out here, too!" Chispo declared. "It seems that no more than the Atlanteans got here from Earth that they just tossed a bunch of cargo and data away."

"Maybe they thought they'd never need it again, since they were no longer on Earth," Rudy commented, suggesting a possible reason.

"What do you think these plaques are about?" Robert asked Morris.

"My instinctive feeling is that these may be programming instructions, maybe data or keys to a puzzle we may soon be solving." Morris carefully worded his answer so that he would spark enough interest in his friends for what he personally knew was yet to come. However, he had to keep a lid on telling them too much until the time would be right.

Morris was of a different sort, and he definitely had special talents. He was able to see the future. It was he who had dreamed of and made initial contact with Tom, the galactic salesman, earlier this year, and Tom had made a deal with Morris and his friends to help him build a galactic communications device to link his home world with Earth and also other star systems. Tom had given them the gift of transporting themselves by a thought process utilizing a pink glow of energy and whirring wind, and they had already travelled to various places on Earth in addition to travelling to Sirius B, Vega, and the Pleiades.

One month ago, when they travelled to Antarctica and met Rinto and Fraxino from Al Nitak, Morris was suddenly compelled to leave the group. He had other duties to fulfill, including visiting Delikadove, the world of the dolphins on the other side of the galaxy. While that was true, he later revealed that the real reason he left the group was that the communications block between Earth and the Orion star system would not have let a diversified being like Morris physically arrive, and he had been afraid for his own safety.

Now that his friends had successfully destroyed the Atlantean dodecahedron crystal transmitters hidden in the mountains of northern Mexico, the block was cleared, and Morris had recently rejoined the group. He was enjoying his time with them here in Zotola.

"Puzzle, like what?" Robert asked Morris, wanting to know what sort of puzzle they might soon be solving.

"My feeling is that Tom will soon be approaching us about another mission for us to accomplish."

"What sort of mission?" Rudy asked Morris.

"I have no idea what it is. It's just a feeling I have."

"Let's get this box and contents carried over to the craft, dudes," Fraxino said to everyone.

"Rinto's not going to believe it, man" Chispo added.

All of them started taking stacks of bronze tablets out of the box, being careful to keep them in the same order. They started carrying them across the boulder field on the way back to the vehicle-craft. They actually felt energized, with the excitement of having found another crate.

"It's just unbelievable what they tossed out soon after arriving here," Morris commented.

"I know. Why?" Chris wanted to know.

"That's what I want to know," Chispo agreed.

"They probably forgot what the purpose of these plates was," Andrew speculated. "After living here a few generations, like Rudy said, they probably saw no use for them."

"What about museums?" Robert asked everyone. "Why didn't they safeguard these in museums?"

"They likely could have done," Morris answered, "but then they might have suffered a cultural setback, having lost some technology somewhere along the time line, and they therefore had no use for them, and these materials became forgotten."

"That sounds likely so," Robert agreed.

"Or it could be that someone purposefully buried it in the crevice, hoping someone way down the time line would dig it up," Rudy added.

They made their way back to the vehicle-craft, arriving in ten minutes. There, they loaded the box into the vehicle and carefully placed the tablets back into the box in the same order.

"All right, dudes," Chispo declared. "Let's head back to Zantaayer."

It was now early afternoon, and the weather had become hot with Al Nitak almost directly overhead. Fraxino let Chispo do the driving. The trip took just over an hour, and Fraxino played some Zotolan pop music in their on-board holodisk player. On the way back, Chispo drove them over the crest of the Ciruclar Mountains and made the descent on the narrow winding highway into Zantaayer. They were afforded spectacular views through the trees of the forested mountain slopes of the city and of the ocean beyond. They arrived in the mid afternoon.

Soon after pulling into the Zapatero's driveway, Rinto came outside to greet them. He had heard them arriving.

"Rinto, you're not going to *believe* what we found this time," Fraxino told his brother.

"Let me guess, a second sacred story stone?"

"Another bronze crate," Fraxino informed him.

"Really? Cool!" Rinto responded, perking up with enthusiasm.

As they stepped out of the vehicle-craft, they helped Fraxino lift the heavy bronze crate out of the back, and they carried it into the house.

"Mom and Dad went out to do some errands," Rinto informed them. "They'll be back in a few hours."

"Good. At least we don't have to hear Mom's complaints about our dragging home more junk," said Fraxino.

Rinto laughed at his brother's comment.

While Glecko Zapatero supported his sons' unique projects, his wife Sosta had a different viewpoint on the matter. Her two sons had dragged home all kinds of rocks and other parts and supplies when they did their Velosa cruiser craft project last year, and she had just about had enough of the sight of clutter that had been hidden in the row of bushes around the edge of the yard. At times she nagged them about it. Even still, Rinto and Fraxino had been thoughtful about keeping their clutter out of sight as much as possible.

"Here, let's get this crate into the next room where the other one is," Rinto suggested, "and maybe Mom won't even take notice."

Everyone continued carrying the crate and set it down next to the box of holographic plates.

"Robert, show Rinto what I found," Rudy requested.

"Oh, yeah. The egg-shaped crystal." Robert reached for his daypack, opened it, and took it out.

"Chispo and Robert and I went to a different area . . ." Rudy began.

"Rudy, you mean you speak English?" Rinto asked with surprise.

"Yes, I do now, incredible as it may seem," he explained. "You see, when we pried open that crate, I reached for an orange crystal, and suddenly I received this whole rush of instantaneous thoughts. They had come from Morris, and instantly I know English and I can speak it."

"That's incredible!" Rinto told Rudy. "Another sudden language acquisition. That's three now, isn't it?" he asked Fraxino.

"That's right. Dad's learning English, Chispo being instantly given Spanish by Rudy, and now Rudy being instantly given English by Morris."

"Good, that makes it easier for us," Rinto stated. "Now all of us can speak English."

"Let's take the lid off this and have a look at the tablets," Chispo suggested.

They lifted off the heavy bronze lid, and they carefully started examining the bronze tablets. Many of them were impregnated with hieroglyphic script. The script was indeed Atlantean. Rinto, Fraxino, and Chispo recognized the characters as being similar to the writing that appeared on the walls inside the ice cave in Antarctica.

"What do you think these tablets are about, Rinto?" Robert wanted to know.

"I'm not exactly sure," Rinto began. He further inspected the tablets. Since some of them had squares and pieces of crystals (some of them holographic) fastened to the tablets, Rinto began to telepathically read the data by plunging the etherical part of his mind into the energy of the material. Via this technique, he was able to probe the data. "The best I can make of it, these tablets look like a set of programming instructions in numbered sequence, possibly to program some sort of computer or device."

"Really?" Robert responded. "Morris, weren't you saying these tablets might be programming instructions or data keys for a puzzle we may soon be solving?"

"That's right. I was," Morris calmly replied.

"What, you mean you know some destiny to this?" Rinto asked Morris.

"I'm not saying I know, but it is a feeling I'm getting."

"Hmm . . . Interesting," Rinto commented.

Chispo was looking at the tablets as several of them were. "Dudes, I keep receiving subtle information from these tablets about souls and spiritual existences."

"You mean like soul travel?" Rudy suddenly suggested.

"Exactly, man," Chispo replied. "How did you think of that?"

"I just picked up that feeling as you said it," Rudy told Chispo. "Maybe I read these tablets in a way, too."

With what Rudy just said, Morris realized that Rudy had indeed picked up more abilities in that brief moment than just learning the English language. He wasn't quite sure yet how much extra information he had suddenly acquired from Morris. It began to concern him. How much information, if any, did Rudy happen to pick up concerning Delikadove, the dolphin world? Morris knew some things that planet Earth was not yet ready for. Perhaps a little too much of Morris' energy field had been repeated into Rudy's character being, and he either hoped that some of it would soon wear off or that there had been a genuine good reason for what had happened.

"Can your crystal base computer read these tablets?" Andrew asked Rinto and Fraxino.

"No, not very well," Rinto admitted. "Fraxino, what purpose do you think those crystals have in that corner compartment of the crate?"

"Man, for some reason, I feel like we're not supposed to even touch those crystals until the time is right."

"Aw, Fraxino, what can it hurt to touch them?" Rudy now asked. He started to reach for one.

"Rudy, wait!" Morris quickly told him. He reached out and grabbed Rudy's arm. "I believe your friend, Fraxino, speaks the truth. You already saw what happened when you touched that orange one. We must be very careful with those crystals. There's no telling what Atlantean programming instructions are in them . . . and intended for certain individuals at the right time."

"You mean there's a predestined plan to these crystals, too?" Rudy asked.

"I'm afraid very much so," Morris verified. "I would leave those alone until I can assure you it's safe to handle them."

"Morris, how can you be so sure of that?" Rudy argued. "I already touched one, and I'm just fine. More, I now know English."

"Yes, you do, and you're very lucky," Morris told him. "At the same time, I'm afraid you may have picked up more from it than was intended."

"Like what?" Rudy wanted to know.

"I'm not even going to say. I would be telling too much, but I do urge every one of you to take my precautionary advice for your own safety. I'm only telling you my feelings for your better good. Time and patience are important as you investigate these pieces."

Chispo stared at the crystals and then began talking. "Man, these crystals are predestined special gifts for certain selected individuals at the right place at the right time. Every one of them are catalyst crystals meant to serve a purpose in that puzzle Morris tells us about."

Morris was somewhat spellbound at Chispo's sudden comments. He knew Chispo was right, and he now realized that he had underestimated Chispo's genuine ability to telepathically read information and data programmed into crystals and the ether around them.

"Chispo, I'm going to go ahead and tell you something," Morris informed him. "I've known this since before I met you, and with that comment you just made, that confirms it for me. You definitely have a link to Delikadove, the world of the dolphins. Your character shows it, and you are right about what you just said about those crystals in that crate."

"Wow, man! That's far out!" Chispo responded. "Man, you weren't with us when we went to see those ancient paintings in Mexico, but one of the walls contained depictions that really surprised me. There were coincidences in it right down to my phone number, man! More than that, there was a depiction of a dolphin, a Eucalyptus twig, and a drawing of an exploding sun, maybe representing Danetar, the dying sun of the dolphin's old home world. Robert and I talked about the possibility of our having some link to the dolphins."

"Oh, you do indeed, Chispo," Morris verified, "and so do you, Robert. Another one of you here also has a strong link, but I'm not yet going to say which one of you has it. That's something for you all to explore and discover for yourselves."

Rudy was realizing the actual amount of voluminous knowledge that Morris possessed in his mind, and he knew that Morris knew a lot more than he let on. It was beginning to bother him how Morris seemingly said much less than he actually knew. More that that, with the extra knowledge Rudy picked up, he could somehow sense that Morris' recent trips to the world of the dolphins involved some major project in mind. He wasn't sure what it was, but he already had an idea that it would involve this crateload of tablets.

"You know," Steven brought up. "I just wonder why these tablets have both hieroglyphic script, and some of them also have square-shaped pieces of crystals and holographic material impregnated in them?"

"That's a good question," Rinto responded.

"It probably had something to do with being more versatile," said Andrew, "as far as being used to program different types of equipment."

"Or it could be that some people simply read the hieroglyphic text," said Rinto, "while others could telepathically read the same information or instructions from the crystals and holographic material."

"It's sort of like it's listed in two languages," Chris speculated.

"Exactly," Fraxino agreed.

"And I'd say for those who read the hieroglyphic text," Morris added, "they probably entered the programming instructions manually."

"That's good thinking, Morris," Robert said to him.

"You want to look at any more holographic plates?" Rinto offered, changing the subject.

"Let's take another look at the index, man," Chispo said to everyone. He placed the index plate on the tray. Everyone looked on as the index list showed up on the screen.

"*Linkage of Souls and Friendship*, plate number 90. Once he placed it on the tray, text soon showed up on the screen, and he began narrating.

"Atlantean society has always had the remarkable knowledge that all human beings carry a force with them which keeps them animated and alive. It is known as the life force or soul, and souls come from a higher level of existence which consists of spiritual beings.

"These spiritual beings or souls reside in a different level of existence from the physical world. They are non-physical in form, and many of them reside in small groups. They live together and interact together and learn in the world of spirits together, and when they incarnate on the physical level to live human lifetimes, they are usually very good friends or family to each other.

"These souls are linked together because they are usually on the same level of advancement since their origin, and they therefore carry nearly the same natural frequency of vibration which is the key to their compatibility of friendship while they live physical lifetimes.

"Friendship is a very important trait to soul advancement. As friends have experiences together, their souls travel together and learn. Their friendly interactions with each other accelerate their advancement to higher levels.

"As many souls interact and learn together in the world of the spirits, they, on their higher levels, can also plan physical lifetimes together. Through their linkage together, they can set up or set into motion various synchronicities and coincidences which can later cause them to come together and be friends during physical life. Through the strong friendship quantum energy systems that they have, they can cause the systems to work in their favor to bring them together, sooner or later, after they incarnate and are born."

"That sounds like a form of destiny," Fraxino commented.

"Very interesting," Morris commented. "That last bit rings similar to the *Friendships and Their Own Life Force* plate we looked at this morning."

"Yes, it does," Rinto agreed.

"So," Chris commented, "friendships have a life force of their own and can actually link up certain people by causing them to meet each other."

"That's right," said Morris.

"Most people who are good friends usually have a strong linkage of souls," Chispo told them.

"And they are compatible with each other," Andrew stated.

"Do we want to go see *Vision from the Ciruclar*?" Rudy asked everyone, changing the subject.

"Sure, man," Chispo agreed. "Let's go. What time does it start, dudes?"

Rinto and Fraxino both checked the time. "In less than an hour," Rinto answered. "Let's go ahead and turn this off, and we'll leave shortly." Rinto switched off the controls to the crystal base computer.

They placed the lid back on their new found bronze crate, and they got ready to leave. Glecko and Sosta had not yet come home. They were still out doing errands.

"The movie theater is on the highway where we passed by it earlier," Chispo informed them.

They walked out of the house, piled into the vehicle-craft, and Rinto drove all nine of them to Zantaayer's movie theater called Myrtillo Cinema.

CHAPTER 2

THE ALASKA PROJECT PROPOSAL

Rinto drove them into the parking lot, and they all stepped outside. Rinto, Fraxino, and Chispo together paid for the others to enter, and they walked into the theater. There was a decent turnout of people attending.

The movie lasted nearly three hours and was very interesting to them indeed. It was about an archaeological expedition team who went searching in the southern section of the Ciruclar Mountains for Atlantean artifacts. One of the members in the group, Quinoteh, had earlier had a vision of some of the first settlers arriving in the fleet of spacecrafts from Atlantis to their new world here on Artenia. The scenery in his vision matched that of the Ciruclar Mountains with the view of the valley where the city of Zantaayer would later be built, and the Elizabeth Ocean seen beyond it.

Quinoteh led the team to the spot where he had seen the vision, and there they dug and sure enough found some artifacts. They found a bronze box containing various rocks and crystals. One of the more interesting pieces was an orange Calcite sacred story stone. They were rare indeed. Only between ten and twenty of these stones had ever been found throughout Artenia's history. The stones were known to come from Vega and were thought to be several hundred thousand years old.

As Quinoteh inserted the etherical part of his mind into the holographic material that had been impregnated onto the piece of Calcite, he extracted a story of a vision and a quest for galactic communication and soul travel between various intelligent races of different star systems. The stone had been carefully guarded and treasured by Atlantean leaders as a quest for the future, and when they had arrived in their fleet of spacecrafts to their new world atop the Ciruclar Mountains, the leader, Cresma had a welcoming ceremony and had carefully stored several artifacts in the mountains to later be realized and discovered by someone at the appropriate time in the future. Quinoteh was the one, and through their discovery, they made efforts to re-establish contact with their ancient homeland of Atlantis.

Throughout the movie, Chispo, Rinto and Fraxino quietly translated to Andrew, Chris, Morris, Robert, Rudy, and Steven to keep them filled in. They couldn't help but laugh at times for what they already knew about Atlantis and also since they had actually, several weeks ago, found one of those rare sacred story stones at the ancient galactic dump site. The stone they had found contained and revealed the mysterious origin of the *Liriodendrons*, the Tulip Poplars, known to the Artenians as the Flowering Sun Tree.

Although the movie was fiction, it was filmed and made available to the public with the purpose of generating interest in Zantaayer's residents . . . well, actually, Artenia's residents . . . about their past history, heritage, and artifacts.

Though the nine of them didn't realize it, the theme of the movie seemed to run somewhat along the same parallels of what they had been doing, digging up crates of ancient artifacts in the ancient galactic dump site, and it might have even represented what they would be doing in the future.

When they exited the movie, it was dark outside. They all climbed back into the vehicle-craft, and Rinto drove them back to the house.

"Really an interesting movie," Morris commented.

"I liked it, too," said Rudy.

"Man, am I glad they didn't give away the location of our secret site, the ancient galactic dump site," Chispo declared.

"Yeah, you're not kidding," Fraxino acknowledged.

"After all, as far as the movie's concerned," Rinto explained, "it looks a lot better and has more purpose to have the artifacts buried along the ridge of the Ciruclar Mountains, in addition to the vision of the scenery it offers."

"It just looks more pleasing to the public, doesn't it," Chispo stated.

"Exactly," Rinto agreed.

"So, while the movie lets the public think the artifacts are so aesthetically set on the mountain top," said Steven, "we know the truth about where the real stuff is buried."

"It's got to look that way for the movie so it will look good," Chris pointed out.

"Exactly," Rudy agreed. "If the movie showed the artifacts buried way out in that old dump site, who would want to go see the movie?"

"That's right," said Robert. "There wouldn't be any scenery."

"That was more of a historical movie, wasn't it," Andrew commented.

"Actually, historical fiction," Fraxino clarified.

"At the same time, it did have some adventure to it," Chris added.

They continued talking about the movie, and they were very soon pulling into the Zapatero's driveway. It had been a long day for them, and they spread out their bedrolls and sleeping bags on the floor. In a short time, they all drifted off to sleep.

Glecko and Sosta had been away for the afternoon and evening, and they soon arrived home. They quietly entered, walked by them, and went into the back part of the house where they also went to sleep.

Rudy was awakened by their having entered. He got to thinking about those crystals in that crate they had found earlier today. Thanks to the one he had already touched, he now knew and understood the English language. Of course, he also knew and understood very well Morris' sincere warning, but then Rudy reasoned to himself that touching those crystals couldn't really do any harm to him, and stubborn as Rudy was, he had to go check those crystals out, regardless of the warning. He just could not resist.

He waited until Glecko and Sosta had settled down to go to sleep in the back of the house. When he heard no one stirring at all, he quietly got up and sneaked into the room where Rinto and Fraxino had their crystal base computer. As he entered the room, he walked up to the crate, placed his hands on the lid and began to remove it. It proved somewhat difficult to remove and, as it turned out, proved impossible to remove with complete silence. As he did so, the lid made a clank with the sides of the box. Both Robert and Morris were awakened by the noise.

Though Rudy didn't realize it, Rinto and Fraxino's crystal base computer was simultaneously sending a telepathic alarm to Rinto and Fraxino that their belongings were being tampered with and for immediate action to be taken to prevent potential harm from occurring. Fraxino jumped up from where he was sleeping and rushed into the room, soon followed by Rinto, Robert, and Morris. Fraxino arrived just in time and caught Rudy just beginning to reach for one of the crystals.

"No!" Fraxino yelled, and he threw his arms around Rudy and pulled him away from the box. They both fell to the floor.

"Rudy, what do you think you're doing?" Rinto asked him as he entered the room.

"I wanted to see the crystals," he answered, as he and Fraxino were getting up from the floor. Rudy, at the moment, was both embarrassed and very surprised at having been caught.

"Rudy, do you realize how dangerously close that was for you?" Morris now asked him, arriving at the scene.

"What's it to you?!" Rudy firmly told Morris. "I wanted to examine those crystals!"

"You mad idiot!" Morris scolded him. "Have you completely forgotten the warning I gave you earlier today about not touching any more of those crystals?"

"No, of course I haven't forgotten!" Rudy angrily answered. "What's it going to hurt?"

"That crystal you were reaching for," Morris now more calmly told him, "would have wiped your personality clean away. You would have been like a zombie."

"How do you know?" Rudy argued. "You weren't in the room. You didn't see me reach for it."

"I could see the event playing out in my mind," Morris answered, "but the reality suddenly got shifted in your favor, thanks to your friend, Fraxino, who grabbed you and saved you from what would have been most disastrous for you."

"Rudy," Robert now explained, "my friends and I have known Morris for some time, now. When he gives out a sincere warning, he does it for our good, and it needs to be heeded to. He knows what he's talking about."

By now, some of the others were also entering the room, having been waked up by what had happened.

"What happened, guys?" Chispo wanted to know.

"Rudy just about touched one of the crystals in that crate," Robert answered.

"Man, you don't know how close you came to losing it!" Chispo firmly told Rudy.

"You need to think about the consequences to you and others," Fraxino explained to Rudy. "Really, what would we have done with you if I had not reached you in time?"

"We don't have any repair techniques for restoring personalities," Rinto added.

"Not all of Atlantean technology is benign," Morris told Rudy.

"Dude, Morris is right," Chispo confirmed. "Those Atlanteans did some vicious mood controlling experiments! That's why there's so much turmoil on your world, Earth. Don't let your curiosity get the best of you."

"More than that," Morris informed Rudy, "Atlantean suppression technology was very dangerous. I warned you fair and square this afternoon, but I knew you would sneak in here anyway. I could see it in my mind. I could have warned you a second time, but you wouldn't have listened to me. You needed to learn your lesson the hard way. It's a blessing for you that Fraxino wrenched you away from that crate just before you could get your hands on those crystals. Some Atlantean materials were marked dangerous and were dumped as a result. In a way, those crystals can compare to toxic or radioactive waste of modern-day Earth."

By now, Rudy was calmed down, and he was beginning to realize what he had done. Chills went down his back for fear of what he now knew could have happened to him. "I didn't consider it nearly that serious," he admitted.

"I know you didn't," Morris said to him. "You acted on impulse and stubbornness."

"Just think of the possible consequences before you do things," Chispo advised. "It will save you a lot of trouble."

By now, with everyone talking to Rudy, he had no choice but be convinced about how important it was to not touch those crystals and to realize possible consequences prior to taking action.

"Let's all go back and get some sleep, guys," Fraxino suggested to everyone.

All of them returned to the room where they had been sleeping, and they climbed back into their sleeping bags.

Even though Rudy knew he was wrong to have done what he did, the scolding he received and the surprise at being caught didn't sit 100% well with him. He felt a slight amount of resentment that he didn't have his way at being able to touch and examine those crystals. At the same time, he was aware that Fraxino had gotten to him in time and had saved him from what would likely have ruined his personality. He had to be grateful for that much. No matter what, with what just happened in addition to missing his brother, Roel, he began to wish to go back home to Mexico. He thought about it as he drifted off to sleep with the rest of them.

Morning arrived with nice weather and clear blue-green skies. All of them got up and went into the kitchen where Glecko and Sosta fed them breakfast. There were various cereals and fruits.

"Here's a new one for you, guys," Glecko announced as he showed them a new box of cereal. "*Kellogg's* Bran Flakes Esperaña." He set the box of cereal on the table. "I just brought it home from the supermarket last night."

"You have *Kellogg's* cereals on Artenia, too?" Robert asked, somewhat surprised.

"We do now, as of this week," Glecko answered.

"Huh!" Steven commented and he laughed. "Earth's companies are having all kinds of influences here on this world. It's coming in from all different angles."

"Looks like *Kellogg's* has now expanded to a galactic level, too," Andrew remarked, laughing.

"Dad, how can they be able to sell this in Earth's alphabet?" Rinto wanted to know.

"I know. How can they get away with this?" Fraxino complained. "Why aren't they forced to conform to Artenia's standards and print the name in Artenian script? After all, very few Artenians know English."

"*Kellogg's* Bran Flakes Esperaña," said Rinto, shaking his head. "Totally Earth's alphabet."

"Look at that," Fraxino commented. "It even goes on to boast how it has Pyridoxine: for better hearing and mental acuity, and it's written in English. What's this world coming to?"

"I'm sure *Kellogg's* will soon get the message," Glecko told everyone reassuringly. "Since it's a new product by a new galactic company here on Artenia, I suspect they wanted to introduce it in the alphabet and language of its place of origin."

"I'll bet they're exporting it directly from *Kellogg's* on Earth," Chispo suggested, "until they can set up manufacturing of it, here on Artenia."

Steven was the first one to the box. He opened it and poured a bowl for himself. He began to munch on the flakes of cereal. "It tastes good enough . . . looks very much like Bran Flakes on Earth. I'll have to take a couple of boxes home to my dad. He's suffering from a little bit of hearing loss."

"He is?" Robert asked with concern. "I didn't know that."

"Yes, it's been going on for about a year now. He hasn't wanted anyone to know about it, and he's basically kept it to himself."

"Sorry to hear that," said Robert.

"Maybe this Bran Flakes *Esperaña* will do the trick," Chris said reassuringly to Steven.

"Thanks."

Robert looked at the box of cereal some more. He read the nutrition information. "Good! It doesn't have any BHT in it."

"That's right," Glecko proudly stated.

"You mean you already knew that?" Robert asked. "It's all over our cereals back on Earth."

"I know it is," Glecko admitted. "You see, that's one of Earth's scandals . . . has to do with a government cover-up scheme and cancer study. BHT, or by its real name: Butylated Hydroxy-toluene, is a poisonous and dangerous byproduct of modern plastics production which began in the late 1940's on your world Earth. They had to figure out how to get rid of the chemical, and it dawned on them that preserving food was the answer, all under contract and agreement with top secret Earth government officials and cancer societies around the world. It's a nasty preservative which is strictly prohibited here on our world of Artenia, and *Kellogg's knows* it!"

"Golly!!" Robert declared, somewhat shocked.

"Glecko, how can you be sure of that?" Steven asked Glecko, doubting.

"I used to teach chemistry," he answered, "and I know about that chemical. Here on our world, it's a strict mandate that all hazardous chemicals and byproducts be sent *straight* to Al Nitak, which is by far, a *superior* incinerator to anything we could have on this world."

"Now that's smart thinking," Robert complimented. "Why can't they do that on our world, also?"

"Scandals, corruption, and undercover cancer studies," Glecko simply replied, his arms crossed.

"So," Chispo proposed, "what do we all want to do today?"

"There's a really neat back road that runs the ridge of the Ciruclar Mountains," Fraxino informed them. "It passes right by the scene where they found that crate and sacred story stone."

"Really?" Robert responded. "Let's go."

"Yeah, I'm for that," Steven agreed. "Who knows. We may find something of interest."

"You never know," Morris responded. "By the way," he brought up, changing the subject, "I haven't seen any televisions or radios."

"Man, there aren't any," Fraxino answered.

"Really?" Morris responded with concern. "How odd. I wonder why? It probably won't be long with galactic trade influence from Earth."

"Not on Artenia, man," Chispo proudly stated. "They're against government regulations. It's like I was telling you all the other day, before Morris came here, TV's and radios were interfering to some of our native people, in addition to being disturbing to whales and dolphins and other life in our oceans. Over half a century ago when the governments of our world started to broadcast electromagnetic waves, they received so many disturbing complaints that they had to abandon their plans. People like the Atascosa down south are very perceptive, and their rights not to be disturbed by electromagnetic waves had to be respected. Man, our phone company, Astrelcom, is not even allowed to use microwave repeater towers for long distance communication. All of it is done with trunk cables and now more recently, fiberoptic cables."

"That's really interesting," Morris commented. "I'm glad to know the native people and ocean life are respected by this world's government."

"No matter what, we have newspapers, and most people have phone service," Rinto now informed Morris.

"Also, if there were a national emergency," Fraxino added, "Astrelcom has a step-by-step calling procedure, and just about everybody could be notified in twenty minutes."

"That's good to know," said Morris.

They continued talking as they ate breakfast, and as they were finishing, there was a knock on the door.

"I wonder who that could be?" Glecko commented to everyone. He got up and went to the front door of the house to answer it. It was Tom, the galactic salesman.

"Good morning," said Tom as Glecko opened the door.

"Well, hello there," Glecko greeted him. "I'll bet you're looking for your friends. They're all here. Come on in."

Tom stepped inside. He had on his white Sirian robe, as always, and he carried his walking staff with the iron ball on top of it. Glecko led the way and took Tom to the kitchen where they were just getting up from eating breakfast.

"Hey, Tom," said Morris. "What brings you here?"

Everyone else followed in and greeted him.

"I have another project for you guys, if you want it," Tom replied.

"Really?" Robert responded.

"I had a feeling you'd be contacting us soon," Morris commented. "Where are we going this time?" as if he didn't already know.

"Do you remember my good friend, Caymar, from Sirius B?"

"Oh yes," Morris replied.

"Well, it's like this," Tom began. "I'll begin by explaining something. You all may have wondered why I've had so little time to accompany you all, that is, that I've always had to return to my work and business transactions."

"Yes, I have wondered about that at times," Morris admitted.

"Yeah, that's true," Chris added. "You've always sort of come and gone."

"Well, the explanation," Tom continued, "is that the Galactic Federation has had in mind a . . . what would best be described as a huge galactic switching station involving the equivalent of literally millions of Earth's telephone lines connecting numerous civilizations across the galaxy."

"No kidding!" Steven responded with enthusiasm.

"Wow, man!" Chispo also responded.

"It's the largest galactic communications project ever undertaken by the federation, and we have just completed drawing up the preliminary proposals and plans. It's taken us years, and the project will take another 14 or 15 years to reach completion. Caymar and I have been assigned the task of engineering and building it."

"This sounds like a really enormous project indeed," Morris commented.

"Gargantuan is the word for it," Fraxino added.

All of them now got up and walked into the room where their backpacks were.

"Tom, we're about to take a daytrip to the southwestern ridge of the surrounding Ciruclar Mountains," Rinto now told him. "If you like, you can come with us and explain your proposal and project to us. It will give you a chance to have a view of this region."

"That's a splendid idea," Tom agreed. "I'll come with you. We'll be going in your cruiser craft, I presume?"

"That we will," Rinto confirmed. "Everyone ready to go?" he now asked the others.

They all answered yes, threw some belongings into their daypacks, and they walked out of the house to the vehicle-craft and climbed in. Rinto did the driving, and he backed them out of the driveway.

This time, he took them on a different route. Instead of going through Zantaayer's central district, he drove them to the highway and crossed it at a location very near the Myrtillo Cinema where they had seen *Vision from the Ciruclar* the night before.

"We saw this really neat movie last night," Chispo explained to Tom, "about an archaeological expedition to the ridge top of the Ciruclar Mountains, and they find some Atlantean artifacts, including a sacred story stone which relates a story of a quest for soul travel and galactic communication."

"Is that right?" Tom responded with surprise. "That's very similar to the project I have in mind for you fellows."

"Really? Where is this project?" Andrew wanted to know.

"It's in Alaska."

"Alaska? That's a remote place," Andrew remarked.

"That's why we chose its remote northern mountains for our project site," Tom informed them.

"Alaska," Rinto said to his brother. "Now that's a place we've never been to."

Soon after crossing the highway, they left the commercial district and were driving along a two-lane paved road. In just a few kilometers, they reached the foot of the Ciruclar Mountains. The concrete pavement ended, and Rinto drove them up the forested mountain slopes on a winding gravel road. Over the next half hour as they climbed in altitude, they traversed numerous hairpin curves.

Tom noticed how crystal clear the air was here on Artenia compared to planet Earth's atmosphere, and he was really taken by the views of the city and the ocean beyond, seen below them through the numerous Southern Beech trees of the forest.

"For those of you who only recently know me," Tom brought up, speaking mostly to Rinto, Fraxino, Chispo, and Rudy, "my actual name is Tomarius. Most people call me Tom for short. I work with the Galactic Federation on various projects, and I live on the planet around the binary star system of Sirius A and B. Robert and his friends, including Morris, came and visited me on Sirius B a little over a month ago, and my friend, Caymar, took them on a walking adventure in our polar district up north. Aside from that region, Sirius B is generally a hot, dry planet with desert-like terrain consisting of numerous varieties of Cactus plants endemic to our world. There are also Cypress-Pine trees and Tamarisk shrubs which were brought from your planet Earth."

"Man, you got it right about your planet being hot and dry," Chispo agreed. "I remember it very well during that brief moment when I went with Robert to meet you."

"I don't believe we've ever known your real name before," said Robert. "All you told us was Tom."

"Yes, that's my true name, *Tomarius*," Tom told everyone. "Robert, when I met you and your friends for the first time on your parents' farm in Tennessee when you were involved in building that galactic communications device, I had said that for those who speak English, my name is Tom, which as you now know is short for and derived from my true name, *Tomarius*. For those of you who more recently know me, not only am I a galactic salesman for the Galactic Federation, I am also a communications engineer."

They continued talking with Tom as Rinto continued driving them up the mountain. They told him about the second crate they had just found and how its plaques could very well be programming instructions or data or keys to a puzzle they may soon be solving. Tom mentioned that the contents of that crate may serve very useful for the upcoming Alaska project. More than that, Tom was even more surprised about the special compartment of crystals and how Rudy had suddenly telepathically learned English upon touching one of them.

They finally reached the ridge top where they intersected the gravel road running the forested ridge of the mountains. Rinto made a right turn and drove them a short distance to a small turnout where he parked.

"All right, dudes," Chispo decided to announce. "This is where we step down. Part of *Vision from the Ciruclar* was filmed just a few hundred meters from here."

All of them stepped outside.

"Beautiful views from up here, aren't they?" Tom remarked.

"Yes, you're not kidding," Steven agreed.

A moderate breeze was blowing from the west, and the temperature was a pleasant 20° Celsius. There was a small, partially forested knoll to the south of the ridge road, and they started walking toward it. They recognized it from the scenes they had seen in the movie last night.

"I wonder if there really are any artifacts up here," Chris said to everyone.

"My feeling is there aren't," Morris answered, "but you never know. There might be something."

They climbed the small knoll with exposed limestone rocks. There was a mixture of Pines and Southern Beeches throughout the region. When they reached the mostly bald top, they were afforded nothing less than spectacular views of the whole region.

"My goodness!" Robert commented. "You can see the whole Ciruclar mountain range from up here."

"Just spectacular!" Tom remarked.

"Out of this world, isn't it?" Fraxino jokingly told everyone.

Some of them laughed.

"I understand now, at least according to the movie," said Andrew, "why Cresma would have stored a crate of important data up here."

"Instead of at that desolate dump site," Rudy added.

"Yeah, really," Chris agreed.

"Sometimes scenery makes more sense and has more order than one realizes," Morris told everyone.

"I can sense that this is an excellent location for me to officially present and offer you my next project," Tom announced. "That of going to Alaska, especially since from this location, as you tell me, the characters in that movie find a sacred story stone telling of a quest for soul travel and galactic communication."

Everyone listened as Tom continued. He paced back and forth with his walking

staff in hand. "This is therefore synchronized with our plans with what the Galactic Federation has assigned me to undertake . . . in Alaska. A few days ago, Caymar and I were investigating the remote rugged mountains of northeastern Alaska in efforts to decide where to build the station. Some of it will be above ground, the group of receiver/transmitter towers, and the rest will be buried within the mountains in underground tunnels that will soon be made.

"As I was earlier saying, this grand switching station will connect numerous galactic civilizations across the galaxy, including this world. In addition to communication via gravity waves, it will involve soul travel. The station will contain the equivalent of literally millions of telephone lines. In subtle and unrecognized ways, millions of planet Earth's telephone numbers will be made available from participating countries, all in preparation for the station's grand opening at the turn of the millennium."

"That's nearly 15 years from now," Chispo commented.

"That's right," Tom responded. "Over the course of that time period, many new area codes will be added to the telephone system of the United States and Canada, all under contract and agreement with Galactic Federation rules and guidelines. Other countries, such as Great Britain and Australia, will also be participating."

"What sort of subtle and unrecognized ways will there be?" Steven wanted to know.

"Nearer the time of the project's completion, there will be small hidden charges levied on all monthly and quarterly telephone bills, such as 'Universal Connectivity Charges' and 'Carrier Line Charges' that will generate more than ample funds to pay for the project. Also, there will be massive restructuring of the national area code schemes, and numerous additions of new area codes will begin in a few years, under the reasons that they are necessary for extra phone lines, population growth, cellular telephones, FAX machines, beepers, and computer modems. While part of that will be true over the next 15 years, a larger percentage of the new numbers will be made available in the form of companies secretly buying up large blocks of numbers for future use, special use numbers, and that sort of thing."

"That's really going to happen?" Andrew asked in disbelief.

"That you will see occur," Tom confirmed. "These plans are all under contract and agreement with federation rules and guidelines, like I was earlier saying."

"That will be interesting," said Andrew.

"What's really come as a surprise to me," Tom went on to explain, "and this is what I've decided not to tell the federation, is that while Caymar and I were exploring the wet, snow-melting mountain slopes, we came across a most curious artifact."

"What . . . What did you find?" Robert wanted to know.

"We came across what looked like the corner of a bronze crate."

"Really? A bronze crate?" Rinto now asked in disbelief.

"That's right," Tom replied, "and when we removed the dirt away from it with our ice picks that we had with us, we pried the lid off of it."

"I'll bet you found another box of holographic plates from Atlantis," Steven guessed.

"No, they weren't holographic plates, like you fellows found here," Tom informed them. "What we found when we removed the lid was a frozen body . . . time frozen, that is."

"Is that *right*?" Steven responded, no doubt surprised.

"You're kidding!" Robert responded.

Everyone showed surprise, and feelings of excitement ran through them.

"I take it the body is from Atlantis?" Morris asked Tom.

"Caymar and I believe it is, but we know of no means to revive the body nor how to unlock the time freeze. That's why we haven't told the Galactic Federation about it. We don't know how many more of these bodies there are. Caymar and I hid the crate and re-covered it with dirt right away. That's why I've come to you all about this. Maybe one or more of you have or know of some techniques to unlock the time freeze and revive this body or bodies, depending on how many more you all might find.

"I feel like it's very important to revive them, and I feel sure there must be several of these time frozen bodies buried among those mountain slopes. There's no telling what vital information they may have and what they can tell us about the region, why they were placed there, and what they can tell us about soul travel and galactic communication, in addition to their knowledge of their past culture, and possible knowledge about time travel."

"Time travel," Chispo responded. "That is far out!"

"That's right," Tom confirmed. "If you fellows can find and revive the bodies, I will personally pay the group of you Earth currency of U.S. $33,000 cash. The Galactic Federation is paying me far more than that to oversee and supervise their 15-year project. If you do a really good job on this project, I'll even pay you a bonus, especially if the bodies you revive can aid us in time travel."

"You can count us in as far as I'm concerned," Fraxino declared.

"Dudes, I know I'm in," Chispo declared.

"Me too," said Robert.

"Tom, I'll see what I can do, as well," Morris assured him. "As you know, I'm also involved with some projects with the land dolphins on their world, Delikadove, but I'll be in on this, too. The dolphins might have some insight on this project, as well. They're very smart beings as most people now know."

"Very good," Tom said to everyone. "The location of our site is between and also involves three mountains in northeastern Alaska. Their names are Mt. Isto, Mt. Chamberlin, and Mt. Michelson. They are only around 80 kilometers from Alaska's northern coast of the Arctic Ocean, and the mountains are surprisingly tall, at nearly 3,000 meters in altitude. At this time of year, the snow is rapidly melting, and access will be good until late September."

"Wow, man!" Chispo remarked. "That does sound remote."

"I'm not supposed to mention this," Tom added, "but Australia is also participating in a sub switching station in their remote Nullarbor Plain. They will connect the stars of the southern hemisphere vantage point, those stars that are out of sight from northern Alaska."

"So, that's why Australia is a participating country," said Andrew, now realizing.

"Exactly," said Tom. "Now I will transmit the visual images to all of you of northeastern Alaska's mountains." He appeared to concentrate, and everyone soon saw clear visual images of the partially snow-covered mountains. They were beautiful in appearance with numerous mountain streams coming down the hillsides. Around 35% of the land appeared to be covered with snow.

"How did you do that?" Rudy wanted to know. "You placed an image in my mind as clear as a real picture." He was more surprised than anyone because it was his first time to telepathically receive an image like that.

"That's known as transmission of visual images via telepathy," Tom explained. "Many of us where we come from on Sirius B communicate like that, but on planet Earth, most people have forgotten that type of communication."

"What about the people from the days and times of Atlantis?" Rudy asked Tom.

"They communicated that way, telepathy via their minds."

"So," Rinto cleverly brought up, "with what Tom's just telepathically transmitted to us, we've now had our own *vision* from the Ciruclar."

"Right on, Rinto!" his brother agreed.

The others laughed some.

"So, fellows," Tom concluded, "I will be in contact with you from time to time throughout this project. I'll let you make preparations, and if you like, I can arrange to meet with you all in northeastern Alaska when you arrive."

"How soon are you thinking?" Morris asked.

"How about exactly two days from now?" Tom proposed.

"That will be fine," Morris answered.

"That's fine with me, too," said Robert. "That will give us time to make plans and get organized."

Earth time, it was 9:30 PM, July 24, 1985. Here on top of the Ciruclar Mountains, it was now late morning.

"That sounds good with us, too," Rinto said to Tom.

"Anyway, I will now teleport home to Sirius B, meet with Caymar, and we'll meet you there in two days."

"See you then, Tom," said Robert.

He walked to the edge of the knoll a short distance away from them, and they saw him instantly and quietly disappear.

"Well, it looks like we've got a big new project on our hands," Steven commented.

"That we do," Fraxino agreed.

They walked back down the partially forested knoll and returned to the vehicle-craft. There, both Rinto and Fraxino telepathically transmitted the visual image of northeastern Alaska's mountain scenery to the Ulexite main controls crystal and the crystal array of their craft, as they planned to use their craft to travel there.

"There, that's got it," said Rinto.

"If we're all ready to go," Fraxino enthusiastically announced, "let's return home and make plans and preparations for *Alaska*!"

Some of them took a last look at the scenery from up here, and then all nine of them climbed into the vehicle-craft. This time, Fraxino did the driving, and he drove them northwest along the ridge road.

"Fraxino," Rinto asked his brother, "do you think we need to make a stop by our cave?"

"Yeah, good thinking," Fraxino agreed. "I can already think of several crystals from our collection that might help us on this new project."

"Then let's stop by there on the way home."

"All right," Fraxino agreed. He now spoke to everyone. "Rinto and I need to make a quick stop at our secret cave to pick up some supplies. We'll just follow this road a few kilometers, and after we visit the cave, we'll take the usual road down the mountain back home again."

That sounded fine to everyone. Neither Morris nor Rudy had seen the cave, and they were looking forward to it.

The winding gravel road weaved its way through Pine and mostly Southern Beech forest. Along the way, the road had its ups and downs but was mostly level as it followed the ridge top of the Ciruclar Mountains. At times, there were other trees such as Poplars, Black Locusts, and Eucalypts, but the majority of the trees were Southern Beeches.

In half an hour, they arrived at a small intersection where Fraxino turned left. He took them down that road for a short ways as it descended into a gully, and he parked at a wide spot in the road. He pointed to a path.

"That's the path that leads down to our secret cave," Rinto now announced while his brother was indicating. "It takes around 20 minutes. Bring your flashlights and daypacks with you."

All of them grabbed their daypacks as they stepped out of the vehicle, and they began to walk down the path.

"Dudes, you won't believe the setup that Rinto and Fraxino have in their secret cave," Chispo proudly told Rudy and Morris. "They've got it all figured out, man."

They followed the narrow path and made the somewhat treacherous descent through the forested gully, sometimes letting themselves down and over boulders. Birds of various colors could be seen flying above the trees, and they gave out their calls in the cool mountain air.

After some 20 minutes, they arrived at a dropoff which had rock walls on each side. Here, they climbed down a rope that Rinto and Fraxino had earlier installed, and the cave's entrance came into view. It was tucked back and underneath the gully itself.

"This cave is a difficult one to reach," Rudy told everyone.

"That's right," said Rinto.

"It's the difficult access that gives us the security we desire," Fraxino stated.

"Even though we don't really need it on this world," Rinto added.

"If you think this is inaccessible," Chispo boasted, "wait till you see what they've got inside."

All of them finished climbing down the rope, and they were now standing at the cave's entrance.

"Welcome to our secret cave," Rinto said to everyone, especially to Morris and Rudy, who had not been here before. "Our research room is about ten minutes back, then up, and to the right."

"You mean there's no locked gate?" Rudy asked. "And there's no trash at all?" Rudy was quick to notice because the large cave in the mountains above Bustamante, Nuevo León did have a locked gate, and the entrance and grounds outside it had plenty of trash.

"We don't need a locked gate here on our world," Fraxino explained. "People here aren't like they are back on Earth. They don't come up here to party, vandalize, and leave beer cans and trash all over the place."

"That's right, dudes," said Chispo, mostly to Rudy and Morris. "When people here on Artenia visit the mountains, they come for useful and responsible reasons, and most of all, they respect the environment."

"That's good to know for this world," said Rudy.

"Yes, it's a shame, really," Morris commented, "that caves and the wilderness back on Earth bear the brunt of such littering and irresponsibility."

"It doesn't seem to concern very many people on Earth," said Rudy.

"Tell Rudy and Morris the reason why no one's discovered your secret room and projects," Robert said to Rinto and Fraxino.

"Yes, how do you keep would-be intruders out?" Rudy wanted to know.

"That's coming up," said Rinto. "We've definitely got that safeguarded."

"Like I was saying," Chispo now boasted in a friendly manner, "Rinto and Fraxino got it all figured out, man. Their research room is accessible only via a high ledge well within the cave, and if that's not enough to satisfy you, the room is well recessed from view from below the ledge. They have to scale the ledge by way of a rope."

"And every time we enter and leave," Fraxino added, "we attach the rope and take it down."

They entered the cave and walked back through the dark tunnels for several minutes. Along the way, Rinto momentarily stopped at a large boulder. He reached behind it, retrieved the rope and slung it over his shoulder.

"You even keep the rope hidden, do you?" Morris asked, and he laughed a little.

"That we do indeed," Rinto replied.

"They've got this place pretty secure," Steven said to Morris and Rudy.

"If that's not enough security for you," Fraxino added, "we've programmed our crystals to cause unwanted intruders to just lose interest and leave the area before they even reach the upcoming ledge."

"Is that really true?" Rudy asked, somewhat in disbelief.

"Yeah, man," Chispo explained. "The crystals transmit telepathic messages to the energy field of any would-be intruder that there are other areas of the cave much more interesting, and he or she simply decides without realizing it to always go to other areas. It's much more effective protection than the doors and locks your people on Earth use."

"You mean that really stops *every* would-be intruder?" Rudy asked.

"Well, I will admit," said Rinto, "there might be a select few who are immune to such methods, but the way our crystal protection works is effective for just about 100% of the population."

"Those are ingenious protection measures," Morris complimented. "People act according to instincts more than they realize," Morris went on to explain to Rudy. "Because of that, along with the fact that their crystals, with their instilled intelligence, communicate directly with the instinct level or portion of the person's energy field, they can therefore manipulate any intruder's decisions without his or her consciously realizing it."

"How did you know that, Morris?" Fraxino wanted to know. "That's a radical, impressive explanation. I was about to tell them the same."

"From my work with the dolphins," Morris answered, "I've learned a lot about how crystals work. I mean, I knew a lot already, but because of my recent work, I've instinctively gained a lot more knowledge about them. It impresses me how much knowledge you Atlantean descendants retained about them."

"Actually, we're not the norm," Fraxino admitted. "Even here on our world, what Rinto, Chispo, and I can read, interpret, and do with crystals is considered a special gift."

"Oh, really?" Morris responded.

"That's right," Fraxino replied. "It sort of runs in our family, and also in Chispo's."

"That's right," Chispo verified. "My dad's aunt has special abilities above and beyond the norm."

After a few more minutes of walking through winding corridors, they reached the ledge which sat several meters above them. Rinto proceeded to sling the loop end of his rope to the top of the ledge where it caught on a hook they had previously installed. One by one, they climbed the rope, treacherous and scary as it seemed to some of them.

"I'm not saying that people here on Artenia would come here and do intentional harm," Rinto now explained to everyone, "but it's still a good feeling to have such crystallized protection for our cave's research room up here in the Ciruclar Mountains."

"In case you might be wondering," Chispo explained to Morris and Rudy, "Rinto and Fraxino have already telepathically communicated to the crystals that it's okay for us to be here."

"I was wondering about that," said Rudy.

For several more minutes, Rinto, Fraxino, and Chispo led everyone down more winding corridors until they came to an opening where their research room came into view. It was approximately ten by ten meters with the ceiling being an average height of three meters. All around the walls were various sizes of crystals of different colors, the majority of the ones being clear quartz. They were securely fastened to the walls. Their vibrant energy could be felt within the room. In one end of the room was a metal platform, its sides encased in glass, and to its left was a large shelf with all different types of minerals and flasks and bottles of liquids.

"This is where we grew the special crystals in our crystal array that we use in our craft," Fraxino announced, pointing to the platform. "We placed each base crystal on our platform. Next, we programmed our base crystals to be grown in just the right form and fashion, and with the help of our meditation and concentration at the right times and the right amount of added impurities, we were accurately successful with just what we needed."

"To grow the crystal array in our craft," Rinto added, "we telepathically communicated to our crystals around the walls what we needed accomplished, and with their expertise in knowledge, they caused the base crystals to take on and incorporate the right amount of impurities during their growth such that they would accomplish the wanted tasks in our craft."

"The power of the mind within these crystals is radical, dudes," Fraxino declared.

"This is truly an impressive setup you fellows have here," Morris complimented.

Rudy was also impressed, and he again felt a strong sense of familiarity with the whole setup, even though he couldn't quite pinpoint in his mind what it was.

Rudy kept wondering why he, at times, would feel such familiarity with various places here on Artenia, light years away from Earth. It began to bother him that he couldn't figure it out.

"Why can't more people do this back on Earth?" Rudy wanted to know.

"Well, it's like I was explaining," Fraxino answered, "we're not the norm. There are only a very few of us here on Artenia who can do this. Most people on Earth, and here on Artenia as well, haven't yet achieved the right level of telepathic communication required to properly communicate with crystals. Rinto and I, and also Chispo, are blessed with that gift, and through practice, we have achieved the right frequency of communication with these crystals, and we've brought forth amazing and favorable results."

"So, which of these crystals do we want to take with us on the Alaska project?" Rinto asked his brother.

Fraxino appeared to concentrate a few seconds. "Those two large quartz crystals to the right of the shelving," and he indicated, "and that piece of purplish-green Fluorite."

"Good choices," said Rinto. He walked over to them and gently unfastened them from the wall. Next, he opened his daypack and placed one of them inside of it. "Here, Fraxino and Chispo. Each of you take one."

"All right, man," said Chispo as he came over to him.

Fraxino also came over. "Anything else?" he asked Rinto.

"No, I guess that's all," he answered. "Anyway, that's our setup, here. This, of course, is where we grew the large Kaolinite crystal that we recently took and used in Mexico."

"I suspected that," said Rudy.

"If you dudes are ready," Fraxino announced, "let's head out of here."

They left the room, and over the next several minutes, they made their way back to the top of the ledge. They climbed down the rope. Rinto unhooked it and took it with him. On the way out, he hid the rope behind the same boulder, and a few minutes later, they were back outside at the bottom of the dropoff in the gully.

"Where did you get all those crystals that you have on display in your research room?" Morris wanted to know.

"We've collected them over time," Rinto answered.

"Many of them came from that galactic dump site," Fraxino also answered. "We also search mountain slopes, creek beds, and from time to time, we go to rock and mineral shows to trade."

"There were some impressive pieces in there," Morris told them. "I could sense that some of them were literally glowing with energy."

"That they do," Fraxino agreed. "Those crystals help us grow other new crystals the way we want and need them to be."

All of them climbed the rope to the top of the dropoff, and they hiked the 20 minutes up the steep and treacherous gully back to the vehicle-craft parked by the roadside. They climbed in, and Fraxino drove them back down the mountain to Zantaayer. Around 40 minutes later, they were pulling into the Zapatero's driveway. It was now mid afternoon.

"Man, I don't know about you all," Chispo answered as they stepped out of the vehicle, "but for some strange reason, I think it's important that we go and get Orolizo in on this project."

"You mean Orolizo of the Atascosa?" Chris asked.

"Exactly," Chispo answered. "I think he knows a lot."

"That's a good idea, Chispo," Rinto told him. "Let's make plans to head down there."

"All right, man," said Chispo. "I'll quickly go home and get some things I'll need." He stared over at his house as he looked through the row of bushes dividing their yards. "Excellent! Mom's car is not home. She won't be able to saddle me with chores. I'll be back in a little while." He walked through the Zapatero's backyard to the row of tall bushes, crossed under them, entered his yard, and walked to the back of his house. Half an hour later, he returned with extra food, water, and clothing. He also had with him his new green Fluorite ball that Morris had previously indirectly given him by way of Robert.

Meanwhile, Rinto, Fraxino, and the others were making plans. They were discussing details with Glecko and Sosta. Fraxino sorted through the crystals they had used in Mexico, and he took some of them out of the compartments in the craft and also took some of the pieces out of the special briefcase of crystals they had taken with them to Mexico.

While Robert and his friends waited and talked about different things with Glecko and Sosta, Rinto and Fraxino dashed up to the attic and sorted through their collection of rocks and crystals they had stored in various boxes. They were up there nearly an hour.

Morris was busy telling Glecko and Sosta entertaining stories about their previous adventures. Glecko, at times, translated from English to Artenian so Sosta could understand. Morris talked about his initial dream and contact with Tom, the galactic salesman, and how he had offered Morris a clear quartz crystal ball, told him all about it, went on and on about it, told him how important it would be in his life, and about how it later turned up in real life when they visited the telephone exchange, the step office, in Eagleville, Tennessee back in March. That was just the start of their adventures.

Finally, Rinto and Fraxino came down from the attic, this time with two carefully prepared briefcases. They opened them up for everyone to see the exotic display of various colors of crystals, carefully placed in certain configurations and arrays.

"Dudes, how do you two do it?" Chispo asked them in a joking manner, and he smiled.

"Just instincts, I guess," Rinto replied, laughing.

"We're just naturally good at it, I suppose," Fraxino added. "Concentration and effort are what it takes."

"But we haven't even been to Alaska yet," said Robert. "How do you know which crystals you'll actually need?"

"We just think of the possible situation and use our instincts to choose them," Fraxino answered.

"If we realize we need more," Rinto added, "we can always return here for them."

"Yeah, that's true," said Robert.

"So, if everyone's ready," Fraxino announced, "let's head down to the Atascosa."

"Are we spending the night or just going for the afternoon?" Rudy asked.

"It's down south in southern Zotola, 1,200 kilometers away," Rinto answered.

"It's several hours away, flying time," Chispo informed Rudy and Morris.

"We're definitely going to spend the night," Rinto told them. "So, bring your backpacks and supplies."

All of them took their backpacks out of the house, took them to the vehicle-craft, and loaded them into the back. Then they climbed in.

Glecko and Sosta came outside to see them off.

"You guys are really on the go, since you met these new Earth friends of yours," Glecko told his sons.

"I know," Rinto said to his father. "Since we're meeting the galactic salesman in Alaska two days from now, we thought we'd accomplish as much as we could prior to that."

"That's thinking ahead," Glecko complimented. "Best of luck on your next mission."

"Thanks, Dad," both Rinto and Fraxino said. Sosta also wished them well in Artenian.

They were now all inside the vehicle-craft. Rinto did the driving and backed them out of the driveway. Glecko and Sosta waved at them as they left.

"You definitely have some kind and supportive parents," Steven commented.

"Especially your dad," Morris added.

"Thanks," said Rinto. "We do feel fortunate in that respect. So, which route do we want to take?" Rinto now asked his brother.

"Dude, let's take the road through the city, and we'll exit via the south side."

"Right on, brother!" Rinto responded with enthusiasm.

He made a left turn and took that road to the highway that entered the city center from the west. Once in the center, he made a right turn. They passed by commercial establishments and stores. Rinto pulled into an Exxoll station on the right.

"Golly, man!" he declared. "Gone up again!"

"11.9 duocibols per liter," said Fraxino as he read the price on the pump.

"Man, it wasn't even a week ago when it went up to 11.8!" Chispo complained.

The attendant came to them and filled the vehicle-craft's hydrogen tank. After paying just over 8 zúbolas, they got back on the two-lane highway and headed toward the southern ridge of the Ciruclar Mountains. They passed by some factories on the way, and then they arrived at the foot of the mountains.

Rinto whizzed up the forested mountain road and took the hairpin curves with the greatest of ease. After 20 minutes of ascending, they crested the ridge of the mountains. As Rinto followed the highway and made the gentle descent into the outstretching desert valley beyond, he waited for an opportunity when there was no other traffic in sight.

"We're airborne, dudes!" Rinto shouted enthusiastically. He pulled back a lever, switched off the engine, and the craft proceeded to leave the surface of the highway. Now under the power of the on-board crystal array, the craft swiftly accelerated and climbed steeply until leveling out at an altitude of 8,000 meters.

"Rinto's put this craft in high gear," Chispo told everyone with enthusiasm. "Sit back in your seats. We're going to zoom down there in less than three hours, man!"

Fraxino popped the holodisk album by Zantaayer's group, *The Hydragyros*, into the on-board player, and they enjoyed listening to its songs. That particular group of young pop artists had exceptional talent. Their album had become an incredible success, already achieving top 12 status on Zotola's pop charts.

The craft continued to accelerate until they reached a cruising speed of 1,000 km/h. They were now heading due south to the Cloerinne Mountains of southern Zotola where the Atascosa people lived.

CHAPTER 3

THE ATASCOSA LINK

As they were cruising along, they could see well below them the desert valley stretching out nearly to the horizon with the Placatera Mountains seen beyond that. They crossed several more desert valleys and mountain ranges before finally approaching the Cloerinne Mountains.

"Tell me about the Atascosa people," Morris requested as they were flying along.

Chispo was the first one to answer. "Several weeks ago, we drove down there . . . took us two whole days, man! We had kept receiving subtle messages and signs that we needed to find and meet with those people because we thought they might have some link to Mexico and also to Atlantis."

"Right," Morris responded.

"Well, we met this guy named Doulos," Chispo continued, talking to Morris and Rudy. "He lives in a small town called Hichicera on the southern side of the Cloerinne Mountains, and he took us on a three-day hike well within the mountains to reach the Atascosa people. Man, those people live in a valley that is only accessed from below by climbing several hours through a dangerous and steep gully! The trail was narrow as everything, and we sometimes feared we'd fall right into the violently rushing Makeeseldruff River, sometimes only inches away from us. Dudes, one wrong move would have sent us plunging into that dangerous river, followed by a sure death sentence when we would have crashed over a gargantuan waterfall several hundred meters tall!"

While most of what Chispo said was true, he was having fun exaggerating the story to make it sound more hair raising.

"They make themselves inaccessible," Fraxino added comment, "so they'll be left in peace by the general public."

"I can relate to that," said Morris.

"Anyway," Chispo went on, "we also met this cool dude named Orolizo, and he told us he'd been having a bunch of disturbing dreams about his soul link, who we now know to be Pegaso in Bustamante. He also showed us a quartz crystal sphere, and he sent it to his soul link by way of me. And Steven here was love at first sight with Orolizo's sister, Lumela, and . . ."

"Now, Chispo," Steven interrupted, smiling, "we don't need to get into that."

"Yeah, but the disturbing dream you had," Chispo went on, "helped us identify that Pegaso was the soul link to Orolizo."

"Oh, okay," said Steven. "What happened was I stayed over at Orolizo's house, and I dreamed that this big Mexican guy was making violent moves toward me, and I woke up, terror stricken. I hurried back over to Zocanto's house where the rest of us were spending the night. That was definitely the end of any relationship between me and his sister, Lumela."

"Yes, but it was all for a purpose," Chris now explained to Morris and Rudy. "Steven's falling in love caused him to be at the right place at the right time to have that dream to later identify Orolizo's soul link."

"Yep, life has more purpose and order than you'd think," Morris told everyone.

"That's true, man," Chispo agreed.

"Destiny is a strange process," Fraxino remarked. "As those at higher levels of existence plan out their lives, we at these lower levels are sometimes affected by their actions and outcomes."

"Such is life, according to those holographic plates we looked at," said Andrew.

"*Destiny, Alternate Realities, and Dreams*," said Robert, quoting the title of the plate.

"That plate told us that destiny originates from higher levels of thought in alternate realities," said Steven. "An amusing concept, indeed."

"Do you know anything about the origin of these people we are about to visit?" Morris asked.

"Doulos did tell us about some of their history," Rinto replied. "The Atascosa people are endemic to this world, and their ancestors have always lived on Artenia since humans began around 72 million years ago."

"Did you say 72 million years ago?" Morris broke in and asked.

"That's right," Rinto answered and continued. "That's some of the information we got from those holographic plates. There have never been very many of the Atascosa people, and one of their characteristics is that they have a green tinge to their skin, a genetic trait left over from bygone days many millions of years ago when some of the genetic characteristics of trees were combined with the genes of their long ago ancestors. Because of that, they could manufacture some of their own food from direct sunlight, a process very similar to how photosynthesis works in tree leaves.

"The genetic trait was installed as a long term experiment to increase the race's chances of survival during possible food shortages, but the genetic combination didn't go over so well with most of them. A large majority of them died of unexpected diseases, leaving only a few lucky ones who carried the correct genetic characteristics to accommodate the photosynthetic genes, and they reproduced and furthered the Atascosa race as we know them today.

"In ancient times, they came to gather and made their home in the meadow and canyon along the banks of the Makeeseldruff River, tucked well within the Cloerinne Mountains, a place so removed from the general public that they became considered a legend."

"Sounds like an interesting group of people," Morris commented.

"You've got to be joking that they have genetic characteristics from the trees," said Rudy in disbelief.

"You'll believe it when you see their green color tinge in their skin," Chispo assured him.

"In a subtle way, these people can be considered walking trees," Andrew jokingly remarked.

They laughed at his clever comment.

The Cloerinne Mountains came into view, and Rinto began to lower the craft's speed and altitude as he approached the range. He and Fraxino began to look for familiar landmarks to help them navigate the craft to land in the remote, high mountain canyon where the Atascosa lived.

"There it is," said Robert as he recognized the area. "The Makeeseldruff Gully."

"Let's land in the open meadow by the river above the gully," Fraxino suggested to his brother.

Rinto steered the craft and brought it in for a landing in the lower section of the meadow. The craft gently touched down, and he drove it a short distance alongside the smooth, flowing Makeeseldruff River, soon reaching the edge of the woods where Zocanto's stone house was.

"The river's back to normal again," Chispo commented to everyone.

"Why do you say that?" Rudy asked him.

"Man, it was up last time," Chispo answered. "It stormed and rained heavily the night before we left. Dude, I'm here to tell you we almost didn't make it out of here! If you think our ascent was dangerous, that was nothing compared to. . ." and he proceeded to relate the story of their harrowing descent down the gully two weeks ago, exaggerating all points where possible to make it sound like it was *really* a dangerous venture!

As Rinto parked the craft, several of the Atascosa people saw, what to them was a spacecraft, landing in the meadow, and they didn't know what to think. They began to rush over to it to investigate. Zocanto also saw them landing, and he came out of his house and also walked over to them. Rinto opened the door of the vehicle-craft, and he and Chispo were the first ones to step outside.

"It's okay everyone," Zocanto called out in the native mountain dialect to the other Atascosans now flocked around the vehicle-craft. "I know them." He paused. "Rinto, Chispo, welcome back to our people," he now told them in Artenian.

"Thank you, Zocanto," Chispo answered, "and how have you been?"

"We've been fine," Zocanto answered. "How did your mission to Mexico go?"

By this time, the others began to step down from the vehicle-craft to the welcoming gestures from the green people. Neither Morris nor Rudy had been with them the last time they had come, and they were certainly put in their place in an impressed way about the olive green color to their skin. As they looked friendly enough, they were not afraid.

"We had radical success . . ." Chispo began to tell Zocanto, when he noticed his good friend Orolizo walking toward the group.

"Excellent. . ." Zocanto responded, when he realized Chispo was now directing his attention to Orolizo.

"Chispo, Rinto, everybody, you've come back," Orolizo called out to them with a smile.

"What's going on, Orolizo?" Chispo greeted him, glad to see him.

"How did everything go?" Orolizo asked everyone. He shook hands with them, glad to see them. "I see you have two new people with you."

Chispo proceeded to introduce Morris, and then Rudy, to the others. With that done, Chispo, Rinto, and Fraxino proceeded to relate the whole story about their mission to Mexico, the ancient paintings they found, how they located and eliminated the transmitter devices, and the rest of it.

Though Zocanto and his wife Cawrenfra, who had also come to the sudden gathering, invited them to come on in and stay, Orolizo stepped forward and asked all nine of them to come and stay with him and his family. After all, he wanted to hear all about their adventures, including their contact with his soul link in Mexico.

As they began to take their backpacks out of the vehicle-craft, Zocanto gestured to the other Atascosans to return to what they were doing. Zocanto was the leader of his people, which were not very many, only a few hundred. They were never very numerous, always having remained in one group in this location for eons of time.

Orolizo led the way, and they walked along the forested path upstream along the river. The dominant trees were Pines, Hemlocks, and Cedars. There were small stone houses tucked in the forested slopes on either side of the open meadow, which ran for several kilometers. In twenty minutes, they arrived at Orolizo's stone house.

They all walked inside and placed their backpacks inside the front main room. Since there was no electricity, the inside of the stone house appeared darker than one would expect, being lit only by candlelight and the forest filtered sunlight that came in through the windows.

Orolizo was one of the more gifted people of the Atascosa, and while he spoke a decent amount of Artenian, most of the Atascosans spoke only the native dialect of Atascosan.

Chispo, Rinto, and Fraxino had filled Orolizo in on some of the story during their walk, and now they proceeded to tell the rest.

"That's impressive work, the way you guys went about eliminating the transmitter devices," Orolizo remarked. "I'm really impressed."

"Man, those two gurus are geniuses!" Chispo remarked, referring to Rinto and Fraxino. "They can do anything they put their minds to."

"I believe it," Orolizo responded. "So, my soul link in Mexico . . . tell me all about him."

"We found him, man," Chispo told him. "He's the same dude Steven had that nightmare about when he spent the night with you, and his name is Pegaso."

"I thought he would be the same one," Orolizo responded.

"After visiting the ancient paintings, Chiquihuitillos," Chispo continued, "we went to the town of Bustamante, Nuevo León. It wasn't long before we met Roel, whose brother Rudy is here with us. We were soon welcomed by them and stayed with their family. We went to some huge caves up in the mountains, and on the way there when we were still in town, Steven spotted him. I mean, his first reaction was fear! We got him calmed down and everything. It turned out that your soul link is one of Roel's good friends, and after we got back from the caves, we went over and met him, his parents, and his two sisters. Man, you won't believe what Pegaso's last name is . . . Orolizo."

"You mean it's the same as mine?" Orolizo asked in surprise.

"That's right, man," Chispo verified.

"That is a coincidence, sure enough!"

"It certainly was confirmation for us," Chispo went on. "We found him to be friendly enough, and as it turned out, three of the seven of us at that time stayed with Pegaso Orolizo's family. Chris and I stayed several days, and Steven, who easily enough got over his fear from his previous nightmare, also stayed with us."

"Excellent, and did you give him the clear quartz crystal ball?" Orolizo wanted to know.

"Oh yeah, man," Chispo assured him. "I did that the first night I stayed with him, and I also later gave him the letter you wrote him, along with a Spanish translation."

"That's great. Thank you."

"Oh yeah, no problem, man," Chispo kindly told him. "We enjoyed our stay in Bustamante for several days, and we went into the mountains several times to investigate and search for the transmitters. Roel and Rudy became our guides and good friends and accompanied us nearly everywhere. They also served as our protection. Pegaso always had to work, as it turned out, and he never came with us.

"One night, we were in the plaza jabbering with a bunch of guys, and some of them asked me how I liked Pegaso's sisters. I casually answered they were pretty and would please me for a girlfriend, thought nothing more of it, until the next day when we all found Pegaso suddenly changed and cold shouldered toward us.

"When I went to talk to him about it, he flared up and attacked me, man! He knocked both Steven and me across room until I delivered him a really hard blow to his stomach, doubling him over in pain. Man, I had to, or the crazy dude would have killed me! With that, including having to explain the incident to his parents, we got out of there and moved over to Roel and Rudy's place."

"Wow, Chispo!" Orolizo remarked. "I knew my soul link had flareups, but I didn't think it was that bad. Why in the world did Pegaso turn against you?"

"Because I had said his sisters were pretty and would please me for a girlfriend."

"You're joking!"

"I'm serious, man!" Chispo insisted. "That Pegaso was a tiger by the tail! He was so protective of his sisters, that he attacked anyone who even made nice comments about them."

"That kills me," Orolizo remarked. "That is insane!"

"That wasn't all," Chispo went on, now in such a fervent vibrant manner that the others made no input. "Pegaso was so angry that he wanted revenge, and he gathered up some of his buddies to sabotage our vehicle-craft. Rinto and Fraxino's crystallized protection prevented them from carrying out their actions, but only thanks to Roel's presentiments and prior warning, bless his soul. Instead, Pegaso and a friend of his tossed a whopping firecracker into Roel and Rudy's house, and I mean to tell you, their mother reported them to the police and had them arrested!"

"Well, good!" Orolizo stated. "They deserved it."

"That's right," Chispo continued. "They spent three days in jail, and the nine of us, including Roel and Rudy, fled in our craft to Zacatecas further south to visit Roel and Rudy's relatives, after which we returned to Artenia for several days, so these two gurus," pointing at Rinto and Fraxino, "could grow their Kaolinite deactivating aparatus to take back to Mexico."

"So," Orolizo now said, "you successfully destroyed the transmitters, and peace and friendship finally prevailed over the town."

"We did," Rinto now answered, "and Pegaso and his friend both came to us and apologized."

"Well, that's good, and where is Roel now?" Orolizo wanted to know.

"He decided to stay in Zacatecas for the summer with his relatives," Chispo answered.

"He was afraid to return to Bustamante," Fraxino explained, "even though we told him Pegaso had apologized, and that things were now safe."

"Pegaso had given Roel an angry stare, implying he wanted to kill him," said Rinto.

"He also stayed there because he took a special liking to one of the girls," Chispo reminded Rinto.

"Yes, I know," Rinto responded.

"There was a purpose to all of that," Orolizo told them. "It was important that my soul link learn the lessons you provided him, and thanks for fighting back and socking my soul link in the stomach, Chispo. That put him in his place."

Chispo laughed at his comment and said, "You're welcome."

"Where's your family?" Rinto wanted to know.

"My sister Lumela isn't here right now. She will be here soon."

"Your parents?" Chispo asked.

"They've already passed away," Orolizo answered with sorrow.

"Man, I didn't even realize it," Chispo told him, surprised. "I'm sorry about that."

"Thank you."

"Yes, they had an accident while exploring some of the higher reaches of our mountains. They were making their way up a narrow gully when several rocks dislodged and tumbled down upon them. That was three of our years ago, and my sister and I now continue to live here by ourselves." Everyone expressed his sympathy for Orolizo.

They continued to visit and talk about events. Orolizo finally brought up the important question. "So, what brings you fellows back here?"

"Man, it's amazing how we haven't gotten to that yet," Chispo remarked.

"Tom, the galactic salesman we told you about last time," Rinto explained, "contacted us only yesterday, and he's got a huge project of installing a galactic switching station in Alaska. He wants us to . . ." and Rinto and Fraxino explained all the details including the puzzle of the time frozen bodies.

"Hmm . . . that is an interesting predicament about the time frozen bodies," said Orolizo.

"I had suggested we come down here and talk to you about it and see if you had any ideas," said Chispo.

"I'm glad you did," said Orolizo. "I'll think about it and see if I can come up with anything." He paused a moment and then said, "Would you like me to come with you?"

"By all means yes," Rinto now answered.

"We were hoping you would," Chispo said to him.

"Great, then count me in," Orolizo agreed. "What about my sister Lumela?"

"Bring her also," Chispo said. Then he showed a twinkle in his eye as he added, "She can keep Steven and Andrew company."

Orolizo laughed at that comment.

"Chispo," Robert brought up, "did you tell Orolizo about our second trip to the galactic dump site?"

"No, I haven't yet," he answered. He then proceeded to tell Orolizo. "Man, we went back to that ancient galactic dump site I was telling you about and found another crateload of bronze plates. They had hieroglyphics casted into them, and others had segments of crystals, some of them holographic, implanted within the bronze."

"How interesting!" said Orolizo.

Chispo, Rinto, and Fraxino told him all about it, that the crateload of plates may be keys to helping them solve their upcoming puzzle.

"I don't suppose you have movies down here," Chispo continued, "but we just saw a really neat movie up in Zantaayer called *Vision from the Ciruclar* about a leader named Quinoteh who finds a sacred story stone telling of soul travel and galactic communication . . ."

"Wait, did you say sacred story stone?" Orolizo broke in and asked.

"I did, man," Chispo confirmed. "Robert here found one."

"You mean you all *found* one? Where?"

"In that galactic dump site south of Zantaayer," Chispo answered.

"Is that a fact?" Orolizo responded with enthusiasm. "You mean the orange Calcite rocks with holographic strips pasted on them?"

"Exactly, man! How did you know that?"

"Oh, I know about those," Orolizo told them. "I have one."

"Do you really?!" Chispo responded with surprise. "How did that get by us?"

"Where did you find the one you have?" Fraxino wanted to know.

"It was in a small cave in the upper reaches of the mountains near here," Orolizo answered.

"Cool!"

"Those are very special rocks indeed," Orolizo told them. "There's a story behind their existence. Do you know it?"

"Nothing more than they came from Vega," Chispo replied. "Each one related a sacred story, and they made nice decoration pieces in the homes of the Vegan humans."

"That and the fact that only a very few of them have been found," Fraxino added.

"Then I'll tell you," said Orolizo, and he began. "As you may already know, the long ago ancestors of your Earth's Atlantis came from Vega or Lyra in the Lyran constellation. In that star system, the Lyran humans of Vega had a long standing tradition of keeping sacred story stones as family heirlooms. Each stone told a sacred story in holographic format via telepathy by reading the holographic filmstrips fused onto what was usually orange Calcite.

"It was the culture in those days that each prominent family had a duty to cherish and be guardian of a sacred story stone, the total sum of sacred stories telling the history of their race. Each family was therefore assigned guardianship of a certain sacred story to keep and hand down through the generations as family heirlooms. This was their duty to their race.

"A few of the stones stayed with the last remaining Lyran humans on Vega, but most of them were taken to Earth around 150,000 years ago by Lyran colonists from Vega and were kept by prominent, distinguished Atlantean families. Through the ages, many of the stones were either forgotten or lost, and when Atlantean settlers came here 10,130 of our years ago, they brought some of them with them. Some of them were dumped, their meaning long since forgotten by those who dumped them, but some of them were carefully placed in caves, crates, or other safe places by those who still understood . . . in hopes that one day in the future, someone would find them and recapture the stories."

"Wow! That does make a lot of sense," Rinto remarked.

"I agree with that," said Fraxino.

Chispo translated the story to English for the others.

"Man, you say you have one of these sacred story stones?" Fraxino asked Orolizo.

"I do. Let me go fetch mine. I'll be right back." He walked into the back room, and a minute later, he came back with a beautiful piece of orange Calcite in his hand. It was slightly larger than the stone Robert had found. This one was around 18 centimeters across, while Robert's was 15.

"Wow!" Chispo declared when Orolizo handed it to him to look at. "This specimen is in excellent condition, well preserved."

"I believe it was always in safe keeping, never dumped like others were," said Orolizo.

"I agree," said Chispo. He looked at it some more. "Man, the holographic filmstrips are perfectly intact, not a bit of fading nor wearing nor chips, like the piece Robert found." Chispo now telepathically probed the etheric part of his mind into the filmstrip. He started laughing. "Man, those Lyrans certainly cared about the trees!"

"That's right," Orolizo agreed. "Trees were very sacred to the Lyrans, and that holographic filmstrip relates a story about the origin of some of Earth's fruit trees."

"Far out!" Chispo declared, as he telepathically saw that the story was about just that. "Orolizo, the one Robert found relates the origin of the Flowering Sun Tree, the Liriodendrons on Earth, that they came from Vega with the early Lyran humans who colonized Earth, and that it was a sacred tree of superior characteristics."

"That's amazing!" said Orolizo. "Like I said, the Lyrans considered trees very sacred."

"They must have," Fraxino now said, "because we keep finding clear quartz crystal eggs with various tree cone images grown within them."

"Really?" Orolizo responded. "I think part of your major project plan may be involving the trees. My feeling is some of your answers may come from them or correlate to them."

"Could be," said Rinto.

"What tree cone images have you found in those egg-shaped crystals?" Orolizo asked them.

"I found the first one several years ago," Chispo answered. "Again it was in that galactic dump site. It had a ghostly image of a Pine cone within it. The feeling I get is that they were literally grown by a pre-Atlantean highly technological civilization on Earth and are probably as old as the sacred story stones. Both Robert and Rudy here have each found one since, one with an image of a cone from the Flowering Sun Tree, and the other image a seedball cluster from the Buttonball Tree."

"Interesting indeed!" Orolizo remarked with enthusiasm. "I'll tell you the story this stone's holographic filmstrip reveals."

"Excellent! We're listening," Fraxino decided to comment.

"When Lyran humans from Vega first settled Earth in the Sol system more than a million years ago, they had a need to grow their food and at the same time combine and carry Earth's genetic codes for survival. In addition to genetically modifying Earth's native humans at that time, they also genetically modified some of Earth's native plants and trees, namely a tree known as the Celtis. From this original Earth tree, numerous hybridized and genetically modified trees were produced with somewhat similar but much larger fruit. While the original Celtis species remained for the birds, the modified species served as an excellent source of fruit for the increasing population of Lyran human colonists.

"The leaves of all the deciduous fruit trees have similarity in appearance to the original Celtis and also have identical leaf growth patterns. It is believed the Celtis is endemic to Earth, however, it first shows up in the fossil record very soon after the devastating meteor that struck Earth's surface nearly 65 million years ago, and it may be of extraterrestrial origin as part of what was brought to restock Earth's plantlife at that time."

"That's a far-out radical story!" Fraxino declared with enthusiasm.

"What tree could that be?" Rinto asked.

"I don't know what you would call it in your English language," Orolizo admitted. "The word *Celtis* may have carried through . . ."

(Chispo finished translating the story to Robert, Morris, and the others.)

"*Celtis* . . . sounds like the Hackberry tree," said Robert.

"Oh, yeah," Chris now said. "They've got those tiny green berries. Birds eat them and plant them all over the place."

"It's basically a weed tree . . . volunteers all over our fencerows back at home," Andrew said with a chuckle.

"So, that's the forerunner of all deciduous fruit trees," said Steven as he realized it.

"From which the other genetically modified species were derived," Morris added.

"Yeah, that makes sense," said Chris.

"My theory is the Celtis likely has an ancient connection to the human beings," Orolizo speculated, "having been a gift species to their race from the time of their beginnings. Wherever humans live, you are likely to find the Celtis growing in abundance on the same planets."

Chispo continued translating to English for the others.

"I don't disagree with any of that," Morris came forth and commented.

"I don't either," Robert agreed.

"But I will say this," Morris began, and as a result decided to lecture, "that while the early Lyran humans may have had a good handle on genetics and how to modify species, our present day humans on Earth hardly know the first thing about genetics, and with their scant knowledge they have no idea the serious repercussions that can result from such careless, thoughtless maneuvers. Present day humans with our present Earth technology have barely scraped the surface on genetics and have no idea what underlying meaning and history lie within the genetic strands of DNA. There is so much we don't know.

"The basic building blocks of life, such as amino acids, viruses, and the like are known to easily survive for eons of time in outer space, and they float around all over the galaxies and the universe, attached to bits of matter, meteors, and comets. Most people believe it is genetically impossible for humans and other similar species to evolve on separate worlds and star systems, but for the known fact that I have just stated, similar life is bound to evolve and produce similar species out of the whole lot of millions of species for any planet of similar atmosphere and gravity."

"Oh, I agree," said Steven. "I remember that Mr. Mayfield talked to us about some of that in our science class back in February."

"That's right," Chris recalled. "Some of the class didn't believe life could have evolved similarly elsewhere."

"In addition to that," Morris went on, "humans, animals, trees, plants, you name it could have been brought from one or more of many star systems and could have easily adapted to Earth's biochemistry to such a degree that most would never suspect that they were ever of extraterrestrial origin in the first place.

"It's absolutely *ludicrous* how so many humans on Earth believe everything originated solely on Earth with absolutely no extraterrestrial background at all. Further, much of Earth's present life and species were brought via spacecraft and/or teleportation, having been translocated from other worlds and star systems. The dolphins, whales, and Eucalypts all came from Delikadove, the world of the dolphins on the other side of the galaxy 35 million years ago."

Chispo, Rinto, and Fraxino took turns translating to Orolizo what Morris and the others were discussing.

"To go on about it further," said Morris, "a trained eye can easily enough see that some of Earth's plantlife has oddball characteristics, especially in their leaf growth patterns. There is no fossil evidence for Cactus as we all know, since they recently arrived on Earth from Sirius B."

"All of us know the weird way the Flowering Sun Tree grows its new leaves," Chispo mentioned.

"And the Sycamore or Buttonball Tree, as well," Robert added.

"Exactly. Plants and trees are part of the evidence of extraterrestrial origins of certain species," Morris pointed out. "Their having been brought to Earth in the more recent millions of years really stands out because they are slow to adapt, and they change slowly over time. Animals and sea life change and evolve much more rapidly."

"I hadn't thought about it that way," Rinto admitted, "but that sounds right. I agree with that."

"Oh, and I'm going to throw this in, too," Morris added. "Hundreds of years ago there was a conspiracy among the scientific community, back when top scientists were classifying the trees with scientific names. There was a lot of ancient information about the trees left over from Atlantean times, and this information was hidden on purpose. A lot of the scientific names for the trees came from that ancient data, for example, the name Liriodendron for the Tulip Poplar, or as you call it on this world, the Flowering Sun Tree. When you trace its name back to the early Greek word *Leiron*, it strongly suggests Lyran, where Vega is. The older languages have more sense to them than you realize. I actually checked on different levels and discovered the conspiracy, something the present day scientific community has already forgotten . . . what their predecessors did. Anyone in power can rewrite history, and that's just what they did. They hid the information."

"Why did they do something so stupid such as hide important data like that?" Steven wanted to know.

"The religious belief systems of the time prohibited the belief in extraterrestrial interference," Morris answered.

What Morris said rang right to everyone. They knew he was right, and they realized what a loss the hiding of that data was to scientific communities of the future.

"Man, that's just how the humans are!" Chispo declared. "They sweep the truth under the rug for reasons at the time, and the truth gets distorted later."

"Like the distance discrepancy from Earth to the Orion system," Fraxino mentioned.

"Exactly," Chispo agreed.

"So, fellows, what do we need to do in preparation for the Alaska project?" Orolizo asked, changing the subject.

"Well, Tom met with us this morning," Rinto informed Orolizo. "We took him to the site of the movie filming atop the Ciruclar Mountains. He officially proposed the project to us there, and he telepathically gave us the images of the northern Alaska scenery. We're supposed to meet him there in two days."

"We've been to our secret cave, making a quick stop by there today," Fraxino added. "We collected some crystals we thought we'd need, gathered some more from our rock collection, and came down here for you and also your sister, if she also wants to join us."

"Then I guess we'd better get busy," said Orolizo. He looked out the window. "Here comes Lumela now." She was walking toward the house with two baskets in her hands, as she had been in the orchard.

Steven looked also, and his feelings immediately flared up. He had thought his feelings for her had gone, but now he realized differently, and he found his eyes fixated on her perfect attractiveness with her olive-green facial complexion of nothing less than *beauty*. It surprised him as his hot/cold/warm feelings took a stronghold on him. Chispo and Chris were the first to notice Steven's sudden change.

"Your beautiful princess has *arrived*," Chris told him, teasing.

Steven didn't even pay attention since he was so fixated on her. Lumela walked in the door, greeted by her brother Orolizo and his guests. Needless to say, Andrew was also under the influence of her attraction spell. Steven was so overwhelmed that he considered running out of the house and into the meadow below them to break the trance, but then she was so attractive that he was unable to leave.

Morris now appeared to be observing the events in a different manner, and as he saw what had suddenly happened to Steven and somewhat to Andrew, he began to concentrate. In a matter of seconds, Steven and Andrew experienced great relief. "Steven, Andrew," Morris now told them. "I hope you don't mind, but I just redirected the energy flows to break the trance you two were suddenly under and brought you two back to normalcy."

"I do feel suddenly much better," Steven responded. "Thanks, Morris, for lifting that off of me."

"No problem," he told Steven.

Immediately, Orolizo started talking to his sister about the sudden proposal and the Alaska project, the time frozen bodies, and the rest of it. As everyone else watched Orolizo and Lumela talk about it, they saw a smile come across her face. As she showed interest in the project, she agreed to it and was counted in.

"It's settled," he told everyone. "We're coming with you."

"Cool!" Chispo declared. "It will be a pleasure having you two come along with us." He and Orolizo shook hands. Lumela would have shaken hands, but she was still somewhat shy.

"Listen, darkness will be here in an hour," Orolizo told them. "All of you can stay here overnight. There's plenty of floorspace and extra beds, as well."

"Thanks, Orolizo," Chispo responded.

"The pleasure is mine," he told them. "Lumela," he now said to his sister in Atascosan, "could you prepare enough food for all of us to eat while I take the guests on a tour of the meadow, or do you prefer to come with us?"

"I'd rather come with you all," she responded. "I find that one," pointing to Steven, "rather attractive."

Orolizo showed a look of pleasant surprise on his face. She had always been so shy before, but in this situation she wanted to accompany Orolizo's new friends, rather than be a cook in the kitchen!

Though Morris didn't let on, he had taken away some of Lumela's shyness at the same time he had broken Steven and Andrew's gripping trance a few moments ago.

"Right, then let's all go for a tour," Orolizo announced, "since two of you have never been here before."

Lumela set her baskets of food and fruit down. Orolizo briefly went to the back room and placed his sacred story stone back in its place. With that done, they all walked out the door and descended through the forest to the meadow.

"You know, I'd like to go to Mexico," Orolizo said to Chispo, "meet my soul link, and see the ancient paintings. They might provide some clues for the project we're about to undertake."

"Excellent idea!" Chispo told him. "I was thinking the same thing. Morris has yet to see the paintings, anyway."

"Hey, Morris," Chispo now called out to him in English. "What do you say we go see Chiquihuitillos, the ancient paintings in Mexico?"

"Yes, certainly. I'm looking forward to it."

"You know," Robert brought up, "I think the trees may be a link to this project after all."

They continued talking and making plans as they walked up the grassy canyon meadow alongside the Makeeseldruff River until they reached its mouth, where its waters could be seen swiftly discharging out of the base of the tall cliff from a cave within that reached back several kilometers. The river gathered its waters from various underground streams originating in the highest reaches of the mountains above them.

Next, Orolizo and Lumela took them along the Base Cliff Trail which ran the upper rim of the forest on the other side of the meadow. As the name suggests, the trail ran along the base of the tall cliffs towering 100 to 200 meters above them. For several kilometers, the trail wound its way along, passing by streams and waterfalls that were surrounded by Hemlocks, which were the dominant trees at this level above the meadow which was now well below them. Birds and squirrel-like animals could be seen going from tree to tree.

They stopped to rest and relax by one of the larger falls, and some of them explored and enjoyed having a look around. Orolizo also told them about some of the secret caves and passageways that allowed their people access to the upper reaches of the mountains, a land of mostly rock and crags with occasional copses of trees in small gullies.

After relaxing at the falls, they continued along the base of the cliffs. Al Nitak could be seen through the trees setting in the turquoise, almost green, western sky on the mountains opposite the meadow. They soon made their way back down to the meadow near Zocanto's house, and now in darkness, they returned to Orolizo's house on the forested path alongside the river.

The stars were now coming out. Morris spotted the Earth's sun which showed up very near Sirius A. Chispo also pointed out Al Nilam and Mintaka, the two brightest and nearest stars in the sky, at 2.75 and 5.0 Artenian light years away respectively. They were the other two stars of the Orion Belt, and everyone gazed at the stars, wondering if their planets also had life on them.

They arrived back at Orolizo's house. Everyone entered, and both he and Lumela prepared supper for all of them. They had a major project ahead of them, so Orolizo and his sister got some things packed for the trip.

Earth time, it was 8:30 AM, Thursday, July 25, 1985. The time had completely shifted out of phase here on Artenia, as it was more or less the equivalent of 8 o'clock at night here.

After eating supper, they went to sleep. They realized what time it was in Mexico, and they knew they would have to get up several hours before dawn to arrive at the ancient paintings in Mexico and have a chance to see them before darkness would fall there. At the same time, Orolizo was looking forward to the trip and adventure, and also meeting his soul link.

Eight hours later, everyone got up. It would be two more hours before Al Nitak would break the horizon. In darkness, aided by flashlights and candlelight, they packed their bedrolls and backpacks and exited the stone house with Orolizo and Lumela, closing the door securely behind them. They walked the twenty minutes downstream alongside the Makeeseldruff River and arrived at Rinto and Fraxino's vehicle-craft at the bottom of the meadow.

All of them climbed aboard. Lumela was the first female to join their group since Suzanne on planet Aleyone in the Pleiades. She had lured James away from them, and other members had come and gone. Since several of Robert's Earth friends had returned home to Tennessee, there were now an equal number of extraterrestrials, that is, Artenian members as Earth members. Each would have a part in the upcoming project and would contribute his (and now her) part. There were now a total of eleven people on this project: Andrew, Chris, Robert, Rudy, and Steven from planet Earth, Morris . . . well also from planet Earth but could also be considered from Delikadove, the world of the dolphins, and Rinto, Fraxino, Chispo, Orolizo, and Lumela from Al Nitak's planet Artenia. With this many, it was a tight fit inside the vehicle-craft.

Rinto started the engine for a short while and drove them to the foot of the meadow, pulled back the lever, and switched off the engine. The craft left the ground, now under the control of the Ulexite main controls crystal and also the crystal array. Rinto telepathically caused the craft to swiftly accelerate and gain altitude.

"Rinto and Fraxino got this craft all figured out, man," Chispo boasted to Orolizo. "They've got this radical controls crystal made of . . ."

Chispo continued to boast, and they were very soon several hundred meters above the terrain below. Rinto telepathically transmitted his command to the controls crystal. They now felt the forcefield accompanied by a faint green glow overtake them. For a brief moment, they felt as if they were dematerializing, and then they were suddenly fine.

It was now bright and sunny, and they were now flying over the remote desert valley in northern Mexico, heading south toward the double mesa of Chiquihuitillos where the ancient paintings were. It was 4 PM, Thursday, July 25, 1985.

Rinto lowered the craft's altitude of 1,000 meters as they neared the double mesa, and he carefully brought it in for a slow and gentle landing on the rough, one-lane dirt road heading south. Touchdown was made, and he started the engine, placed the transmission in first gear, engaged the clutch, and proceeded at a crawl toward the mesa.

It was a sunny and hot afternoon of 40° Celsius, and around three hours of daylight remained. Plenty of desert plants occupied the area, including the Palma Real, a type of Yucca tree very similar to the Joshua Tree, Nopal plants, Mesquite shrubs, and various Cactus plants.

"Check this out, dudes," Chispo said to Orolizo and Lumela. He inserted a holodisk into the on-board player, and they listened to music from the album done by *The Hydragyros* from Zantaayer.

In fifteen minutes, they were pulling up to the left mesa of Chiquihuitillos. Rinto parked and everyone stepped outside. The heat of the afternoon was certainly noticeable.

Morris was looking forward to finally seeing the paintings and interpreting their meaning.

Orolizo and Lumela were overwhelmed by the difference of it all, and Orolizo was emotionally taken, for he had experienced numerous dreams of being in northern Mexico. Both he and Lumela were impressed at how blue the sky was here in Mexico on planet Earth, since skies back on Artenia had a slight green, sort of a turquoise color to them.

CHAPTER 4

ANOTHER VISIT TO CHIQUIHUITILLOS

The mesa sidewalls could now be clearly seen. Everyone stepped out of the vehicle-craft and walked up the steep slopes to the base of the cliff walls. While the whole area appeared uninhabited, there were in fact, a few ranch houses interspersed throughout the valley.

It was somewhat of a scramble as they made their way up the steep slopes. In addition to having to dodge various thorny bushes, Cactus, Yucca, Agave, Lechuguilla, and Zotól plants, the soil was loose, and at times they slipped and fell. After some considerable effort and offering each other helping hands to make their advance, they arrived at the base of the brownish-beige cliffs. The ancient paintings were now right before them.

"This is really far out!" Orolizo remarked.

"Impressive drawings and paintings indeed!" Morris commented.

Most of the drawings were done with red paint, and some of the depictions contained orange, as well. There were drawings of what appeared to be people, tools, plantlife, animal representations, suns, and moons. There were also drawings of more exotic things like concentric circles, chains of diamond-shaped cross hatched squares, spacecrafts, and other vehicles.

As they looked at the paintings, they advanced along the base of the cliff.

Morris added comment. "These paintings look like they were done by amateurs, but then they probably have a lot of hidden meaning to them."

"What about genetics?" Robert brought up.

"They could very well be telling a message about that, too," Morris agreed, "DNA patterns and the rest of it."

They talked about several of the drawings as they made their way now west along the cliff's base. Then they arrived at the scene of the 37.5 cross hatched diamonds in seven columns. This was where Chispo and Robert had discovered quite a coincidence and therefore thought they had some link to the dolphins. They didn't say anything to Morris about it.

Sure enough, when they came to this scene of paintings, Morris stopped, stared at the drawings, and his mouth dropped open in surprise.

"Now that's a scene that really does surprise me!" Morris declared.

"Really?" Chispo asked, not letting on what he and the others already knew about it.

"Indeed it does. I've got a tingling feeling going through me!"

"No kidding!" Steven commented.

"What do you read from it?" Robert asked Morris.

"You already know what it says," he told Robert.

Morris had already sensed that Robert and Chispo were keeping low keyed about it to see if he could pick up on it himself.

"Yes, that's true," Robert admitted. "I just wondered what you think?"

"Somebody long ago had a vision," Morris began, "and it was indeed about Delikadove, the world of the dolphins." He paused and looked at the images some more. "These paintings depict and represent much of what I've seen on my visits there recently. This confirms it for me. There is a reality to what I've seen." While what Morris had seen and experienced on his visits to the dolphins over the past month seemed very real, he sometimes doubted his own senses. He was very glad to see that someone else had tuned in to the same information. "It even shows a drawing of Danetar, their sun, as it's breaking up, as that's what happened 35 million years ago, which is why the last remaining dolphins had to leave and come here to Earth." He continued looking at the drawings. "It really amazes me how there are hidden codes and meanings, including artifacts, like this brilliant set of depictions, which indicate and tell the story of the origin of dolphins on Earth, along with other ancient stories of Earth and other star systems."

"Look at that drawing," said Robert as he indicated. "It looks like a Eucalyptus twig."

"Yes, I know," Morris now more calmy said. "That confirms that, too. The Eucalypts and other similarly related Australian trees came with the dolphins when they arrived on Earth."

"You did see the little orange depiction of the dolphin leaping off the platform over here, didn't you?" Steven pointed out to Morris.

"Where?" It had not yet caught Morris' attention, and he now stared at it in surprise. "Absolutely brilliant! It's a drawing of both a dolphin and a whale simultaneously."

"Wait, how do you see a whale in it?" Fraxino wanted to know.

"Look at the whole of the orange, ignoring the dolphin," Morris pointed out.

They looked at it. "Oh, yeah," Fraxino commented first, realizing. "Now I see it."

Rudy looked at the dolphin/whale image, and he gained a different viewpoint on it. "Take another look at it," he directed. "It's not a drawing of a dolphin or whale. It's a human face with a hood or some sort of cap around its head. That jagged platform represents its collar. So, it looks like I've debunked your theory," he jokingly said with a smile to Morris.

Morris took Rudy more seriously than intended. He and the others now looked at the drawing again.

Robert was also staring at it. "Rudy, how on Earth do you see a drawing of a human in that?" he asked him.

"It's right there," Rudy insisted.

They weren't yet seeing the human image in it, and they continued to stare at it.

"Right you are!" Morris suddenly exclaimed when he realized it and saw it. "Brilliantly done, Rudy. That confirms my theory even more . . . that the humans, dolphins, and whales are of all one race!"

"What?" Rudy asked, confused. He had not expected Morris to take what he had pointed out in such a positive manner. "Are you crazy? How can they be of one race?"

"If you go back far enough along the time lines, not entirely linearly, of course," Morris explained, "the dolphins, whales, and humans come from the same stock . . . common ancestors."

"The same stock?" Rudy asked.

"That's right," Morris answered. "Much of life evolves and diversifies that way."

"Yes, I know that," Rudy responded, "but I never thought about dolphins being related to us."

Rudy and Morris continued talking about that theory some more, as the others looked at the drawings and made their interpretations and comments. Orolizo was taken by some of the drawings, as was Lumela.

They advanced to other drawings and looked at them. Morris was very impressed with what visions the people who drew these depictions must have seen.

"I have a very strong feeling the people who drew these were recent Atlantean descendants, having migrated here, and they drew what they saw and remembered.

"Morris," Chispo brought up, "I remember you said you knew that Robert and I have a strong link to the dolphins."

"That's right, I did say that," he answered.

"What link do you see?" Robert now asked.

"Well, it's not really important in this reality," said Morris.

"What do you mean, Morris?" Robert asked him. "There are so many coincidences in those paintings."

"You and Chispo did correctly interpret the paintings," Morris explained, "but the coincidence lies in the fact that your link to the dolphins, Chispo, is in a parallel universe, like I was explaining to you the other day, shortly before we took off to Zotola."

"Parallel universe?" Chispo now asked.

"That's right, Chispo," Morris confirmed. "It's like I was telling you, in that parallel reality, you and Robert became quite imcompatible over different issues and problems with stress and your resentment from your parallel existence on planet Earth. You took on habits that Robert's parallel self didn't like, and the problems caused your friendship to be very temporary. It failed.

"As for your link to the dolphins, there was a dolph, a land dolphin, who was brilliant, quite a maverick among his kind, but he also had a lot of bad traits. He was your past life, Chispo. Although you're a good fellow in this reality, your parallel self on Earth is a different story, and like your past land dolphin's life, your parallel self would rather lose a friend like Robert than face the issues and problems and fix them."

"Man, if I have problems with people, I talk them over and solve them," Chispo insisted.

"I know you do, and that's excellent," Morris acknowledged. "However, your parallel self on Earth doesn't."

"Oh, I see," said Chispo, realizing.

"I don't know if it was very wise for me to have told you that, but since you asked me what I saw, I have decided to tell you. I know it doesn't sound so glorious as you might think, but that's it. It has to do with parallel universes and alternate realities."

"Thanks for telling us, Morris," Robert said to him.

"Morris, didn't you say another one of us here also has a link to the dolphins?" Rudy asked.

"Yes, I did, but I'm going to leave that for you to figure out."

No more than Morris said that than Rudy telepathically received the answer from Morris, and he now knew who he was . . . and what the link was. He would wait and tell the others later, when Morris wouldn't be around them.

They had been looking at the paintings for two hours. The sun was getting low in the sky. They descended the steep sloping hillside back to the valley floor and walked back cross country to the vehicle-craft parked on the east side of the double mesa.

They talked about what links or information the paintings might provide for their upcoming Alaska project. Rudy had something else on his mind about how past humans communicated, and he wanted to know what Morris thought. He decided to ask him.

"I think the past humans communicated in various ways," Morris replied to Rudy.

"As in what ways?" Rudy wanted to know.

"By verbal speech, writing, pictures, and telepathy, visual image transmission and . . ."

"Are you crazy?" Rudy broke in and argued. "They didn't use verbal speech back in those days, the days of Atlantis!"

"What makes you think they didn't?" Morris asked Rudy.

"Our history books tell us that civilizations prior to 6,000 years ago communicated with pictures. They didn't talk."

"That's ridiculous! Of *course* they talked," Morris insisted.

"Well, I never thought they did," said Rudy.

"People know so little about prior civilizations," Morris complained. "It's ludicrous to think they didn't speak in those days! They had vocal cords then as now, and right back to the Lyran humans and much further back, they did."

"More than that," Rudy pointed out, "all the professors in school believe they didn't talk."

"And where did the professors get their supposedly correct information?" Morris asked.

"From the history books," Rudy answered.

"Which were wrong about that in the first place," Morris stated.

"Oh," Rudy commented. Although he realized Morris was right, he didn't want to admit it. After all, how was Morris such an authority? How did he know so much? It made Rudy feel jealous, and it bothered him.

"The people of long ago, previous civilizations were very sophisticated at times through history," Rinto now explained. "They used a multitude of communications means, and even though they used telepathy, drawings, and other means, it wouldn't stop them from using verbal speech."

"We know they did," Chispo added. "Our Artenian language comes from Atlantean."

As Rudy thought about it, he realized that Rinto and Chispo were also right.

"Bueno, sí, comunicaban con voz, también," Rudy now said in Spanish, admitting that they also communicated with verbal speech.

"What did he say?" Rinto asked Chispo.

Chispo translated Rudy's comment.

Though Morris said nothing of it, he felt very relieved, because with what Rudy had just argued, he had picked up very little extra information when he had telepathically received the English language from Morris the other day when he had touched that orange crystal. If Rudy had indeed received extra data during that telepathic thought transferrence, then it had either worn off, or he had already been caused to forget it. If Rudy had retained the extra knowledge, he would have already known that long ago humans communicated by speech, and he would not have argued otherwise. That was confirmation enough for Morris.

After all, Morris had been quite concerned about how much extra knowledge Rudy had obtained. He knew that all knowledge has a responsibility to it, and some of what he knew about the dolphins, he knew the world wasn't ready for yet. It wasn't a case of Morris being paranoid, but it was more that the dolphins didn't want certain information to be let out on general release to be known by others, and not by Rudy either!

"Let's go to Bustamante," Rudy said to everyone.

"Right, let's go," Rinto agreed.

Everyone climbed aboard the craft. This time Rinto didn't start the engine. He just pulled back a lever, and the craft silently left the ground. They flew eastward as the craft's main Ulexite controls crystal telepathically levitated and guided the craft.

"Dudes, we're *sailing* over to Bustamante!" Rinto shouted with enthusiasm.

He telepathically caused the craft to swiftly accelerate and pick up altitude. They were pressed back in their seats as they raced toward the crest of the mountain range to the east of them. The mountains stood well above the valley floor at an average of 1,800 meters in altitude. Once they levelled out and crested the mountains, the town of Bustamante came into view well below them at the foot of the mountains on the east side.

"Let's make a quick landing on the Cypress ridge," Chispo suggested. "I want to show Orolizo and his sister the results of what your deactivating device did."

"Okay," Rinto agreed. He turned the craft around to the right, and they soon touched down on the narrow ridge of limestone bedrock which had Arizona Cypress trees and shrubs interspersed along with other plants, such as Lechuguilla and Siempre Viva.

As they were stepping out of the craft, Chispo said to Orolizo, "Take a look at that, man," pointing to the fresh, broken rock. "Look how this part of the ridge got blown away!" He indicated more and pointed out how some of the boulders had tumbled all the way down the mountain's steep slopes to the valley floor way below them.

"It was a spectacular sight!" Fraxino added.

Orolizo and Lumela were impressed at the force with which the energy had been released, and Orolizo now better understood how the numerous bad quantum energy systems had been literally blown out of existence at the time.

"Man, when we realized those flashing lights and energies got out of hand," Chispo explained, "we ran for cover and literally dove between the rocks on that mountain over there!" indicating the Lion's Head Mountain several kilometers to the north of them.

"You mean it was that bad?" Orolizo responded with concern.

"Man, it was!" Chispo confirmed.

"More than that," Fraxino answered. "Chris here got zapped by one of the rays."

"That's right," said Rinto. "We saved him and brought him back to life, using our on-board crystal first aid kit."

"Smart thinking," said Orolizo.

"We had not expected such violent results," Fraxino explained, "but then there were more energy systems to be cleared than we thought."

Chispo translated the conversation they had been having with Orolizo in Artenian to English for the others.

Morris proceeded to explain how he came on the scene right after the occurrence. He had detected the energies of the explosion from the other side of the galaxy.

"They didn't realize how strongly entrenched those quantum energy systems were, and the energy release resulting from neutralizing all of them was therefore enormous. I'll go on to explain that humans are more programmed than you all would think, and on so many levels they don't even realize. Programs can be added to any individual, unrealized by him or her. Intelligent energy systems out there in the ether and reality can latch onto any individual and benefit or cause harm, alter a personality for better or for worse, and even existing programs can be corrupted or dismantled. At times, for people I know and have regard for, I've been known to dismantle unfairly placed bad energy systems and programs placed on them. I've only interfered if it's to their benefit."

"You've been able to do all of that?" Rinto asked Morris.

"Hmm . . . those dolphins *have* taught you a lot," Steven added comment.

"Oh that I knew how to do before I had anything at all to do with the dolphins," Morris clarified. "You see, those Atlanteans who set up a lot of those quantum energy systems here on Earth understood the different, more basic levels of reality. They did their programming on what we would call lower levels, and the energy systems ran their course with a life of their own, seeking out individuals to contaminate. You might compare different levels of programming to computers, such as programming in MS-DOS compared to Windows."

"How did they figure out how to do that?" Andrew wanted to know.

"There are shortcuts in reality, and everything in the universe throughout time is connected. I can detect any certain living individual, say 4,000 miles away, in a matter of seconds, and can manipulate, install, or dismantle energy systems around the person with ease."

"How can you do it remotely?" Robert asked.

"Thought," Morris simply answered. "In a different level of reality, they are right by me. It's easy for me to see the multiple parallels of reality. Quantum realities play a large part in our lives, and different realities cross themselves at various junctions and turning points in our lives. We are not static to one universe. There are many parallel universes out there, and we shift across the boundaries from time to time.

"I'll go on to explain that people who have good luck have a natural ability to subconsciously cause the right vibrational frequencies of events to come together to a junction. It's all a matter of timing. Destiny works along the same lines with the thoughts and intelligence from beings on higher levels of reality."

Chispo translated Morris' comments to Artenian for Orolizo and Lumela.

"Oh, yeah," Chris responded. "One of the holographic plates we viewed talked about that sort of thing."

"In other parallel realities," Morris explained, "we've done things we wish we could do in this reality, and vice versa. Many different actions have been played out across the whole of realities."

At times, Morris was known to ramble on like this. His friends usually let him do so, because what he said was so interesting and nearly always seemed to ring right. Although his explanation was impressive, Rudy was most impressed in that it was really annoying to him how much this Morris guy knew! Rudy thought to himself, *What sort of project am I getting myself into?* It also bothered Rudy that Morris seemed to have an unlimited amount of intelligence.

Although Rudy felt comfortable with his friends, he felt more than somewhat incompatible with Morris! They seemed to be at odds, at least according to Rudy, ever since he had wanted to touch a second crystal in that crate the other night in Rinto and Fraxino's house. Rudy now wished to be with his family, his friends in Bustamante, and to be with his brother Roel who had stayed behind in Pinos, Zacatecas. He was really having second thoughts about continuing with this group. Although fun and interesting to be with, along with the adventures, he really missed his own kind in Bustamante, and now that he was seeing his home town right at the foot of the mountain, the town beckoned him to come home and stay.

While the others discussed their interesting and intelligent ideas, Rudy sort of walked off by himself and continued thinking which way he wanted to go. The adventures of continuing with them was very tempting, but he also really missed home. After all, he was the youngest one of them all, at age 15. This was a turning point for him, and he was undecided.

Orolizo and Chispo, including Rinto and Fraxino, and Lumela, were really going to it, discussing ideas and concepts. They were speaking entirely in Artenian. More than half an hour went by, and as Andrew, Chris, Robert, Rudy, and Steven didn't understand the conversation, they started exploring the ridgetop. Andrew, especially Steven, from a distance also explored the beautiful features and perfect outlines of Lumela, as they watched her participate in the discussion with Orolizo, Chispo, and the others.

Morris didn't understand verbally what the Artenians, that is, Zotolans were saying, but he picked up their gestures and feelings from other levels and gained a fairly accurate understanding of the subjects they were discussing, in addition to telepathically reading their thoughts, even though they didn't realize it.

The sun was now setting in the western sky, and that added some interest and beautiful scenery to their brief visit up here. Chispo and Orolizo realized it was getting dark.

"Man, where did the time go?" Chispo said to Orolizo. "We've been jabbering for nearly an hour!"

"Oh, man you're right," Orolizo acknowledged. "How did we do that so easily?"

"I know," Chispo agreed. "We start talking, and the time flies away."

From the moment Chispo and Orolizo had met a few weeks ago during their first visit to the Atascosa people, they had struck up an immediate good friendship and felt like they had always known each other. Rudy was taking notice and was feeling somewhat second place. He had also become good friends with Chispo, but now seeing this, he had a stronger desire to return to Bustamante.

"We've been here long enough," said Orolizo. "Let's go on down to Bustamante. I want to meet my soul link."

"Right, let's go," said Rinto. "Hey everyone!" he now shouted out to Andrew and the others who were a few hundred meters away exploring and looking around. "Time to go."

Everyone walked over to the craft, climbed in, and Rinto flew them down to Bustamante. It was now twilight, and they quietly made their flight down the mountain, cruising just above the treetops, passing through the gully, and making their landing near the cono building at the road's end some three kilometers from Bustamante. Rinto now started the engine and drove them down the straight gravel road. They entered town at the left hand bend in the road.

It was now dark, and the street lights were turned on. It was Thursday night, July 25, 1985. Nothing special was going on. Rinto already knew the way from their previous trips to Bustamante, and he drove them to Roel and Rudy's house. They passed the plaza in the town's center on the way.

Bustamante was a small town with around 3,000 residents. In some ways, the whole town was like a large family. Most of the residents were lifetime natives, and they were related and connected to each other in various ways. There were no banks, no law offices, no fast-food restaurants, and no convenience stores. There were no traffic lights. Bustamante did not even have a fuel station. The nearest one was a Pemex station in the next town ten kilometers away.

Most of Bustamante sat in the middle of an oasis, and there were Pecan trees and Avocado trees throughout the town, except for the upper reaches nearer to the mountains. The center of the town sat five kilometers from the foot of the towering mountain range, and its main feature was the Lion's Head Mountain, elevation 1,860 meters, locally called Cabeza de León, because its outlines did indeed have the appearance of a lion resting and facing south.

As they proceeded through town, they passed numerous houses made of adobe and of concrete blocks. Nearly every street corner had a small place of business. The road they were on was one of the main streets through the town. Nearly every house came right up to the sidewalks. Most of the streets were quite narrow, and in some places it was difficult for two vehicles to pass by each other. Nearly every street followed the same style.

Only two days had passed since they had been away from Bustamante, but to Rudy it seemed a lot longer. They had been busy since then, briefly visiting Roel in Pinos, Zacatecas, going to Zotola where they viewed more of Rinto and Fraxino's holographic plates, seeing the movie: *Vision from the Ciruclar*, receiving a visit from Tom about his Alaska project proposal, touring the secret cave in the mountains, and visiting the Atascosa people.

Rinto parked the vehicle-craft on the streetside by the house, and everyone stepped outside. Nora and Idalia, Rudy's sisters, ages 11 and 6 respectively, were the first ones to emerge from the house. They ran to them with happy smiles on their faces and greeted them in a welcoming manner. María, their mother, came outside next.

"Hola muchachos. ¿Cómo están?" she greeted them, asking them how they were doing.

Rudy came to her and gave her a hug and told her they were fine.

"¿Qué hicieron? ¿Cómo les fue en tu viaje?" she asked, wanting to know what they did and how their trip went.

"Muy bien," Rudy answered, telling her that it went very well. He began to tell his mother all about it.

Somebody else stepped out of the house.

"Roel!" Rudy said to his brother. "Ya viniste," commenting with surprise that he had already come home. Rudy was quite surprised to see his brother because he had clearly stated that he would be staying in Pinos for at least another month, having been afraid to return home to Bustamante for the danger that had already occurred earlier.

"¿Cuándo llegaste?" he said to Roel, asking him when he arrived.

"Acabo de llegar. Hace media hora," telling Rudy that he arrived half an hour ago.

They shook hands, Mexican style, glad to see each other, and as everyone entered the house, Rudy proceeded to tell his family all about his adventures with his new friends. He told them with enthusiasm, and with Chispo's help in the story telling, they really had María on edge with their tall tales, especially when Rudy nearly lost it, when he nearly touched that crystal. He surprised them even further when he started talking in English to the others! Rudy explained how he acquired English, and his family was at a loss for words for their surprise.

Roel explained that his feelings told him he needed to return to Bustamante as soon as possible. He had sensed that Rudy had missed him and had also sensed that Rinto, Chispo, and Fraxino would soon return, which they had just done, confirming Roel's predictions. He had thought about what Rudy had told him, that the danger was indeed gone, and his feelings had told him the same during the last couple of days.

"¿No has hablado con Pegaso?" Rudy asked Roel, wanting to know if he had spoken with Pegaso.

Roel shook his head no.

"Este Orolizo quiere ir a conocerle," telling Roel that Orolizo wanted to go meet Pegaso.

Roel asked why, and Rudy explained that Orolizo is Pegaso's soul link.

María asked her son why Orolizo and Lumela were of a green color, and Rudy and also Chispo explained the story of the Atascosa race of people from the mountains of southern Zotola.

"Bueno, vamos con Pegaso," said Rudy, offering to everyone to go see Pegaso. All twelve of them walked the few blocks to Pegaso's house.

Orolizo was indeed struck with the familiarity of the place, as he had had numerous dreams of the place through his connection with his soul link.

They arrived at the side door of Pegaso's house. His parents answered the door. She greeted them happily and offered them to come inside and wait in the living room.

"Pegaso," his mother called out. She also announced to him that his friends from another star system had come to visit him.

Pegaso emerged from the back of the house. A smile came across his face when he saw his friends. He greeted everyone and apologized to both Roel and Rudy for the firecracker incident. They shook hands and made up for the past differences.

"¿Qué tal, Pegaso?" Chispo said to Pegaso, greeting him.

They shook hands as friends again. Pegaso now took a look at Orolizo. He felt certain he had seen him before, but he couldn't quite place it. Both Chispo and Rudy proceeded to introduce Pegaso to his soul link, and the two of them shook hands. Suddenly, Pegaso was overwhelmed by a telepathic force of energy, followed by Orolizo and also Lumela. The three of them were somewhat stunned and the others looked at them in amazement. As Pegaso's mother commented, followed by Roel and Rudy, both Orolizo and Lumela understood what was said. Orolizo surprised himself when he started speaking Spanish. Though he had dreamed of Mexico numerous times and had heard the Spanish language spoken, he had never been able to speak it . . . until now!

"Y el cristal de cuarzo, ¿cómo te gustó?" Orolizo now asked Pegaso, wanting to know how he liked the quartz crystal he had given him by way of Chispo.

"Sí, me gustó mucho," Pegaso answered, telling Orolizo he liked it very much. He went on to explain that he had seen it clearly in a dream back a year ago, and that he was quite surprised to receive it in real life.

The link of their souls and connection of friendship took such a stronghold that Orolizo and Pegaso started chatting with each other in Spanish as if they had always known each other, which they had, on a different level.

The others looked on with interest as they watched the friendly interaction occurring.

"I've had the same feelings of a strong connection with certain dolphins I've recently met," Morris told everyone.

"I guess soul links naturally hit it off very well," Steven commented.

"That's right," Morris confirmed. "It's because they already know each other, like that holographic plate on friendships told us . . . their friendship quantum energy system has a life of its own and knows how to manipulate destiny to cause them to be brought together, sooner or later . . . like you see here."

"It's one of the greatest feelings of reality, isn't it?" Robert commented.

"That's right," Morris agreed. "Friendships have a lot of importance in a person's life."

"I agree," said Chris. "They do."

"Well, dudes," Chispo said to everyone with a smile, "those two are going to be jabbering the rest of the night. Let's go walk around town."

"Yeah, good idea," Andrew agreed. "May as well."

They all walked out of the house. Pegaso's mother wished them well as they left.

Orolizo and Pegaso continued chatting enthusiastically with each other. Pegaso went to his bedroom and got the quartz crystal and the letter Orolizo had sent him. They chatted with interest about them, and when Pegaso looked at the letter written in Artenian script, he really got a shock when he could actually read it! He surprised himself even more when he discovered he suddenly knew how to speak Artenian as well. So, he and Orolizo now chatted in Artenian, surprised at themselves. They wondered how they suddenly acquired each other's languages, and Orolizo suggested the possibility that their friendship link was so strong that, with a life of its own, it had enough intelligence to spark the reality of sudden language acquisition in both of them at their time of physical meeting. The force must have rubbed off on Lumela also, since she was Orolizo's sister, and was nearby at the time.

Meanwhile, the others decided to take a walk to the town plaza. Lumela came with them. She was enjoying speaking her suddenly acquired Spanish language, and she was now able to speak directly with Rudy and Roel, and also with Andrew and Robert, who also knew Spanish. She and Andrew began talking with each other as they walked to the plaza. Meanwhile, poor Steven, who had felt such an attraction for Lumela, felt left out because not only did he not speak Artenian, he also couldn't speak Spanish!

As they walked along, Roel and Rudy talked to each other, catching each other up on their recent adventures, but Roel out of the corner of his eye was looking at Lumela from time to time. He found her quite attractive. Her perfect beauty and olive green complexion were just out of this world . . . literally! Roel was like that, always on the lookout for a beautiful young woman. As they walked along, he casually slipped over and nearer to her. His feelings were turning on for her.

They passed the social center and continued the two blocks to the plaza, where on one side, the town church stood, and on the other side of the block, the police station and presidencia stood. Stores, a restaurant, and a bus station lined another side of the block.

Some of Roel and Rudy's friends were also at the plaza, some walking and others seated on the park benches. They called out to them and some whistled at Lumela's beauty and asked them which one was dating her. Since Lumela now understood Spanish, she knew they were talking about her.

After chatting with some of their friends around the plaza, they walked into the Cantu's store at the corner. Roel and Rudy bought some fruit drinks and other food for snacks. Robert looked at the place where the *No fío porque cobrar es un lío, y el negocio es mío* sign used to hang. There was no sign hanging there now. Chilo had taken down the original sign expressing mistrust in his customers, right after the device was deactivated in the mountains. He had suddenly gotten a compelling urge to remove it, as he had suddenly gained more confidence and trust in his customers.

When Robert spoke to Chilo, he greeted him in a friendly manner and asked him how their adventures had been. Robert filled him in on what they had done. Chilo reacted with surprise, especially when Robert told him they were about to go to Alaska to do a big project up there.

Next, Chilo opened a drawer, pulled out a new sign, and showed it to Robert. It read as follows: *Se fia solamente a personas mayores de 90 años, y acompañados de su abuelito!* (We sell on credit only to persons above 90 years in age, and accompanied by their grandfather!) At first, Robert took it seriously, but then he saw the smile on Chilo's face, and they both laughed heartily at the sign, which if serious, would be literally impossible! The others now also saw the sign and also started laughing. After a few more moments when the laughter died down, Chilo put the sign back in the drawer.

All of them walked out of the store and back into the plaza. They talked to more friends. As they were seated and standing around the park benches, they noticed another young female, an exquisitely beautiful muchacha who walked by. She was accompanied by other female companions. Andrew immediately took a strong attraction to her. Almost instinctively, his eyes looked straight toward her like a magnet! He gently elbowed Roel who was standing by him at the time.

"¿Roel, quién es esa chica?" Andrew asked Roel, wanting to know who that chick was.

"Se llama Perlona," telling him her name was Perlona. Immediately, Roel could sense that Andrew was turned on. He smiled. "¿Te gusta?" Roel asked Andrew, wanting to know if Perlona was appealing to him.

"Sí . . ." Andrew answered, already wishing to be with her.

As they continued to talk and chat, Andrew just watched as the gorgeous young female walked by. *Never mind Lumela*, Andrew was thinking. *I just want to know this Perlona chick.*

After a while, they walked back to Roel and Rudy's house a kilometer away. They briefly stopped by Alvaro's house on the way back and talked with him. Alvaro was another of Roel and Rudy's friends. He too was taken by Lumela's beauty. After chatting with Alvaro a short while, they walked the remaining distance back to Roel and Rudy's house. Lumela turned left and returned to her brother Orolizo at Pegaso's house.

María made accommodations for them all. There weren't enough beds, needless to say, but she cleaned and mopped the floor for them so they could spread out their bedrolls. After all, she was very grateful to them because they together had recently given Rudy $8,000 so they could buy their house and now own it instead of renting it.

Tom, the galactic salesman, had paid the group U.S. $25,000 cash for the project of successfully eliminating the transmitter devices in the mountains above Bustamante. It had been a top priority of the Galactic Federation. Out of the $25,000, they had decided to help Rudy by buying their house, with the condition that they could come to visit and stay there whenever they would be in northern Mexico. The house had cost $8,000.

María and her husband had already made repairs to the cracks in the walls. They had exterminated the hundreds of cockroaches that used to crawl the walls at night, and they were also repairing the run down toilet and shower.

After eating some supper and visiting for a while, they all went to sleep for the night.

Morning arrived. It became light at 6:30 AM. Half an hour later, they began to get up. As they were packing up their bedrolls, María fixed them all some breakfast.

Orolizo and Lumela had stayed overnight at Pegaso's house. They were sure Orolizo and Pegaso had talked well into the night.

As they were eating breakfast, Andrew came up to them. "Guys, I've thought about it. I'm going to stay here."

"What?" Robert asked in surprise.

"It's Perlona, isn't it?" Rudy immediately asked him.

"Yes, you guessed it, Rudy," Andrew replied. "Besides, I've taken a real liking to Bustamante. I've always liked the Spanish, Latin American culture. After all, I was born and raised in Peru."

"I didn't know that," Rudy responded. "Dice que nació en Peru," Rudy now told Roel, telling him that Andrew was born in Peru.

"¿Dónde vive esa Perlona?" Andrew asked Roel, wanting to know where Perlona lived.

"Como tres cuadras de aquí," telling him that she lived three blocks away.

"Whew doggie!" Andrew called out enthusiastically.

Robert, who now had a chance to comment, said, "Well, Andrew, sorry to lose you from our group, but I guess you've made your mind up, haven't you."

"I've been with you guys long enough," Andrew pointed out to them. "I want to do something else now."

Though Steven said nothing of it, he was liking the sound of this. Now he'd have a chance to know Lumela without Andrew's interference! As he thought more about it, excitement built up inside him also.

Meanwhile, Robert felt taken aback with Andrew's comment, which implied that the Alaska project wasn't worth that much to Andrew. He asked him, "What about the $33,000 he offered to the group of us?"

"No, that's okay. I've already been paid from that last project," Andrew declared. "I'm satisfied with that. What I want to do now is relax . . . with *Perlona*." He had the appearance of savouring her name as he said it, and he smiled.

They knew the love bug had bitten him. There was no longer any use in talking him into continuing with them.

"Where are you going to stay?" Robert asked him.

"Here with Rudy's family. Where else?"

"I thought you might want to stay with her," said Robert.

"No, Robert, that would be too forward. I need a few days to get to know her first!"

"Este Andrew quiere quedarse aquí," Rudy now said, telling his mother that Andrew wanted to stay in Bustamante.

"Aquí puede quedar. Aquí tiene su casa," María answered, giving consent and saying Andrew could stay with them.

With that, it was decided. Andrew was going to stay and spend the rest of the summer in Bustamante, Nuevo León. He was a nice person, but when it really came down to it, he strived for what he wanted for himself without regard to previous commitments. That's the way Andrew was. He had his decisions made and he was going to separate from the group and the adventures. Later in the day, one of Roel's friends would take Andrew over to Perlona's house and introduce them to each other.

"Well, now is as good a time as any," Chris decided to announce.

"You're leaving us, too?" Chispo asked him.

"Yes, I've been thinking about it," Chris explained. "I've had enough adventures. I've enjoyed my time with you all, but as I think about it, I want to spent the last month of my summer at home in Tennessee. Besides, I sense danger. I nearly died . . . well, actually did die . . . when that final energy beam zapped me. Thanks to you, Rinto for saving me. Also, it's cold up in Alaska, and mosquitos must be rampant."

"Are you sure you don't want to continue with us?" Robert asked Chris.

"Really, I want to go on home," Chris answered.

"Well, okay Chris," said Robert. "I guess you'll transport yourself home by thought?"

"Right."

Out of the original eight who had gone to Sirius, Vega, and the Pleiades during the first part of the summer, only Robert and Steven remained . . . and also Morris, at the present moment. Rinto, Fraxino, and Chispo had joined the group, followed by Rudy . . . and Roel, for their stay in Mexico.

Robert remembered he had stored a rocking chair here at Roel and Rudy's house when they had returned to Zotola. The chair was a native craft, made in Bustamante by some neighbors, and he had bought it as a souvenir.

"Chris, since you're going home," Robert requested, "would you take my rocking chair with you and take it to my house in Tennessee?"

"Yeah, sure," Chris consented.

"Good, thanks."

Rudy, who had been listening, went to the back room, retrieved the chair, and brought it to Robert. Chris said goodbye to everyone. Next, Robert and Chris, with the chair, walked out of the house and across the dirt street to an abandoned adobe house. They entered. Chris sat in the chair, and now with no one except Robert looking on, he brought on the energy forcefield by thought. Very soon, a pink glow enveloped him along with the sound of whirring wind. In seconds, both Chris and the chair dematerialized, followed by the disappearance of the pink glow and whirring wind. He along with the chair were now back in Tennessee. Robert walked out of the abandoned house and returned to the others.

They finished breakfast. Rudy walked Andrew over to Perlona's house to introduce him to her. Roel and the others went over to Pegaso's house to see how Orolizo and Lumela were doing.

When they arrived at Pegaso's house, his parents were in the kitchen, and they welcomed them inside.

"Buenos días," said Roel, greeting Pegaso's parents. "¿Está Orolizo?" asking if Orolizo was there.

"Está bien dormido, y Lumela también," answered Pegaso's mother, telling Roel that both Orolizo and Lumela were sound asleep. She went on to explain that Orolizo and Pegaso had talked until 3 AM, and when Lumela returned after walking with the others to the plaza, she joined in the conversation, as well. Then both of Pegaso's sisters arrived home, joined in the conversation, and the five of them talked the hours away. She explained that it was like the five of them already knew each other, and they felt like siblings.

A quick thought suddenly raced through Roel's mind that perhaps Orolizo and Lumela were going to stay in Bustamante.

"Pegaso," his mother called out to him. "Te hablan tus amigos," telling him that his friends had come to talk to him. She left the kitchen, walked down the hall, and knocked on his door. "Pegaso," she called out again. She returned to the kitchen. "Ahorita vienen," telling them they would be coming in a little while.

Pegaso, followed by Orolizo, both sleepily dragged themselves out of the bedroom several minutes later. They came forward to the kitchen. Lumela and Pegaso's sisters were in a different room and continued to sleep.

"Good morning, everyone," Orolizo greeted them in Artenian.

"What's up, Orolizo?" Chispo asked him.

"Chispo, everyone, it's like this," Orolizo began. "Lumela and I hit it off really well with Pegaso and his sisters."

"Man, how could we keep from noticing?" Chispo responded with a smile.

"They've invited us to stay and spend the summer with them," Orolizo now informed them. "More than that, they're taking a trip to Puerto Vallarta, and they've invited us to come with them."

"Dudes, we go to southern Zotola for you," Fraxino now pointed out, "bring you with us here to Mexico with the intent of going on to Alaska from here, and you already cut and run on us?"

"Didn't we tell you the galactic salesman is paying us?" Rinto now mentioned.

"No, you didn't mention that," Orolizo replied, "but then we don't use money among the Atascosa."

"True, but you do here," Rinto pointed out.

"Yes, but that's okay," said Orolizo. "They've invited us to stay here. So, that's what we're going to do."

Chispo translated the conversation both to English and Spanish for the others to understand what was said. Meanwhile Rinto and Fraxino kept talking with Orolizo to see if they could talk him into joining them to go to Alaska. It just no longer interested Orolizo. He and Lumela were staying, and that was it.

In a way, they felt like they had been used by Orolizo. As a result, without even mentioning it, they decided to leave it up to Orolizo and Lumela about how they were going to return to their people in southern Zotola. Perhaps Andrew, who was also going to stay in Bustamante, would transport both of them back when they would be ready later on. That or Rinto and Fraxino might be kind enough to come and take them back to Artenia in their craft at a later date.

Roel, Robert, Steven, Morris, Chispo, Rinto and Fraxino said goodbye to them, left the house, and walked back to Roel's house. Roel informed them he had already sensed that Orolizo and Lumela were going to stay.

"I had a feeling those two were going to stay here," Morris also told everyone. "I just knew it."

"Are we going to have anybody left at all?" Robert asked everyone with concern.

"We're staying with you on the project," Fraxino assured Robert, speaking also for Rinto and Chispo.

"I'll stay with you all, at least for the beginning of the project," Morris told them. "However, I must get back to my project with the dolphins after that."

"The dolphins have a link to the project, don't they, Morris?" Chispo asked him with a smile.

"Well, I'm not supp . . ."

"Yes, they do, don't they?" Chispo insisted, still smiling.

"Yes. Yes, they do indeed," Morris admitted. "That's why it's important for me to return to them. Once we get things started in Alaska and we investigate those time frozen bodies, then I must rejoin the dolphins to coordinate the engineering from their end."

"I knew there had to be a good reason," Steven declared with a smile.

"I sort of thought that, too," said Robert.

"So, Morris," Chispo brought up, "who's the other one among us that has a link to the dolphins?"

"You're fishing, Chispo," Morris told him in a joking manner.

"Fishing?" Chispo asked.

Morris thought about it as they continued walking toward Roel's house. "Okay, I'm going to tell you who he is. I'll put you out of your misery. I'm going to tell you now . . . He's Rudy."

"Rudy? Really?" Chispo reacted with surprise.

"That's right," Morris answered. "He and I may be at odds, but then that goes back many eons of time ago. If he decides to stay here, he's really missing out on an adventure."

"What makes you think he's going to stay?" Robert asked.

"It's my feeling he will," Morris answered. "This is his home."

"Man, we never thought about it being Rudy," Chispo told Morris.

"Let's put it this way," Morris pointed out. "How do you think Rudy instantly gave you the Spanish language? That's a trait left over from the time of the dolphins."

"Yes, you do have a point there," Chispo admitted.

"You and he and also Robert are linked to that world of Delikadove," Morris continued. "That's why the three of you have so easily become the good friends you are on this adventure."

"I agree, now that you put it that way," Chispo said to Morris.

"When you go back far enough along the time lines, there are ancient reasons why certain people have such a strong connection and become friends so easily here in our time period. I know who each of the three of you were. Chispo, you already know, but as for Robert and Rudy, I'm going to leave it to you all to figure that one out."

By now, they were back at Roel and Rudy's house, and they walked inside. They packed their backpacks and took them to the vehicle-craft. Rudy returned a half hour later without Andrew.

"Where's Andrew?" Robert asked.

"He stayed with Perlona's family," Rudy replied.

"You're kidding!" Steven remarked.

"You mean they took him in, just like that?" Chispo asked.

"Perlona's father liked Andrew right away," Rudy explained. "He needed a worker on his ranch, and even though the pay was only a little, Andrew took him up on it, seeing it as an opportunity to cultivate his relationship with Perlona. So, Andrew's now staying there with them."

"Well, I will say!" Robert remarked.

"It's amazing what the love bug will do to some people," said Fraxino.

"Well, I guess we're not going to have any females on this project after all," Steven commented with sorrow. He had wanted to cultivate a relationship, too . . . with Lumela, but then Pegaso and his sisters had lured her away from him. He had been glad that Andrew had now directed his attention to another female, but now Steven had lost anyway. *Well, such is life,* he thought to himself.

Though Chris never said anything about it, the real reason he had just gone back to Tennessee was to see if he could re-establish his relationship with his former girlfriend with whom he had broken up last year. He had just had a dream about her last night, and she had been constantly on his mind since. While the reasons he stated were true, he also used them to cover up the real one.

Robert's thoughts were as follows: *The girlfriends can wait till later!* His desires were to take off and have adventures with his friends, do projects like they had been doing, and enjoy the unique summer vacation. Cutting out and going home early were out of the question.

Chispo, Rinto, and Fraxino were also for the adventure, especially Chispo. Rinto and Fraxino, for all the projects they were into, would best be described as lab gurus. It was highly unlikely that others had done projects similar to Rinto and Fraxino's, converting a vehicle for spaceflight and teleportation to other worlds, not to mention, their expertise with crystals.

"Anyway, let's get the vehicle-craft loaded," Fraxino said to everyone.

"Tom's going to be there in less than two hours, right?" Chispo asked.

"That's right," said Morris, as he looked at his watch.

"Yo no voy. I'm not going," Rudy suddenly announced in both Spanish and English.

"You too, Rudy?" Robert asked.

"What happened? Why not?" Chispo now asked.

"It's like Chris said," Rudy reminded them. "Mosquitos are rampant, and it's cold."

"That's not a reason to cut and run on us," Rinto said.

"And what about the money?" Steven asked Rudy.

"I've already got the house, thanks to all of you. You can come and stay anytime, but I'm not going to Alaska."

"What about Roel?" Robert asked.

"I'm staying here," Roel answered. "It's like Rudy said. It's cold, and the mosquitos are rampant." Roel didn't say, but he also had beautiful Lumela on his mind.

"You're not coming either. Why really?" Robert asked Roel.

"I just got home last night, and . . ."

"Roel! When did you learn English?!" Rudy suddenly broke in and asked.

Roel looked at his brother, smiled, and said, "No te digo," telling Rudy that he wasn't going to tell him. Though Roel had kept quiet about it, he had absorbed the English language from Rudy overnight while they were asleep together. He enjoyed the game of keeping it a secret from his brother. Since they were brothers, they had a close telepathic connection. Roel also had a special knack of sensing other levels of realities, and he was known for his good instincts at finding things either hidden from him or lost.

Rudy looked at his brother with a stare. "You got it telepathically in your sleep." Roel acted like it wasn't true. "Yes, you did. I know you did," Rudy insisted. They both started laughing.

"Rudy," Morris now pointed out, "you're missing out on quite an adventure."

"What's it to you? Since Roel's not coming, I'm not either."

"You went with the group before," Morris said to him.

"Yes, I did, but now you've come back on the scene and joined us, and how do you know so much, anyway? You have such imagination!"

"I just learned it through time," Morris replied. "Okay, fair enough. Stay here then."

Morris could sense that Rudy felt at odds with him. They had argued several topics. While Rudy was not jealous, he was still bothered by the voluminous amount of information Morris knew.

Then Roel recalled that the galactic salesman was paying. "Rudy," he now reminded him. "¿Qué tal del dinero?" asking Rudy about the money offer.

"Ya tenemos la casa," Rudy answered, telling Roel that they already have the house.

Rudy and Roel continued talking over the possibilities in Spanish as everyone else stood and listened.

"No, no quiero ir con este," Rudy argued, stating that he didn't want to continue because Morris was with them.

"Pero pronto se va a los delfines," Roel pointed out, reminding Rudy that Morris was very soon to return to the dolphins.

"Sí, ya sé, pero es que sabe todo!" Rudy said with some disgust, complaining that Morris knew everything. "Por eso, no quiero ir," further stating that was the main reason he didn't want to continue with them.

Roel then told Rudy that since there was a money offer reward involved, he wanted to come along. Roel also pointed out that he wanted to buy a car with some of the money. They could go travel to the south of Mexico, visit the beach, travel to other places as well, buy a second home at a resort area. Roel was carrying on and on about it, explaining how they could enjoy the money.

"¡No me gusta el sur de Mexico!" Rudy suddenly declared, telling his brother that he didn't like the south of Mexico.

"¿Pues, el carro?" Roel said, reminding Rudy about buying a car.

"Tampoco," Rudy answered, saying he wasn't interested in that either.

What Rudy really felt was a dislike for Morris, and he just didn't want to continue with them. Morris' commanding ways and irritating knowledge about the crystal Rudy was about to touch just never sat right with him, and he had since then felt a tinge of resentment toward Morris about it. For that reason, he was stubbornly refusing to continue with them. He wasn't angry at his brother, but under the circumstances, he was answering Roel in such a manner because he didn't want to be with Morris. Since Rudy was determined to stay, Roel unwillingly accepted that and decided to stay also.

With that done, they all walked out of the house. María and her sons, Roel and Rudy, walked out of the house with them, and as the others climbed into the vehicle-craft, they wished them well. They shook hands. Both Robert and Chispo felt sadness at parting with Roel and Rudy.

There were now only six of them: Rinto, Fraxino, Chispo, Robert, Steven, and Morris.

This time, Fraxino did the driving. As he drove them away, they waved goodbye. Two blocks down the street, he made a left turn and drove them out of town on the canyon road, a one-lane gravel road.

"I can't understand why Rudy suddenly backed out on us," Robert commented to everyone.

"Man, what's he afraid of?" Chispo asked.

"Of how much I know," Morris answered.

"What do you mean, Morris?" Robert wanted to know.

"It's like Rudy said, he's intimidated by my vast knowledge and what I know. Perhaps he doesn't want me to know things about him that are private. Also, when he telepathically received the English language from me when he touched that orange crystal, he at that time realized how much I know, and it somewhat scared him off."

"I don't see why that would stop him," Rinto said. "Rudy seems pretty straightforward."

"Yes, he is," Morris partially admitted, "but he's been changing as far as that goes. Also, he and I are incompatible, like I said, from eons ago on the world of Delikadove. I will say this. I saw a negative energy system come onto him this morning. That's what caused him to react angrily to me and to Roel. It caused him not to reason as well. I'm surprised he didn't throw a tantrum. He did very well, considering, because he's a good and sincere fellow at heart."

"You saw a bad energy system come onto him this morning?" Steven asked Morris.

"Yes, I detected its presence, even though I didn't say anything about it."

"Couldn't you have done something about it?" Robert asked.

"I could have done, but I decided to let it run its course so I could see how well Rudy would do. He did quite well. It was kind of him to wish us well and tell us we're welcome to come back."

"Yes, I agree," said Chispo.

"Rudy and Roel are going to want to rejoin you all," Morris told them.

"They are?" Robert responded.

"How do you know?" Chispo asked.

"I'm going to dismantle that energy system later today, once we're in Alaska."

"How are you going to do that?" Rinto wanted to know. "We're not with Rudy anymore."

"I can do it from anywhere," Morris answered. "You see, reality is very pliable, and there are shortcuts. It's like I was saying, on another level, he's actually right with me."

"You didn't set up the bad energy system in the first place?" Steven asked.

"I could have done something like that, but I didn't," Morris replied.

"Then where did it come from?" Chispo wanted to know.

"It floated in from another region," Morris explained. "It likely hitched a ride on Roel, seeing he just arrived yesterday. Bad energies are slowly returning to Bustamante, balancing out their absense since their total wipeout at the time those two crystal transmitters were eliminated in the mountains. That region had a clean slate once that happened. But don't worry. It won't ever be as bad as it was before those transmitters were eliminated."

"That's good to hear," said Rinto.

"So, Rudy's going to be all right?" Robert asked.

"Oh yeah. He will be fine. You'll see. You can go back for him once I've left you all and returned to the dolphins."

That made them feel a lot better, especially Robert and Chispo.

"So, we only have an hour and a half before we need to be in Alaska, right?" Rinto asked his brother.

"That's right, man."

"We can't fly there in that short time," Rinto realized. "It's too far. We'll have to teleport."

"Dudes, we're putting this cruiser craft in flying mode and popping over to Alaska!" Fraxino enthusiastically announced. He pulled back the lever, switched off the engine, and they left the ground. They were now well into the canyon. Fraxino telepathically caused the craft to swiftly accelerate, and in minutes, they were passing over the tops of the mountains and were now flying over the desert valley to the west.

As they picked up further speed, both Rinto and Fraxino telepathically transmitted the scene of Alaska to the Ulexite controls crystal and crystal array. In seconds, the faint green glow overtook them. They felt as if they were dematerializing, but then they were suddenly fine.

CHAPTER 5

THE TIME FROZEN FINDINGS

They were now flying over mountains and glaciers in northeastern Alaska. The sky was clear and blue overhead, and the sun shined bright with its light reflecting off the glaciers and small lakes. It was early morning, around 5 AM, Alaska time, but then at this latitude and this time of year, the sun shined 24 hours a day. The day was July 26, 1985.

"Wow! What a change!" Steven declared.

They were now flying at an altitude of 4,000 meters, and around 30 kilometers ahead of them could be seen three mountains to their north. The mountains stood tall, and snow and glaciers still partially covered their slopes.

Fraxino lowered the craft's air speed velocity of 1,000 km/h and lowered their altitude as they came in for a landing.

"Man, this scenery is beautiful!" Fraxino declared.

"Dude, you're not kidding!" Chispo agreed.

"I've already located him," Morris suddenly announced as he looked ahead.

"Who, Tom?"

"That's right," Morris replied. "Fraxino, steer the craft a little more to the right and make a landing in that ravine tucked into the left side of that biggest mountain ahead of us."

"Right on!" Fraxino responded, complying.

"Morris, I don't see him," Rinto said.

"I can assure you with almost 100% certainty that he's there," Morris told him. "He's got to be there. I can sense it."

As they neared the high mountain ravine, Robert asked, "Morris, how are you able to set up and also take down energy systems?"

"You mean like what I'm going to take down and remove from Rudy?"

"Right."

"All energies have certain patterns to them. I'm able to see them through my extra senses of other levels. When I see something unfairly placed, I usually step in to redirect the energies, dismantle the system, and remove it. I am what could be called a quantum energy system weaver. I already knew something of the art of energy weaving, but the dolphins have taught me a lot more during the past month. In the near future, you'll witness humans discovering that dolphins are excellent for healing and curing. All they do is redirect the energy patterns and wake up certain ones necessary for healing within and around the human body, and in days, the disease vanishes. The country of Mexico will be well ahead of the United States on that discovery."

"Energy weaving . . . That is an amusing concept," Steven remarked.

Fraxino steered the craft to the right and flew into the ravine, which had the appearance of being precariously tucked into the western slopes of Mt. Isto, the easternmost of the three mountains, the other two being Mt. Chamberlin and Mt. Michelson. All had an elevation of nearly 3,000 meters.

"There he is," Fraxino stated as he now saw Tom from a distance.

"Looks like he's got somebody else with him," said Chispo.

"That's probably Caymar," said Robert. "Yes, it is. I recognize him."

"Huh!" said Steven. "There's a building there."

By now, Fraxino was making a touchdown on the grassy arctic tundra. Tom and Caymar were outside next to their grey building 100 meters away, and they now looked toward them, at first with surprise, and then with relief when they recognized them.

"Caymar, our friends have arrived!" Tom happily told him in the Sirian language.

"What an interesting craft they've arrived in!" Caymar remarked.

As Fraxino opened the door and they stepped out of the craft, Tom and Caymar walked over to greet them.

"How are you doing, Tom?" Steven spoke first.

"You all have arrived safely," Tom announced as he walked toward them. "Well done!" He first shook hands with Morris and then the others. "This is my good friend Caymar," as he introduced him to the six of them. Robert, Steven, and Morris already knew him from their trip to Sirius B at the first of the summer.

Caymar now shook hands with them, and as he did so, a strong feeling of true friendship was transferred from him to the six of them. That was Caymar's way. He showed genuine friendship to those he met, and his handshake was neither a vise grip nor too weak. Peace of mind was immediately felt, as well, and they already felt as if they had known him for years. Caymar and Chispo were the same height, and they also happened to look similar to each other.

Tom looked at the six of them. "More people have left your group, haven't they?"

"Yes, they have," Robert admitted. "Andrew found a sudden female friend in Mexico, and Chris suddenly and simply went back home to Tennessee. They had both had enough."

"Of course, you know there's a reward for . . ." Tom began.

"Oh yes. We know," Robert acknowledged. "Even still, they weren't interested."

"How strange!" Tom remarked.

All of them took a look around them. The scenery was phenomenal! This ravine would better be described as a cove which was a small valley tucked between two westerly extending ridges from Mt. Isto, whose snow-covered summit sat some 1,000 meters above them. A small glacial lake sat some 200 meters beyond them further up the cove, and above and beyond that was a glacier which emptied into the lake. There were almost no trees in the region, only a few small shrubs of White Spruce interspersed throughout the lower part of the cove. The sounds of waterfalls and streams of rushing water were prevalent everywhere, and a small brook ran the length of the cove, from the lake to the lower reaches of the mountain. West of the cove at the foot of Mt. Isto was a vast area of partially snow-covered hilly terrain with tundra and barren ground, as well. Herds of Caribou and Reindeer could be seen at times, as well as the dangerous polar and grizzly bears! It was moderate and sunny with a temperature of 10° Celsius.

"So, what have you done the last two days?" Tom asked them.

"We went to visit Rinto and Fraxino's secret cave in the Ciruclar Mountains," Robert answered, "went to visit the Atascosa people, went to northern Mexico, saw the ancient paintings, and also visited Rudy's family in Bustamante."

"Rudy decided to stay in Mexico for now," Morris explained. "Once I return to the dolphins, he and his brother will likely rejoin the group."

"He didn't take much of a liking to you, did he?" Tom asked Morris.

"That's right."

"I could sense that the other day when I proposed the project," said Tom.

"Yes, he and I were simply at odds," Morris explained, "an incompatibility that dates back eons of time when I had a life on Delikadove, the world of the dolphins."

"It's interesting that reasons for present day feelings have their origins from so long ago," Tom commented. "Anyway, we just arrived half an hour before you did."

"No kidding!" Steven responded.

"Then we timed it pretty well," said Morris.

"You did indeed," said Tom. "Caymar and I found two of those time frozen bodies, each in a bronze crate, when we were here the other day. They are both buried up there on that ridge above us," and he pointed to the north.

"Those Atlanteans have an affection for those bronze crates!" Morris declared, laughing.

"Let's go have a look at them," said Robert.

Rinto and Fraxino closed up the vehicle-craft.

"Fraxino, bring the pick and prybar," Chispo said to him. "We may need them."

"Good thinking." Fraxino went to the back of the vehicle, opened the door, and dug the two tools out of the back compartment.

With that done, they all began the climb out of the cove, and they scrambled up the somewhat steep slope of the side of the ridge. Most of it was dirt and small boulders, but there were a few tufts of grass, as well.

"Tom, whose grey building is that?" Steven wanted to know.

"Caymar and I had that teleported down from Sirius B. We needed a place to get out of the weather and the elements, to live in and have our facilities, instead of teleporting back and forth to Sirius B every little while."

"It just arrived when we did," Caymar informed them, "and we had a small crew come with us and secure it to the ground."

"It's a nice building, the size of a normal house," said Tom, "with plenty of insulation and the rest of it."

They continued talking as they climbed the ridge, and in a period of fifteen minutes, they were standing on top of the ridge, a finger which extended west from Mt. Isto and always sat above the snow and glaciers, even in the winter.

"Caymar and I have decided to firmly secure the receiver/transmitter towers to the top of this ridge. Though the winds and winter may be severe at this location, they will never be toppled by snowpacks and glaciers."

"Nor by avalanches," Caymar added. "We have plans to bring in a galactic crew of some 100 Sirians to excavate the tunnels and rooms well within this mountain, to later install the switching equipment."

"Anyway, where are the crates of time frozen bodies?" Morris eagerly wanted to know.

"Right," Tom acknowledged. "Follow me."

They followed the crest of the ridge uphill, toward Mt. Isto's summit, for five minutes. Then Tom and Caymar stopped and pointed. The others could see that the ground had been recently disturbed.

"This is one of them," Tom indicated. "The other one is some 200 meters further up the ridge."

"Let's get this thing uncovered," Morris now directed.

"Right on, dude!" Fraxino declared.

They all began to unearth the crate, now for the second time, since Tom and Caymar had earlier unearthed it the other day. Fraxino and Rinto helped dig the dirt away with the pick and prybar. In five minutes, they had it completely unearthed, and they all lifted it out of the hole. It was heavy!

"Okay, let's go dig up the other one," Rinto said to Tom.

For the moment, they left the crate and advanced further up the ridge. Caymar indicated where it was, and they had it unearthed in minutes. Next, they carried the crate down the ridge and placed it by the other one.

"Do you think there are any more?" Rinto asked Tom and Caymar.

"We really don't know," Caymar admitted.

"My feeling is there are," Morris told everyone.

"Where then?" Robert wanted to know.

"I have no idea where," Morris admitted. "I'm not picking up anything on them, except that there are more of those crates hidden up and down this mountain."

"Let's walk up and down this ridge and search," Steven suggested. "Maybe Caymar will sense another one."

"I've walked up and down this ridge numerous times," Caymar told them, "and these are the only two that Tom and I have found."

"Very well, then," said Morris. "I suppose it's time to carry these two crates down to the cove below us."

"What about Roel and his good locator instincts?" Robert brought up and suggested.

"That's a good idea," said Rinto.

"After all, Rudy did tell us how Roel was good at finding lost items around the house," said Chispo.

"Maybe Roel's good locator instincts could find the other crates," said Steven.

"Robert, why don't you go fetch him?" Morris directed. "Bring him to us. You know how to transport others by thought, right?"

"Oh yes. I still do."

"Good, then tell him we need him right away," said Morris. "Don't tell him what it's about. Just bring him."

"All right, I'll go right now." Immediately, Robert brought on the energy of the pink glow and whirring wind, and he thought himself to Bustamante. He arrived in the abandoned adobe house across the street from Roel and Rudy's house.

Meanwhile, Morris, Tom, and the others started carrying the two crates carefully down the steep sloping side of the ridge to the cove below them.

They had hardly begun the descent when they heard the sound of whirring wind again.

"Already?!" Steven exclaimed.

In seconds, both Robert and Roel materialized on the ridge.

"Luckily, he was right there at home," Robert immediately announced. "I told him it was urgent. We stepped across the street, entered the abandoned house, and now here we are."

Roel was very surprised at the sudden change in scenery for him. "¡Caramba!" he exclaimed, still in disbelief that he was suddenly somewhere else. "You . . . magicians . . . It's for certain! Where are we?"

"We're in Alaska, man," Chispo told Roel.

"What is it that you need that is so urgent?" Roel now asked, getting used to his new surroundings.

"Look at those two crates," Robert now told him. "We think there are more."

"We can't find any more of them and thought maybe you could," Rinto said to Roel.

"That I can find those?" Roel asked in disbelief.

"Yes, seriously," said Rinto.

In seconds, Roel's locator instincts took control. They watched his facial expression change. With hardly thinking about it, he took off walking up the ridge toward the summit of the mountain. The others had to be quick to follow him because he didn't wait for them. In less than a minute, Roel suddenly declared, "There!" He pointed. With that, he quickly proceeded further up the ridge.

Robert went and stood over the spot. "I'll stay here. The rest of you follow Roel."

In less than ten minutes, Roel indicated two more locations. Steven occupied one of the spots and Caymar another. For ten more minutes, Roel searched but found no more.

None of the three locations showed any evidence of a crate being buried, but when they began digging at the three locations Roel indicated, they sure enough found bronze around half a meter under the dirt.

"Well done, Roel!" Chispo commended him. They shook hands in declaration of triumph.

These next three crates were not so easily uncovered. They were lodged next to boulders, and it took them nearly two hours to finally bring them up out of their holes and place them on top of the ground.

"Okay, now we've got five of them," said Chispo.

They carried the crates down the ridge and placed them next to the other two. It took four of them to carry each heavy crate, so they took more than another hour just to get all five crates down into the cove. They placed them near the vehicle-craft.

"Right, let's remove the lids and see what we've got," Tom directed. "Caymar and I only inspected one the other day."

They pried the lid off the first bronze crate, the same one that Caymar and Tom had inspected.

"Far out, dude!" Chispo declared when he saw it.

Inside was the same human body that Tom and Caymar had seen when they had earlier opened the crate. It appeared to be a male, and he was clothed in what looked like some sort of uniform, made of a very different fabric, somewhat similar to nylon. Blue and purple were the main colors of the clothing. There seemed to be some sort of invisible shield that prevented them from being able to reach into the crate and touch the body.

"Really amazing what those Atlanteans could do," Morris declared.

"I just want to know why they're up here on the other end of the world," Steven said to everyone.

"That's what I want to know, too," Robert agreed.

"We may soon find out," said Morris.

"Let's get the lids off those other crates," Tom directed.

Rinto and Fraxino took on that task while the others continued looking at the body. Morris started figuring out how to revive him.

Steven noticed an emblem or symbol attached to the body's shirt. "No way! No . . . no way!" He started laughing.

"What is it, Steven?" Robert wanted to know.

"Isn't that the same symbol we saw painted at Chiquihuitillos, the one Rudy and Morris talked about . . . representing all one race?"

Robert looked at it. "Good gracious! You're right!"

"I'm not believing this!" Steven declared with surprise.

"Now, that does indeed surprise me!" Morris told everyone. "That symbol really is important."

"Dudes, that confirms who did those paintings," Chispo declared with confidence.

"That is indeed an ancient Galactic Federation symbol," Tom informed everyone.

"Really?" Robert responded.

"Yes, indeed," Tom replied. "I have seen that symbol in our ancient historical documents about Atlantis. All one race is exactly what it represents, and with that symbol on his uniform, these crates and bodies are very likely from Atlantis."

"Cool! I can't wait to revive them," Chispo declared.

"You say you just saw that symbol painted with those ancient cliff paintings in Mexico?" Caymar asked.

"Yes, we did," Chispo confirmed.

"Amazing!" Caymar remarked. "Atlantean people did do those paintings."

"A group of them must have settled there in Mexico," Tom stated.

"That's what we've been suspecting," said Chispo.

"How amazing!" Steven declared, laughing. "To think that the same symbol of *all one race* shows up here on this man's clothing after we see it in rural Mexico."

Roel looked at the man in the crate. He realized he was looking at something very ancient, very different.

"Yep, another human indeed, this one also a male!" Rinto shouted in triumph as he got the lid pried off the second crate.

Next, they pried the lids off the three crates Roel had found. All three were females. All five of the humans were of brown skin with black hair and dark brown eyes. They varied in height from 5 feet 6 inches to 5 feet 9 inches.

"So, Morris," Fraxino asked him, "how are we going to revive them?"

"I'm working on that now. They definitely are time frozen. They wouldn't have lasted otherwise . . . very ingenious way of preserving bodies, far better than freezing them to absolute zero, which destroys cells throughout the body." He paused and meditated. "I already know what to do. I need all of you to stand back, as I will have to weave an energy matrix forcefield around the five crates and bring time to a halt . . . suspend it, that is."

"How . . ." Robert began.

"All of you get at least 100 meters away for your safety," Morris suddenly directed. "Rinto, move your craft away from here also."

"Oh, yeah," Rinto acknowledged. "Thanks, Morris. I'm glad you thought of that." As the others walked further away from Morris, Rinto walked to the vehicle-craft, got inside of it, started the engine, and drove it over to where the others were now standing.

Everyone else watched with utmost curiosity from a distance as Morris thought and meditated. A low note and a whirring sound could be heard as sparkling energy was brought on to surround him and the five crates. A purple glow appeared for 15 seconds, then faded away, along with Morris and the crates. They had disappeared.

"They've all gone!" Steven exclaimed, as a sharp feeling hit him that they might have just permanently lost all five crates.

"Don't worry," Chispo assured him. "I'll bet he took them to the dolphins to unlock the time freeze."

"Now, he did say he was going to bring time to a halt," Tom reminded them, "which means he and the crates would therefore be invisible to us . . . by entering into and becoming our past."

"As Morris suspended time for himself," Caymar explained, "he is now synchronized with them and can wake them up from their level of time frozen sleep."

"I'm going over there to look," said Steven.

"No!" Tom ordered. "We must stand back and wait. We can't be in their way when they return, no matter how long it takes . . . in *our time*."

Steven immediately realized that Tom was right.

"Robert," Roel brought up, "why didn't my brother want to come?"

"Maybe this is what Rudy wasn't supposed to see," Rinto answered for Robert.

"Who knows," Chispo speculated. "Rudy probably understands how to unlock the time frozen bodies, and he and Morris might have fought over which method was the best one."

"That's likely true," Roel admitted. "My senses and my mind already made me aware of that." Roel had extra senses, and he sometimes knew things that were seemingly impossible to know by normal means.

"Yeah, I agree," said Robert. "Seems like Rudy and Morris always were at odds."

"They didn't get along all that well, anyway," Steven remarked.

They continued to stand and watch. The minutes went by as they talked and speculated.

"I'm getting worried they're not coming back," said Robert.

"I hope they're . . ." Chispo began.

Suddenly, a distinct whirring sound was heard along with a purple glow increasing in intensity. All of them watched with awe as the purple glow lasted for some 20 seconds and then slowly faded away along with the whirring sound. There stood Morris and the five crates, some 100 meters away.

"Wow! They made it back!" Rinto declared.

"Cool!" said Fraxino

"Far out!" Chispo remarked.

Morris walked to one side of the five crates and proceeded to give instructions to the crates by moving his arms as if he was performing a magic spell. The lids of the crates lifted themselves off, seemingly on their own, until everyone saw that the five occupants were the ones doing it, as they were now alive and well. The lids clanked to the ground, and the occupants rose up and stepped out of their crates respectively.

Morris was proudly grinning, pleased with his accomplishment, to say the least.

"You've done it, Morris!" Tom joyfully exclaimed as he and the others walked toward him, the crates, and the five now alive Atlanteans.

The Atlantean now living bodies started walking around, somewhat dazed and also surprised. Some of them sat down on the ground to get used to their new surroundings, so they could adjust to living and flowing time again.

"I'm just not believing you've actually done it!" said Steven, laughing.

"Dude, this is a miracle!" Chispo declared to Morris, and he walked up to him and shook hands with him.

"How'd you do it? Tell us," Robert eagerly wanted to know.

"Oh, I don't know . . . just threw in a little dolphin magic, and here we are!" Morris stated, laughing.

"Magic sure enough!" Steven declared.

"Fine job, well done," Caymar told him.

"I knew if anyone could do it, you were the one," Tom told Morris, commending him.

"He's a brujo. It's for certain," Roel quietly told Robert.

"Yes, I know," Robert agreed.

"So, tell us," Tom requested. "How did you do it?"

"Like I said, a little dolphin magic . . ."

"You mean you actually transported yourself and the crates to the dolphin world?" Steven broke in and asked.

"No, not to their world," Morris clarified, "but I did telepathically call up a land dolphin expert who understands time suspension, and he came to me, in my frame of reference, after we disappeared from your sight. The crates and I never left the spot, only I slowed down time for us, and while we remained still in time, we became your past and disappeared from your sight."

"We suspected that," Fraxino commented.

"Once out of your sight, the expert land dolphin aided me in waking up the bodies by transmitting a telepathic force to each body and unlocking their still time freeze. Then we let time run again and accelerated it a little faster than normal to catch up with, to us, your future time frame of reference, until we latched onto it and synchronized with it. My dolphin friend instantly teleported himself home, and the rest of us are now here."

"Absolutely brilliantly done!" Tom praised Morris.

By now the living Atlantean bodies had become more oriented, and they faced Morris, Tom, Robert, and their friends.

"What a relief to have our lives back!" one of the females declared in Atlantean.

"Where are we?" one of the males asked everyone.

"What time are we in?" another one of the females wanted to know.

"Fraxino, did you understand them also?" Rinto asked his brother in Artenian.

"Yeah, one of them just stated her relief at having her life back," Fraxino replied in Artenian.

"That's exactly what I understood!" Rinto stated in agreement.

"And another one asked where we are?" Chispo added.

"And what time period we're in, right?" Rinto asked both Fraxino and Chispo.

"Right on brother!" Fraxino enthusiastically declared.

"Dudes, we can understand them!" Chispo declared.

"It's almost the same as Artenian!" Rinto declared with enthusiasm. "Yahoo!!" and he threw his arms up in the air, displaying triumph.

"Guys, they speak our native Artenian language," Fraxino said in English to Morris, Robert, Steven and Roel.

"You mean you guys can understand these five revived Atlanteans?" Robert asked.

"That we do," Fraxino confirmed.

"No kidding!" Steven responded "Your Artenian language is the same as their Atlantean language?"

"Just about," Fraxino answered.

"That is amazing!" Steven declared. "You'd think with 12,000 years . . ."

"We would have thought that, too," said Rinto.

"But then with one world language since the arrival of the Atlanteans to our world . . ." said Chispo.

"It makes sense after all . . ." Fraxino said.

". . . that it would remain pretty much the same," Rinto added, completing the statement.

Meanwhile, the five Atlanteans began talking to themselves, glad to be free from their time traps, as they saw it. One of the females then walked over to Chispo and repeated the question about where they were. She made eye contact with him as she asked him, and immediately they felt a strong sense of familiarity. Her name was Chameur, and Chispo found her brown eyes and friendly gaze to be so familiar. Chispo's green-brown eyes caught her attention, as well. She could immediately sense that he had a vibrant, lively personality.

"You're way up in the northern latitudes in a place called Alaska on planet Earth," Chispo came around to reply.

"Are we still in the same world where Atlantis is?" one of the males now asked in Atlantean.

"Yes, that much you are," Fraxino now replied, "but on the opposite end of the world."

Morris walked over to Chispo, Rinto and Fraxino. "You mean you three can really understand these five Atlanteans?"

"Yes, we do," Rinto answered, "amazing as it seems."

"That is indeed amazing!" Morris stated. "Your one world language must be what kept it standardized all this time."

The five Atlanteans were now talking to themselves. Chispo, Rinto and Fraxino were listening to them.

"And we were right in the middle of that project when they time trapped us, weren't we?" one of them said to another.

"Yes. Yes, that's right," another one recalled.

More memories were coming to them.

"Oh, yeah, and they conspired against us and locked us in these crates," another one recalled.

"Where were we, last?"

They looked around at their surroundings. Moments went by. Chispo, Rinto and Fraxino really had a strong urge to ask the five of them what they were talking about, but they said nothing, because they didn't want to interrupt their thinking and recalling.

"Yes, that's right," one of the males recalled. "It was here in this valley."

"Yes, it was," a female agreed. "It's changed since then."

They looked up the cove at the glacier. "Where did that come from? That wasn't here."

"You mean that glacier wasn't there then?" Chispo asked them, not resisting speaking any longer.

"No, not now . . . I mean . . . Yes . . . It is now," a female replied, totally confused with her sense of time.

"What time period is this?" one of the males asked.

"Man, we think you guys are from Atlantis," Fraxino answered, "and if that's true, you've been time trapped, as you call it, for 12,500 Earth years."

"Ahh . . . 12,500 Earth years!" he responded in a surprised tone.

Another one of them intuitively sensed that about that much time had gone by.

"We come from a large double island continent in the southern sea of this world," another one said.

"That would be Atlantis," said Fraxino.

"What sort of project did you guys have going on?" Chispo wanted to know.

"We're still recalling that," one of the females answered.

"Memories are still coming back to us," a male answered.

At that time, one of the females turned her attention to Morris. She extended her hand to Morris and told her sincere thanks to him and his dolphin friend who had teleported in to unlock their time trap. The others followed. Rinto translated their comments to Morris, and he told them he was glad to have been of help.

"Morris, we're so glad you and the crates with the bodies made it back to us," Robert told him.

"I was worried about it myself." Morris admitted.

"You were?" Robert responded.

Tom and Caymar had not made comment for several minutes, just observing what was happening.

"Morris," Tom now told him, "that was a considerable risk what you did."

"Indeed it was, Tom," Morris agreed. "I'll say this, that my dolphin friend who came guided me through the process with his expertise."

"Why didn't he show up with you and the crates?" Chispo wanted to know.

"He teleported right back to his world. He didn't want to reveal himself to the rest of you."

"Oh," Robert simply responded. Chispo reacted with a similar comment.

"Come," Tom offered to everyone. "Let us enter our building right over there. You five are probably hungry, and we can talk everything over and make plans."

Chispo translated Tom's invitation to them, and they accepted with thanks.

Everyone walked over to the building and entered. While Tom and Caymar began preparing a meal of fresh fruits, vegetables, and live grains, the others talked.

They were talking to Morris more about how he did the unlocking procedure. Chispo and Rinto translated the conversation to the five Atlanteans. Tom and Caymar gave glasses of fruit juice to everyone.

"Man, I was telling Roel that his brother Rudy didn't come," Chispo told Morris, "because he probably understands how to unlock the time freeze and would have argued with you about which method was best."

"That's partly true Chispo, but while Rudy and I are incompatible, I still would have welcomed his help."

"Oh, really?" Robert responded.

"We thought maybe you didn't want Rudy interfering," Steven added.

"Well, if you think about it a moment," Morris explained. "Rudy is the one who took the dislike, not me. If he had come with us and wanted to help me, I would have discussed it with him first to see if his understanding of the unlocking technique was there, and if it had been there, then I could have been able to tell straight, not by Rudy's comments, but by the undertow of feelings that reveal the truth of words about his ability."

"Well, good," said Steven.

"By all means, I would have given Rudy a chance," Morris assured them, "and I would have been glad to have had the help."

"Anyway, what are your names, or do you have names?" Rinto asked the five Atlanteans.

"Oh yes, we have names," one of the males answered. "That's for certain."

"My name is Latorna," said one of the females. "I was the leader of the project that, to us, we were just working on."

The two other females introduced themselves as Seglima and Chameur. The two males were named Quicho and Tecoloteh. Chispo, Rinto and Fraxino introduced themselves and also introduced the others to them.

Latorna began to explain the project. At the same time, Roel suddenly spoke to Robert and said, "I want to go back home to my house."

"To bring Rudy back here with you?" Robert asked.

"No, I just want to go back home," Roel stated. "I feel nervous, actually very uneasy."

Robert looked at Roel in a strange way.

"What about Rudy?" Chispo now asked.

"I think he wants to stay home," Roel said.

"Morris, everybody," Robert called out. "I'm going to take Roel home. I'll be back soon."

Morris nodded a gesture of approval and carried on listening to the Atlanteans via translation done by Rinto. Robert and Roel walked outside into the sunny mountain cove, and in seconds, he transported Roel back to Mexico.

"The project we were doing," Latorna began, "was growing and creating a device-craft for soul travel."

"Wow!" Chispo remarked.

"In addition to that, time travel," Quicho told them.

Rinto translated to the others.

"We had the device-craft grown and ready for programming and testing," Latorna continued, "when corrupt government officials from our home country of Atlantis apprehended us and doomed us to the fate in which you found us."

After Rinto translated that part, Tom and Caymar's eyes opened wide, and their interest perked up.

"Ask her where the device-craft is," Tom said to Rinto.

Rinto asked her, and she responded, "If it's still in existence, it's under this mountain and well within it, and the entrance would be under what is now that glacier up the mountain from us."

"You mean this mountain, here?" Fraxino asked with surprise.

"The best we can remember, this is the mountain," she answered.

"The scenery has changed considerably," Tecoloteh told them.

"Aw, the government officials probably destroyed your device," Chispo told them.

"No, that wouldn't have happened," Chameur now told them. "They would have been interested in it for their use."

"Oh, yeah. Good point," Chispo acknowledged.

"Do you think it's still there?" Fraxino asked her.

"It more than likely still is," Chameur answered.

"They wouldn't have been able to use it, however," Seglima brought up, "because they wouldn't have known the correct sequence of telepathic frequencies to make it work."

"In addition to the programming plates," Latorna added.

"True," Seglima responded.

"There's a good possibility it's still there just like we left it," said Latorna.

"You don't think they time froze it also?" Rinto asked her.

"I don't think our device-craft would have let them," she answered.

"That's good," said Rinto.

Tom and Caymar announced that the food was ready to eat, and everyone served himself. They were hungry, especially the five Atlanteans, and they found the food to be truly out of this world, and delicious.

Robert arrived and walked in alone.

"Hey, what's going on, Robert?" said Chispo, greeting him.

"What about Rudy?" Steven asked.

"Roel and I both talked to him, and he stubbornly didn't want to come be with us. He said since Morris was involved in the project, he had contaminated it, and for that reason, he didn't want to join us. He said he didn't want to be with us since we like Morris, in addition to it not being convenient to him."

"Well, I will say!" Steven declared.

"Man, that's wild!" Chispo remarked. "I thought Rudy was our friend."

"I was surprised, too," Robert admitted. "He's suddenly so changed, and he was somewhat cold shouldered when I talked to him."

"Dudes, that's Earth people for you," Chispo complained. "They're your friend when they want to be and when it's convenient to them."

The Atlanteans were looking on, wondering what the problem was. Rinto proceeded to explain what had happened.

"Actually, I'm not at all surprised," Morris told everyone. "I had a feeling Rudy would stay away from you guys."

"What? You're kidding!" Robert told him.

"Morris, I thought you told us Rudy would rejoin us after you leave us and return to Delikadove," Chispo reminded him.

"Yes, I did say that," he admitted, "but I knew in truth Rudy had found us to be too much for him. He just couldn't take it any longer . . . because it made him think too much, in addition to his being homesick for his people in Mexico."

"Then why did you tell us the opposite?" Robert wanted to know.

"I didn't want to let your hopes down, especially yours and Chispo's."

"Oh, I see," said Robert.

"Sorry, next time I'll remember to be more straightforward with you all," said Morris. "You see, Rudy, well many people for that matter, find people like us to be great people at first, and even though in truth we are indeed great people who are genuine, when they get to know us better, they become somewhat scared off and take a dislike to us. That's been my feeling about Rudy ever since I first saw him, and I'm sorry if it disappoints any of you."

"But we just bought that house for him!" Robert pointed out.

"I know we did," Morris admitted, "and it was very noble of us to do so. For the help we gave him and his family, it will be appreciated in some form or fashion down the time line, and I know we're going to receive compensation for it."

Everyone thought about what Morris said, and their own feelings told them he was right. They felt sad about losing Rudy from their group.

"What if we go back and see Rudy and his family?" Chispo asked.

"You can if you like," Morris replied, "but I suspect you'll find that Rudy will turn his back to you with indifference."

Chispo gave Morris a look of disbelief.

"It's like I just said," Morris went on. "Rudy has taken an uneasy feeling to us and is afraid to rejoin any of us. It's up to you whether you want to go back and see him. I just don't want any of you to be made to feel hurt."

"All right, man," Chispo said mournfully. "Thank you for telling us."

The others also thanked Morris.

"Anyway, guys," Rinto announced, "so much for Rudy. We've got a radical project ahead of us, and who knows what sort of exciting adventures with it!"

"Right on, brother!" Fraxino enthusiastically declared.

"Where's that device-craft of yours?" Chispo asked the Atlanteans. "Let's see if we can help you find it."

"We're going to need to excavate and dig through that glacier," replied Tecoloteh.

"I know, man," Chispo admitted.

"We've been wondering," Latorna asked everyone. "How did you know where to find us?"

"It was Tom and Caymar who came across two of you, by chance," Rinto answered.

Chispo translated to English for the others, and Caymar told them, "We don't know exactly why we chose this mountain. It just felt right to us."

"And we certainly were surprised when we discovered your crates," Tom added.

"More so when we found one of you in it, you, Tecoloteh," said Caymar.

"And with their knowledge about soul travel," said Tom, "and their device-craft they say may still be within this mountain, I must declare that destiny is really perfect sometimes."

"I knew there was a good reason why we chose this location," said Caymar. "I could really feel it."

Rinto translated Tom and Caymar's comments.

"You say you found two of us initially?" Tecoloteh asked them. "How did you find the rest of us?"

"That guy who just left us, Roel," Chispo answered, "is the one who found the rest of you."

"He has radical locator instincts well beyond the norm," Fraxino informed them.

"That Roel walked up and down that ridge and found the other three of you in ten minutes, dudes!" Chispo informed them. "We had to move fast to keep up with him and occupy the spots he marked for us."

"Once we dug the five of you up," said Rinto, "we struggled to carry you and your crates to the location where Morris woke you up."

"All of us got away from Morris and your crates," said Fraxino, "and from a distance, we watched and waited."

"Well, fellows," Tom suddenly brought up, "it's like I had said. If you can find and revive the bodies, I will pay you U.S. $33,000 cash, and the work has been miraculously accomplished."

Caymar retrieved a metal box from the closet and brought it to everyone. Tom opened the lid and pulled out a thick envelope with a good stack of $100 notes. He pulled the notes out of the envelope and spread them out on the table.

"Thank you for a job well done," Tom commended them. "Divide the money among yourselves as you wish." The Atlanteans were observing with considerable curiosity. Chispo explained to them what Tom was doing.

"Thank you, Tom," said Robert with enthusiasm. The others also thanked him.

Several of them looked at Morris. Robert spoke first. "Morris you deserve the better portion of this money for reviving the bodies."

"True enough, I will admit," Morris acknowledged. "Thank you very much."

"How much of it do you want?" Robert asked.

"Whatever you think is fair is fine with me."

"What do you think, everybody?" Robert asked the others.

"How about 50% of it?" Steven suggested.

"Sounds all right to me," Morris answered.

"Does everybody approve of it?" Robert asked the others.

Everybody nodded his approval.

"All right then 50% of $33,000 is $16,500," said Robert. He handed half the stack to Morris. "Count out 165 of the notes for yourself."

"Thank all of you ever so much," Morris told them sincerely.

"Do we divide the rest equally among ourselves?" Robert asked the others.

"What about Roel?" Rinto brought up, "Only thanks to him, we found the other three crates and bodies."

"That's true, and he just left us," said Robert, "but then as we know, we overpaid Rudy. Morris, what do you suggest?"

"Yes, definitely pay Roel something," Morris suggested. "After all, he did come up here with you and indeed found those three remaining crates. If each of the five of you: Robert, Steven, Chispo, Rinto and Fraxino take $2,500, that's $12,500, and subtracted from $16,500, that leaves $4,000. Actually, those numbers add up quite nicely. Yes, that's what I suggest."

"What do you think, everybody?" Robert checked.

"I don't have any problem with it," Chispo answered.

"After all, Roel's not Rudy," Fraxino approved.

"All right with me," said Steven.

"Me too," said Rinto.

Robert counted out 25 notes for each one of them and for himself, and then counted out the remaining 40 notes to take to Roel. He distributed the money appropriately. Next, he picked up the 40 notes. "I'll be back in a few minutes." He walked out of the building and transported himself to Bustamante.

"Let me tell you five Atlanteans the project Caymar and I are undertaking . . ." Tom began. Chispo translated to them as Tom explained the whole project at hand about the galactic switching station using the equivalent of millions of Earth's telephone numbers, it being one of the largest projects of the Galactic Federation, and the quest for soul travel to be included. ". . . and if that device-craft you five were working on can be of help to us, we'll be glad to have our crew melt that glacier away so it can be located," Tom offered.

After Chispo finished translating Tom's offer, Latorna was the first to respond. "What are we waiting for? Let's get to work and locate the entrance."

Tom and Caymar agreed to it, and Tom stepped outside and teleported away to Sirius B to fetch his crew and necessary equipment. He would be away for several hours.

By now it was nearly the middle of the day.

"Come on," said Chispo to everyone in both languages. "Let's go and explore the ridge and glacier."

"Good idea," said Rinto. "Maybe our new five Atlanteans will recall more of their project."

All of them stepped outside, and Caymar came with them. They left the building and began to make their way up the cove toward the glacier.

Suddenly, there was a whirring sound, and they turned around to witness Robert materializing. Immediately he saw them up the cove and started walking toward them. He had a content look on his face.

"Hey, Robert," Rinto greeted him. "What did Roel say?"

"He was ecstatic. He was beyond glad to get that money, I tell you!"

"Well great!" Rinto remarked.

"Did you see Rudy?" Chispo asked.

"Yes, I did." Robert said, now more sullen. "Morris, you were 100% right. Rudy ignored me and put his back to me the whole time. He just sat in front of the stereo and turned the volume up, but never mind Rudy. Roel shook hands with me in the friendliest manner you could imagine. He sends his sincere thanks to all of us, and that any time we're in Mexico, we have our house to stay in. He also told me he's going to get after Rudy right good and set him *straight* about us."

"Well, how kind of him," said Morris.

"Roel has such a kind and welcoming nature about him," Robert added.

Robert and Chispo now realized the painful truth that Rudy was simply not their friend, despite their having felt a special friendship with him, complete with an inner understanding for one another that could best be described as a sense that made them feel like they had known each other since time began. All of those good feelings they had for Rudy were still no guarantee of friendship. He had come to feel uneasy and had taken a dislike to the group. Robert and Chispo and their friends had already been of use to him.

They weren't sure what sort of new energy system had come over Rudy, but whatever it was had changed his natural frequency of vibration. He had therefore lost his genuine character and intuition. Furthermore, Rudy had never stopped and thought enough to truly realize the value of his new friends, and he never figured out why he had found Artenia so familiar.

Though they had not realized it at the time, their true friend was Roel, even though he had abandoned the group and stayed behind in Pinos, Zacatecas, which he had done because of potential danger that existed in Bustamante at the time. Roel had a welcoming nature about him and knew how to appreciate, much more so than Rudy, as they now knew. It was Roel who had the intuition, understanding and compassion, despite their previously having thought otherwise.

"You know", Steven commented, "I'm glad we gave Roel that $4,000. I feel compensated already."

"Compensation has already arrived," Morris told everyone with a smile. "Our gift in buying Roel and Rudy's house for them has now been properly appreciated."

"Morris, right again," Fraxino told him with a smile.

"Now, this time I'm glad you're *right*!" Robert told him enthusiastically.

"Right on, Morris!" Chispo declared with enthusiasm.

"Thank you everyone. Thank you very much. I need to tell you that I'm already overdue to return to the dolphins on Delikadove, but I'm too curious about that Atlantean device to leave just yet."

"Yeah, stay a little while longer with us," Steven said to him.

"Who knows," Rinto reminded everyone. "We might have to unlock it somehow."

"That thought had entered my mind, too," said Morris.

Robert joined them on their walk up the cove. They made their way along the left side of the cove. They passed by the small lake, and in a short while they reached the foot of the glacier. They now climbed around the left side of the glacier, following along the sloping ridge next to it. It became just about too steep to advance any further, but with helping hands, they managed the scramble in the appropriate places.

Rinto looked at the all-one-race symbol on Tecoloteh's blue and purple clothing. He wasn't sure if the clothing could be considered a uniform, but he suspected it was.

"Tell us about that symbol," he asked Tecoloteh.

"That is an icon to represent all one race," he began. "The icon has its orange color for several reasons, one of them to remind us where we came from, the star system Vega, over a million years ago. Further, orange Calcite is one of our favorite crystals, especially since Vegan tradition required the guardianship of sacred stories by means of holographic material fused onto orange Calcite rocks and crystals. Prominent families each guarded a portion of the whole story of our race, and we kept that tradition going . . ."

"Man, you're not going to believe this," Chispo interrupted, "but we've already seen two of those sacred story stones."

Tecoloteh's mouth dropped open in surprise. He was speechless.

"Yeah, man, we found both of them on our world Artenia, one in an old galactic dump site and the other one in the guardianship of a race of green people called the Atascosa."

Tecoloteh expressed his surprise and then said, "Atlantean refugees must have taken those stones with them when they left our world and settled yours."

"That we know to be true, man," Chispo confirmed.

"To continue my telling you about the icon," Tecoloteh went on, "our region called Atlantis had various races of humans and humanlike beings as well, one of the races having transformed from the dolphins of the sea. Each race had various characteristics, and to recognize the importance of sentience among all the intelligent races, we derived an icon that when viewed in different ways would show an image of a human face, a dolphin, and a whale all combined, a very clever derivation from illusionary graphics from a high level of technology that we had until the devastating collapse of our society when the whole Earth slid."

"Wow! Interesting indeed," said Rinto.

Chispo translated to English for the others.

"So, I take it you five must have still been alive and well when that disaster happened," Rinto said to them.

"Yes, but it wasn't long after that when we were caught and time trapped," Latorna now answered. "You see, what happened was that the Atlantean government had become corrupt, ever since 2,500 years ago, from our time frame of reference, when a very important Flourite peace keeping crystal suddenly disappeared from Atlantis, likely stolen and whisked away in an alien spacecraft. From that moment on, without its positive vibrational influence, things began to turn for the worse . . ."

"We know about that, too," Fraxino broke in and informed them. "We have a box of holographic plates from that same dump site on our world, and one of the plates reveals that story."

"You have a box of holographic *plates*?" Latorna asked with surprise.

"Indeed we do," Rinto confirmed. "We just found them last month."

"With 144 plates, and compiled by Atlantean historians, right?" she asked, with enthusiasm rising.

"How did you know?" Rinto asked, quite surprised.

"You're talking to the compilers," Latorna informed them.

Rinto, Fraxino and Chispo showed such surprise they had to sit down where they were on the edge of the glacier by the ridge. They really were speechless!

Chameur now spoke. "I was the major compiler and creator of those plates. Latorna was the leader of creating the device-craft, and I programmed those plates with our stories and spiritual observations, as well."

"Far out!" Fraxino responded.

"That's wild!" Chispo came around to comment. "You all compiled those plates?"

"We did and what a surprise that you fellows have found them!" Latorna stated. "Destiny really does make the pieces of the puzzle fall in place perfectly."

"It's making sense why our paths have come to a junction and why we've met each other," Chameur added. "Have you read our stories?"

"Yes, we have," Rinto replied, "and they are rather remarkable, to say the least."

"They provide a lot of insight about friendships, souls, energy systems, and the rest of it," said Fraxino.

"But they also relate the sabotage that took place," Chispo added.

"Those are indeed our plates," Chameur told them. "That crate of plates was with us inside this mountain when the apprehenders caught us and time trapped us."

"How long after the disaster was that?" Chispo wanted to know.

"Nearly a year," she answered.

"Tell us. What happened?" Fraxino asked them.

Quicho decided to relate this part of the story. "As we had said before, the device-craft we were building was for use in soul travel and time travel as well and is hopefully still within this mountain. We had been working on it for several years, here in this remote region of the world, and our purpose was to solve the problem of many unwanted energy systems the unscrupulous Atlantean scientists had created from lower level programming in their mood control experiments."

"Morris here is aware of that," said Rinto, "and we read about those mood control experiments in the holographic plates."

"Right then, well, we wanted to eradicate the bad energy systems worldwide. We had our programming tablets fresh off the press, as you might say, and suddenly the worldwide disaster happened. That set us back quite a bit. We got the damages repaired and regrown. Meanwhile, Chameur compiled and created those historical documents on the 144 holographic plates. Just before we could load the programming instructions into the device, we were found out by Atlantean government officials who immediately apprehended us and would not give us a chance to explain that we were doing something good for the world.

"Furthermore, a fleet of several spacecrafts loaded with a total of 65,000 Atlantean residents and their belongings had taken off to Al Nitak, never to return to Earth. 400 of the most unscrupulous scientists and government officials were made to stay behind on Earth, and it was some of them who found us. Matters were made even worse since we had been doing our projects in secret. Since you tell us you found our holographic plates in that dump site on your world, we can now speculate that the crate was taken from us after they time trapped and buried us, and one or more space vehicles must have gone to your world."

Rinto and the others thought about that. "Yes, I believe there was another spacecraft that returned to Earth around a year later, if I remember our ancient history correctly. The leader, Cresma, sent the craft to search for any possible survivors who wanted to leave Earth and come to Al Nitak. Do I remember right, Fraxino?"

"I believe you do."

"We knew Cresma Atenkor well," Tecoloteh told everyone.

"Really?" Rinto asked. "Wait . . . Atenkor . . . Is that his last name?"

"Yes, Cresma Atenkor," Tecoloteh verified. "That's what we called him."

"Never had we known his last name," said Rinto.

"All the documents we've ever seen just refer to him as Cresma," Chispo told Tecoloteh.

"Right, anyway, Cresma was a fine man who wanted only good for his people," Tecoloteh went on to explain. "It was he who organized the mass fleeing of the 65,000 residents and through galactic trade deals obtained a fleet of spacecrafts for the purpose. He was in on our project too and gave financial support, as well."

"Cool!" said Rinto.

"You know," Chispo speculated, "maybe Cresma sent a search party looking for you all, and being unable to find the five of you, he had the crate of holographic plates collected and brought to Al Nitak."

"That sounds reasonable, but then why was that crate found in that dump site instead of in safekeeping?" Latorna asked.

"That's what we want to know," Chispo replied.

"We think somewhere down the time line," Fraxino told them, "their true value and meaning were forgotten and for reasons of not understanding the plates, their being obsolete, or even dangerous materials for that matter, they were carried well out of Zantaayer and dumped with other goods in a remote desert valley at the foot of the Placatera Mountains."

"Yes, that theory of reasoning makes sense," Chameur commented.

"Did we tell you we had a second crate, complete with bronze data plates, specifically to program the device-craft's main computer?" Latorna decided to bring up.

"No you didn't," said Rinto.

"Oh, yeah," Chispo recalled. "You said something about programming tablets fresh off the press, didn't you?"

"Yes, those," Latorna verified.

"Want to tell 'em, Fraxino?" Rinto asked his brother.

"We found a second crate, as well," Fraxino now informed her. "It was last week. We couldn't decipher what it was about, only that the 144 tablets were likely programming instructions for some sort of radical massive computer."

Latorna's eyes lit up with enthusiasm and hope, along with the other four Atlanteans.

"Did the tablets have little holographic squares impregnated in them along with weird script-like writing?" Latorna wanted to know, enthusiasm rising in her voice.

"Exactly!" Rinto answered. "They did indeed."

A joyous smile came across Latorna's face along with the other four Atlanteans, and they jumped and extended their arms toward the sky in sincere thanks for the amazing synchronicity! They looked at Rinto, Fraxino and Chispo as if they were gods from the stars, having come to Earth to rescue them.

After the excitement died down, Latorna said, "Let's find our device-craft in this mountain, and then you can take us to your world to retrieve the two crates."

"By all means," Fraxino agreed. "We'll be glad to help."

"Thank you. How did this work out so well?" Latorna asked the others.

"Maybe this was all meant to happen this way for a time far into our future, which is now," Tecoloteh speculated.

"That we were meant to be preserved," Chameur told them, "and revived much later to help Tom and Caymar with their important project."

Chispo, Rinto and Fraxino now translated those latest realizations to English for the others to understand what was going on.

"What? No way!" Steven reacted.

"You're kidding!" Robert remarked.

"I'm usually not surprised by things," Morris told them, "but this impressive synchronicity is a miracle in itself and has got me . . . *gob smacked*, to quote a British expression!"

"Rinto, Fraxino," Chispo teased them with a twinkle in his eye, "how do you two always pull it off so well?"

"Good programming on other levels," Rinto replied with a smile.

"That is really amazing!" Steven declared.

One of the most impressive synchronicities I have ever seen," said Caymar. "Our project really is meant to happen."

"Actually, there is truth to what Rinto just said," Morris told everyone.

"There is?" Robert responded.

"Oh yes. You see, people who know how to achieve the right level of thinking can bring events to a junction at exactly the right time and cause wonderful events to blossom forth. It's all a matter of timing and hitting the right vibrational frequency. Those who operate free of fear and boundaries find that there is a free flow to realities and that we cross boundaries all the time. Those who are good at timing and right vibrational frequencies and bringing it to a junction create good luck. That's how destiny works. It's amazing when you think about it."

"Destiny works that way?" Steven began to ask.

"To go on further," Morris continued, "many events, like this synchronicity here before us, are set up by our subconscious minds and higher selves on other levels ahead of time, to later be consciously realized and occur in our reality. I must say, every one of us here had an important part in this and that we've done very well, in addition to others who have gone on and left us. We have a lot to be grateful for."

Chispo translated Morris' theory to the Atlanteans.

"Your friend, Morris, has a lot of insight," Chameur told Chispo. "He has studied other levels in depth and carries our level of consciousness with him, in addition to bringing in conscious levels from other worlds throughout our galaxy. With the events of these realities now coming to this grand junction, we can be thankful that our project was indeed meant to happen for the improving of humans here on this world, now being long-line descendants from Atlantis."

"To explain our project further," Latorna told everyone, "our main purpose of the project was, as we said, for soul travel and in addition to that, time travel. By soul travel, we wanted to offer those here on Earth a chance to ascend and leave behind the bad energy systems our government's unscrupulous scientists had created during their earlier mood control experiments during the previous 2,500 years. Further, some of our programming of the device-craft's central computer was going to release new positive and good energy systems to circulate throughout the world, locate any bad energy systems, latch onto them, and eradicate them, now having explained in more detail what we wanted to do."

"The government officials who apprehended us," Quicho added, "would not give us a chance to explain, as we had told you, but all five of us now have the strong feeling that they knew very well what our plans were, and for their devious and unscrupulous ways, they couldn't afford to have their bad energy systems eradicated. They were still carrying out mood control experiments, and after the disaster, began wielding domination over other peoples in different and new regions of the planet. They just could not conceive of how to settle other parts of this world in a kind, loving and friendly way, causing them to be welcomed by different natives with appreciation, which is what our device-craft's programming would have brought about."

Rinto and Fraxino translated the comments to the others.

"You five are very noble Atlanteans indeed," Caymar commended them. "Tom and I are honored to have you alive and well with us on this project."

Rinto translated.

"The honor is ours also," said Latorna, "and we five are grateful to all of you for what you've already done in finding us and bringing us back to life."

Caymar was made to feel very good by her comment.

They were continuing walking up the ridge by the glacier, sometimes on the edge of the glacier ice and other areas on the dirt and rock of the sloping hillside.

"If we remember correctly," said Seglima, "we are close approaching the entrance. Isn't it about here?" she now said to Tecoloteh, and she pointed out into the glacier.

"I believe it's directly under the middle of this glacier," he told her. "Our entrance is probably covered by some 50 meters of ice."

"It's going to take a gargantuan amount of melting to access it," Fraxino told them.

"If we had considered that a huge glacier would be in this cove in the future," said Latorna, "we would have put the entrance into the mountain from the ridge."

"Let's look at the good aspect of it," Chameur pointed out. "Our entrance likely became covered only a few years after we were apprehended, which meant the people of Earth have known nothing of it and have likely not disturbed it since then. It's a blessing in disguise."

The other four of them looked at Chameur, marvelling at her comment.

"Chameur, you always have impressed us with your insight for good reasons," Seglima told her.

"Thank you, Seglima."

"What sort of work did you all do normally?" Fraxino asked them. "What was your profession?"

"As best as we can put it," Quicho answered, "we were brought up as scientists and trained in that field, and through the years of training, the five of us came to know each other and became the best of friends. We realized and took a dislike to the corruption of the main stream Atlantean society of science, and we officially left our careers behind."

"I was the influencing factor," Chameur now told them. "I explained to these friends of mine how the scientific community of Atlantis had gone sour and that a project of devising a means of soul and time travel would be both enlightening and refreshing, considering the knowledge of the other problems Quicho has told you about."

"Were the five of you alone on this?" Chispo asked them, "or were there other mavericks like yourselves?"

They stepped out onto the glacier and carefully walked to the center of it.

"The five of us were the only ones who broke away from the mainstream, believe it or not," Latorna told them, laughing a little.

"Then the world disaster happened," Tecoloteh told everyone. "Cresma, especially since he knew us, offered to take us and our entire project with him and the 65,000 fleeing Atlanteans in that fleet of spacecrafts. While we sincerely appreciated his offer, we declined and stayed here."

"Why didn't you guys take Cresma up on it and go to Al Nitak with him?" Chispo wanted to know.

"We felt a responsibility to our world and its future," Tecoloteh explained, "and we wanted to clean up and correct the problems that had occurred over the past 2,500 years. Of course, now add another 12,500 years. In one respect we don't blame the 65,000 Atlanteans who fled in Cresma's fleet to Al Nitak. They had suffered generation after generation of problems, turmoil and grief, and their fleeing was their salvation, which they deserved. At the same time, they dropped everything and ran away from their problems. For us however, even though the

65,000 had yet another good reason for leaving since the disaster happened, we felt our calling to remain here and finish our project to aid and cause emotional relief not only to those who stayed but also to all other races on this world, as well."

"Suddenly, a large craft could be seen arriving down in the cove next to Tom and Caymar's building.

"Hey, what's that?" Steven called out to everyone, catching a glimpse of it out of the corner of his eye.

Everyone else looked, somewhat feeling on edge.

"I don't know," Robert answered.

"Probably Tom and his crew returning," said Rinto.

They watched as the craft gently landed in the cove. Soon, Tom stepped out of the craft along with at least 20 other Sirians.

"Yep, it's just Tom and his helpers," Robert commented.

Tom could be seen looking around the cove, likely wondering where everyone had gone. Chispo gave out a loud whistle to get Tom's attention. Sure enough, he heard it and turned around to look up at the glacier.

"We're up here, Tom!" Chispo yelled out.

Several of them waved their arms in the air. Instantly, Tom was within several meters of them via teleportation.

"Wow! That was quick!" Rinto declared.

Some of them were somewhat startled but then realized what Tom had just done.

"Yes, I'm here now," said Tom.

"We momentarily forgot how you can teleport yourself around," said Steven, laughing.

"But it is convenient, isn't it?" said Tom. "Anyway, have our Atlantean friends decided where the entrance was?"

"Yes, they have," Rinto replied. "They say it's pretty much directly under us at the bottom of this glacier."

"This is going to prove to be cumbersome, to say the least!" Tom stated.

"This is a gargantuan amount of ice to melt away," Fraxino told him.

"Yes, it is," said Tom. He thought a few moments.

"Do you think it might be better to tunnel through this ice to the entrance?" Robert asked.

"That's a good idea," Tom acknowledged, "but where exactly is the tunnel is the problem."

"Yes, that will be difficult to fathom," Robert admitted.

"Why don't you teleport the glacier away instead of melt it?" Steven suggested.

"That's another good idea," Tom replied. "This you might find hard to believe, but that is beyond my skill and also that of my crew."

"You managed to teleport Kingston Park's telephone step office to that Earth museum on the Planet of the Islands," Steven reminded him.

"Yes, that was within my skill," Tom admitted, "but this glacier is a totally different thing and much larger."

"True," Steven agreed.

Tom paced back and forth over the area on the glacier while the others watched. Finally, he spoke. "Rinto, ask the Atlanteans if one or more of them can guide me and my crew if we excavate."

Rinto translated Tom's question to them.

"I believe, as we penetrate the glacier," Latorna answered, "identifying the location of the entrance will become easier."

Rinto translated the answer to Tom, who then pondered it a few more moments.

"Penetrating via excavating a tunnel will be far faster than melting the glacier," Tom declared. "We will excavate."

He faced his crew and telepathically communicated to them his plans. They entered the craft immediately, and it soon quietly left the ground and flew toward them, gently landing on top of the glacier and nearby. Tom walked over to the craft which was at least 200 meters in length and 40 meters wide. It was more than 40 meters in height, as well.

Everyone watched while he entered the craft, caused a large door to open downward at its other end, and a fleet of excavating machines rolled down the door which now served as a ramp. All of them were driven by members of his crew, and they all made noises similar to internal combustion engines just like the ones of Earth. They were powered by hydrogen fuel and were the property of the Galactic Federation.

While everyone else still watched with some amazement, Tom directed the digging to begin. The machines, some equipped with saws, others with jackhammers, and still others with backhoe shovels and blades, went to work digging and cutting through the sheer ice.

Once that was started, Tom walked over to the Atlanteans and asked them to come over to the digging spot to direct them where and how to dig. Chispo accompained them to translate the directions, and Robert, Morris, Rinto and the rest of them stayed a distance away, observing everything from the edge of the glacier.

The Atlanteans made it clear to Tom that the tunnel was likely directly below them at a vertical 90° angle. At their smart suggestion, Tom and his crew moved the operation several hundred meters down the glacier nearer the cove. Again they proceeded to dig, this time in a nearly horizontal manner directly up-glacier-stream. The tunnel they made was 5 meters wide and 4 meters high. Their rate of penetration was around 10 meters an hour. Excavators entered and left the tunnel, some chipping and sawing away at the ice, while others carried the rubble out of the tunnel and dumped the ice bits over on the far side of the glacier. Caymar, Robert, Morris, and the others observed the digging for more than an hour.

Tom telepathically communicated with his workers as they continued with the digging, also under the guidance of the Atlanteans. Tom also communicated to Caymar that if the others were bored, he could take them down to the building to rest and relax or do other things, since the digging operation would likely take until the next morning, (if that could be determined since there was no night at this time of year in northern Alaska). That was a good suggestion.

Two of the Atlanteans, Latorna and Quicho, stayed with Tom and his crew. Morris also stayed and helped with the guidance using his instincts. Rinto swapped places with Chispo and did the translating.

The others: Chispo, Fraxino, Robert, Steven, and three of the Atlanteans: Tecoloteh, Chameur and Seglima all accompanied Caymar and walked down the glacier and ridge to the building in the cove. It took them nearly half an hour to make the descent.

The day, timewise, had gone by. Alaska time, it was 6 PM, which meant that for the time they were used to, it was already 10 PM central time. Here in Alaska, the day was still bright and sunny, and as they would find out, would remain so, all "night" long.

Upon entering the building, Caymar offered, "Would you all like something to eat? Are you hungry?"

Everyone gladly accepted, and he prepared supper for everyone. Soon they were munching away on Sirian food complete with live grains and prana.

"This is good and tasty, Caymar," Steven told him.

"Thank you. We believe in good nutrition, as you know."

"Man, you Sirians don't fool around," Chispo said to Caymar. "I'm really impressed with the efficiency of Tom's digging operation."

"Yes, we get right to business with things," Caymar acknowledged. "We hope we're in time for the new millennium with our complete project."

"Man, at the rate you guys are going," Chispo told him, "you'll have that station completed and waiting for use years ahead of schedule."

Caymar laughed. "You might be right."

"Chispo, Fraxino," Tecoloteh brought up, "tell us what stories those two sacred story stones related."

"Both of them told an ancient story about the trees," Fraxino replied.

"The one that Robert, here, found in that galactic dump site," Chispo proceeded to explain, "reveals the origin of the Flowering Sun Tree, known scientifically as the Liriodendron. The story reveals the fact that it came from the planet around the star Vega in the Lyran constellation, and that early human settlers brought it with them as a sacred reminder of their home world when they came here to Earth between 1 and 2 million years ago. They settled an area which is presently known as China, and only two species of Liriodendron exist in the world! Man, the tree is definitely of extraterrestrial origin, in addition to the weird way the leaves on the tree grow." Chispo related the rest of the story's details to them for the next several minutes.

Note: For the complete revelation, see this novel's prequel: Mission Beyond the Ice Cave: Atlantis-Mexico-Zotola, pages 57-61.

"That story is indeed true and accurate," Chameur told them. "There were sacred reasons why our human ancestors from Vega's planet Xiawp brought that tree with them, in addition to its having superior qualities in many respects. The Flowering Sun Tree, or as we call it in Atlantis, *Xluaipoplee,* is of an ancient race of trees, and its method of growing in a spire is characteristic of it prehistoric connection with the coniferous trees throughout the galaxy. 200,000 years ago, planet Xiawp was destroyed by comets, and the Axitw people, who had numbered around 50,000, had to flee their world. Some of them arrived on Earth and founded the civilization of Atlantis."

"Wow!" Chispo responded. "I had wondered if it was something like that."

"What was the other story?" Seglima now asked.

"It was about the original fruit tree, the Celtis, from which the others were derived," Chispo replied. He and Fraxino both told what Orolizo's sacred story stone related.

"That was a major triumph in genetics of our Atlantean ancestors from long ago," Seglima told them. "Other experiments were done on different trees prior to that in training for the fruit tree derivations from the original progenitor, which you call Celtis."

Chispo translated the conversation.

"You know," said Robert as he thought about it, "there are some anomalies among the trees of Earth, like the Desert Willow of the southwestern United States having the same flowers and seed pods as the Catalpa tree."

"Now, how do you know about a detail like that?" Steven asked Robert.

"You know about my interest in trees. I've been out West before, and I've noticed that and wondered how. I believe I've just had my question answered. Now it makes some sense to me."

Chispo told the Atlanteans what Robert just said.

"You have a very observant friend," Chameur told them. "I don't know if you've read all of our holographic plates."

"No, not all of them," said Fraxino.

"Right, well there is one that talks about the trees. Every species of tree has its own special properties and functions for the world in which it lives. In their own relative actuality, trees spin, you know. That's why their trunks are round and why their limbs are spread out evenly around the trunk. Trees bring in an untuned world with them."

Chispo and Fraxino were looking at Chameur with puzzled faces.

She saw their reaction and explained further. "No, they don't spin physically, but they indeed do spin in a different way in their own level of reality. Trees bring in an untuned world with them is the same as saying that trees make harmony of a disorderly world. They are aware of a different level of reality, and their life force comes from this untuned world, a place were beings are free of programming, quite the opposite of most people on this Earth. In a way, trees are free spirits, who are unregulated and they grow in their numerous species on our world to show us the way to harmony."

Both Seglima and Tecoloteh looked at Chameur. "It never ceases to amaze us how you make sense of so much out there in the world," Seglima complimented.

Chameur had an uncanny awareness of the spirit world and the important messages it had to offer. She was rare among her people, and her unique abilities and insight were the reasons she was involved in the project with the other four Atlanteans.

Chispo thought about what Chameur had just told them. He was indeed impressed by her insight. Fraxino translated to the others who were also impressed.

Robert thought about Chameur's comments also. "You know, that actually does make some sense. I never had thought about it that way before."

"If nothing else, she paid a high compliment to the trees," Steven added.

"Yeah, that's for sure," Robert agreed.

"Since we're talking about trees," Chispo decided to bring up, "there are some more artifacts we found at the galactic dump site."

"What else did you find?" Chameur asked.

"Several clear quartz egg-shaped crystals," Chispo answered. "I found the first one several years ago, and in the last month we've found two more . . ."

"Do they have ghostly white images of tree cones grown within them?" Chameur broke in and asked enthusiastically.

"Exactly!" Chispo responded. "How did you know?"

"Those are ancient historical artifacts grown by our long-ago ancestors who lived where Atlantis came to be. They are between 150,000 and 200,000 years old."

"That's the same feeling I got when I read that crystal!" Chispo declared with surprise.

"They are wonderful artifacts indeed and come from a time when humans were in close contact and communication with the trees. Numerous families had them in their homes, but by our time, things had changed. There were only a few of them left, and they had become museum pieces. Much of the insight and messages from the trees had become forgotten."

"Which trees did you find represented, Chispo?" Seglima wanted to know.

"The first one was a Pine cone image, and the other two had seed cone images of that Flowering Sun Tree, and the Buttonball Tree."

"The crystal with the Pine cone image was more unique," Fraxino added, "because it had seven engraved white lines running around its equator. Around 30 tiny stars were also engraved on its surface."

"There were several of those egg-shaped crystals made that had those seven engraved equatorial rings," Chameur told them. "They stood for the seven sacred pathways, and the stars stood for enlightenment. The rings were not necessarily perfect. There was some slight jaggedness in places, and we refer to that as synadarkabie, which is an ancient word meaning there are some imperfections to life and to each pathway. For that, there are some imperfections to the seven circular equatorial rings."

"Far out!" Chispo remarked.

"Radically impressive explanation!" Fraxino declared.

"On that crystal I found however," said Chispo, "those equatorial rings are just about perfect."

Fraxino translated Chameur's explanation to the others.

"Tell us, what was it like in Atlantis?" Fraxino requested.

"We lived in one of the more northerly sections of Atlantis, on the northern island of the two," Tecoloteh began. "To the north of where we lived ran a finger of tall and rugged mountains extending to a big continent north of us, right into the equatorial tropics and beyond. Where we lived, which was then at a latitude of 45° south, it was a cool, moist, temperate climate with fairly steady temperatures maintained by the Southern Ocean which was nearby.

"We are from a small town called Atenkor, which is Cresma's last name as you now know. Cresma was from there also, and it was his ancestors who founded the town several hundred years ago . . . of course, now add another 12,500 years. The terrain was rather mountainous, and much of the farming was done by terracing.

"There was a coastal metropolis around 30 kilometers from Atenkor. It was called Ennohoness and it was a city of fine stone structures, some left over from the prehistory of Atlantis tens of thousands of years ago. It was the major center of learning, and most of the distinguished scientists studied there, many of whom, as we have told you, became corrupt and obsessed with mood control during the final 2,500 years."

"It was from that city that the Fluorite peace keeping crystal was stolen," Chameur now told them. "In those days, the city was called Texclozantess, which had been its name as far back as records went. With the mysterious disappearance of the crystal, it was decided that the name of the city would be changed, and the name Ennohoness was chosen."

"The mountains were beautiful and were well forested," Tecoloteh told them. "Southern Beech trees and Fern Trees of various types grew there along with other exotic plants, trees and heaths. The five of us used to take plenty of walks in the mountains and rejoice in the natural beauty of the place.

"We had a remote hide-away place where we initially went to make our plans for our device for soul travel, but when people started getting suspicious as to why we were away so much, we moved our project here to Alaska, which was at that time under a milder climate than today."

Chispo and Fraxino translated to the others.

"I really wish I could go back in time and visit Atlantis," said Robert.

"Me too," said Steven.

"I would too, man," said Chispo. "It's probably under quite a lot of ice today."

Fraxino translated, and Seglima made a comment. "Maybe we can travel back in time, once we complete our device-craft by finally programming it."

Excitement at the upcomming possibilities built up in them.

"That would be really cool!" said Fraxino.

"Did you have a lot of technology?" Chispo wanted to know.

"Yes, we had quite a decent amount and we were also free of air pollution," Seglima answered, "We cared for our environment and atmosphere. We had flying vessels, and we were very advanced with our knowledge of crystals and computational technology."

"Ma'am, you might find this hard to believe," Chispo told her and pointing at Fraxino, "but this one and his brother Rinto are really a couple of gurus. They're way above the norm. You wouldn't believe what those two have done with crystals! They grew intelligence into their crystals and converted their Velosa cruiser craft, which is parked outside, so that it would fly, and they can even teleport to other worlds. We've been coming to Earth for over a year now, and we've also been studying our Atlantean ancestral roots."

"Rinto and I were really impressed with your holographic plates," Fraxino told them, changing the subject. "That plate number 36 about the *Origin of the Hieroglyphics* was radically impressive. That they originated from computer icons and visual telepathic communication was really a . . ."

For further reading, see: Mission Beyond the Ice Cave: Atlantis-Mexico-Zotola, plate #36, pages 64-67.

They continued chatting about various subjects for several hours. Chispo and Fraxino translated back and forth. The Atlanteans told them more about their homeland and culture. Robert and Steven filled them in on what had happened on Earth over the past 12,500 years, and Chispo and Fraxino told them plenty of stories from their world Artenia, where the 65,000 Atlantean refugees had settled.

Several hours later, Morris and Rinto walked into the building. It was time to spread out the bedrolls and get some sleep.

"They've made some good progress up there," Rinto told them with a smile in both languages. "Still got a ways to go yet, however. Latorna and Quicho are going to stay up there with Tom as he and his crew work through the night. I've got to hand it to them. They've got energy."

Tecoloteh, Chameur, and Seglima were not ready to sleep. They'd been doing that for the last 12,500 years, and they were so glad to be free now. They walked up the glacier and joined Tom and his crew to help oversee the excavating.

CHAPTER 6

DEVICE CRAFT UNDER THE GLACIER

The next day, July 27, 1985, arrived, not that it ever got dark. Tom and his crew had worked five additional hours, a total of ten, having penetrated 100 meters into the glacier with their horizontal tunnel. They decided to call it off and get some rest as well, to continue the project today. Tom and the five Atlanteans had entered the building and gone to sleep with the rest of them, the crew having rested in the huge spacecraft parked up on the glacier.

At 8 AM, Alaska time, the Atlanteans woke up, soon followed by everyone else. Robert and Steven dug some food out of their backpacks and ate some breakfast. Chispo, Rinto, and Fraxino fixed their own breakfast as well, while Tom and Caymar fed themselves and the Atlanteans some food from Sirius B.

"So, how much further do you think we'll have to dig?" Tom asked the Atlanteans.

Chispo translated the question.

"The best I can tell from the time we stopped," Tecoloteh answered, "and from my memories of the way the cove was, we probably lack another 50 meters."

Chispo translated.

"Then we'll probably reach it sometime today," Caymar now said to Tom.

"Hopefully."

All of them finished breakfast, and Tom and Caymar went up the glacier, followed by the others. The two of them entered their large spacecraft parked on the glacier, and in less than 20 minutes, their crew started up their machines and went to work.

Latorna and the Atlanteans guided them by overseeing their digging. So far, they were still unable to see through the remaining ice to distinguish if there was some sort of entrance, so they continued the tunnel in a straight, horizontal direction.

Morris, Robert and Steven, along with Chispo, Rinto and Fraxino spent some time observing the digging operation. They also helped carry bucketloads of ice and rubble out of the tunnel. The further back they tunneled, the more work they had to do per meter of penetration, because of the work it required to carry the rubble the increasing distance to the glacier outside.

The hours went by. Lunchtime came and went.

I see rock! one of the Sirian crew telepathically related to Tom.

Good man, Dotsero! Tom telepathically replied. He and Caymar were both outside on the glacier observing the ever increasing pile of dumped ice and rubble. They both hurried back to the entrance and entered the tunnel. The other crew members stopped digging momentarily. Tom inspected the end of the tunnel.

Somebody bring some water to throw onto the end of this tunnel, Tom telepathically directed to his crew. *We need to see better through the remaining ice.*

In a few minutes, one of the crew brought a bucket of water from their craft, and he sloshed it onto the ice.

"That's better now," Tom said out loud.

The Atlanteans entered the tunnel. Several Sirian crew members shined lights through the ice at the tunnel's end. It was a strange experience, peering through some ten meters of ice at the bottom of the glacier. They could see the rock underneath it through the still and frozen water.

"Where is our entrance?" Latorna asked Quicho.

"I'm still searching for it," he answered, shining one of the Sirian crew's lights through the ice.

Another one of the Sirian crew arrived with a more powerful light, and he placed its beam right up to the end of the tunnel and shined it through the ice. Now the rocks below and in front of them were illuminated much better. He shined the beam toward the left.

"I think I see it!" Tecoloteh announced to the others with enthusiasm. He indicated to the others where.

A dark area indicating an entrance could barely be seen some 20 to 25 meters further and to the left.

Seglima looked where Tecoloteh had indicated. "That does look familiar! I believe you're right."

The others expressed their agreement and directed Tom and Caymar to have their crew make a 30° lefthand bend in the tunnel and go slightly upwards.

They started up their machines again. Excitement built up as they continued the digging operation. Nearly three more hours went by before they finally reached the entrance. The Atlanteans confirmed that this entrance was definitely the one.

"It's completely plugged with ice!" Latorna commented to the others with genuine concern.

"I hope the ice didn't totally fill the cave and project room," said Quicho.

Tom and Caymar looked at the ice-filled entrance.

I think we better melt the rest of this ice instead of using our conventional digging and penetrating, Tom telepathically directed to his crew.

They agreed to the changeover process, and over the next fifteen minutes, the crew drove their machines out of the tunnel and back into the large spacecraft. They soon emerged with metal tanks and hoses, and they re-entered the tunnel. They were carrying flame throwers. The others watched as they lit the nozzles at the ends of the hoses and proceeded to melt the ice. As the water dripped and ran to the floor, others gathered up the water with buckets, carried it out of the tunnel, and dumped it onto the glacier.

After an hour of melting, they had penetrated 10 meters into the entrance, The tunnel floor had become very slippery and some of them slipped and fell while carring the many bucketfuls of water outside to the glacier.

Suddenly, 12 meters into the entrance, they broke through, reaching the end of the ice barrier, finding the rest of the way to be dry and free of ice. All of them yelled joyous triumph. They had succeeded. They continued melting the ice, making the hole larger, until they were able to walk through and enter the rest of the dry tunnel.

"Looks like we've got us another ice cave," Rinto announced to everyone.

"Right on!" his brother agreed.

"This does remind me of that ice cave we entered in Antarctica last month," said Morris.

"That's right," Robert recalled. "That wall of ice hadn't reached that wall where we saw those hieroglyphic inscriptions with crystals interspersed throughout. This place got spared also."

For further reading about the ice cave in Antarctica, see: Mission Beyond the Ice Cave: Atlantis-Mexico-Zotola, chapter 1.

The Atlanteans, more than the others, advanced with nervous anticipation, wondering if their device-craft or any part of it would be there. They knew their research room well. They walked the 200 meters up this winding tunnel with its gentle upward grade, until the tunnel suddenly widened and entered their project room.

"Yahoo!" Quicho called out in Atlantean.

The other Atlanteans called out similar exclamations of joy.

There it stood, their device for soul travel and time travel, just like they had left it, minus the two bronze crates of plates and tablets. It was quite a sight to see, with its colors of gold and green, which reflected the light of their flashlights with an array of rainbow colors.

The outer shell of the device looked very much like a miniature spacecraft of some sort. It had an oval shape, rounded in all respects, and its dimensions were approximately 2 $1/2$ meters in width, 2 meters in height, and 7 meters in length. It was similar to Rinto and Fraxino's Velosa cruiser craft in that its body or shell had been grown over a period of several months using a mixture of silicon and other metals, such as Vanadium, to give it strength and durability.

Tom and Caymar and their crew were rather impressed, to say the least. They were beyond words as they telepathically communicated with each other and marvelled at a unique piece of technology over 12,000 years old.

"Dudes, I am seriously impressed!" Chispo commended the Atlanteans. He laughed with amazement.

"Radically impressive piece of work!" Rinto declared.

"Far-out, and the *colors*," Fraxino told them, marvelling.

Morris, Robert and Steven looked at the device-craft in wonder and amazement. They felt tingling energy for their excitement at seeing such a spectacle, in addition to feeling really privileged and honored to be a part of this.

The Atlanteans walked to the far end of their device-craft, glad to see it all intact. The rest of them watched as Chameur changed her expression and appeared to meditate. An activation of noise was heard within the device-craft and then an audible click. It was a telepathic relay device within, and upon recognizing Chameur and the other Atlanteans, it unlocked and opened the door for them.

"Oh . . ." she commented, breathing a sigh of relief. "Thanks be to the goodness of all, it's still here, after all this time."

Everything was intact, just the way they had left it. The invaders had not been able to do anything with the device-craft, as Chameur had managed to telepathically lock it. Unfortunately for them at the time they were caught and apprehended, both bronze crates were sitting outside the device-craft on the project room floor, and those two items had been confiscated as a result.

Latorna was the first to enter, followed by Chameur and the others. All the others watched as they started to check the controls within, making sure they were still in working order.

Tom, Caymar, their crew, and the others just watched in silence.

Suddenly, CRAAACK . . . MOAAAN . . . CRAAACK . . .

All of them, including the Atlanteans, were startled.

"It's just the glacier outside and above us making noise," Rinto told everyone, recognizing the sound from the ice cave in Antarctica the month before.

"Man, I thought it was their device-craft!" Chispo declared, his startled feelings easing.

A thought ran through Tom's mind, and the shifting and cracking sound of the glacier had made him aware of it. He directed his telepathic thoughts to his crew.

Take our spacecraft home and return with our Titanium-Vanadium expansion reinforcing kit. We've got to line and brace the entire ice tunnel right away before the glacier flows and breaks it.

With that thought transferrence, the entire Sirian crew left immediately.

"We've got to attend to the tunnel straight away," Tom told everyone. "I have to leave right now with my crew. Caymar will explain to you." With that, Tom and the crew hurried out of the project room and made straight for their spacecraft outside on the glacier.

Everyone suspected what the hurry was, and Caymar proceeded to explain, verifying their thoughts.

They continued to watch as the Atlanteans tested their on-board equipment.

"What do you think of this device-craft of theirs, Morris?" Robert quietly asked him.

"Really an impressive piece of original technology that is . . ."

At that moment, a holographic projection suddenly appeared in front of them, just outside the body of the device-craft. It was a 3D movie in miniature, and it proceeded to show the whole apprehending procedure, complete with a telepathic mind reading of the apprehenders themselves. There were four of them, and the movie showed how they entered with disarming crystals specifically designed at overcoming the will power of the five Atlanteans and making them obey the apprehenders.

The 3D holographic movie projector was a clever piece of equipment, and Latorna and her friends had created it by growing crystals with the right combination of added impurities to achieve the desired result of telepathically recording every move and thought the apprehenders made, to be stored as a holographic movie within their device-craft. The apprehenders never realized they were being telepathically recorded, and they only made matters worse for themselves when they stole the two bronze crates and took them with them. One of the crates, the one with the programming tablets, had a special telepathic message relayer and responder crystal which later used a remote image forcefield to relay the events back to their device-craft in the project room.

The 3D holographic movie showed the apprehenders taking control of the five Atlanteans. Four of them were outside the device-craft at the time, but fortunately Chameur was inside, and already being aware of the alarming circumstances, she quietly exited the device-craft, closed the door, and telepathically locked it before they even realized she was there.

The apprehenders next escorted them out of the project room, and they left through the cave tunnel, emerging into the cove, which at that time was thickly forested with Spruce trees. There was no glacier at all, but the weather was cold, and the Spruce trees that then grew in the cove in those days would soon most of them be killed off at their new and harsher latitude.

The apprehenders had arrived from Atlantis in a flying vessel, and they took the five Atlanteans on board where they had five time-freeze bronze crates ready and waiting for them. The apprehenders' oppressive and domineering will power caused all five of them to be in a trance state and step right into the crates and lie down. The apprehenders swept a forcefield over them, and they were time frozen. Next, they placed the lids over them and flew up to the ridge above the cove, and they haphazardly buried them with an on-board excavator as quickly as possible. Their fear was of being caught by Earth's Atlantean satellites at the time, and the rules were for the apprehenders to bring the Atlanteans to their superiors in Antarctica (Atlantis) to be taken aboard the final craft headed for the star Al Nitak. Of course, since the devastating crustal displacement, the world had become pretty much lawless. Corruption was rampant, and the apprehenders didn't feel like obeying the superiors' rules, much less give the five Atlanteans a chance to explain their project in the first place before apprehending them!

Next, they flew back down into the cove, landing directly in front of the entrance where they exited the vessel, entered the cave, brought the two crates out, and loaded them onto the flying vessel. They re-entered the cave with plans of breaking into the device-craft, and they spent an hour making efforts to break the telepathic code to enter. They wanted to *physically* break in, but they reasoned that would be ruinous to the device-craft and defeat their purpose. They were unsuccessful and had to give up.

So, they exited the project room and walked back through the cave tunnel to the cove outside. Immediately, they flew their vessel to Antarctica where the final spacecraft was waiting for them to take the last group of Atlanteans wanting to flee planet Earth to Artenia around the star Al Nitak.

Cresma Atenkor was unaware of the scandal about the time freezing of the bodies. His request was to send out a search party, not apprehenders, to look for his five friends in the north polar region, now Alaska, and offer them a final chance to come to Al Nitak's planet Artenia to live in peace and harmony.

Unfortunately, Cresma's genuine request had fallen into corrupt hands, as most of those who had stayed behind were dishonest scientists, the ones who had been responsible for the most recent mood control experiments. As a result, the scandal of the time freezing of the five Atlanteans: Latorna, Chameur, Seglima, Quicho, and Tecoloteh had occurred.

The story was revealing itself more and more to the appalled faces of those watching the 3D holographic movie playing out its events. They had been unaware that the whole scandal had resulted from Cresma's genuine request to save them and have them brought to his world. The apprehenders were very dishonest indeed. No wonder they time froze and buried them in haste.

As the movie continued to play out the sequence of events, the apprehenders barely arrived to Antarctica in time before the large spacecraft, already loaded with 3,750 fleeing Atlanteans, was to soar away from Earth.

The apprehenders delivered them the two crates, telling their superiors that each one had a living, time-frozen body inside and that they had only found these two people in the project room at the time. They lied and said they had time-frozen them for their own safety because the two of them had been confrontational, and their lives had been threatened.

As the large spacecraft was just about to leave, there was no time for the superiors to ask questions as to why the apprehenders had done what they had done, much less check to see what the two bronze crates really had inside them. They took the two crates on board the large spacecraft, and as soon as the apprehenders had re-entered their flying vessel to leave, the spacecraft left the ground. It was seen to swiftly accelerate and then suddenly disappear, leaving a quick green flash behind. It would be entering Artenia's atmosphere in a mere few seconds.

The apprehenders had other devious plans. They were going to return to Alaska to unearth the five crates, revive them, and make use of them for their own needs. They wouldn't have gone to the trouble to bury the crates in the first place, but they had to cover their tracks in case they had been caught and in case there had been an investigation of their scandal. As the two crates with "frozen bodies" were already arriving on planet Artenia, they were now free to dig up the five crates with the *real* time frozen bodies.

They proceeded to fly in their vessel back to Alaska, but somebody or something from above delivered them their bill. They met with technical problems aboard their vessel and crashed into what are now the High Andes mountains of South America. All of them were killed. Natural law had paid them off.

The five Atlanteans and the others continued to watch the movie, finding out the real reasons for what had happened to them. They were glad to know the apprehenders had met their doom with natural law, and they breathed sighs of relief and thought, *Good riddance!*

The next part of the movie showed the large spacecraft entering Artenia and landing on the southeastern rim of what came to be called the Ciruclar Mountains with the newly established city of Zantaayer, Zotola below and to the northeast.

"Oh wow!" Fraxino commented. "They're showing our world now."

"Man, this 3D movie is out of this world!" Chispo declared.

"That looks like Zantaayer," said Robert.

"It is," Fraxino verified.

"Wow! It's Quinoteh's vision from *Vision from the Ciruclar*," Rinto told them.

"So, that's what it *really* looked like," said Chispo, realizing.

"The hillsides are mostly grassy pasture," said Steven.

The Ciruclar Mountains were only sparsely populated with trees, growing only in selected locations in those days. It would soon become thickly forested with mostly Southern Beech (*Nothofagus*) trees, which over the next several hundred years, would become established after having been brought to Artenia by the Atlanteans.

The 3-D holographic movie next revealed the fate of the two crates. Once the spacecraft had landed, other residents from the new city of Zantaayer arrived in their crystal powered flying vessels. This was the first time the five Atlanteans had seen a glimpse of the world where so many of their friends had fled to and settled. It really looked beautiful, and emotions filled them as they saw their good friend, Cresma Atenkor, lead the welcoming party as they walked over to the arriving spacecraft and received the final 3,750 refugees from Earth's Atlantis, bringing the total number of refugees to 68,750. These final refugees had not fled the year before with the rest of them because they had needed more time to settle matters and affairs in Atlantis. Others came from some of the small outlying towns and had been overlooked.

Most of the 65,000 refugees the year before had settled the valley nestled within the circular range of mountains, and had built the city of Zantaayer, Zotola, which would become an important coastal port city of their world Artenia.

"Zantaayer. What an appropriate name!" Chameur commented, nearly crying with joy. Everyone could feel her emotion as she continued to talk. "How sentimental of them."

"How do you mean?" Rinto asked her.

"Zanta was a famous Atlantean scientist who lived 3,750 years ago, and she devoted her life and career to studying the ways of the Sun, its life giving forces and energy patterns. She made numerous discoveries and realizations about how the Sun made life what it is. Out of their high regard for her, they looked back at yesterday and named the city of Zantaayer after her, in memory of her life and accomplishments." Tears came to Chameur's eyes as she finished her explanation.

"Wow! That's something we never knew," said Rinto.

"I had never considered how our city got its name," Chispo admitted.

"I wonder if anyone still knows," Rinto mentioned.

Meanwhile the 3D holographic movie continued to run its course. Numerous flying vessels had by now arrived, and they collected the Atlanteans and their cargo and whisked them away to the city of Zantaayer below. Cresma had not seen his five friends: Latorna, Seglima, Chameur, Quicho, and Tecoloteh, stepping down from the spacecraft. So, he stepped on board and inquired as to their whereabouts.

"We sent your search party as you requested," one of the spacecraft crew flatly answered.

Immediately, Cresma felt a terrible sinking feeling.

"We apologize, but they were not found," he continued to answer. "The search party we sent arrived to us just moments before we left, and delivered us two bronze crates." At that moment, some other men on the spacecraft were bringing the two crates out of a cargo room. "They told us they only found two of them, had a confrontation with them, and time froze them. Here they are." The men carried the crates off of the spacecraft and set them on the ground.

Cresma looked at the spacecraft crew members in a confused way. "Are you sure there aren't any more?"

"Positive," the crew member replied. "Look, I don't mean to be rude, but we're already late as it is! We've got to get this craft returned to the Galactic Federation and go on to our next assignment before we lose it."

"You know, it was very important that they be found and brought here. The five of them are good friends of . . ."

"Look here!" the crew member sharply answered. "I haven't the time to chat with you about it. You've got two of your friends right there. We're late because we had to wait for the search party to return to us! We've got to go right now!"

"But wait a . . ." Cresma began, but the crew members of the spacecraft were already closing the doors, upon which it immediately left the ground, swiftly accelerated to the south, and disappeared in a green flash.

Cresma was considerably disgusted at the curt manner of the spacecraft crew! His thoughts were that the Galactic Federation could just *keep* their spacecrafts! He didn't want any further dealings with that bunch, as they were unfriendly and lacked compassion for others, including customers like Cresma Atenkor, who now was a customer no more! At least he had gotten 68,750 of his people brought here, and for that much, he was grateful. He and his people would now live their lives in peace and harmony.

One of the vessels with some of Cresma's friends still remained there on the ridgetop of the Ciruclar Mountains. They walked over to him and expressed their condolences at the search party's failure to bring all five of his friends to the spacecraft before it left Antarctica. They helped him load the two bronze crates into the vessel, and they flew down the mountain to his residence in Zantaayer.

Later in the day, he and some of his friends took the crates to a specialist in unlocking time frozen goods. Cresma knew it had been highly out of order for that search party to have time frozen two of his five friends, and who knows what had become of the other three? Cresma watched as the specialist proceeded to pry the lids off one of the crates . . . to reveal the 144 holographic plates!

"What from Earth is THAT?!!" Cresma exclaimed as he stared at the crate's contents in total surprise and disbelief. "Open the other crate."

The specialist opened it, revealing the bronze data tablets of hieroglyphic script and holographic implantations, and also the compartment of special use crystals.

"Arghhh!!" Cresma screamed. He knew he'd been had. Either the search party had been dishonest, or the spacecraft crew, or *both*, he thought. It made him angry, to say the least.

The specialist looked at Cresma with sorrow, realizing that he had been tricked.

"Cover them!" Cresma ordered. "Put the lids back on them immediately. There's no telling what sort of sabotage they've handed me, nor how dangerous those materials are."

The specialist placed the lids back on the two crates. They immediately loaded them back into Cresma's flying vessel, and he returned to his residence. Over the next several days, he sent out a newsflash and requested to all 68,750 Atlantean refugees that if they thought they had any dangerous crystals or other materials, that they bring them to his residence so they could be disposed of.

Numerous residents panicked and brought Cresma their precious rocks and minerals, among other sacred items, including a few sacred story stones and egg-shaped crystals. What mattered most to them on their new world was to keep their peace and harmony at all cost. The precious rocks and crystals were of the past, and they were ready to move on to better times. Several days later, Cresma had a large cargo vessel loaded with the goods, and he accompanied the disposal mission with his own vessel, personally carrying the two crates. They flew out of Zantaayer to the south, crossing over the Ciruclar Mountains, and they flew an additional 100 kilometers until reaching the foothills of the Placatera Mountains, where they landed. Cresma and the others stepped outside into the hot desert weather.

"This is far enough away from us and well out of the way," Cresma announced. "None of this stuff will ever hurt a thing out here. Scatter the materials across this region. Now, the crates are a different matter, which I will oversee. I want them carefully buried intact with the lids firmly placed." He was afraid of any possible contamination if they were to be haphazardly dumped.

While Cresma and his friend personally dug the holes and carefully buried the two bronze crates between the rock boulders, the large vessel left the ground, and its driver proceeded to fly over the region. He suddenly released the cargo hatch, and numerous rocks and crystals fell to their doom in a scattered fashion across the terrain. Some fell on soft dirt and remained intact, but others were shattered when they were dashed against the boulders during the fall.

Cresma shovelled dirt onto the two crates to cover them up.

Contact was severed.

End of 3D holographic movie . . . Do you desire a replay? the projector telepathically asked the five Atlanteans.

"Man, that is one radical movie!" Fraxino exclaimed.

"So that's how it happened," Rinto commented, realizing.

"Now we know the origin of that galactic dump site," Chispo stated.

"I never considered that Cresma was the one behind the dumping operation," Rinto admitted.

"That surprises me more than anything," said Fraxino.

The five Atlanteans approved of a replay, and the player reset. Again, they watched the movie play through the events, catching and realizing details they missed the first time through.

Morris had been silent during the first playthrough, but now he spoke. "You know, I'm not all that surprised that Cresma had that mass dumping."

"Why do you say that, Morris?" Rinto wanted to know.

"After all, he was the leader of his people," Morris continued, "and he had them to look after, to keep everything in peace and harmony. I know they were all shell shocked after all that went on in Atlantis, but my feeling is that Cresma over-reacted. If he had just stopped for a few moments and really thought about it, he would have realized the supreme value of what those crates contained. Granted, there was that small compartment of dangerous crystals, one of which Rudy touched, as you know. Instead, Cresma acted on impulse and totally missed the fact that his five friends were the ones who created and compiled the entire contents . . . a great and serious loss to society, not to mention, the mass hysteria and dumping of those priceless crystals and historical artifacts."

They thought about what Morris said. Fraxino translated Morris' comments to the Atlanteans.

"We've always considered Cresma with the highest regard," Rinto told Morris. "Never had any of us ever heard about that mass dumping. I'm beginning to wonder if it really . . ."

"Man, don't go doubting that it really happened," Chispo broke in and told him. "You know we've been to the galactic dump site several times. How else do you think all that stuff got there?"

"And you know how we've always thought those rocks and crystals appear to have been scattered all over that site, as if having been dumped from the air," Fraxino reminded Rinto. "Now we've had our question answered."

"It makes perfect sense, man!" Chispo pointed out.

"It all adds up," Fraxino stated.

"Nobody's perfect . . . not even Cresma," Rinto sadly admitted, feeling somewhat let down.

"Man, I know it's hard to admit things sometimes," Chispo told Rinto, and he placed his hand on his shoulder to express his sympathy.

"That mass dumping operation is not listed in any of Artenia's historical records," Fraxino told Morris, "at least as far as I know."

"Our government swept that truth under the rug, too!" Chispo stated.

"No wonder so few people know about that galactic dump site," Fraxino added.

"And the government still has such little interest in it," Chispo added. "Wonder why?"

"Guys, I just feel so sad for the loss of those priceless crystals, as well as the truth for 10,130 of our years," Rinto told them.

"Let's look at it this way," Fraxino pointed out. "At least we, by some form of destiny, have located both crates and some of the priceless crystals, and we're still maintaining our quest of finding out the truth of our ancient Atlantean heritage."

"Yes, you're right," Rinto told his brother. "I'll come around in a little while."

They continued to watch the 3D holographic movie as it played through its second showing.

"I'll tell you what I think," Morris decided to mention. "All of us here have come together by some means of destiny, as Fraxino just said. We are truth seekers and are here to restore the song, and what I mean by the *song* is the historical truth. Look at it this way. Even though the search party and others, including Cresma, acted in senseless ways, and even though they were wrong to act that way, it was meant to happen that way, their higher level beings having influenced it. They weren't tuned in to their higher selves well enough, however, but as a result of their combined actions, you've recovered some of the precious items, especially those two crates, and we have come together to solve the rest of this mission."

"Well said, Morris!" Chispo commended him. He went on to translate Morris' statement to the Atlanteans. Chameur, including the others, commended him on his insight.

They watched the 3D holographic movie replay to its end, where Cresma threw dirt onto the crates, burying them.

"Right, well, this is where I must leave all of you to it," Morris announced.

"Yeah, we know you're already overdue to return to the dolphins," Steven responded.

"True, but it was a pleasure being with all of you," Morris continued. "I'm glad I stayed, especially to meet you five," looking toward the five Atlanteans, "and to see that holographic movie with its startling truth."

"Morris, we'll miss you," said Robert. "Take care, and say hi to the dolphins for me."

The others followed and wished Morris well.

"Thank you. I'll miss all of you, too," Morris told everyone, "and I'm still in on this project, from here on from the standpoint of the dolphins. It's all part of the whole picture and assignment from the Galactic Federation, which thankfully is friendlier than it was to Cresma, by the way," and he laughed. "The dolphins have their part in this intergalactic station being built here."

Fraxino translated Morris' comment to the Atlanteans, who shook hands with Morris and wished him well.

"You'll be seeing me from time to time," Morris went on. "However, I do feel it is my duty to make you aware of something, as this might ease this project's timely completion. It's been my increasing feeling that the existence of the subconscious mind is a myth. It's a learned response which gives human beings the excuse of committing unacceptable actions, like the mass dumping of those precious crystals and artifacts. While there are higher levels of consciousness and higher level beings, the human mind can become unified and be consciously aware of different levels, in addition to merging the conscious and subconscious into one program. Let that movie be a lesson to you. Senseless actions would be far fewer if the humans would learn to do with their minds what I've just stated.

"With that said, I must leave you. All the best."

"Morris, what about . . .?" Rinto began to ask.

Morris put his hands on either side of himself and brought on the energy of the pink glow and whirring wind. Then something unique happened to everyone's astonishment. Sparks of silver and white energy took over, replacing the pink glow, and the area of energy expanded, and then, *Vanish*!

"Oh . . . my goodness!" Robert declared.

"What was that all about?!" Steven wanted to know, and surprised beyond belief.

"Man, did you see what I thought I saw?" Chispo asked everyone.

"Chispo, I think I did," Robert answered.

"Did you see him transform to a dolphin at the very last instant?" Chispo hurriedly asked Robert.

"Yes! Yes, I did indeed, Chispo."

"Far-out!" Chispo exclaimed. "Far-out!"

"Dudes, you don't think Morris is a . . .?" Fraxino began to ask.

". . . a dolphin?" Rinto finished for him. "Guys, I saw the last glimpse, too!"

The Atlanteans were surprised beyond belief, as well. They made their comments of surprise and disbelief.

"Well . . ." Steven started to say but said no more.

Everyone felt tingling sensations throughout their bodies . . . for what Morris may have really been all along!

"Man, if Morris has been a dolphin in disguise all this time," Chispo commented, "then no wonder he's such a diversified being with tons of special talents."

Everyone thought about their entire friendship with Morris, and some of the mysteries about him now made some sense.

"I just don't know what to think yet," said Rinto.

"But we know what we saw, dudes," Chispo reminded everyone.

They talked for some time about Morris, getting over their absolute surprise.

Tom arrived with his crew, and they walked into the project room. They had been away for $1^1/2$ hours.

"Tom, how's it going?" Robert asked him.

"Man, you just missed the 3D holographic movie," Chispo told him.

"That's okay," said Tom. "Caymar will telepathically play it to us."

"Oh, all right, man," said Chispo.

Caymar had also been there during the whole movie viewing. He had remained silent, just observing it all.

"We've brought the Titanium-Vanadium expansion reinforcing kit," Tom informed everyone. "The process is going to take around three to four hours to entirely line the inside of the ice tunnel so that it stays safe and unharmed by the ever shifting glacier above. After all, our plans are to have that as our permanent entrance into this mountain where we want to build our subterranean galactic switching station. What we want to do is penetrate further into this mountain and excavate the large room necessary for the station, as this project room is not large enough. Is this okay with all of you?"

"It's fine with all of us," said Rinto. He translated Tom's comments and proposed plans to the Atlanteans.

"That's fine with us," Latorna consented, "but what about our device-craft? It's probably in your way."

Rinto translated.

"At its present location, it is," Tom answered, "but we can move it to the side of this room and place a protection barrier beside it so our crew will never harm it in any way, and so that no accidents occur to it."

Rinto translated.

Latorna requested it to be moved to the side right away. Tom called on his crew to help him, and among 20 of them, they picked up the device-craft and set it near the left wall of the project room. Tom assured her and the other four Atlanteans that they were honest people who would never do anything to harm nor sabotage their device-craft. After all, Robert, Steven, Chispo, Rinto, Fraxino, among others were witnesses and testimony to Tom's honesty.

"Thank you for those kind words," Latorna and the others told Tom. "We are forever grateful to you and your friends for having found us and for having revived us. We will give you our trust and know that you and your crew are far more sincere and honest than those who apprehended us and time froze us."

Rinto translated.

"Fine, then we will begin to line the ice tunnel and forever protect it," said

Tom. "For the duration of the expansion growing and lining process, no one will be able to pass through the tunnel. You'll be out of harm's way here, if you want to remain here, or if you want to go back outside to the glacier, or wait down at our grey building. The choice is yours."

After Rinto translated, the Atlanteans thought a moment. Latorna and Quicho decided to remain in their project room, as they needed to test some more of their equipment on their device-craft. Everyone else chose to leave, and they walked out of the project room, through the cave tunnel, the ice tunnel, and back out onto the glacier.

The sun was low in the northwest sky. The whole day had gone by, and it was 8 PM, July 27. They suddenly realized their hunger. It had been quite some time since lunch.

Tom stayed with the crew to oversee the tunnel lining and reinforcing process, and Caymar accompanied the rest of them down the glacier and ridge to the grey building in the cove.

Through a chemical process, the crew activated a rapid growing process using liquid silicon and other polymer resins, complete with Titanium and Vanadium for added strength and durability. The material took to the ice walls of the tunnel on all four sides, first establishing a thin layer throughout. As the crew kept adding the material, the thickness increased uniformly. At 30 centimeters, the desired thickness was achieved, and the reinforcing was complete. Over a period of 20 minutes, the material became as hard as steel but stronger.

Next, the crew went into the project room and under Latorna and Quicho's direction, they grew a barrier to protect their device-craft, both from above and on the sides. By that time, a total of 3.75 hours had gone by.

Meanwhile, the others in the grey building down in the cove had eaten some supper and had been chatting with each other, making plans.

"Guys, I just can't get over the fact that Cresma had so many valuable materials dumped," Rinto stated.

"I know it's difficult, Rinto," Chispo said to him. "You had such high regard for him."

"In a way, we still can," Fraxino told him, "because on one level, he did the right thing by dumping the two crates."

"That's right," Chispo added. "Man, if he hadn't dumped them like he did, there's no telling *what* would have happened to those crates, much less would we have found them."

"Cresma didn't exactly know why he was doing what he did," Fraxino reasoned, "but for what he did, it worked out in our favor, since we have the crates to deliver back to our five Atlantean friends."

"You know, that makes sense," Rinto admitted, now seeing reason. "Personally, we have Cresma to sincerely appreciate for what he did." He thanked Chispo and Fraxino for pointing that out to him.

"Don't worry, man," Chispo reassured Rinto. "You can re-establish your high regard for Cresma for what he did for us."

"Even though he didn't realize who he was dumping those materials for," Fraxino added.

It wasn't much longer before they all drifted off to sleep. Tom, Latorna, and Quicho came in at midnight, and they went right to sleep.

Morning arrived. There were no clouds in the sky, and the sun shined in the southeastern sky. The date was July 28, 1985.

Soon after everyone had waked up, Tom announced the next step of his plans. "We have successfully lined the entire ice tunnel with a 30-centimeter thick protection shield, strong enough to resist ten times the weight of that glacier above it. It will be our permanent entrance to our galactic switching station. We are going to install some sturdy doors to keep unwanted intruders out, and we'll give each one of you the combination to unlock the doors to come and go as you wish.

"My crew is going to begin the excavation process to create the large room beyond the project room. We will tunnel an additional 200 meters and then expand to build the large room to accommodate the massive amounts of switching equipment needed. You will be glad to know that the excavating will be done by laser cutting the rock in block sections instead of using jack hammers and explosives, which would cause considerable danger to the structural strength of the rock of the mountain above us. We don't want any collapses. At any rate, we are going to install the same reinforcing kit to the walls and ceiling of our big room, once it's created."

"What sort of time do you think all this will take?" Steven asked Tom.

"We're not really sure," he answered. "It depends on the type of rock we encounter within the mountain and how efficient the excavating operation will be, among other factors."

"A couple of days, weeks or months?" Robert asked.

"The excavating will likely take a week, if all goes well," Tom answered.

"That's pretty quick," said Chispo.

"What sort of combination will the doors have?" Robert wanted to know.

"You will need to enter a ten digit number," Tom answered. "You all can choose whatever number you want."

"I know," Fraxino suggested. "What about 10130 to represent the number of our years since the Atlanteans arrived on our world?"

"Good idea," said Rinto, "but that's only five digits."

"And then we could follow that by the total number of refugees, 68750," Chispo quickly brought up.

"That'll work," Fraxino agreed.

"What do you think, guys?" Chispo checked with everyone.

They all agreed. Robert wrote out the number and handed it to Tom.

"Okay, agreed," said Tom. "The number is 1013068750, the combination to enter and leave the tunnel and facilities. We will have the doors fabricated to recognize that number, and also an additional different number that my crew will use." He shook hands with everyone.

Rinto now told the five Atlanteans who were very glad to know that their project room and soul/time travel device would be protected from unwanted and unauthorized intruders. However, it took some extra explaining for them to understand the combination, since it was written in Roman Arabic numbers and also in base 10. So, Rinto proceeded to explain the conversion from their base 12 system which used Atlantean script for numbers. Rinto, Chispo, and Fraxino were glad to learn that the Atlantean base 12 numbering system used the same script number characters as Artenian, their system having remain the same on Artenia ever since 10,130 of their years ago.

With that explanation completed, Tom announced that he and Caymar were going to direct their crew to begin the further excavation immediately.

"What are your plans?" Tom asked everyone.

"We need to go get those two bronze crates from home," Rinto told them.

"By the way, Tom," Robert decided to bring up, "I guess you noticed that Morris has left us."

"Oh, yes. I know."

"Well, the strangest thing happened when he transported himself away last night, and . . ." Robert started to explain.

"Man, we couldn't believe it when we thought we saw Morris transform to a *dolphin*!" Chispo completed for Robert.

"You can indeed believe it," Tom assured them.

"You mean you know?" Steven asked Tom.

"Yes, I've known that about Morris ever since I first knew him," Tom replied. "I have kept that fact to myself at Morris' request."

"Well, I will say!" Robert declared.

"Morris is a very diversified being who is aware of other levels," Tom explained. "He is a very important link to this whole project, bringing in vast amounts of alien knowledge, along with help from other important dolphins, who live on Delikadove across the galaxy and linearly in our 35 million year ago past but who are accessible right across the time line, thanks to Morris' diversified ways and genius. He has been aware of the plans for this major station since before he left you in that ice cave in Antarctica, one month ago."

"We certainly have been aware of his unique and diversified ways, to say the least," said Steven, "but it never had crossed our minds that he was a dolphin in disguise."

"He is," Tom verified. "You can be sure of that."

"Well . . ." Steven started to say.

"That's amazing!" Robert declared.

"I'm really impressed at that!" Chispo declared.

"Right, well," Tom told everyone, "Caymar and I are going to get started right away. Have a safe trip, those of you who go. Enter and leave the tunnel and project room as you like, keeping aware of the entering and leaving traffic of our crew."

"Thanks, Tom. We will," said Steven.

"See you around, Tom," Chispo told him, followed by the others.

Tom and Caymar walked out the door of the grey building and up the glacier to the spacecraft where they would notify their crew and begin work. They would also build a path to make the going and coming easier.

"All right, dudes," Fraxino announced. "Who wants to come with us to Zotola?" He repeated the question to the Atlanteans who talked it over.

"Let's all five of us go," Latorna said to her friends. "I can't wait to see the world where our friends fled, after seeing that 3D holographic movie."

"I want to go, too," Quicho told Latorna, "but I think at least two of us need to stay here and attend to our device-craft. I choose to stay."

"I'm going to stay also," Seglima announced. "We've got to protect what's ours."

"I understand your paranoia," Latorna told her, "but Tom and Caymar are entirely honest. They're not going to do any harm to us nor our project."

"How do you know for sure?" Seglima asked.

"My feelings tell me," Latorna told her, "in addition to our new friends here who know him and can attest to Tom and Caymar's genuine character."

"Latorna's right," Chameur told Seglima. "What happened to us is the long ago past, as you know, even though it just recently occurred to us in our time frame of reference."

"All right, I'm convinced," Seglima gave in, "but I still want to stay, if nothing else, to witness Tom and Caymar's crew and their excavating operation."

"Fine then," said Latorna, "but we do want you to trust them."

"That I will do my best to come around and do," Seglima assured her.

"How will you communicate with them?" Latorna asked both Seglima and Quicho.

"Oh, that's easy," Seglima answered. "Tom and Caymar are pure telepaths. I understand them with the greatest of ease."

"That's great," Latorna told her. "So, then, how many times did Tom and Caymar think about doing sabotage to our device-craft and project?"

Seglima thought a few moments. "Never," she came around to answer.

"There you are," Latorna pointed out. "You've verified their honesty for yourself."

"Indeed I have," Seglima admitted, and she smiled. "You've made your point."

"So, are you coming with us or staying?" Latorna asked.

Seglima and Quicho looked at each other.

"We're going to stay," Seglima answered. "Zotola and Artenia can wait another week for us."

"Very well," Latorna consented. "Chameur and Tecoloteh?"

"We're coming with you to Zotola," Tecoloteh answered.

"Right, then let's go," Rinto now told Latorna, Chameur, and Tecoloteh.

All of them packed their belongings in their backpacks, for those who had them, and they exited the grey building. Rinto and Fraxino's Velosa cruiser craft was parked 100 meters away next to a small copse of Spruce shrubs in the cove.

"You know," Latorna said to Rinto, "we've hardly taken notice of your craft, seeing how we've been occupied by other things."

"Ma'am, I tell you, it's a unique one," Chispo boasted. "You wouldn't believe what those two gurus did to make their vehicle-craft fly . . . more than that, teleporting to and from Earth."

"Oh, I can believe it," Latorna assured Chispo. Though she didn't say it, she was really impressed by Rinto and Fraxino's abilities, and would be even more so a few moments later.

Tecoloteh saw and noticed their five crates over at the other end of the cove. "The five crates everybody! We've got to safeguard them."

"Go and tell Quicho and Seglima to carry them up to our project room," Latorna directed. "These crates we're definitely going to keep!"

Tecoloteh looked at her.

"Go ahead and tell them. We'll wait for you here," Latorna assured him.

Tecoloteh ran back to the grey building.

Rinto and Fraxino opened the side door to their vehicle-craft.

"My! Would you look at that!" Latorna declared with pride. "A piece of our future," she now said to Chameur. "And how does it operate?" she asked Rinto.

"It runs on hydrogen fuel," Rinto answered.

"On land, that is," Fraxino added. "In the air, we use our Ulexite main controls crystal in conjunction with another array of crystals situated underneath it and in direct telepathic contact at all times."

They all stepped inside. Rinto pulled up the trap door between the front seats, revealing the Ulexite cube.

"That is outrageously ingenius!" Latorna stated with a smile.

"So, I take it you grew the derived sequence of added impurities into the array of crystals there under the large cube to give it the intelligence to fly and teleport?" Chameur asked Rinto and Fraxino.

"Exactly!" Fraxino answered. "How did you know that?"

"The information just entered my mind," Chameur admitted.

"Chameur is that way," Latorna explained. "She is the most insightful one among the five of us."

"Dudes," Chispo told Rinto and Fraxino with a smile, "it looks like she just read your crystals."

"Just like you, Chispo," Rinto returned comment. He gave Chispo a look which suggested more . . . such as, more between Chispo and Chameur. Chispo suddenly realized and felt the implication, but he kept quiet.

Next, Rinto took them back outside, raised the hood, and explained to them about their Richmond in-line 6-cylinder motor and the 5-speed manual gearbox behind it. He checked the different components and fluid levels and then closed the hood.

By this time, Tecoloteh came running back. "They're on their way right now to collect the five crates and move them to our project room."

"Very good," Latorna responded.

At that moment, both Seglima and Quicho could be seen leaving the grey building. They came over to Rinto and Fraxino and the others and wished them all a great trip, said their goodbyes, and then walked further to where the crates were.

The rest of them boarded the Velosa cruiser craft, bound for planet Artenia's land of Zotola. Rinto closed the door when all eight of them were safely inside.

"All right, dudes!" Chispo boasted with enthusiasm. "Rinto's going to put this craft in high gear, and we're zooming out of here." He repeated the same boasting remark to the three Atlanteans.

Rinto got in the driver's seat, and the craft left the ground in total silence. To Latorna, Tecoloteh, and Chameur, flying under crystal power was just second nature, but this Velosa cruiser craft certainly did differ in appearance from their crystal powered flying vessels they used in Atlantis.

Rinto caused the craft to quickly accelerate to the north. They cleared the western ridge of Mt. Isto and were now flying high above the icy tundra of the valley. He sent a telepathic command to the controls crystal, and a green glow enveloped them and their craft. They felt as if they were dematerializing for a brief moment, and then they were fine again, restored to normal.

CHAPTER 7

RETRIEVAL OF THE TWO CRATES

They were now flying over the desert valley in Zotola, heading north to the Ciruclar Mountains. Al Nitak was low in the western sky, as it was nearly the end of the day. Rinto lowered the altitude of the craft and turned left just when beginning to crest the southwestern rim of the Ciruclar Mountains. The city of Zantaayer was clearly visible below them and to the north of the mountain range. Beyond that, the Elizabeth Ocean stretched to the distant horizon.

"This is . . . absolutely fantastic!" Chameur commented with emotion in her voice.

"How beautiful a planet our people have settled!" Latorna said to Tecoloteh beside her.

"I'll say! And look at the sky," Tecoloteh remarked. "It's turquoise green."

"The green color is more pronounced in the early mornings and late evenings, like now," Rinto informed them.

"We love it here," Fraxino told them. "People are friendly and honest."

"And there is no air pollution," Chispo added.

"Every vehicle is powered by hydrogen here on our world," Rinto boasted. "No fossil fuels, like on Earth."

"Not saying that your people of Atlantis used fossil fuels," Fraxino added comment.

"No, we didn't," Latorna answered.

Fraxino popped a holodisk into their on-board player, and they impressed their Atlantean friends with some Zotolan music, including the album by *The Hydragyros*.

Rinto brought the craft in for a landing as he approached the rim of the mountains. Southern Beech trees whizzed by as he lined up the craft with the gravel road and made the landing. Immediately he applied the brakes and slowed down to reasonable speed. He started the engine, placed the transmission in second gear, engaged the clutch, and drove them several kilometers along the rim road, heading north.

"Look at these wonderful trees," Chameur stated with happiness. "Just like they grew in Atlantis."

"Yes, they were brought here by your people," Rinto verified. "Before, as we saw in that 3D holographic movie of yours, these mountains were mostly grassy hillsides."

"They've become remarkably well established," Chameur commented.

"They do offer us cool moist shade compared to what would otherwise be hot and sunny terrain," Chispo agreed.

"That's very true," said Chameur. "They bring life to the area." She went on to explain the name of that type of tree.

Chispo translated to English for the others. "Chameur just said the name in Atlantean for these Southern Beech trees is *Noirtrel Alaktt*. In Artenian we just call them Nortralakt Trees, and she said the name gets its meaning from the fact that this type of tree likes to grow in pure stands, covering the mountainous terrain thoroughly. It's an ancient tree that adds character to the mountains and provided refuge for Atlanteans when they went on retreats in the mountains."

Rinto drove them through the forest along the winding gravel road for nearly half an hour before turning right and making the switchbacking descent into Zantaayer. By now, it was twilight, as Al Nitak had set. They could now see the lights of the city being turned on.

At the bottom of the mountain, the pavement began, and they passed the residential houses the few kilometers until they reached the Zapatero's house. Rinto drove them into the driveway.

"Yep, Dad's home," Rinto said to everyone. "There's his classic car, the Tolejo sedan."

"Rinto and Fraxino's dad is very proud of his *Tolejo*," Chispo proudly boasted to the Atlanteans. "He takes super care of it and keeps it in *immaculate* working order."

Once Rinto parked, everyone stepped outside. Latorna, Tecoloteh, and Chameur were very impressed . . . such a different way of life than their culture of Atlantis, they were realizing.

"Chameur, do you feel a slight sense of tingling energy, like I do?" Latorna asked her.

"Yes, I do."

"We're at 98% Earth's gravity here," Chispo explained. "You'll feel more energized and vibrant here than back on Earth."

"Oh, yes," Latorna responded, realizing. "That would explain it."

"Look at these houses," Tecoloteh brought up, speaking to Latorna and Chameur. "How different!"

"Technological styles do change through the times," Latorna commented.

"It looks like they are made of some type of artificial stone," Tecoloteh told them.

Rinto explained to them that most houses were made out of bricks and also stones, but that most of them were of brick.

"Back at our homeland in Atlantis," Tecoloteh explained, "we used a semi-growing process, not too different from the way Tom and his crew lined that ice tunnel. We would program a pattern and grow the walls, floors and ceilings to a desired thickness, using a resinous liquid with a mixture of various polymers and metals for strength and durability. The liquid would dry as it was being appropriately applied and the homes would last many thousands of years before deterioration of the compound matrices of the material."

"We had other houses grown by a slow growing process using silicon and other mixtures of metals," Latorna mentioned. "The process took several months. They were as permanent as stone houses."

"Our device-craft was grown that way," Tecoloteh told them. "That's why it's lasted so well after all these years."

"In addition to other instilled intelligence to cause self preservation that we included with it," Latorna added, "which some houses also had."

"Cool! Radical!" Fraxino remarked.

"What an interesting method!" Rinto commented.

"Also most homes were grown in the shape of a pyramid," Latorna told them.

"Of course, we had some stone houses, too," said Tecoloteh.

By now, all of them had stepped out of the vehicle-craft, and they were entering Rinto and Fraxino's house. Glecko and Sosta had been in another part of the house and now realized that their sons were home. They came to them and greeted them.

"Welcome back home, sons," Glecko told them in Artenian. "How was your trip?"

"Dad we've done a lot in the last few days," Rinto answered.

"That's my boys, always on the move," Glecko complimented them.

"Looks like some of your friends have left and different ones have come with you now," Sosta remarked.

"Who are these three?" Glecko asked as he looked at Latorna, Tecoloteh, and Chameur. Then he saw the orange emblem design on their clothing. His eyes lit up with surprise. "Ohhh . . . would you look at that!" he remarked, before the three of them had a chance to introduce themselves. He went on to say, "They've got the ancient all-one-race symbol on their uniforms. Are these three people from *Atlantis*?"

"Yes, they are, Dad," Rinto replied.

"Oh, law!" Sosta now remarked. "What have you boys gotten yourselves into this time?"

Both she and Glecko gave Rinto and Fraxino looks of disbelief.

"It's like this," Fraxino began. "We found five time frozen bodies that Tom, our galactic salesman friend, told us he and Caymar found two of . . . and our friend, Morris, revived them!"

"No! You don't mean it," Glecko remarked with enthusiasm.

"We do indeed, Dad," Rinto verified.

"It's true, man," Chispo told Glecko.

"My, what a treasure find!" Glecko exclaimed. "I knew you guys could do it. Three living people from Atlantis. So, where are the other two?" he asked, now realizing only three of the five had come with them.

"Two of them stayed in Alaska," Rinto answered, "to help with the galactic switching station."

"In addition to their device-craft of time and soul travel," Fraxino added.

The surprise of it all eased. The three Atlanteans had been quiet, but now they finally had a chance to talk, and they introduced themselves.

"Come on inside, everyone," Glecko offered. "Tell me all about it."

They entered the Zapatero's home, set down their backpacks and belongings, and for the next hour, they related all their latest adventures.

". . . and let me tell you about that symbol on your uniform," Glecko told the Atlanteans and looking at Tecoloteh. "That symbol is very sacred and shows up in our ancient historical documents."

"Dad, you didn't tell us you knew about that symbol," Rinto told him.

"You've never shown me that symbol before," Glecko responded. ". . . wasn't any reason to talk about it before."

"But how do you already know?" Fraxino asked his father.

"We never knew about it until we saw it on those ancient paintings in Mexico," Rinto added.

"And now on these Atlanteans' uniforms," Fraxino further added.

"I'm surprised you hadn't seen it before that, sons," Glecko said to them. "After all, there are several books that discuss it, down at Zantaayer's central library."

"I guess we never thought about it," Rinto admitted.

"Glecko, how did you know about that symbol?" Chispo wanted to know. "Hardly anyone knows about it."

"I have to admit, that is a good question," Glecko replied. "One of my teachers in school was really interested in other intelligent races, and with his interest in icons, he had come across it when looking through some ancient documents at the library. It interested him so much that he made a point to talk about it to every one of his classes. Since he taught ancient history, it was appropriate."

"Why does hardly anyone know about it now?" Steven asked Glecko.

"Times change. Things that were important then become unimportant later and forgotten."

Tecoloteh proceeded to explain the whole history behind the all-one-race icon, why it was orange, what it represented, that Atlantean colonists came from Vega, and so on. Though Glecko knew a decent amount of details, for the ancient documents he had read, he soon realized that Tecoloteh knew a considerable amount more about the icon than Zantaayer's ancient documents.

Glecko talked with them about other subjects, as well. Meanwhile, his wife Sosta, who had less of an interest in their discussion, had gone to another part of the house, to do other things.

"Did they tell you about the new movie, *Vision from the Ciruclar*?" Glecko asked the Atlanteans.

"Yes, they did," Latorna answered.

"I highly recommend you three see it," Glecko advised.

"We do indeed want to see it," Latorna told him.

"The three of you will probably get a good laugh at Quinoteh's vision," Chispo told them with a smile, "after having seen the real thing on that 3D holographic movie of yours."

Sosta came into the room after a while and motioned everyone to come into the dining room area.

"There's supper for all of you if you want it," Glecko offered them.

They gladly accepted and followed Glecko into the kitchen, and on to the dining room area, after serving themselves. They continued to chat about various subjects while eating, talking about the times and history of Zotola and also how life was in Atlantis.

"Come on back and see our computer setup," Rinto said to the Atlanteans, now finishing supper.

"That's where we've got all your plates," Fraxino told them.

Everyone got up from the table and walked into the room with the computer setup. The Atlanteans had wanted to see the two crates and holographic plates and bronze data tablets as soon as they arrived at the Zapatero's house, but they didn't want to be disrespectful by being too pushy. After all, Chameur, more than the others, knew the two crates were in safekeeping here.

As they followed Rinto, Fraxino, and Chispo and entered the room, a sense of joy came over them as they saw and recognized their lost belongings. Immediately, Latorna, followed by the other two, rushed over to the two crates by the back wall of the room. They took the lids off the crates.

"Oh, there they are, still intact," Chameur commented with relief as she looked at the 144 holographic plates.

Meanwhile, Tecoloteh and Latorna examined the bronze data tablets in the other crates.

"They're all here," Latorna told them. "All the holographic pieces are in place. Excellent!"

"This is really great!" Tecoloteh remarked. "We do indeed appreciate you for finding these crates and for all the help you've given us."

"We're glad to do it," Fraxino told them. "Not a problem."

"We are so glad to have these back," Chameur told them. "It really is a miracle."

"You're not kidding," Chispo agreed.

Meanwhile, Rinto was switching on the controls to the crystal base computer, which the Atlanteans found very interesting. They commended Rinto and Fraxino for their original genius to have combined the power and intelligence of crystals with the present day technology in Zotola.

"There's a holographic plate on herbs and plants I'd like to take a look at," Chameur requested. "It's plate number 7." She took it out of the box and handed it to Rinto, who placed it on the viewing tray.

It wasn't long before information soon showed up on the screen, both in Atlantean script, and then in English at Rinto's command.

"*Medicinal Herbs and Plants of Atlantis*," Chispo said, as he read the plate's title.

The plate was a data base of some 100 different medicinal plants that grew in the wilderness of Atlantis. They were able to scroll through the listings, complete with color photo images.

"Look at that one," said Rinto, when he saw a photo of an attractive looking spring, a water hole in a quaint forest meadow of yellow grass and Southern Beech trees. A small, brownish-grey flowering plant could be seen at the water's edge.

Text showed up under the picture and Rinto narrated.

"Quanac, (*Quastris illustris*), a small, brownish-grey ground dwelling plant consisting of a single flower bloom with a velvet red interior . . . no leaves. Habitat: perched by the water's edge on wet banks and only at sources of water, such as at springs and water holes. Known to thrive deep within the temperate rain forests, especially those of the Noirtrel Alaktt (Southern Beech trees). Excellent for allieviating stomach aches and pains by causing the nerves of the inner stomach lining to communicate better.

"Quanac has its origin 800 million years ago and is from a star system 230 light years away called Quastris illuminosa (Qtu) whose large planet Quanac, together with its three moons: Acnqu, Cauqa, and Ncnqn, comprised four heavenly bodies. Planet Quanac, consisting of 95% water and 5% land, was designated as a marine reserve for ocean life in the galaxy.

"85 million years ago, the Quanac plant was brought to Earth to serve the special purpose of maintaining the ecological balance of the rivers by purifying and oxygenating the atmosphere. In the daytime, it received and captured the sunlight, and at night it was known for telepathically emitting vibrational waves to strike the water's surface and produce the cycle of oxygenation."

"Interesting plant," said Robert. "It looks familiar. I don't know why."

Meanwhile, Chameur had been reading the other text of Atlantean script. She, along with Tecoloteh and Latorna, were impressed at Rinto and Fraxino's computer setup and at how well it could call up and interpret the data, including photographic images, on those holographic plates that were created and compiled so long ago. To think that data compiled 10,130 Artenian years ago could be deciphered and read by modern day equipment.

"I wonder if any of the Quanac survived the disaster," Latorna commented.

"We can only hope those who stayed behind took some of them to other parts of the world," said Tecoloteh.

"Or perhaps even brought them here to Zotola," Latorna mentioned.

Rinto scrolled down to the next plant. It was another species of Quanac. As they continued to examine the herbs and plants listed, they saw a total of 4 species of Quanac listed, all of them variations of a dull, brownish grey, ground dwelling flower bloom with a velvet red interior, and all of them growing in the same type of habitat, perched by the water's edge on wet banks only at sources of water.

"Oh, yeah!" Robert realized and told everyone. "I know what that flower looks like . . . the Wild Ginger."

Meanwhile, Chameur made comment. "Back in Atlantis, we had another name for that plant, *Gintzyell Luz*, for its telepathic ability to receive sunlight and emit vibrational waves. It was very important for its ability to maintain the ecological balance of the rivers. I also showed you that particular herb because it was widely used for treating stomach aches and pains, which were somewhat prevalent throughout Atlantis."

"You can probably understand why there were so many cases of stomach aches and pains," Latorna mentioned.

"From the numerous bad energy systems and turmoil, right?" Chispo responded in a sincere manner.

"That's right," Latorna answered.

"We wonder if any of you have seen or heard of this type of plant here on Artenia?" Chameur asked everyone.

"No, I never have," Rinto answered.

"I haven't either," Chispo replied, "but there might be some information on it at Zantaayer's central library."

"If you like, we can go search for it," Fraxino offered to them.

"There are plenty of mountains and springs, especially west of here," Rinto told them.

"Man, there are even more of them up north toward Caloma," Chispo told Rinto.

"Yeah, but the information we just read says the Quanac grows in Southern Beech forests," Rinto pointed out, "like we have here around Zantaayer. Up in Caloma, most of the trees are conifers."

"Oh, all right, man," Chispo admitted.

"That is something I want to research before we return to Alaska," Chameur told them.

"I'll be glad to take you down to the library," Chispo offered to Chameur.

"We'll come with you also," Tecoloteh said to Chispo.

"I'm very curious as to the ancient documents, as well," Latorna added. "When can we go?"

"They'll be open tomorrow," Chispo informed them.

"Dudes, let's go see *Vision from the Ciruclar*," Fraxino reminded everyone. "It's going to be starting in less than an hour."

"Don't worry, man," Chispo assured him. "We haven't forgotten. What other plates do you want to see?" he now said to Chameur, Latorna and Tecoloteh.

They looked at a few more plates. Some of them, they had seen earlier, but then Chameur was spot checking various plates to be sure all the data was still intact, and she and the others were relieved to find that indeed everything had been remarkably well preserved.

Then Rinto shut down his crystal base computer system, and they left. Rinto drove all of them in the vehicle-craft to the nearby Myrtillo Cinema on the highway. They really enjoyed the movie, and the three Atlanteans got some laughs for what they knew to really be true. However, they did appreciate that Quinoteh's vision and quest were for genuine reasons and that the purpose of the movie was to generate public interest in Artenia's residents about their ancient Atlantean history.

By the time the movie finished, it was well into the evening. Fraxino drove them back to the house where they all spread out their bedrolls and slept for the night.

That night, Robert had a dream about that Fluorite peace keeping crystal that had mysteriously disappeared from Atlantis. He clearly saw the large, egg-shaped crystal in the dream, and he was aware of it being cleverly stolen in the night and whisked away in a spacecraft, destined for a faraway star system's civilization that was at war. On the way, they became afraid for their safety. They made a quick stop at one of the planets in the Pleiades and deposited the crystal high up in some mountains. Then the thieves proceeded toward their home nearer the center of the galaxy.

Robert woke up from the dream, somewhat surprised at the clarity of it all. *You don't think it could be . . .?* he thought to himself. He now realized it was already morning, and he immediately went to wake up Steven.

"Steven! Wake up!" and he gently tapped him on his shoulder.

"What? What," Steven woke up and responded.

"Steven, I just had this dream . . ." and Robert told him all the details. ". . . and do you think that's the same Fluorite crystal we found high up in the mountains of Aleyone of the Pleiades and took to Mt. Timpanogos in Utah?"

Steven thought for a moment. He started laughing. "Oh my goodness! Robert, I believe it is. I hadn't even thought about it . . . being the same one!"

"Nor had I," Robert admitted. "I mean, we were certainly aware that it was stolen from Atlantis over 15,000 years ago . . ."

". . . which coincides with 2,500 years ago from the story we read on those holographic plates!" Steven finished for him.

"It's the same one, Steven!" Robert declared. "Why didn't we associate that and think of it sooner?"

"I know," Steven admitted. "How did that get by us?"

By this time, Robert and Steven's conversation had waked up the others.

Chispo was the first one to wake up. "Wait a minute. Did you say you dudes *found* and *took* that stolen crystal back to Earth?"

"Yes, we did," Robert replied.

"Oh, yeah," Rinto realized, just waking up and catching the conversation. "I remember now that you guys told us you took a crystal back to Earth, back when we first met you in Antarctica."

"Man, I hadn't even thought about it being the same crystal either!" Fraxino stated.

"Something probably kept you and Steven from realizing it," Rinto told them.

"Must have been," said Steven.

"I guess it must really be so," Robert admitted. "People are caused not to associate and realize certain things until the right moment."

"Some sort of destiny must have controlled that," Rinto told everyone.

Chispo now related the sudden revelation to Chameur, Latorna and Tecoloteh. Their eyes opened wide in amazement.

"You mean Robert and Steven here and their friends actually *found* that Fluorite peace keeping crystal and returned it to Earth?" Chameur asked Chispo.

"They say they did."

"Chispo," Robert requested, "tell them it was Tom who knew about its disappearance over 15,000 years ago, and it was he who sent us on the treasure hunt when we were visiting Aleyone and having adventures there over a month ago."

Chispo told them.

"Well, what are we waiting for?" Latorna proposed. "Let's go back to Earth. I want to *see* that."

"We can go ahead and take our two crates back to our device-craft in Alaska while we're at it," Tecoloteh suggested.

"Guys, I've got a favor to ask you," Rinto requested to the three Atlanteans.

"Yes?" Chameur responded.

"Can we take the next few hours to copy all the holographic plate data into our computer and crystals before we take your crates back to Alaska?"

"Yes, certainly," Chameur consented.

"Thanks," said Rinto. "I want to compile a complete history book of Atlantis, its way of life, culture, and peoples, and restore any misconstrued historical information, as well."

"We'll be glad to help in any way we can," Latorna assured them. "We're forever grateful to the group of you for finding what was stolen from us."

"Don't you want to hang around Zotola for several days before we return to Alaska?" Chispo asked them.

"Yes, certainly we do," Latorna replied. "It's just that we feel anxiety because we want to return our two crates to our device-craft."

"We can visit the mountains in Utah where your friends left the Fluorite peace keeping crystal, and then return here," Chameur suggested.

"That way, Quicho and Seglima can commence the programming," said Latorna, "while we return here and see your world of Artenia."

"Okay, good plan," Rinto approved. "Chispo, do you want to take Chameur and the others to the central library while Fraxino and I do this programming?"

"Yeah, sure man," Chispo approved.

"I'd like to come, too," Latorna requested.

"And I'll go ahead and stay here with Rinto and Fraxino," said Tecoloteh. "I want to tell them about the crystals with the bronze data tablets."

"Robert, Steven, want to come with us?" Chispo offered.

"Yeah, sure," they both replied.

They walked out of the house, across the backyard, crossed under the row of tall bushes, and into the Colancha's backyard. Robert and Steven were glad to have been invited by Chispo to come with him also, that he still included them, even when with females. Chispo was indeed of decent, genuine character, and they appreciated him.

They got into his Velva Dibe, and he drove them to central Zantaayer. He also took them on a quick tour of the University of Zotola and the beach.

Meanwhile, Tecoloteh entered the computer room with Rinto and Fraxino to begin the complete transference of data. As Rinto put the index plate on the tray, he turned on the computer. Tecoloteh began looking at the bronze data tablets in the other crate.

"Man, did we tell you what happened to Rudy, who's now in Mexico?" Fraxino said to Tecoloteh.

"No, what?"

"When we found that second crate, he put his hand on that orange crystal . . ." Fraxino began.

". . . and he instantly picked up another language," Tecoloteh finished for him.

"Exactly!" Fraxino answered with surprise. "How did you know?"

"That orange crystal is our language acquisition crystal," Tecoloteh explained, "specifically programmed to cause telepathic transferences of energy and intelligence to occur between the person touching it and the person nearest him at that moment."

"Which was Morris, wasn't it?" Rinto asked Fraxino.

"It was him," Fraxino verified, recalling the scene.

"That crystal is only to be used under strict and necessary situations," Tecoloteh advised them.

"What are those other crystals used for?" Fraxino asked.

"They are part of the programming procedure, as they have a lot of the bad energies recorded in them."

"Whoa!" Fraxino exclaimed. "Let me tell you. That same Rudy sneaked in here wanting to touch another crystal, but I caught him and saved him just in time."

"We had sensed that the crystals were dangerous to touch," Rinto explained, "and only to be handled by the appropriate people at the appropriate times."

"You sensed correctly," Tecoloteh verified. "I personally programmed those crystals with all the various bad energy systems of Atlantis, to be carefully loaded into our device-craft so it would telepathically figure out a neutralizing energy system for each one. Not even we handle them by hand. We use special shielding gloves that are on board our device-craft. That fellow has you to *thank* for preventing him from touching any more of those crystals, Fraxino."

Tecoloteh talked with Rinto and Fraxino some more about that compartment of crystals, and he helped them load the data from holographic plates 1 through 100, as plates 101 through 144 consisted entirely of programming and instructional keys for their device-craft's computer to make sense of the stories and information on the holographic plates and interpret it for soul travel, in addition to learning how to interpret the energy systems.

It took all morning long for Rinto and Fraxino to load all of the data into their crystal base computer system. Fraxino went upstairs to the attic for more crystals, and he also brought down a sizeable cube of Ulexite, an extra piece they had, which they had ended up not using in the Velosa cruiser craft project last year. When they finished with plate 100, Rinto caused the computer to copy and transfer all the data to that extra piece of Ulexite cube.

One wouldn't have thought it was possible to store that massive amount of data into a decent size cube of Ulexite, but then with Ulexite's unique characteristics of millions of in-line fibers, it indeed had enormous storage capacity. After all, matter was mostly empty space, and for that, information could be stored indefinitely within the energy matrix of matter itself. In addition to that, Rinto and Fraxino knew the correct telepathic frequencies to be able to store and retrieve data, and by their telepathic link to their crystal array of their computer, they caused the system to accurately store all of the holographic plate data into the Ulexite crystal fibers.

Rinto then checked the Ulexite cube for accurate information storage. He called up various sections of data as a means of spot checking.

"Done and secured!" Rinto triumphantly announced, after his spot checking.

"Right on, brother!" Fraxino declared.

Tecoloteh had spent some of the time looking through the other crate's bronze data tablets, in addition to enjoying reading the data on the screen as Rinto and Fraxino went through all of the holographic plates.

"I must say," Tecoloteh admitted, "I had not realized what a massive amount of data our friend, Chameur, had compiled."

"It's a treasure," Rinto commended.

"Rinto and I thank her very much," Fraxino added.

"This is definitely our next project," Rinto told them, "to compile a complete history of Atlantis and our ancestral heritage."

Around five hours had passed, and Chispo had still not returned. He knew those two gurus, Rinto and Fraxino, would be occupied quite a while.

Their first stop had been the library. Latorna and Chameur had really enjoyed searching through the ancient documents. Some of the people discussed had been personal friends of theirs, and they missed their homeland. Chameur, with Chispo's help, located data pertaining to the all-one-race symbol, which both of them found very interesting.

After the library, Chispo had taken them on a quick tour of central Zantaayer including various flea markets. He showed them the campus of the University of Zotola and also took them through the Cloak Hall anomaly.

Their last stop was the beach on the north side of the city. As it turned out, Chameur and Chispo were talking more and more with each other and less so with Latorna. The five of them walked along the beach, watching others swim in the ocean and play in the sand. Latorna, Robert, and Steven walked along behind Chispo and Chameur. They slowed down to let Chispo and Chameur walk further on, and they watched the two of them as they joined hands.

"Robert, are you thinking what I'm thinking?" Steven brought up, pointing ahead at Chispo and Chameur.

"Yeah, I see it too," Robert answered. "They're taking to each other, aren't they."

"You think they'd make a good couple?" Steven asked Robert.

"They certainly do connect well enough."

Latorna, Robert, and Steven stopped for a while and looked out at the Elizabeth Ocean stretching to the horizon. It was 20 minutes later when Chispo and Chameur finally realized their three companions had purposefully stayed behind. They turned around and then hurriedly returned to them.

"Sorry, dudes," Chispo apologized, arriving with Chameur. "I guess the two of us got carried away."

"Oh yeah. We noticed," Steven told Chispo with a smile.

"Let's go back home," Chispo announced. "We've been out of the hair of those gurus long enough."

They walked back to Chispo's Velva Dibe, and he drove them back home along the north of the city by the coastal road, after which he turned left and drove the several kilometers to the southwestern region of Zantaayer, where they lived.

Upon arriving, Chispo drove up the Zapatero's driveway, and all of them stepped out of his car and walked inside.

"We're back, dudes!" Chispo called out to Rinto, Fraxino, and Tecoloteh. They walked back to the computer room.

"Chispo, where have you and Chameur been hiding?" Fraxino teased him.

"Aw, come on!" Chispo responded with a smile. "How are you supposed to know?"

"We notice those things, man," Fraxino replied. "After all, we're not total 100% gurus, you know."

"We've completed the data transfer from the plates," Rinto informed them. "We were just here looking at some of the plates until you guys would be returning." He switched off the controls. "Fraxino, we need to take this Ulexite cube to our cave in the mountains. It's very important to protect our backup data."

"Yeah, I agree," Fraxino told his brother, "but can't that wait until we get back from Alaska?"

"I want this important data safe and secured before we leave and take those crates to Alaska," Rinto insisted.

"Rinto, if you're worried about your backup crystal being in the same house with your computer," Chispo offered, "I can store that Ulexite cube over at my place for now."

Rinto thought for a moment. "Okay," he consented. "That's a good idea, Chispo."

Chispo picked it up, walked out of the house, and carried it across the backyards to his house where he stored it safely within his clothes wardrobe and out of sight. He returned to the Zapateros a few minutes later.

Rinto and Fraxino were already outside, checking over their Velosa cruiser craft. "Yep, it's good to go!" Rinto stated as he closed the hood. "Let's get the two crates loaded."

Between all eight of them, they picked up the heavy bronze crates, carried them out of Rinto and Fraxino's computer room, out the back door of the house, and loaded them into the vehicle-craft. They brought their backpacks and other supplies out of the house and loaded them also. With that, everyone climbed aboard.

"Oh, yeah!" Chispo suddenly realized, seeing his car parked behind the vehicle-craft. "Let me take my car home." He quickly stepped down, walked to his car, got in it, drove it around to the next street, and into his driveway. He quickly returned on foot through the backyards.

Once Chispo stepped on board, Fraxino started the engine, and he backed them out of the driveway and onto the street. Glecko and Sosta were away from the house on errands, or they would have seen them off to wish them well.

"It's back to Alaska, dudes!" Fraxino shouted enthusiastically as he placed the transmission in first gear and proceeded to drive away.

Rinto placed another holodisk of Zotolan pop music into the on-board player.

Fraxino quickly went through the gears and drove them along the road to the foot of the southwestern section of the Ciruclar Mountains. The pavement ended, and he drove them up the winding gravel road to the rim, arriving some 30 minutes later. Now along the forested rim road, he pulled back the lever, and the craft proceeded to leave the ground. He switched off the engine, and the craft swiftly accelerated, whizzing by Southern Beech trees and leaving them behind as it gained altitude.

Fraxino caused the craft to fly toward the west, and then he and Rinto sent the telepathic signal to the main controls crystal. The green glow briefly enveloped them, and then they were suddenly flying over the Arctic Ocean of Earth's polar region.

CHAPTER 8

THE EXOTIC PEACE KEEPING CRYSTAL

"There it is!" Rinto declared as he looked to the left and saw the north coast of northeastern Alaska. They were flying in a westerly direction over the Arctic Ocean, and it was clear, sunny weather. Alaska time, it was 5 AM, July 29, 1985.

Fraxino turned the craft toward the left, and they flew toward the three high mountains of Mt. Isto, Chamberlin, and Michelson, which were at present 100 kilometers away. Twenty minutes later, they arrived, and Fraxino flew the craft in for a landing, directly on the glacier near the tunnel entrance.

There was quite a pile of rock and rubble on the opposite side of the glacier, as Tom and Caymar's crew had been busy, excavating the big room. Their large spacecraft was still parked on the glacier, as well.

"Dudes, Tom and his crew don't waste any time!" Chispo declared, laughing.

"They've already made quite a pile of rocks, haven't they?" Robert commented.

"Okay, let's get these two crates unloaded," Rinto directed to everyone.

One of Tom's crew vehicles emerged from the ice tunnel, carrying another load of geometrically shaped laser cut rock. The Sirian vehicle (in more practical terms, a dump truck) stopped when the members saw Rinto and Fraxino's craft. They telepathically sent for Tom and Caymar, who were inside the project room at the moment. Tom sent a telepathic message to the crew to help them carry the two crates into the project room, as Quicho and Seglima were there, tending to their device-craft.

One would have thought they would have been asleep at this early hour, but since it never got dark at this time of year, they hadn't paid attention to the hours of the day.

The crew members drove over to Rinto and Fraxino, stepped out of their vehicle, and showed them the gesture of offering to carry the crates into the tunnel. Rinto understood, and they unloaded the two crates from the vehicle-craft and loaded them onto the bed of the Sirian vehicle. Once Rinto and Fraxino closed the doors to their vehicle-craft, all of them climbed onto the bed of the Sirian vehicle, and the crew drove them into the ice tunnel and through it to the project room.

Quicho and Seglima had been unaware of the sudden arrival of their friends. Then the Sirian vehicle stopped, and everyone stepped off the bed, unloading the two crates with them. The Sirian crew drove their vehicle further into the new tunnel they had created.

Quicho and Seglima emerged from the device-craft, now sensing something unusual. Smiles came across their faces when they saw their friends standing by the two crates.

"You've already returned!" Seglima happily declared.

"Are the crates all right?" Quicho quickly wanted to know.

"Everything is fine," Latorna quickly assured them.

"The contents are perfectly intact and well preserved," Chameur told them.

"Along with the data tablets and crystals," Tecoloteh added.

"Excellent! That is just excellent!" Seglima triumphantly declared.

By this time, the two of them had walked over to them and were enthusiastically shaking hands with all of them.

"Let's hurry and finally get these holographic plates loaded into the device-craft," Quicho urged them.

"And the data tablets and crystals, as well," Latorna added.

Immediately they carried the crates into the device-craft and set them on the floor inside.

"Tell me. How was it in Zotola?" Seglima wanted to know.

"It really is a beautiful place," Chameur answered her. "Their city of Zantaayer is nestled in among the beautiful Ciruclar Mountains . . . just out of this world, and the Noirtrel Alaktt (Southern Beech trees) have become so well established on their mountain slopes."

"The people and atmosphere have such a sense of peace there," Latorna informed them, "so much better than it was in Atlantis."

"The computer setup these two have," Tecoloteh told them and pointing at Rinto and Fraxino, "and the way they could read the holographic plates' data is remarkable, to say the least."

"Let me tell you something else amazing," Chameur brought up. "That Fluorite peace keeping crystal has been found and returned to Earth."

Quicho and Seglima both gave looks of total surprise.

"You don't mean it!" Quicho remarked.

"The one that was stolen 2,500 years ago?" Seglima asked.

"Exactly," Chameur answered.

"But how?" Seglima asked excitedly. "How and where?"

"Tom knew about it," Tecoloteh now explained. "He sent these two," pointing at Robert and Steven, "and their friends more than a month ago to search for it, and they found it high up on a mountain on a planet in the Pleiades."

Quicho and Seglima gave them confused looks, and Rinto, Fraxino, and Chispo explained the whole story in detail, about how Robert, Steven, and their friends found the crystal high up in the mountains of Aleyone in the Pleiades and then took it to Earth, and they told them the piece was now resting high up on a ledge on the eastern side of Mt. Timpanogos in Utah.

A few moments of silence passed after they finished telling the remarkable story.

"Let's go!" Seglima proposed enthusiastically.

"That's our next visit," Rinto told her.

"Quicho, close up the device-craft," Seglima directed.

"Don't forget the green quartz interpreter recorder," Tecoloteh reminded Quicho. "We'll certainly want to record the peace keeping qualities."

"Good thinking," Quicho acknowledged. He entered the device-craft, located the appropriate hand-sized crystal in one of the compartments, exited the device-craft, closed the door, and telepathically caused it to lock.

Next, they walked out of the tunnel and out onto the glacier. As the ten of them were climbing into Rinto and Fraxino's vehicle-craft, another Sirian vehicle was seen exiting the tunnel with another load of laser cut rock.

Once everyone was packed inside the craft, Rinto pulled back the lever, and they left the surface of the glacier. He caused the craft to swiftly accelerate as they flew over the cove and banked a turn to the left.

"Rinto, how far away is Utah?" Fraxino asked his brother.

"Almost as far away as Mexico, right?" Rinto answered.

"Dudes, I think it's around 5,000 kilometers from here," answered Chispo, who was sitting right next to Chameur.

"It's going to take us five hours at normal flying speed," Fraxino realized and told Rinto.

"Guys, we're going to enter the upper atmosphere and step up our speed to 2,500 kilometers per hour," Rinto announced to everyone. He repeated the same announcement to the five Atlanteans.

The craft turned upward and swiftly accelerated at a 15° angle, pressing everyone back in their seats. All of them felt the thrill of the acceleration, but Chispo and Chameur felt even more. For the way the seat was shaped, they were pressed closer to each other, and a special indescribable energy came over them and caused their feelings to turn on for each other. They had taken a liking to each other in the first place, and now it was definitely certain that Chispo and Chameur had a liking (or might they say *love*) for each other. If it was possible for them to have gotten closer to each other, they did. They put their arms over each other's shoulders and leaned their heads together, thoroughly enjoying the feelings of pleasure that flooded over them.

The other Atlanteans, and also Rinto and Fraxino, were immediately telepathically aware of Chispo and Chameur's experience. Robert and Steven took notice as well, as they were sitting in some seats behind them. Robert was somewhat surprised, because he remembered Chispo's comment the first day he had known him, the day he and his friends had first travelled to Artenia with Rinto and Fraxino.

"... the fun and adventure. When I'm ready to settle down, I'll find a girlfriend and maybe later marry, but that's going to be a while yet."

Robert could clearly hear Chispo's comment ringing within his mind. Famous last words. When the right female comes along, the time is then . . . no longer later.

Of the five Atlanteans, Chameur was the extra female without a partner, as the other four were, for all practical purposes, partners. Quicho and Seglima were very good friends and had stayed behind in Alaska while the others had gone to Zotola. Tecoloteh and Latorna were unannounced partners and enjoyed their time together. So, Chameur was open to finding a partner, and as far as she was concerned, she was no longer in search of one. Chispo fit the bill very well. Whenever she would look into his irresistible green-brown eyes, his eye contact was so genuine and *peaceful*, enough to put *anyone* at ease. He was alive and vibrant with plenty of spark and enthusiasm, and he had genuine character, as well. Not only that, he had the rare gift of being able to read crystals.

Rinto leveled out the craft after ten minutes of accelerating and climbing. They were now cruising in a southeasterly direction at 2,500 km/h and at an altitude of 30,000 meters. Though the sun shined, the sky was dark at this high altitude. They would reach Utah in two hours.

"You know," Rinto realized, talking to Quicho and Seglima, "we didn't even go look at what Tom's crew was excavating."

"They've made considerable progress," Seglima informed them.

"What are they going to do with that gargantuan pile of rocks and rubble?" Fraxino asked them.

"They were just going to leave it there," Quicho answered, "but at our suggestion and request, they're going to laser cut the stone blocks appropriately and build several buildings in the cove."

"After all, once the galactic station is open," Seglima pointed out, "high government officials are going to need a place to stay."

"Some of the stone is going home with the Sirians, as well," Quicho added.

"Good thinking," Fraxino approved, "because that amount of rubble could become dangerous, piled on the edge of that glacier."

"That's true," Seglima agreed. "We also advised Tom and his crew to excavate the big room in the shape of an interior pyramid . . ."

". . . and then line it with their strong resin material," Quicho finished for her.

"Weren't they planning that shape already?" Chispo now asked.

"No," Seglima answered. "They were going to make it cubical rectangular with appropriately placed ceiling supports."

"Tom thanked us for our superb ideas," Quicho told everyone, "and he wonders why he and his crew and the Galactic Federation hadn't planned it that way in the first place."

"The major design change is going against Galactic Federation mandate," Seglima explained. "So, Tom's not going to say anything until the excavating is finished. He sees no problem in the design change, seeing that the floor will maintain the same dimensions, in addition to the major improvement by the deletion of the vertical ceiling supports."

"Which would have been dangerous, anyway," Quicho added, "seeing that crew vehicles could have run into them, possibly knocking them over."

"So, what did you all do in Zotola?" Seglima wanted to know.

"We went and saw that movie, *Vision from the Ciruclar*," Rinto replied. "Fraxino and I copied all the holographic plate data into our crystal base computer system because we want to write an accurate history book on Atlantis, its heritage and culture."

"Excellent and noble idea," Seglima told them. "For what those holographic plates don't say, we can tell you a lot, as well."

"Cool!" Rinto responded.

"I carried Chameur, Latorna, Robert, and Steven to central Zantaayer," Chispo told Seglima and Quicho. "We saw the central library, the university, and took a walk on the beach."

"When they returned," Rinto continued, "we loaded the two crates into our craft and came straight to Alaska."

"And now we're here," said Fraxino.

"So, how did you guys communicate so well with Tom and his crew?" Chispo asked Quicho and Seglima.

"Verbal language didn't do us any good," Seglima answered, "since we don't speak Sirian, but visual image telepathy worked like a charm, just like we thought it would."

"We Atlanteans are used to communicating with visual image telepathy and metaphorical symbols, as well," Chameur told Chispo. "It was our way of life because there were other races living in Atlantis who either didn't speak the same language or didn't have the same characteristics of speech like we humans do. Visual image telepathy is universal among everyone."

"We do have a decent amount of telepathy intact," Rinto told them, "but it sounds like you Atlanteans are much more skilled at it than we are."

"Most Artenians have very little of the art left," Chispo explained. "It's gotten away from most of us over the millenniums, since our ancestors settled our world from Atlantis. We're actually rare among our people."

"Especially for what we've done with crystals," Fraxino added.

"Tell us," Rinto asked. "Was Atlantis, or as we know it now, Antarctica, the only civilized continent on Earth then, or were there others?"

"We were the main center of world trade and commerce," Latorna answered. "We also had galactic trade with various other races, therefore our major use for telepathy."

"There was also a newer settlement up in the northern hemisphere," Tecoloteh informed them, "most of which became flooded, following the world disaster. Some of them stayed behind and settled remaining lands in the mountains both west and east of there. They used our levitation technology to build the pyramids as a means of safeguarding what they knew and had, in hopes that if there were another disaster, contents and technology might survive."

"Where did you get your levitation technology?" Fraxino wanted to know.

"Oh, that's an ancient art that was brought to us eons ago from another world," Chameur answered. "The land of Mu was an older continent on Earth that sank some 20,000 years earlier, and they knew the art, as well."

"Those pyramids were built to help those who stayed behind to re-establish their bearings," Tecoloteh continued. "Latitudes and longitudes had suddenly changed all over the world, in addition to changed altitudes for the nonuniformity of the Earth's mantle under the crust."

"Did they build a duplicate set on Mars?" Chispo thought to ask.

"Yes, they did," Tecoloteh answered. "In case there had been a major wipeout on Earth, at least there would be some record of the technology in our solar system."

"Our friend, Morris, who revived you," Chispo told them, "was suspecting your civilization had done that."

"Yes, our friend Cresma made sure of that," said Tecoloteh. "That was part of the deal he made, that a duplicate set of records be made and deposited on Mars."

"There were some more records hidden in the high mountain tunnels and caves of the continent due north of Atlantis," Seglima told them, "in addition to stories recorded on cave walls in Atlantis itself."

"Like what we saw and read in that ice cave in Antarctica," Fraxino said.

"Exactly," Seglima confirmed. "Those were written by Atlanteans right after the disaster."

"Yep, that's the story we . . ." Fraxino began.

They continued talking about Atlantis and told each other various stories. Chispo, Rinto and Fraxino translated what they were talking about to Robert and Steven, who added comments and speculation, as well.

Rinto flew them over the Canadian Rockies, western Montana, Yellowstone National Park, and slowed the speed of the craft, lowering its altitude as he veered right and flew over the High Uinta Mountains of northeast Utah. Robert and Steven knew where Mt. Timpanogos was. They guided Rinto and Fraxino.

"There it is. I see it," Steven announced and pointed in the distance.

"It's the last mountain before that big valley beyond it," Robert informed them. "That big lake to the right and off in the distance is Great Salt Lake."

Rinto looked ahead and slowed the speed of the craft even more. They had just cleared the High Uinta range and were now quickly approaching the eastern slopes of the mountain.

"You see that high alpine meadow this side of the summit?" Steven asked Rinto.

"Yeah," he answered.

"Okay, we need to land on one of the ledges on the side of that cliff just beyond the meadow."

"Dudes, that's going to be tight," Fraxino remarked.

"Oh, don't worry," Steven assured them. "There's room to touch down and land."

In a few more minutes, they reached the alpine meadow. Rinto caused the craft to hover.

"Move over closer to those cliff ledges," Robert directed. "Steven and I have got to remember which one it is."

Rinto did as directed, and the craft now hovered by the cliff, slowly moving north while Robert and Steven were looking. This eastern face of Mt. Timpanogos was an enormous cliff, and there were several narrow ledges at different levels, most of them with Fir trees growing on them. They were entirely inaccessible, short of using technical climbing gear and ropes.

"There it is!" Robert suddenly declared. "Rinto, steer the craft down there to the left, and touch down on this end of that ledge."

Rinto gently steered the craft as directed, and in less than a minute, the craft had touched down on the soft moist dirt on a ledge towering some 200 meters above the level of the alpine meadow east of them. This particular ledge was the most inaccessible of them all, and it was 150 meters long. It was narrow, as all of them were, its widest point being 7 meters. Some clumps of Fir trees, some of them full size, grew in selected areas along the ledge. Shrubs, grasses, and moss grew on the soil, which in places was up to a meter deep.

The sun was well up in the southeastern sky. It was 10 AM, July 29, 1985.

All of them stepped out of the craft. Some of them looked over the edge.

"Wow, man!" Chispo declared, laughing. "This ledge is way on up here!"

"Man, you're not kidding!" Fraxino agreed, as he carefully looked over the edge.

"Anyone falling off this ledge is a goner! That's for sure!" Rinto told everyone.

"So, where's the exotic peace keeping crystal?" Chispo asked Robert.

"It's up at the other end."

They had landed on the southern end of the ledge, and all of them carefully made their way north along the narrow ledge, easing their way around the copses of Fir trees as they went. When they got themselves around the last group of Firs, they were at the northern end of the long ledge.

"Good, it's still there," Robert called out to everyone.

The exotic peace keeping crystal was still sitting on the top of the cool moist dirt, just like they had left it last month. It was egg shaped, colored green, and measured 25 centimeters from end to end, and it had a pyramidal shaped piece of Citrine ingeniously grown within it. The five Archaeopteris tree seedlings they had brought with them from the Pleiades were also still there, alive and well, where they had planted them.

"Oh, cool!" Chispo declared upon seeing the crystal.

"Radical!" is all Fraxino could say.

They walked over to it. Tecoloteh reached over and placed his hand on it. It gave out a glow of forest green, which surprised him.

"It's capable of self illumination!" Rinto told his brother.

"Now, that is far-out!" Chispo exclaimed.

Chameur was the next one to place her hand on it. Warm energies reached her, verifying who it was. "This is indeed the long lost Fluorite peace keeping crystal," she told everyone.

As Seglima looked on, she said, "It matches the description of what our historical documents from Atlantis had told us."

"As well as the image documents," Tecoloteh added, "especially with that piece of pyramidal shaped Citrine grown within it."

"We had also heard legends that it was capable of self illumination," Latorna told everyone, "but I had never believed that . . . until now!"

Quicho pulled out of his pocket the piece of green interpreter recorder crystal he had brought with him, and he held it in front of him. The exotic Fluorite egg glowed forest green, and upon Quicho's telepathic request, transferred the necessary peace keeping feelings and energy systems to his crystal. It quickly became warm in his hand. A minute later, the exotic Fluorite egg finished glowing, data transfer complete. He quietly placed the crystal back in his pocket.

"This is an extra added bonus for instilling the peace keeping qualities to our device-craft and our project," Chameur happily told everyone.

"We are more than grateful to you for finding it and bringing it back to Earth," Seglima told them, looking at Robert and Steven.

Chispo translated their conversation.

Robert explained to them that they enjoyed the search. "We were exploring the mountains of a large oceanic island in the southern hemisphere of planet Aleyone in the Pleiades. It was quite a puzzle, and we were given hints, oddly enough, by a group of Archaeopteris trees growing by a spring in a high alpine meadow."

"With *trees*?" Rinto asked.

"Yeah, they made telepathic contact with some of us and gave us clues," answered Robert.

"I tell you, we searched those mountains for days!" Steven boasted.

"I was one of the ones who actually found it on a ledge similar to this one," Robert told them. "Since Archaeopteris trees grew on that ledge instead of Fir trees, like here, we decided to bring some seedlings with the exotic crystal and plant them around it."

"Cool!" Chispo responded.

"Radical, impressive story!" Fraxino had to declare.

Chameur looked at the seedlings. They had already grown several centimeters since last month, and they showed promise at growing to maturity. "These are very interesting trees indeed. They come from an ancient race." She continued to examine the fan-shaped clusters of leaves on the seedlings. The leaves were mostly green with a tinge of yellow and had grey-silver lines on their undersides, and they had resemblance to the Ginkgo leaf.

"Chispo," Robert decided to tell him, "tell her and the others this species of tree grew here on Earth over 345 million years ago but has since then been extinct on this world. Early alien visitors to this world took it to the Pleiades with them."

"Dudes, Robert says . . ." and Chispo told the story to the Atlanteans in Artenian.

"Chispo, tell Robert and his friend," Chameur explained, "that planting these five Archaeopteris seedlings around this crystal was superbly done, a very wise move indeed, because these trees' life giving properties will help weave the energy matrix of the peace giving qualities transmitted by this exotic Fluorite crystal. In the future, mankind will rediscover this tree, and it will later be realized with equal regard as the Ginkgo."

Chispo told both Robert and Steven, and they were impressed.

"Fraxino," Rinto told him, "run back to our craft and dig out a piece of orange Calcite and another piece of our green Kanágran. This I *definitely* want to record for our Atlantis history project."

"No problem, dude!" Fraxino dashed back to the craft parked at the southern end of the ridge, located the appropriate crystals in one of their on-board compartments, and returned in five minutes.

The others meanwhile were still observing the exotic crystal and also looking at the impressive scenery all around them, the alpine meadow way below them, and the glacier feeding a small lake to its north.

"Back in Atlantis," Chameur explained, "we called this tree the *Irquiarluz*, which means *accepted by all*." She looked at the seedlings again and then faced the others. "There's a story behind this tree and why it was brought to Earth."

"Really? Tell us," Chispo urged.

"Way off, on the frontiers of the next galaxy, 120,000 light years away, there's a star called Plenidi. One of its planets, Tuepeic, was dying of volcanic eruptions and toxic gases. That was 370 million years ago. Since the Archaeopteris trees were becoming extinct on their home world, Tuepeic, ten varieties of them were rescued from there and brought to Earth as a temporary world to regenerate them and multiply their numbers. Over the next 25 million years while Tuepeic recovered, Archaeopteris trees flourished across Earth's surface, being the first trees to give shade. At which time their home world was fully recovered, a massive teleportation exercise was carried out, and every single Archaeopteris tree was removed from Earth's surface and returned back home. They vanished from Earth's surface literally overnight."

"How did they manage to get every single one?" Rinto wanted to know.

"You'd think they would have missed a few," Chispo pointed out.

"The intelligent extraterrestrials who were responsible for the moving operation used a telepathic genetic recognition device. Each tree had a certain genetic code, which when given the proper signal, would activate and cause each tree to teleport itself to its home world of origin."

"Smart thinking," Chispo remarked. "By that method, they would have caught every one of them, but how did they get them all replanted back on their home world again?"

"Seems they would have all piled up, bunched together," Rinto added.

"Good question," Chameur replied. "Some of that did occur, but there was a large crew awaiting their arrival, and massive replanting procedures were carried out in 250 different parts of Tuepeic."

"Oh, okay," said Rinto, "and why didn't they leave some of them here on Earth?"

"It would have been incompatible for the animal life destined to evolve on this world, but Archaeopteris trees still exist on Tuepeic today, in addition to their existence in 25 other star systems, and of course, now these five here on this ledge."

"That's good to know," said Rinto.

By this time, Fraxino returned from the vehicle-craft and handed the crystals to Rinto, who then pointed the long and narrow piece of Kanágran toward the exotic crystal and held the orange fist-sized Calcite to its end. Rinto caused the crystal to achieve the right telepathic frequencies of communication, and the exotic crystal glowed a forest green again. The data was successfully copied, channeled through the Kanágran, and recorded into the orange Calcite. At the completion of the data transfer, the exotic crystal ceased to glow.

"Golly!" Rinto suddenly exclaimed. "This Calcite's become hot!" He quickly set it down on the cool moist dirt so it would cool off.

"We also had that happen with some of our crystals," Steven told Rinto, "when in association with that exotic one."

"Wonder why that is?" Rinto asked everyone.

"That crystal was known throughout Atlantis to be very powerful," Tecoloteh informed everyone. "According to history, it was a gift from the extraterrestrials and was grown with some very unique qualities and instilled with remarkable intelligence."

"It does not surprise us that it glows and causes other crystal to become hot," Latorna added.

"You fellows chose an excellent location for this crystal," Chameur commended them. "It's out of harm's way here and will serve for peace on this planet for all time."

"It's amazing it's lasted so long," Quicho remarked.

"With its remarkable intelligence," Chispo mentioned, "it probably has a self refresher program instilled within it."

"That's true, Chispo," Chameur confirmed with a smile. "Our Atlantean ancestors knew how to grow that trait within crystals, so they would self refresh from time to time, restoring the imperfections on their outer surface. How did you think of that?"

"The two transmitter crystals we encountered in Mexico had that trait," Chispo answered her. "There wasn't a blemish on them. They were in perfect condition, like this one."

"Our device-craft is grown with the same self-refresher preservation intelligence," Latorna told them.

"It's a good thing we included that," Seglima told everyone. "It was Latorna who had suggested it when they grew its body."

"I'm glad we included it, too," Tecoloteh told them, "or it would never have lasted so well through 12,500 years."

"If everyone's ready, let's go back to Alaska," Rinto proposed.

"Right, it's time," Seglima agreed.

"What an excellent gift this Earth has, to have this wonderful peace keeping crystal on its surface again," Chameur happily declared. She and the other Atlanteans took one last look at it, marvelling its features.

They walked back along the narrow ledge, making their way around the copses of Fir trees, and boarded the craft. Once everyone was inside and seated, Rinto pulled back the lever, and the craft silently left the ledge.

"Absolutely beautiful area, isn't it?" Rinto commented to his brother.

"Excellent!" Fraxino responded.

Rinto steered the craft to the right and slowly flew along the side of the ledge as the others took one more glimpse. Then the craft turned upward and swiftly accelerated to the north, clearing the summit of Mt. Timpanogos in a period of 30 seconds.

Rinto looked in his rearview mirror and noticed that Chispo and Chameur were sitting by each other again. A mischievous smile came across his face. "Let's see how close you two get *this* time!" he cheerfully shouted, and he caused the craft to accelerate at full force, laying everyone back in their seats!

Chispo and Chameur fell into each other as a result, and everyone laughed heartily at Rinto's remark. Though Chispo and Chameur said nothing of it, they had indeed felt enormous pleasure.

In short order, they were thousands of meters above the land. Salt Lake could be seen way below them to their left. Again, the craft achieved a speed of 2,500 km/h and a cruising altitude of 30,000 meters. They flew back across the Montana Rockies, the Canadian Rockies, and back to northeastern Alaska, arriving at 10 AM, Alaska time, July 29, 1985.

Rinto brought the craft in for a landing, touching down on the glacier somewhat away from the tunnel entrance and out of the way of the large spacecraft.

Tom was outside at the time of their arrival, and he came over to greet them. Quicho and Seglima were the first ones to step outside, followed by Chispo and Chameur and then the others.

"Man, we've got some stories to tell you!" Chispo spoke to Tom.

"Really? How did everything go?"

"We brought the two bronze crates of plates and data tablets from Zotola," Robert told Tom.

"They finally have them with their device-craft," said Steven, telling Tom the Atlanteans finally have their crates back.

"We've just been to the high ledges of Mt. Timpanogos in Utah," Fraxino informed Tom.

"And we saw that impressive Fluorite egg-shaped crystal," Rinto added.

"Oh, yes. The one that Robert, Morris, and their friends retrieved from Aleyone, right?" Tom responded.

"Exactly!" Rinto verified.

"Man, it knows how to glow!" Chispo stated enthusiastically.

"That particular crystal is remarkable," Tom agreed. "It was very special to this world in the times of Atlantis, and since our Galactic Federation historical records made mention of it being stolen from Atlantis over 15,000 years ago, I sent them on that treasure hunt looking for it, since they were visiting planet Aleyone, anyway."

"Cool!" Fraxino remarked.

"For its peace keeping qualities it was known for," Tom explained, "and for this world's present need for peace, I deemed it important that it be found and returned to this world."

Chispo translated Tom's comments to the Atlanteans.

"Very noble of your friend, Tom," Seglima told Chispo. "Tell him we say thank you." At the same time, Seglima telepathically transmitted her appreciation to Tom.

"We've recorded the peace keeping qualities of the crystal," Rinto told Tom, "as well as the Atlanteans, to install in the central programming of their device-craft."

Tom expressed his approval of that, and they walked into the ice tunnel. They also told Tom that some of the stories from the holographic plates talked about the Fluorite peace keeping crystal and that it had just dawned on them that it and the exotic crystal were one in the same.

"And Rinto and Fraxino and I are going to compile a complete history of Atlantis," Chispo told Tom.

"Accurate and true," Rinto added.

"You fellows have pulled a wealth of information to you," said Tom. "Any time you fellows want to look through our Galactic Federation historical records, you're welcome to, even though these five Atlanteans can probably give you more reliable information."

"Thank you, Tom," Fraxino sincerely told him.

"We'll probably take you up on that," Rinto told Tom, "if nothing else, to make comparisons."

"Man, we'll have to check them out," Chispo also said to Tom.

They finished walking through the ice tunnel, and they next walked through the cave corridor. A Sirian crew vehicle drove by them, carrying another load of laser cut rock outside to the glacier.

Upon reaching the device-craft, Tom said he'd talk to them later, and he walked on further to continue supervising the excavating. Meanwhile Chameur telepathically unlocked the door of the device-craft, and they entered.

The others watched as Quicho placed the green recorder/interpreter crystal on what would best be described as a scanning tray. A forcefield was seen to arrive from below. It glowed yellowish-green, and over a period of 30 seconds, all of the recorded peace keeping qualities were telepathically transferred to their central computer crystal to be integrated within the already existing programs, for their intelligence to be used accordingly. The glow ceased.

"There," said Quicho. "The data is already absorbed." He took the green crystal off the tray and placed it back in its compartment.

"Anyway," Seglima announced, "our next project is to finally program the central computer crystal with our data tablets and the numerous stories from our holographic plates."

"It's going to take us something like two days," Quicho added, "barring any complications."

"We have to program it in a certain sequence," Seglima informed everyone, "and we have to be aware of the whole process with no distractions to accomplish the task."

"In addition to the telepathic monitoring required," Quicho told them.

Chispo translated Seglima and Quicho's plans to the others.

Quicho and Seglima were the experts who were more aware of and familiar with the programming procedures than Latorna, Tecoloteh, and Chameur. They knew the programming procedure only required two people. While Latorna was also decently familiar with the programming procedures, she was more the leader of the whole project, and her area of expertise had been organizing the project in all respects. Tecoloteh had been of immense help in gathering necessary materials, including programming the special compartment of crystals. Chameur had been the expert in compiling the stories onto the holographic plates, including feelings and peace giving qualities, not to mention, her beyond-the-norm spiritual attributes.

Chameur smiled, looked into Chispo's green-brown eyes, and said, "Want to go do something while Quicho and Seglima are busy *programming*?"

Feelings of excitement suddenly flashed through him. "Yeah, sure," he came around to reply. Thoughts of going to Caloma raced through his mind.

"Is there any help you guys might need with the programming?" Fraxino offered.

"Not any more that we can think of," Latorna answered, "and we are very grateful for what you've already supplied us."

About that time, Tom and Caymar walked into the project room from their excavating further within the mountain.

"What's going on, Tom and Caymar?" Fraxino greeted them.

"We've come to talk about further plans with our project," Caymar announced.

"While we've made plans for the procurement of the switching equipment to be installed within the big room," Tom explained, "we are in need of a considerable quantity of in-line fiber Ulexite, of pure quality, and seeing that you have some of it in use in your cruiser craft, we would like to obtain some from the same source."

"About how much of it are you thinking?" Fraxino asked Tom.

"Twenty cubic meters."

"Wow!" Rinto exclaimed.

"All in one piece or several pieces?" Fraxino asked.

"All one piece with the dimensions of one by four by five meters," Tom answered.

"Dudes, that's gargantuan!" Fraxino remarked.

"We need it to channel the millions of telephone lines to our sending and receiving crystals," Tom explained, "which, as with our earlier project this year, will be sending and receiving, utilizing gravity waves."

"Tom, I want to ask you something," Robert brought up.

"Yes, what?"

"Here in Alaska, it's so remote from civilization. How are you going to get the millions of phone numbers, to be made available, moved up here?"

"That's a very good question," Tom replied. "Why do you think the Alaska pipeline was built a decade ago in the 1970's?"

"To bring oil south to the 48 states," Robert answered.

Tom smiled. "That was just the *front,* you might say. The media never mentioned this because it was top secret information, but when they laid that pipeline down, they also laid down a massive bundle of fiberoptic cables to bring the lines up here."

"In addition to that," Caymar now explained, "satellites will be used, as well."

"You will see over the next 15 years," Tom continued, "that numerous cell telephone towers will be installed in many locations in your country nationwide, as well as in other countries. While those towers will send and receive phone calls locally, they will also be *secretly* used as a means of literally beaming, via satellite and fiberoptic cables, any available blocks of phone numbers worldwide to our switching station to be dialable and usable by any *being* throughout the galaxy."

"Man, that's brilliant!" Chispo declared, and he laughed.

"So *that's* how it's going to work," Robert realized and commented.

"That is amazing!" Steven commented, laughing. "It never crossed my mind that the Alaska pipeline would serve any other purpose."

"In the literal sense," Tom pointed out, "that pipeline was totally unnecessary. Oil tankers and tractor trailer rigs can carry any amount of that oil down south, but it had to be built to serve the Galactic Federation needs for this project."

"You know," Robert admitted, "I always thought it was ridiculous that they built that pipeline, anyway. My parents and I agreed that it was a waste of money. Now that I know its real reason for being built, it's finally making some sense to me."

"There are reasons for everything," Caymar told everyone, smiling.

"Even though they may be top secret," Tom concluded.

Meanwhile, Chispo translated their conversation to the Atlanteans. They had a good laugh at the secret tactics that were used to keep the truth away from the public eye. Everyone realized that Earth's government had gone to a lot of extra expense to lay down that oil pipeline, while if they had just been truthful and straightforward with the general public, they could have dug the long trench and simply laid down the bundle of fiberoptic cables.

"Four meters wide," Fraxino commented, referring to the proposed slab of Ulexite. "That's going to be a tight fit through this tunnel."

"Yes, but the tunnel is wide enough," Tom assured him. "We made sure of that."

"I figured the Galactic Federation would have had everything ready to supply," Steven told Tom and Caymar.

"They do," Tom admitted, "and we have access to Ulexite via galactic trade, but when I saw your main controls crystal," now looking at Rinto and Fraxino, "in your cruiser craft, I realized that it is of much purer form than what we can obtain from our suppliers."

"Where did you obtain such excellent Ulexite?" Caymar asked them.

"There is a major Ulexite mine near the south coast of our region," Rinto answered.

"Southern Zotola, that is," Fraxino clarified.

"Would our crew and I be able to obtain some of it from that mine?" Tom asked.

"Sure, man," Fraxino replied. "They sell the material by the cubic meter."

"Around how much does it cost?" Caymar asked.

"It's moderately priced," Fraxino told them, "reasonable, but it would only be payable in Zotolan currency."

"I would have thought so," said Tom. "I'll have a word with the federation and see if the appropriate currency can be obtained." Suddenly, he silently vanished.

"Oh!" Rinto reacted.

"Man, where did he go?" Fraxino wanted to know.

"It's like he said," Steven answered. "He went to have a word with the Galactic Federation."

Still, Rinto and Fraxino were surprised. They weren't used to seeing people teleport away, even though it was second nature to Tom, Caymar, and their crew from Sirius B.

Chispo and Chameur began talking to each other. "I've got family and relatives up in Caloma," he told her. "They live in the upper reaches of a city called Zwever, surrounded by some cool mountains. We can go up in there and . . ."

"Maybe we can find a Quanac flower," Chameur told him.

"With pleasure," Chispo told her, smiling.

While Chispo and Chameur continued making plans, Rinto and Fraxino talked about returning to Zotola to help Tom obtain that slab of Ulexite.

"Yeah, we'll just make our appearance over the Zuehl Sea and fly north to the mine in the canyon near the south coast," Rinto told his brother.

"You think they sell slabs that large?" Fraxino asked his brother.

"Good point," said Rinto. "Tom and his crew may have to excavate it themselves with their laser cutters."

"Probably will," Fraxino agreed.

"You don't think it's going to scare the people at the mine to meet Tom and his crew?" Rinto asked his brother with concern.

"Man, I don't know. We certainly can't pick it up for him, not with our cruiser craft."

"And it's too wide to legally go down our roads," Rinto pointed out.

Meanwhile, Robert, Steven, and the other Atlanteans were thinking about what to do next. Quicho and Seglima entered their device-craft and began to make preparations for the programming. Latorna and Tecoloteh talked with Chispo and Chameur about the possibilities of visiting more of Zotola for the next two days, to stay out of Quicho and Seglima's hair.

Suddenly, Tom appeared in front of everyone in the project room, slightly startling some of them.

"You're already back!" Steven declared.

"Where did you disappear to?" Rinto asked Tom.

"I just visited the Galactic Federation, and yes, they have supplied me with some Artenian currency from Zotola. Their bank vault had just gotten it in. From the equivalent conversion rates, and value per cubic meter of federation participating suppliers of Ulexite, I have brought you 1,200 Zotolan zúbolas, of your currency." Tom handed Fraxino the money.

"That will definitely cover it, and some to spare," Fraxino assured Tom, as he accepted the money from him.

"Very good," said Tom.

"If you all are ready," Caymar proposed, "let's go look at the mine."

Rinto and Fraxino agreed to it. For the time being, Tom and Caymar would leave their crew to their excavating and accompany Rinto and Fraxino to the mine to view the Ulexite and make plans on how to quarry it and bring it to Alaska. Chispo and Chameur had their plans made to go visit Caloma, and Latorna and Tecoloteh decided to accompany Rinto and Fraxino also, for nothing better to do.

"Tom," Robert asked him, "what more do you need me and my friends to do?" referring to Steven and possibly others back in Tennessee.

"I can't think of any projects for you fellows, right now," Tom replied, admitting the situation. "Perhaps you want to enjoy some adventure?"

Robert hesitated to speak.

"Tom, what about Chris and Richard Bell?" Steven brought up. "They have that thousand line step office from Kingston Park, Georgia."

"You mean on the Planet of the Islands?" Tom asked.

"Of course," Steven answered. "Is it going to be tied into this station here?"

"Yes, that block of numbers is definitely in our plans," Tom replied. "It will be our main access to that planet and star system."

"Good," said Steven.

"I haven't had a chance to let Chris and Richard know about it," Tom admitted. "If you two want to go and let Chris and Richard know about it . . . Other than that, enjoy some free time, because there's nothing pertinent for you to be of assistance here, right now."

While both Robert and Steven could have felt a little put off, they didn't. After all, they'd been of plenty help earlier this year, especially with the building of the original galactic communications device, built on the farm where Robert lived in middle Tennessee. They appreciated Tom on several counts, that he granted them the gift of transport by thought, in addition to the two Galactic Federation payments for past projects successfully completed.

"Rinto, what if Steven and I come with you all?" Robert asked him.

"Well, we'd be glad to take you guys, but we're going to be kinda busy securing that piece of Ulexite."

Robert looked at Chispo.

"No hard feelings, dudes," Chispo said, "but Chameur and I are going to make for Caloma, to visit relatives and the mountains." He showed a gesture implying that he and Chameur wanted to be together . . . by themselves.

"Yes, I understand," Robert said to Chispo. "You two want to be alone."

"That's right," Chispo admitted.

What had suddenly happened? both Robert and Steven thought, concerning their friends. If they didn't feel put off by Tom, they did this time, by their new friends from Zotola.

"Why don't we accompany you to see the mine?" Robert asked.

"Robert," Rinto flatly replied, "we've got to concentrate on the task at hand."

"After we get that Ulexite brought back here," Fraxino added, "we'll have time to show you guys around some more of Zotola."

"Well thanks, Fraxino," Robert told him.

"About how long do you think?" Steven wanted to know.

"Give us three or four days," Fraxino answered, "and you can transport yourselves to our house. We'll do some more exploring and travelling around."

"All right. Sounds good," said Steven.

"Cool!" Fraxino agreed.

"Don't worry," Chispo assured them. "We'll do some more things."

"Okay," said Robert.

Fraxino and Chispo's comments made Robert and Steven feel better.

While Quicho and Seglima stayed with the device-craft in the project room, the rest of them walked out of the tunnel and out onto the glacier. Tom, Caymar, Latorna, Tecoloteh, Chispo, Chameur, Rinto and Fraxino entered the vehicle-craft. Robert and Steven briefly entered, retrieved their backpacks from the craft, and stepped down again.

"See you around, dudes," Chispo called out to Robert and Steven, now standing on the glacier.

"Later on," Fraxino also called out.

They waved as Rinto closed the door. It was a strange feeling, watching their friends take off and leave. The craft silently left the glacier and with the greatest of ease, swiftly accelerated and sailed over the western ridge of Mt. Isto.

"Steven, what are you thinking?" Robert asked him.

"I just want to know one thing?"

"Yeah, what?" Robert asked.

"Why did they carry Latorna and Tecoloteh with them?"

"Good question," Robert answered. He thought a moment. "Oh, I know."

"What?"

"Rinto and Fraxino's history project," Robert stated. "They need them for that."

"Yes! Of course!" Steven realized. "That makes sense. You know, when you think about it, we didn't really contribute that much to Rinto and Fraxino, anyway."

"Except for my knowledge and Andrew's knowledge of Spanish," Robert brought up.

"But then Chispo learned that anyway, straight from Rudy, as we know," Steven pointed out.

"Yeah, that's true," Robert admitted, "but we are the ones who knew where that exotic crystal was on Mt. Timpanogos."

"Now, on *that* one we did contribute!" Steven declared.

"That's right!" Robert agreed.

"Oh, so be it," Steven said with a smile. "At least they took us with them for the past month. It's time we went our separate ways for a while."

"I guess so," Robert admitted. "Want to go to Chris and Richard Bell's?"

"Sure, let's go tell them what's happening."

Both of them proceeded to bring on the energy of the pink glow and whirring wind, and in seconds, they transported themselves away to the Garnet star system, some 3,000 light years away.

CHAPTER 9

SEPARATE PROJECTS AND ADVENTURES

Robert and Steven made their appearance under a large Cypress-like tree in the grand arboretum owned by Chris and Richard Bell's family. It had been nearly two months since they had come here with their Tennessee friends and Tom.

They had briefly met Chris and Richard Bell, who were brothers appearing to be in their early 20's, when walking the Overland Track through Tasmania's Cradle Mountain-Lake St. Clair National Park. By chance, they had crossed paths with them again in the very north of England, and they got to talking about telephone exchanges.

Plans were talked over, and Tom had come into the picture and helped Chris and Richard teleport a recently disused thousand line step office from Kingston Park, Georgia to their residence on the Planet of the Islands. Chris and Richard were glad to receive it, to add to their collection of Earth memorabilia in their Earth museum. Tom had connected the exchange to the galactic communications device, as well.

"We made it, Steven!" Robert declared, looking at the different trees in the spectacular arboretum.

"We sure did," Steven agreed.

"I hope Chris and Richard are home," said Robert.

They started walking through the large arboretum. Chris and Richard's family had travelled all over the galaxy in past years and had collected many different tree species compatible with a temperate climate with normal amounts of rainfall. Earth's Sol system was certainly represented with its vast variety of temperate conifers and hardwoods. After ten minutes of walking, they reached the edge of the arboretum, where they now saw the large concrete block building, housing the Earth museum.

As they reached the door, Robert knocked on it.

No one answered.

Robert knocked again.

Still no answer.

Steven opened the door and called out, "Hey Chris, Richard! Are you here?"

An answer could be heard from the very back of the large building.

The former Kingston Park step office stood there before Robert and Steven. Clicking and clacking sounds from the Strowger switches could be heard as calls were connected and disconnected.

In around a minute's time, a person walked into the step office room where Robert and Steven were waiting. It was Richard.

"Oh, hey! How's it going?" Richard happily greeted them.

"We've really had some adventures since we've seen you," Steven replied. "How about you?"

"We're doing fine," Richard answered.

About that time, Chris walked into the room. "Well, look who's here! How are you?"

"Doing fine, Chris," Robert answered. "What about you?"

"We're fine," Chris answered. "Good to see you all."

"Where are the rest of you?" Richard asked Robert and Steven.

"They went their separate ways," Steven replied.

"Some of them just got tired of it and returned home," Robert told Chris and Richard.

"James fell in love with an alien in the Pleiades," Steven informed them with a smile.

"Suzanne is her name," Robert added.

"And Morris comes and goes to and from the dolphin world," said Steven.

"Paul had to go home and help his father with his cabinet business," said Robert.

"Andrew stayed with a *chica* in Mexico," said Steven.

Chris and Richard laughed, and Richard came around to say, "Say the others cut and ran on you, did they?"

"Right," Robert answered.

"But you both stayed with it and are still travelling?" Chris asked them.

"Yep, we've got a month left," said Robert.

"So, what all have you done? Where have you been?" Richard asked.

"After we came here, we went to Sirius B, Vega, and the Pleiades," Robert began.

"That took nearly a month," Steven told them.

"Tom came to us and told us about an exotic peace keeping crystal that was stolen from Atlantis and was hidden in the Pleiades," said Robert.

"And we went searching for it and found it," said Steven, "returned it to Earth, after which we went to Antarctica."

"One thing led to another, and we met these . . ." Robert continued, and he and Steven related all of their experiences about Rinto and Fraxino Zapatero and their neighbor, Chispo Colancha. They told them about the ice cave in Antarctica, the ancient galactic dump site, the Atascosa, Mexico, the transmitter devices, the communications block they had cleared, and Alaska.

". . . and most recently, we've been in northern Alaska helping Tom with a huge galactic switching station, which will have the equivalent of millions of Earth's telephone numbers, to be opened for use in the new millennium," Robert concluded.

"Wow!" Richard remarked. "You guys *have* had some adventures!"

"So, tell us," Steven asked. "What have you and Chris been doing?"

"We've been connecting customers from this world to our step office," Richard answered, "adding more items to our Earth museum, as well as travelling to different star systems in the galaxy, collecting trees for our arboretum."

"Really an impressive arboretum," Robert complimented.

"Thank you," said Chris. "We're glad our family was able to create such a museum of temperate climate trees from throughout the galaxy."

"You know what we found out about the Eucalypts?" Robert brought up.

"No, what?" Chris responded.

"They came from Delikadove, the world of the dolphins 35 million years ago, and arrived in what is today's Australia," said Robert.

"Did they really?" Richard remarked. He looked at his brother and said, "I always wondered if they were alien to Earth, indigenous to somewhere else."

"I remember feeling that when we were in Australia," said Chris. "They seemed like more recent arrivals, like they had come later, and from somewhere else."

"Come. Let's take a walk through the arboretum," Richard offered.

As they walked along, they talked for some time, catching each other up on their adventures. Robert also told them about the Tulip Poplars, that they originated from Vega's planet Xiawp. Steven told them about the Atascosa and his attraction for a young female named Lumela, Orolizo's sister.

Chris and Richard showed them their new additions of tree species, some of which looked very exotic. One was a close relative of the Tulip Poplar, and each leaf was literally a cluster of small Poplar-like leaflets. They called it the Poplar Reale. This version had been rescued from Vega and brought here from another star system. It had never been taken to Earth.

"Chris, do you have any Archaeopteris trees, like what used to grow on Earth over 300 million years ago?" Robert wanted to know.

"Yes, we do," he answered. "Follow me."

They turned right as Chris and Richard led them to a different area of the arboretum, and they arrived at a small grove of magnificent Archaeopteris trees that produced a canopy over the forest floor. At a glance, they resembled Baldcypress trees. Their trunks were free of branches for some 20 meters in height, with only the upper third of each tree having branches.

"Wow! You do have them," Robert commented. "Where did you get these trees from?"

"Our grandfather obtained these when he was a boy," Chris replied. "We think he got them from the Pleiades."

"Same planet where we saw them, then," said Robert.

They continued looking at the arboretum. Robert and Steven told them more about the galactic switching station and the Galactic Federation's plans.

"Anyway, Steven told them, "we came here to tell you that Tom wants to connect your step office to the galactic station."

"Really?" Chris responded.

"Take us there," Richard requested. "Let's go see it."

"Okay," said Robert.

Robert and Steven each directed Chris and Richard to stand in front of them, and putting their hands on either side of them, they brought on the energy of the pink glow and whirring wind.

*   *   *

The craft made its appearance over the Zuehl Sea, heading north to the south coast of Zotola. Rinto was driving. Al Nitak had just set in the western sky, and it was still twilight. He slowed the speed of the craft as the south coast came into view. By the time they reached the coast and came in for a landing on the coastal highway, it became dark.

"Back in Zotola!" Rinto shouted as they touched down on the highway. He started the engine, shifted the transmission into 4th gear, engaged the clutch, and drove them west.

"Isn't the mine around ten kilometers west of here?" Rinto asked his brother.

"If I remember right, it is?" Fraxino answered.

"Good, let's hope it's still open," said Rinto. "Sometimes, they're still open after it gets dark."

Rinto continued driving them west along the narrow two-lane highway, and five minutes later, they arrived at the road to Milvilona Canyon. They turned right and drove up the winding gravel road, which climbed steeply into the canyon, leaving the coast behind. Three kilometers later they arrived at the entrance to Milvilona Ulexite Mine, as it would best be known in English.

A man was just closing the gate to the entrance, the workers having already left and gone home. He saw Rinto and Fraxino's vehicle-craft as Rinto drove it up beside him. Rinto rolled down the window and spoke to the man, telling him they had come to purchase a large slab of Ulexite with the dimensions of 1 by 4 by 5 meters, a total of 20 cubic meters.

"That's a mighty big chunk of that stuff," the man answered in Artenian.

"We have a special need for it, sir," Fraxino explained.

"I . . . just don't know if we can cut a piece that large," the man informed them. "Our tools are not set up for it."

"Yes, we were afraid that might be the case," Fraxino told the man.

"In addition to the legal restrictions of nothing being wider than three and a half meters to go down the roads and highways," the man pointed out.

"What if we bring our own cutting equipment and airlift the piece out of here?" Rinto asked.

"What do you want with such a big piece, anyway, fellows?" the man inquired.

"It's for a special communications project," Fraxino answered.

"Can we quarry the piece ourselves?" Rinto repeated.

"Not supposed to. It's against policy regulations," he answered.

"Can we talk this over and see if we can come to some arrangement?" Rinto asked.

The man was the owner of the mine, and he frowned at Rinto and Fraxino's persistence. "Fellows, it's against the rules."

Without saying a word, Fraxino handed Rinto the stack of Zotolan currency, and Rinto showed the man the money.

"1,200 zúbolas if you'll sell it to us," Rinto offered with a smile.

The man's interest perked up, as that was more than double what it was worth. Rinto and Fraxino sensed the man's willingness changing in their favor.

"Tell you what," he directed them. "Drive on inside the gate so I can close it, and we'll talk this over."

"Right," said Rinto, and he drove the vehicle-craft through the open gate. The man's vehicle was parked on the roadside just outside the gate. He walked to his vehicle, got inside of it, and also drove through the gate, closing it behind him. As he continued driving up the road, he motioned them to follow him to the site of the mine. Rinto and Fraxino followed him the kilometer to the open pit mine, which for all practical purposes, was a quarry. The man pulled his vehicle up to the edge of the quarry and parked so that his headlights shined across it. Rinto parked the vehicle-craft beside his, and everyone stepped outside.

"My name's Rinto, and this is my brother, Fraxino," as they introduced themselves to the man.

"Ocotiyo," the man told them. "Pleased to meet you fellows." He paused for a moment. "Wait a minute. You two look a little familiar. Have you two been here before?"

"Yes, we have," Rinto answered.

"We came two years ago and bought some Ulexite from you," Fraxino reminded Ocotiyo.

"Oh, yeah," he recalled. "You fellows were going to do a cruiser craft project, right?"

"That's right," Fraxino answered.

"I remember you fellows now," Ocotiyo told them. "Is this the vehicle you installed the Ulexite cube into?"

"It is indeed," Rinto proudly answered.

"Want to see it?" Fraxino offered.

"Yes, certainly," Ocotiyo answered.

He followed Rinto and Fraxino and stepped on board their vehicle-craft. They showed him the Ulexite cube, the main controls crystal, along with the crystal array situated underneath it.

"Very impressive setup you fellows have here," Ocotiyo complimented them. "I'm glad to see that some of the Ulexite from our mine is being put to good use."

"Yeah, we're proud to have it," Fraxino stated.

"So, who have you brought with you?" Ocotiyo asked, changing the subject.

"This is our friend, Chispo," Rinto began, as he introduced him. "Uh . . . the other five . . ."

"Sir, we don't want you to panic," Fraxino now spoke.

"Put it this way . . ." Chispo interjected. "We have a special use for that large slab of Ulexite."

"So, I gather the other five with you are from other worlds, right?" Ocotiyo asked them in a straightforward manner.

"Uh . . . yes," Rinto answered timidly. "How'd you guess?"

"Hey! Not a problem," Ocotiyo quickly assured them. "Why didn't you tell me straight up?"

"You mean you're not going to freak out?" Rinto asked, gaining a little confidence.

"Not at all," Ocotiyo answered.

"Okay, here goes," Fraxino began. "This is Tom, who's a galactic salesman with the Galactic Federation. He's from Sirius B."

"And this is his friend, Caymar, also from Sirius B," said Rinto.

Chispo translated to Tom and Caymar as they shook hands with Ocotiyo.

"This is Chameur, who is straight from Atlantis on planet Earth," Chispo informed Ocotiyo, and he also introduced Latorna and Tecoloteh. "They speak Atlantean, which is nearly identical to our language Artenian."

"From Atlantis, eh?" Ocotiyo reacted with enthusiasm rising, and he shook hands with them.

"That's right," Chispo confirmed. "We just found them last week and revived them. They were time frozen."

"Well, glory be!" Ocotiyo remarked. "Listen, let me tell you. Two or three times a year, I have strange people coming in here wanting Ulexite . . . supposed to aid in astral travel, space communication, and that sort of thing."

"Really?" Rinto responded.

"People like us, right?" Fraxino asked.

"Exactly," Ocotiyo answered with a smile. "So, how do you propose quarrying that large piece of Ulexite out of here?"

"Tom has a crew of more than 20 Sirians and a large spacecraft," Rinto answered.

"And they have laser cutters and the rest of it," Fraxino added.

"Come on down here and take a look," Ocotiyo directed.

They followed him into the open pit quarry, and with flashlights, they shined their beams onto the off-white fibrous rock.

"This is far superior to what Galactic Federation suppliers can offer us," Tom declared.

"That's true," Caymar admitted.

"We'll buy the slab here," Tom told Rinto and Fraxino.

"Yeah, he says he will buy a slab," Rinto now told Ocotiyo, translating what Tom said.

"Very good," he approved. "When are you planning to quarry it, tonight?"

"If that's okay with you?" Fraxino checked.

"Yes, it will need to be tonight," Ocotiyo directed. "Tell your friend Tom to bring his crew in here tonight, quarry the slab they need, and be out of here by 4 AM, because that's when my next group of workers arrive."

Rinto translated to Tom and Caymar what Ocotiyo said.

"I will telepathically notify my crew in Alaska to come here within the hour," said Tom.

Rinto told Ocotiyo who said, "That will be fine, fellows. My main concern is to keep quiet about this. Anything out of the ordinary, especially extraterrestrial visits, hits the newspapers like wildfire, and soon it's all over town with people freaking out. Then I've got reporters and the media all down my throat. I've got to be very careful."

"Oh, yes. We understand," Rinto assured him.

Fraxino told Tom and Caymar about Ocotiyo's concern.

"Tell him we'll be as quiet and subtle as possible," Tom said to Fraxino.

With that, Tom directed Rinto to hand the money to Ocotiyo in payment for the Ulexite slab.

Ocotiyo happily accepted the money. He put his finger over his lips, gesturing to everyone to keep quiet about what they were going to do, as carelessness could result in mass hysteria. They walked back out of the quarry and returned to their vehicles.

Both Tom and Caymar then telepathically sent a message to their crew, presently at the major project in Alaska, directing some of them to come to the Milvilona Ulexite Mine in southern Zotola, and to bring their large spacecraft with their laser cutters on board. He telepathically transmitted a clear visual image of the mine.

"They're on their way," Tom then told everyone.

"Just like that?" Chispo asked.

"You mean you're not teleporting yourself to Alaska to tell them?" Rinto asked.

"No, it's not necessary," Tom explained. "They're already exiting the ice tunnel and loading the spacecraft right now."

"Anyway, fellows," Ocotiyo announced, "I better leave and go home before my wife and children become worried and suspect something unusual. Go ahead and get the piece you need and be as subtle and quiet as you can. Lock the gate on your way out."

"We will," Rinto assured him.

"Take care and all the best with your project," Ocotiyo told them. He shook hands with Tom, Rinto and Fraxino, waved to the others, got into his vehicle, and drove away.

Meanwhile, Tom and Caymar were awaiting the appearance of their large spacecraft. Rinto and Fraxino were talking to Chispo, Chameur, and the other two Atlanteans.

Suddenly, the craft silently appeared in the air around 50 meters above the quarry. It floated over to where Rinto and Fraxino had parked their vehicle-craft and settled down for a landing by touching down on the gravel parking area. For the huge size of the spacecraft, there was almost not enough room for it to park.

Immediately, the back hatch opened. Tom and Caymar walked over to direct the crew as they drove several vehicles equipped with laser cutters down the ramp. Tom rode with one of the crew, Caymar with another, and they directed them into the quarry and showed them the appropriate location to make the laser cuts.

The crew immediately went to work, making the appropriate slices. They made a horizontal slice right across the top of the chosen slab to be extracted. With that

done, the non-uniform surface was removed. Next, they made the four appropriate vertical slices, two of them 4 meters long, and two of them 5 meters long, and all of them 1 meter deep. To make the horizontal slice along the entire bottom of the slab in order to sever it from the quarry, they used a special laser drill and drilled a vertical hole 7 centimeters in diameter, 1.1 meters deep, and slightly offset from one of the slab's corners. Next, they inserted a cylindrical laser cutter into the hole and did a 90° sweeping horizontal laser cut, adjusting the depth of the cut throughout the sweep from 4 to 6.4 to 5 meters, such that the area of the cut produced a perfect 4 by 5 meter rectangle, when viewed from above.

With that, the slab was entirely severed from the quarry, and with telepathic levitation skills, the crew caused the slab to rise upward and literally float over to the spacecraft where it entered its back hatch, followed by one of the crew members. The rest of the crew soon followed, and they drove their vehicles back to the spacecraft, up the ramp into the back hatch, and the door closed.

"That's excellent!" Tom declared. "Rinto, Fraxino, Chispo, thank you three very much for referring us to this site so that we could obtain such a fine slab of Ulexite."

"Not a problem," said Rinto.

"We're glad to have been of help," Fraxino told Tom.

"Glad we talked Ocotiyo into it," Rinto added.

"Where are all of you going now?" Tom asked them.

"We're going back home," Rinto answered.

"Listen, Caymar and I are going to return with my crew to oversee the safe arrival of the Ulexite, and then we'll pop over to your house to talk to you about another project I want to interface with our galactic station."

"When will you be arriving home?" Caymar asked them.

"In about three hours," Rinto answered.

"What's the project about?" Fraxino asked Tom and Caymar.

"It's to do with soul travel and telepathic communication, to be channeled through the phone lines," Tom answered.

"Among other services of Galactic Federation motives," Caymar added.

Rinto and Fraxino's faces showed looks of curiosity.

"Caymar and I will explain the rest to you later tonight," Tom told them. "Our crew is awaiting us."

"We'll see you in a few hours," said Caymar.

He and Caymar shook hands with them and silently vanished, teleporting themselves into the spacecraft, which then proceeded to leave the ground silently. It floated north over the quarry, and when it attained an altitude of 50 meters, it suddenly vanished.

"I guess they'll be reaching Alaska in a few seconds," Rinto commented.

"Dudes, let's go home," Fraxino announced.

They climbed back into their Velosa cruiser craft, and Fraxino drove them out of the quarry. They stopped at the entrance where Rinto stepped outside and opened the gate. After Fraxino drove through, Rinto closed the gate, locked it, and climbed back into the vehicle-craft. Fraxino drove them down the steep, winding gravel road, returning to the coastal highway.

Meanwhile, Chispo was telling Chameur, Latorna, and Tecoloteh what they had discussed with Tom and Caymar.

When they reached the coastal highway, they turned right and headed west. Fraxino quickly went through the gears, accelerating rapidly, and when they attained highway speed, he pulled back the lever and switched off the engine. They became airborne. The craft swiftly accelerated and made a turn toward the north, climbing rapidly in altitude. They would reach Zantaayer in just under three hours.

"What was it Tom just said?" Rinto asked his brother.

"Something to do with channeling soul travel and telepathy into the phone lines, didn't he say?" Fraxino responded.

"Dudes, they're probably going to use a section of that Ulexite slab for just that," Chispo speculated.

"I'd say you're right," Rinto agreed.

"We'll find out in a few hours," said Fraxino.

"How did you guys use Ulexite in Atlantis?" Rinto asked Chameur, Latorna and Tecoloteh.

"We had various means for it," Chameur answered. "Astral travel is its main feature, and it's an excellent choice made by Tom, Caymar, and their crew."

"If they want to interface telepathy and soul travel with their phone lines," Latorna now said, "we can certainly be of assistance."

"To the point of telepathic visual imagery," said Tecoloteh.

"And more than that . . ." Chameur began.

They talked and speculated for some time as Fraxino flew them north across Zotola. The night sky was clear and filled with stars.

When they reached the southern rim of the Ciruclar Mountains, Fraxino brought the craft in for a landing on the main south highway at the point where it crested the mountainous ridge. He started the engine and proceeded to descend the forested slopes along the winding highway, complete with hairpin curves. The lights of the city could be seen through the Southern Beech trees and other trees.

"How beautiful the lights of the city are!" Latorna remarked. "It reminds us of one of our coastal cities back in Atlantis."

"Really?" Rinto responded. "What was it called?"

"Taltipocheh," she answered. "It sat west of us and on the northern coast of Atlantis."

"It was around 150 kilometers away," Tecoloteh told them, "was about the same size as Zantaayer, and was also nestled into the mountains, like here."

Twenty minutes later, they were pulling into the Zapatero's driveway. It was nearly midnight here in Zantaayer. Glecko and Sosta had already gone to bed for the night. Everyone stepped down from the vehicle-craft. A cool breeze was blowing from the north. Rinto and Fraxino walked toward the back door.

"Man, I don't know about you guys," Chispo announced, "but Chameur and I are going up north to Caloma for a few days."

"Excellent!" Fraxino told him.

"Enjoy your *honeymoon*," Rinto jokingly told him with a smile.

Chispo gave him a smirk for that comment, and then they laughed.

"Anyway, see you around guys," Chispo told them.

"Later on, dude," said Fraxino.

Chispo and Chameur walked across the backyard, through the row of tall bushes, and through the Colancha's backyard to his house.

Rinto and Fraxino entered the house, followed by Latorna and Tecoloteh.

"Wonder what Chispo and Chameur are *really* going to do up in Caloma?" Rinto asked Fraxino.

"Oh, who *knows*," Fraxino responded, laughing. "Wonder when Tom and Caymar are coming."

*   *   *

Meanwhile, Tom, Caymar, and their crew safely arrived in the large spacecraft and touched down on the glacier of Mt. Isto in Alaska. The back hatch of the craft opened, and the crew drove their vehicles off the ramp, followed by the floating slab of Ulexite. They proceeded to enter the ice tunnel.

Tom and Caymar walked down the hatch ramp, talking with Dotsero, one of the crew leaders. Most of the crew had stayed in Alaska and were entering and leaving the tunnel with their vehicles loaded with laser cut rock. The arriving crew telepathically communicated to them to disoccupy the tunnel to allow the wide load to enter.

"You and your crew did excellent work, quarrying that slab of Ulexite," Tom commended.

"Thank you, Tomarius," Dotsero responded. "Where do you want the piece stored?"

"Let's store it next to the Atlantean craft," Tom directed. "After all, it could be in harm's way if stored in the big room."

"That's right." Dotsero sent telepathic instructions to the crew to carefully guide the slab of Ulexite through the tunnel and to make sure and place four square-shaped laser cut rocks under it before setting it down.

The crew acted accordingly, and as other members of the crew were presently laser cutting rocks in the big room, they cut four appropriate blocks and brought them to the Atlanteans' project room. The hovering slab of Ulexite cleared the sidewalls of the tunnel by only centimeters as they brought it in, and it was now hovering in the project room, waiting for them. They set the four blocks by the wall and out of the way of the line of traffic, and then the piece of Ulexite gently descended and came to rest upon the blocks. One of the crew went outside to the spacecraft for a large tarp, brought it back into the project room, and covered the Ulexite. It was resting very near the device-craft and was on the same side of the room. Upon later completion of the big pyramidal shaped room and with equipment installation, the Ulexite slab would be moved to its destined location to serve as part of the station's interfacing.

Tom, Caymar, and Dotsero had witnessed the events.

"Caymar, I can't tell you how glad I am to have obtained such a *fine piece* of Ulexite for this project," Tom declared with satisfaction.

"It's a superb specimen," Caymar agreed, "certainly better than any of our suppliers could have offered us."

"You got that right," Tom remarked.

Tom and Caymar walked with Dotsero through the next tunnel and into the big room to see how much excavating had been done.

"It's coming along nicely," Tom commended Dotsero.

"Looks like it's about 50% of the way completed," said Caymar.

"Continue the good work, Dotsero," Tom encouraged him.

"Thank you, Tomarius. We will." With that said, Dotsero walked on and resumed overseeing the crew.

"Okay, Caymar," Tom told him, "let's go tell our friends in Zantaayer our next proposal."

They turned around and walked out of the big room, through the tunnel, passed by the project room, and continued through the next tunnel and ice tunnel out onto the glacier.

"Tom, we still haven't installed the doors to safely secure what's inside," Caymar brought up.

"Oh, that's *right*," Tom admitted. "It slipped my mind. I have to constantly remember we're dealing with planet Earth here. Doors and locks are a way of life. Let's go back inside and tell Dotsero to go fetch the doors from our suppliers."

They re-entered the tunnel, walked to the big room, found Dotsero, and advised him. He rounded up four members of the crew, and together they walked out of the tunnel with Tom and Caymar.

Tom gave directions to Dotsero and the four crew members to take the spacecraft with them to fetch the doors and other equipment from one of the Galactic Federation warehouses. With that said, Dotsero and the others boarded the large spacecraft. It levitated upward and proceeded to fly to the north, cresting the summit of Mt. Isto on the way.

Tom and Caymar instantly teleported themselves to Zantaayer to talk to Rinto, Fraxino and the others. They arrived in the Zapatero's backyard. Rinto and Fraxino and the others were not there yet.

"You know what, Tom?" Caymar brought up.

"What?"

"Only two hours have gone by since we left them at the Ulexite mine. Didn't they say it would take them three hours to arrive here?"

"Yes, that's right," Tom recalled.

"Let's go do something for the next hour while we wait for them," Caymar proposed.

"Good idea. May as well," said Tom. "What do you want to do?"

"Let's see the rim of the mountains surrounding the city."

Instantly, Tom and Caymar disappeared from the Zapatero's backyard.

They made their appearance on the southwestern rim of the Ciruclar Mountains. The lights of Zantaayer could be clearly seen throughout the valley to their north and east.

"Remarkably clear air on this planet of Artenia, isn't it?" Tom said to Caymar. "Indeed it is."

They looked around them at the night sky and the Southern Beech tree forest. The gravel road running the ridge top was less than 100 meters away from where they had made their arrival.

"Come. Let's walk along the road through this beautiful forest," Caymar suggested.

"Sure," Tom agreed. "We've been nearly constantly on the go with this project. This will do us some good."

They began walking northeast, soon joining the road, and followed the winding road through the forest, enjoying the serene beauty, the clean mountain air, and the star-filled night sky. They talked over their further plans about the galactic station and what they would discuss with Rinto, Fraxino, and the Atlanteans.

"I tell you, that Morris is something else!" Tom commented. "I knew he had amazing talents from the time I first entered one of his dreams the early part of this year and offered him that quartz crystal sphere."

"Yes, he is remarkable," Caymar agreed. "I was really impressed how he and one of his dolphin friends managed to revive those five time frozen Atlanteans."

"I'm telling you. So was I," said Tom. "Now, think about it. How many people do you think could have done what Morris did?"

"Probably less than a handful."

"Very, very few," Tom declared. "Thanks to his abilities and his dolphin friends, we have five living people straight from Atlantis to assist us with our project. It really amazes me. I still can't get over it."

"We are very fortunate to know them," said Caymar.

They enjoyed their hour's walk through the Southern Beech forest along the rim of the mountains, after which they silently teleported themselves to the Zapatero's backyard.

* * *

"Wonder what Chispo and Chameur are *really* going to do up in Caloma?" Rinto had asked Fraxino.

"Oh, who *knows*," Fraxino had responded, laughing. "Wonder when Tom and Caymar are coming."

"I don't know. They said they'd be here about now." Rinto looked out into the backyard and witnessed Tom and Caymar making their silent and sudden appearance. "Oh, wow! They've just arrived!"

"Really?" Fraxino responded enthusiastically. He looked out into the backyard to see Tom and Caymar walking toward the back of the house. "Sure enough!"

He and Rinto walked out the door and greeted them.

"Hey! How's it going?" Fraxino greeted them.

"Timed it just about perfect, didn't you?" Rinto said to them.

"Well, actually we got here an hour ago," Tom admitted.

"We just took a walk for the past hour along the rim of the mountains," Caymar explained.

"Excellent views of the city at night, aren't they?" said Rinto.

"That they are indeed," Tom agreed.

About that time, Latorna and Tecoloteh walked up to them.

"So, what is the project of interfacing you have in mind?" Fraxino asked Tom and Caymar.

"Fellows, what we have in mind . . ." Tom began, and he paced back and forth in the backyard as he continued,". . . is to offer various services including the interfacing of soul travel experiences and telepathic communication through the phone lines. In addition to that, we want to interface these services through what are known as personal computers. By the new millennium, which is less than 15 years away, numerous people on Earth will obtain these instruments and will be able to access dialable services, many of which will be secretly connected to and routed through our galactic station.

"Many, many phone numbers are going to be used to accommodate this phase of our project, in addition to other uses throughout the galaxy, hot lines to government officials, among other secret connections to high ranking officers across planet Earth. There will be local servers stationed as well, and they will have connections to our station, as much of the information storage and retrieval will be routed through there."

"On your planet Earth," Caymar now told them, "there are intolerable amounts of intelligence suppression conspiracies occurring, all of them in efforts to prevent the human race of Earth from advancing to galactic levels of intelligence and awareness. These conspiracies need to be broken open and abolished."

"Amen," Fraxino agreed.

"How will that be done?" Rinto wanted to know.

"Galactic Federation motives," Tom answered, "are to build and create these dialable servers, which will come to be called the *Internet*, worldwide, to give the people of Earth better access to vast amounts of information of just about any subject area. We want to establish open galactic trade with planet Earth and abolish the secrecy that is prevalent in this day and time."

"Like Tom said," Caymar reminded them, "we want to interface soul travel experiences and telepathic communication through the phone lines, in addition to interfacing virtual time travel experiences, all as a means of boosting the consciousness of the people of Earth to an awakening to meet galactic level standards."

"Apart from virtual time travel being telepathically available over the phone lines," Tom further explained, "we want the galactic station to be so complete that for those who come and personally visit the station, they can enter various machines or devices, possibly your device-craft, for first hand experiences.

"In addition to Galactic Federation supplied holographic film, we need special storage crystals to be intelligently designed and grown, in addition to other crystal arrays, to successfully achieve our goals of interfacing as we've stated. Telepathic visual imagery, feelings, and virtual time travel experiences need to be converted through certain configurations of crystal arrays and matrices, to be chanelled through the 20-cubic-meter Ulexite slab and transmittable through Earth's telephone lines."

"And for those of Earth who lack telepathic skills," Caymar added, "their personal computers can therefore serve the same purpose."

"Rinto, Fraxino," Tom now told them, "for your remarkable and impressive abilities with crystals and the intelligence you know how to telepathically grow into them, the Galactic Federation has chosen you, in addition to our new Atlantean friends, to take on this project, grow the necessary crystals, and bring our goals and services of our galactic station to *reality*."

"Wow!" Rinto responded.

"That's a radical plan!" Fraxino remarked enthusiastically.

"100,000 Zotolan zúbolas is the Galactic Federation payment reward for a job well done," Tom offered.

Both Rinto and Fraxino's eyes opened wide in amazement.

"100,000 zúbolas?!"

"That's right," Tom verified.

"We'll do it!" Rinto happily agreed, extending his hand to Tom.

"Right on! We'll get right to it," Fraxino assured Tom and Caymar.

They shook hands.

"What about your two Atlantean friends, here?" Caymar now asked Rinto and Fraxino.

Over a period of five minutes, Fraxino translated the whole project proposal to Latorna and Tecoloteh, who showed considerable interest. Tom and Caymar saw their facial expressions as they reacted in a positive way.

"Yes, tell Tom and Caymar we know what to do," Tecoloteh advised Fraxino. "We'll be glad to contribute to the project and help grow the appropriate crystals to bring the station's services to reality."

Fraxino translated to Tom.

"Excellent," said Tom. "Caymar and I are now going to return to the station to tend to the excavating."

"If you have any questions," Caymar offered, "you know where to find us."

"By when do you need all of this?" Rinto wanted to know.

"As soon as possible," Tom answered, "but don't rush. Just be sure and do the job right."

"That we definitely will," Fraxino assured.

They shook hands again, and then Tom and Caymar instantly and silently disappeared from the backyard.

Rinto was somewhat taken aback and startled, still not being used to watching people appear and disappear so instantly.

"Still bothers you, doesn't it?" Fraxino said to his brother.

"Yes, it does," Rinto admitted. "I wish I could figure out how to do that myself."

"Me too."

"Let's go get some sleep," Rinto suggested.

The four of them walked inside the house and slept soundly.

The weather was crisp and cool the next morning with clear and sunny skies. A north breeze was blowing. Both Rinto and Fraxino got up early, energized on ideas on how to grow the crystals to achieve the project goals of the galactic station. They went to wake up Latorna and Tecoloteh, who had also dreamed of some ideas.

As the four of them walked into the kitchen to fix themselves some breakfast, Glecko and Sosta entered to do the same.

Rinto took a box of *Kellogg's* Bran Flakes Esperaña off the shelf. "Take a look at this, guys," he said to Tecoloteh and Latorna. "This is one of Earth's most recent arrivals."

"That's right," Glecko told them. "One of planet Earth's cereal companies, *Kellogg's*, has just broken into the market, here on Artenia."

"Minus the food additives, of course," Rinto added.

Tecoloteh and Latorna found the situation amusing and fixed themselves some of the exotic cereal, as well.

"So, fellows," Glecko brought up as they were munching away on the cereal, "what have you got in the plans, now?"

"Tom and his business partner, Caymar," Rinto answered, "have asked us to grow some intelligent crystals to adapt into their galactic station project in Alaska."

"That's excellent, sons. I know you guys can do it."

"They want us to interface virtual time travel, soul travel, and telepathic communication through the phone lines . . ." Rinto began.

"To boost the conscious levels of the people of Earth," Tecoloteh added.

"They're wanting to create a worldwide dialable service," Fraxino told his father, "to connect to the galactic station and also to many other star systems across the galaxy."

"Including this one, I presume?" Glecko added.

"I'm sure they will."

"They also need storage crystals to be grown," Rinto explained.

"And they want equipment built to accommodate personal visits," Latorna added.

"Perhaps our device-craft will serve part of that," said Tecoloteh.

"What did Caymar say about the worldwide dialable service?" Rinto asked his brother. "What are they going to call it?"

"The *Internet*, right?" Fraxino replied.

"*That's* right," Rinto recalled, "and Caymar told us there are intolerable amounts of intelligence suppression conspiracies going on around planet Earth."

"That's very true, sons," Glecko responded.

"Really, Dad? How do you know?" Rinto asked.

"Well, you know even the newspapers have mentioned it, in addition to other reports, documents and studies I've researched and read down at the central library. It really is atrocious some of the scandals and conspiracies our cousins on Earth get away with these days."

"Like what?" Fraxino asked his father.

"To start with, you already know about the scandal on food additives and preservatives in cereals and other Earth foods. Money was definitely slid under the table on that one, but I'll tell you a *real* shocker about money being slid under the table."

They gestured Glecko to continue.

"It's to do with Sodium Fluoride, which is a white powdery byproduct of aluminum production. When the production of aluminum on planet Earth went into full force over this past century, the manufacturers soon had a vast surplus of Sodium Fluoride, and they didn't know how to get rid of the stuff. Well, somebody got the bright idea . . . *drinking water*. Since some 40 Earth years ago, more and more of the city water suppliers have been adding small amounts of Sodium Fluoride to the drinking water. Worm gears meter the powdery compound into the water, and you know how it got approval and began?"

"No, how?" Rinto responded.

"A check for $50,000 was written to the dental association so they would promote Sodium Fluoride and say that it's good for preventing tooth cavities. While partly true, the long term effects of Sodium Fluoride are very bad. Case study reports have shown that intelligence is dulled because the regeneration of brain cells is inhibited, and the chemical synapses of nerve cell communication within the brain is also somewhat inhibited."

"Dad, that's a scandal sure enough!" Rinto declared.

"Yes it is, but that's corruption for you. As you may know," and he looked over at Latorna and Tecoloteh, "here on Artenia, when aluminum is made, its byproducts are flown *straight* to Al Nitak, therefore properly disposed of, but Earth's Sodium Fluoride scandal is only a moderate one compared to others."

"Such as what?" Fraxino asked.

"Such as nuclear power production and the high risk and dangers from that, not to mention possible harmful radiation exposure . . . and the element lead being added to Earth's fossil fuels for driving their automobiles and other vehicles . . . atrocious, that is. I tell you!"

"At least here on our world, we have hydrogen," said Rinto.

"And we can count our blessings on that one, sons," Glecko stated. "Earth's fuel companies *know* we can! Lead is extremely bad for living beings and is known for dulling intelligence, in addition to promoting chronic diseases because it accumulates within the body's tissues. It's a toxin which has no business *ever* being put into automobile fuels!"

"That really is appalling!" Tecoloteh declared. "We had no idea Earth's people would do anything so ridiculous!"

"They do," Rinto told Latorna and Tecoloteh.

"Special interest groups and other factions control a lot of Earth's scandals,"

Glecko went on, "and don't forget to consider that other star systems may be behind some of it, using Earth's people as test subjects for long term studies. Design your project crystals accordingly, and we'll make this galaxy a better place to live after all."

"Right on, Dad!" Fraxino declared.

"Dad, with the way we grow those crystals," said Rinto, "we'll have every one of those scandals squelched and abolished!"

"That's your intelligent genius at work, sons," their father commended them. "With your two friends from Atlantis, I'm sure you'll do fine work."

They continued talking and soon finished breakfast.

"Let's go up in the mountains and get started." Rinto told them.

"Do we need anything out of the attic?" Fraxino asked his brother.

In short order the four of them went up into the attic to sort through Rinto and Fraxino's rock and crystal collection. After half an hour up there, they came back down again, carrying three boxes full of rocks and other assortments, which they carried to the vehicle-craft.

Rinto opened the back door of the vehicle. There sat the extra piece of Ulexite. Chispo had brought it over several hours earlier.

"Oh, yeah," Rinto recalled. "I forgot all about that. Thank you, Chispo." He spoke those words and looked through the row of tall bushes toward his house.

"Good man, Chispo!" Fraxino commended. "Do we need any extra tools?"

"Yeah, some extra chemistry flasks, hammers, pulverizing tools, sulphuric acid, and . . ."

They rounded up the appropriate supplies, including some food. Once the four of them were inside the vehicle-craft, Rinto backed them out of the driveway, and they were off to their secret cave up in the Ciruclar Mountains!

CHAPTER 10

CHISPO AND CHAMEUR

Chispo and Chameur walked across the Zapatero's backyard, through the row of tall bushes, and through the Colancha's backyard to his house. They had plans of driving up to Caloma the next day. Chispo had plenty of relatives up there, and he was looking forward to visiting with them and introducing them to his new friend, Chameur, from Earth's Atlantis.

Chispo opened the back door to his house, and they walked in. His parents were gone as usual.

"Come on back," he offered Chameur. "Let's get some sleep. We've got a long day ahead of us tomorrow to reach Caloma."

They went straight to bed, and it wasn't long before the two of them fell sound asleep.

Both of them woke up around an hour before the crack of dawn. Chispo was the first one up, and he rounded up a few supplies and extra clothing for him and Chameur to take up north. He opened up his clothes wardrobe.

"Oh, yeah," he suddenly said. "The extra slab of Ulexite." He took it out of the wardrobe and looked at Chameur. "Wait up just a minute. I'm going to take this back over to Rinto and Fraxino."

As she was still in bed, she remained there while Chispo did the quick errand. He carried the Ulexite piece across the backyards, and since it was still dark, he opened the door to the vehicle-craft and set the piece on the back floorboard. "They'll be certain to find it there," he said to himself, and he returned to his house.

Chameur was now getting up, and they gathered the supplies they would need.

"Need any extra clothing?" he offered. She agreed that she would. He looked toward his parent's bedroom and started walking toward it. "You can come on in here and use some of Mom's clothing. I'm sure she won't mind. She and my dad are usually out on the road with their jobs, anyway."

He and Chameur walked in, and she picked out some appropriate clothing from Mrs. Colancha's closet and wardrobe. With that done, they carried their supplies out of the house and took them to Chispo's Velva Dibe car, parked in the driveway. It was just beginning to become light outside.

Chameur looked at the fine, smooth features of Chispo's car as he opened the trunk. "What an impressive cruising vehicle you have here."

"Thanks. I like it a lot, and does it ever *cruise*! It's got a lot of power and pep with the Richmond V-8 engine mounted under its front hood."

They placed their items in the back, and Chispo closed the trunk lid. "Good to go, Chameur. Let's cruise!" he declared in a cheerful manner.

She responded with a smile, admiring his cute and energetic mannerisms. She already knew she'd go anywhere with this guy.

They both climbed into the car. Chispo started the engine, and they backed out of the driveway. Once on the street, he enjoyed showing off by quickly accelerating and going through the gears with an unbeatable level of dexterity and expertise. He really enjoyed his Velva Dibe and enjoyed impressing his friends and passengers.

Chispo took Chameur on a route that ran along the north side of the city near the coast as they headed in an easterly direction. Al Nitak was now breaking the northeastern horizon, the direction of the coastline.

"Your city of Zantaayer is such a beautiful place, and the sunrise is beyond spectacular," Chameur told Chispo.

"Yeah, Zantaayer has a lot to offer," Chispo informed her. "It's one of the major port cities on our planet, Artenia. With a population of 120,000 people, it's one of the largest cities on the planet."

"It really does remind me of Taltipocheh, which was one of the major cities on the north coast of Atlantis."

"Zantaayer is where they make numerous products used throughout our world," Chispo explained, "including cars like this Velva Dibe and Rinto and Fraxino's Velosa cruiser craft, and also other types, such as their father's classic Tolejo, and the Skiivona. We have trade deals set up with various galactic member groups, although we keep low keyed about that one," he finished with a smile.

"I can sense that your world has a fine system of peace and trade," Chameur stated.

"We do," said Chispo. He looked down at the fuel gauge. It showed nearly empty. "Wow! I better get some more fuel." There was an Exxoll station another kilometer up the highway, near the northeastern edge of the city. When they reached it, Chispo pulled in.

"Golly! Price has gone up again!" he complained when he saw the price sign posted.

"Of the hydrogen fuel, you mean?" Chameur asked him.

"Yes, it's reached 12 duocibols per liter. Just last week it was 11.9, 11.8 before that, and it was only at that for a week."

"Such is life . . . Chispo."

"Yeah, I know. You're right. Just more inflation. That's all."

Chispo slowly shook his head, drove up to the pumps, and one of the attendants filled his hydrogen tank. He paid the man 9 zúbolas, and then drove away.

They were now on the open road, and they proceeded northeast along the highway which ran for some 100 kilometers along the coast before turning inland. They talked along the way.

An hour after leaving the Exxoll station, Chispo offered, "Want to pull over and take a walk along the beach? The highway is about to go inland."

"Yes, sure," Chameur happily consented, remembering their walk along the beach in Zantaayer the other day.

Chispo slowed the car down and turned left at the next available access to the beach, and he drove the several hundred meters to the sandy dunes. He and Chameur stepped out of the car, closed the doors, and the two of them walked north along the beach for some 20 minutes, enjoying the fresh and breezy sea air from the Elizabeth Ocean. No one else was on the beach at this early hour. The sounds of the waves breaking made a regular rhythm.

They joined hands along the way.

"This is really wonderful, Chispo."

"I really enjoy your company, Chameur. My life feels more complete when I'm with you."

They looked at each other, smiled, drew themselves to each other, and put their arms over each other's shoulders as they continued walking up the beach.

Later they returned to the car, and Chispo drove the whole day as they made their way north, entering Caloma by early afternoon. In Caloma, much of the terrain was green with plenty of farmland and wooded forests, not so desertlike as the inner regions of Zotola.

Along the way, they talked some more, swapped stories and tales, and Chispo also played some music from time to time in his on-board holodisk player.

"Did you all have music back on Atlantis?" Chispo wanted to know.

"Oh yes," Chameur answered. "We had a very fine selection of music down at the central library and music archives of Ennohoness, available through our central communication network throughout the country, in addition to many people having personal collections of their favorite pieces, as well."

"Really?"

"It wasn't too different from here, with your holodisks," she told him.

"Looks like some of the same technology got reinvented here, and . . ."

It took several more hours of driving to reach the Urlachia Mountains. Chispo maneuvered his car through the hairpin curves with the greatest of ease as they made the ascent through the forest and reached the high crest where he pulled over.

"Take a look straight ahead, Chameur," Chispo indicated. Al Nitak was just setting, and the lights of a city were visible way below them in the valley beyond. "That's the city of Zwever, situated in what's called the Vovvitlet Valley. If you look at that river running towards the northeast, that's the Vovvitlet River."

Chameur was really charmed by the serene beauty of the whole area.

"There's a trail that runs the whole crest of these mountains," Chispo continued. "It's called the Wyndham Way. When I brought my friends up here several weeks ago, we walked a section of it."

"This area is spectacular!" Chameur told Chispo. "I suddenly have a strong urge to take an evening walk through the forest up here." She looked at Chispo and gave him a flirtatious smile.

He looked at her inviting expression. Feelings of excitement ran through him. "Sure! Why not?" he replied. He happily opened the door and stepped out of his car.

Chameur did the same. They closed the doors and took off walking east along the trail.

Some high clouds were moving in from the southwest. A moderate cool breeze was blowing, and as Al Nitak set, the colors were truly out of this world, spectacular to say the least.

Both Chispo and Chameur felt energized to be walking together through this high mountain forest. Most of the trees along this crest were Firs and Spruces. Occasional birds could be seen flying overhead from tree to tree and making their calls.

"I really love it up here in Caloma," Chispo told Chameur. "This is my homeland. All of my Dad's family is from Zwever, down there below us," and he indicated. "I used to come up here a lot when I was a child. My parents used to bring me, but times changed. My parents became more busy with their ongoing projects and Caloma got away from them."

"When is the last time you came, aside from a few weeks ago with your friends?" Chameur asked him.

"It was when Grandma Colancha passed away. We drove up here for her service on a cold, snowy winter's weekend, right after the day of Cresma."

"How many years ago was that?"

"Let's see," Chispo answered and thought. "That was 10118. I was just a child then. Twelve years ago. Yeah, I just saw Cliss when I was up here a few weeks ago. He's my favorite cousin. He and I talked about the time when we and our other cousins went playing in the snow that weekend and went sledding down the mountain slopes at dangerous breakneck speeds . . . while our parents and older relatives attended to more *formal* matters. We had a blast! It was too much fun!" and he laughed.

Chameur laughed, gave Chispo a pleasing response, and they walked further down the trail. He continued telling tall tales and hair raising stories, all which gave her more laughs and charmed her even more. She was now realizing that she was falling in love, and she made absolutely no efforts to resist the forces from moving in that favorable direction.

Several of her years ago in Atlantis, she had a loving relationship with a fine young fellow of genuine character. He had been a lively, energetic person who had an ear for her and was really there with her whenever they talked. He was very similar to Chispo, and he even favored him in appearance, so much that Chameur at times had to remind herself that Chispo was a new man in her life, instead of her former lover, whose name was Qwintelo. He had met unfortunate circumstances and had lost his life while exploring the high reaches of the mountains near Taltipocheh.

There was something about the connection between Chameur and her new friend Chispo that caused her to feel energized and that much more glad to be with him. Chispo felt the special energy too, and it was such a soothing, peaceful sensation through him, the likes of which he had never known before, all of which made their relationship grow and take on a life of its own within them. Chameur realized Chispo's genuine character. He was really tuned in with her when they talked, and he showed concern and appreciation, as well.

While Chispo was right in the middle of telling another tall tale, Chameur placed her hand on his shoulder. He stopped right in the middle of his sentence and looked at her as she gazed at him with a look of genuine love and appreciation. Before he realized it, yearning feelings flashed through him and took hold, and with her inviting expression, he suddenly wrapped his arms around her and kissed her, followed by many more kisses of affection. She responded accordingly.

After a couple of minutes, Chispo got hold of himself, the yearning sensation gone, and they stood looking at each other, somewhat surprised at themselves.

". . . Sorry, I don't know what just came over me," Chispo came around to tell her.

"It's quite all right," she responded. "It's just what I wanted, and I thoroughly *enjoyed* it."

"Really?" Chispo responded, smiling.

"Mmm hmm . . ." she confirmed with a satisfied smile.

They wrapped their arms around each other and *kissed again*. After another minute, Chispo separated his mouth from hers enough to say, "Let's uhh . . ." kiss ". . . head back to my car . . ." kiss . . . kiss ". . . and drive on down to Zwever."

"Mmmm . . ." . . . kiss . . . kiss . . .

Later, they finally separated their mouths from each other, disembraced, and began the walk back to the highway.

It was Chispo's first time to have a serious relationship with a woman. While he had known and been casual friends with females as he was growing up, he had never known the likes of someone like *Chameur*, who was many levels beyond any other female he had *ever* known before. Being with her gave him such a sense of peace. He knew Chameur was the right female for him, because when the right person comes along, the friendship and connection are already there from the start.

By the time they reached the car parked at the crest, it had become dark. They got inside and Chispo drove them down the winding narrow highway, descending steeply through the forest. Half an hour later, they reached the valley and entered Zwever, Caloma.

"We're here, Chameur!" Chispo enthusiastically stated. "This is my homeland."

"A beautiful place indeed," she agreed. "How far are we from the ocean?"

"Around 400 kilometers, if you go due west from here. Zwever is more of a city of mountains. Even though right here we're at the base of the mountains, Zwever sits at an average of 1,650 meters above sea level. The highest mountains around the valley reach up to 3,700 or 3,800 meters in altitude. That's why it's a little cooler around here."

They were now heading toward Zwever's central district on the main boulevard, but still on the upper reaches of the city, Chispo turned right and drove on a street that climbed uphill for the last kilometer, arriving at the southern edge of the city at the base of the Urlachia Mountains.

His aunt Esalina lived in a house that had an excellent view of the Vovvitlet Valley, Zwever to the north, and of the surrounding mountains, some whose higher reaches were still covered with snow, even though it was summer. They reached the driveway to her house, and Chispo drove up its steep grade, arriving at the back of her house.

He and Chameur both stepped outside.

"Spectacular residence, your relatives have," she complimented.

"Yeah, my aunt really likes it up here in Zwever," Chispo responded, "and the mountains are right there, just a couple of blocks away."

"Let's go up in those mountains and explore tomorrow," Chameur proposed.

"Absolutely!" Chispo approved.

A woman opened the back door to the house and stepped outside to see who had just arrived.

"Hi, Aunt Esalina," Chispo called out to her.

"Well hi, Chispo! What a pleasant surprise! Come on inside."

Chispo and Chameur walked up to the door. "How are you?" Chispo asked.

"Very well, and you?" Esalina replied. They hugged each other. "You're back so soon."

"Oh yeah," Chispo agreed. "I wanted to . . . This is my friend, Chameur," as he introduced her. "She's from Earth's Atlantis."

"My, my! How exotic!" his aunt remarked. She now looked at Chameur and said, "Welcome to Zwever, Caloma. Do come on in and visit. Both of you bring your things inside and stay the night."

Chispo and Chameur went back to the car, grabbed their bags, and brought them inside. Esalina led the way as they walked to the living room at the front of the house, where they sat down on the sofas.

"Where are your friends, from last time?" Esalina wanted to know.

"We've all gone our separate ways," Chispo replied. "Some went to work on a major galactic station project down on Earth's Alaska, and others went home, tired of running around with us."

"What about that different friend of yours who you brought from . . . Mexico was it?"

"Oh, you mean Rudy?"

"Right."

"He put his backside to us and stayed in Mexico after we solved the problems there and cleared the communications block."

"How strange!" Esalina remarked.

"But now I have with me this wonderful young woman from Atlantis."

"Now *that* one is a mystery to me," Chispo's aunt admitted. "How did you meet her? Is she from the past?"

"Yes."

Esalina's mouth dropped open in surprise.

Chameur decided to pick up the conversation now. "Chispo and his friends are part of a big project in the northern mountains of Alaska. Five of us, including myself, had been working on a soul and time travel device in that area, back in the times of Atlantis, until we were apprehended and time frozen in five different crates." She related more of the story about how they were found by Tom and Caymar, how they were revived last week, and so surprised to find themselves 12,500 years into the future. She related the coincidence about the two crates, the holographic plates, the 3D movie, and more. ". . . but destiny must have had good reasons for what happened, as we soon realized, and from the moment I set eyes on Chispo, I knew he was the man for me."

"What a remarkable story!" Esalina declared. "Chispo, you and your friends have had some rich and exotic adventures, sure enough! I'm very pleased for you."

"Thank you, Aunt Esalina."

"My son, Cliss, rang up yesterday. He's really enjoying his research job over in eastern Caloma."

"Excellent," said Chispo. "Yeah, I remember he left here to begin that job right after my friends and I arrived here a few weeks ago."

"That's right."

"What's he researching?" Chispo wanted to know.

"Rare and exotic plants of the mountain forests," answered Esalina.

Chispo and Chameur looked at each other in surprise.

"Really?!" Chispo asked Esalina with sudden enthusiasm.

"That's right, and he says it's a really great adventure for him."

"Aunt Esalina, that is really far out!" Chispo told her. He now looked at Chameur again, and asked her, "Do you think he might know about the Quanac flower you're searching for?"

"For the ways and flows of destiny, he may very well," Chameur answered.

Esalina, having heard them, offered, "If you'd like to call him and see, I'm sure he'd be glad to hear from you."

"Yes, definitely," Chispo responded. "I'm always glad to speak to cousin Cliss."

"Come on in the kitchen. The phone's in there. I was just beginning to prepare some supper."

Chispo and Chameur walked into the kitchen with Esalina. She dialled up Cliss, soon reaching him, told him his cousin Chispo was here visiting again, and then handed the phone to him.

"Cliss?"

"Hey, how's it going, man?"

"Great! What's going on Cliss?"

"Back so soon?"

"Oh yeah," Chispo answered. "Couldn't stay away from here, man."

Cliss laughed at Chispo's comment and then asked, "Bring your friends back with you?"

"No, man, they stayed back on planet Earth. Rudy gave us the backside and stayed in Mexico, and the two gurus, Rinto and Fraxino, are busy on another project with some revived Atlanteans, growing crystals for use in a galactic station down on Earth's Alaska."

"Revived Atlanteans? Far out!" Cliss exclaimed.

"It's the truth, man. Listen, your mom says you're researching rare and exotic plants."

"That's right. I'm with a research team. We're studying and researching rare plants that came from Earth when Atlantean settlers came to this world."

"Far out! Let me tell you. One of the revived Atlanteans came here with me, and she and I are looking for a rare plant named Quanac."

"Yes, I *know* that one," Cliss told Chispo.

"Really? Cool!"

"It's a rare one . . . grows on wet banks only at sources of water, like springs, and always deep within the forest."

"Exactly! That's it!" Chispo confirmed. "Man, how far are you from here? Can we come and visit?"

"Yeah, sure! I'm 400 kilometers due east of Zwever. Take the highway straight through central Zwever, through the Vovvitlet Valley, and then take a right on the highway to the east. I'm staying in a small town call Echelosa." Cliss proceeded to give the details of the directions to reach the residence where he was living.

"Cool! We'll be there tomorrow," Chispo told him.

"Excellent! Look forward to seeing you."

They said goodbye, and Chispo hung up the phone.

Meanwhile, Esalina had begun supper.

"Did you say your cousin *knows* of the Quanac flower?" Chameur asked Chispo.

"He sure does."

"Amazing, the destiny of that!" Chameur happily exclaimed. "The pieces of the puzzle are really coming together easily!"

"I'll say," Chispo agreed.

Chispo and Chameur continued visiting with Esalina as she cooked supper, after which they ate in the dining room.

"You and Chameur might want to visit central Zwever and see the native crafts at the central markets on your way to Echelosa tomorrow."

"Oh, yes. We're planning on it," said Chispo.

They looked out the big dining room window and down at the lights of Zwever to the north. The combined glow of the lights reflected off the mountainsides, and they could see the faint glare of the white snow on the highest reaches and peaks.

Chispo and Chameur told more tales of their recent adventures. Esalina certainly was surprised when Chameur mentioned that she and the other four Atlanteans knew and were friends with Cresma Atenkor!

After visiting for some time, Esalina took them upstairs for the night.

"Good night," Chispo sincerely said to his aunt. "Thanks for having us,"

"It's a pleasure, and so nice to meet your friend, Chameur. Good night."

Esalina walked to her bedroom. Chispo and Chameur slept in the guest bedroom, and it wasn't long before they were sleeping together soundly.

Morning arrived nice and sunny. The temperature was somewhat cold. Birds were calling out their tunes outside the window and in the backyard. As Chispo and Chameur were waking up, they could hear Esalina walking downstairs.

A few minutes later, they got up and walked downstairs also. Esalina was in the kitchen preparing some breakfast. While Chameur remained in the kitchen, Chispo took their bags outside to his car.

"So, tell me," Esalina asked her. "How big was Atlantis?"

"The best I can tell, it was nearly the size of Zotola and Caloma combined. Atlantis was two large islands, and the southern island was much colder and icier. Few people lived there. I come from the more northern reaches of the north island where we had a mild temperate climate, until the disaster happened 10,130 of your years ago."

"And you say you actually knew Cresma?"

"Indeed I did. He was a personal friend and came from the same town I come from."

"That really is amazing!"

Chispo walked back inside. A few minutes later, Esalina served them some bowls of hot oatmeal. They looked out of the big window at the city of Zwever down below in the valley. Al Nitak's rays broke over the tops of the mountains to the right and reflected off the snow-capped mountains to the left. The morning sky was a clear turquoise green at the moment.

"You have a beautiful day for your trip to Echelosa," Esalina told them.

"So, we take a right on the Great Eastern Highway on the other side of Zwever, right?" Chispo asked.

"That's right," Esalina answered, "and just keep following it to the east. It will take you right there. You can't miss it because you'll reach a major range of mountains around 30 kilometers before reaching Echelosa."

They ate the rest of their breakfast, talking at the same time.

"Well, I guess we'll be cruising, Aunt Esalina."

"Right you are, Chispo. So good to see you again, and what a pleasure to meet your new friend, Chameur. I've really enjoyed the stories."

Esalina walked out into the backyard with them. Chispo hugged his aunt, and they said goodbye. Chispo and Chameur got into his car, and he backed out of the driveway onto the street below. Esalina waved at them as they drove away, and she walked back inside her house.

"You have a wonderful aunt," Chameur told Chispo.

"Yeah, she's a jewel. So, you want to visit the markets in central Zwever?"

"Sure."

He drove them back down the somewhat steep street, reaching the main boulevard again, where he turned right and drove into the city center.

Chispo parked his car on a side street, and he and Chameur walked the three blocks to the plaza where the markets were set up.

"What's the population of Zwever?" Chameur asked Chispo.

"I believe it's 65,000, around half the population of Zantaayer."

A few minutes later, they reached the markets. There were many types of native crafts for sale, including practical use items, as well. Chameur was intrigued by the uniqueness of the crafts, and she saw some similarities to what the markets used to sell back in the cities of Atlantis. Chispo bought her some of the native crafts to take back to Latorna and Tecoloteh, as well as Quicho and Seglima in Alaska.

They walked back to the car, and Chispo took the main boulevard north. At the edge of the city, the 4-lane boulevard narrowed just before reaching the left bank of the Vovvitlet River. Flowering Sun Trees now lined both sides of the 2-lane highway as it wound its way north along the riverside. Three kilometers later, the road made a sharp right and crossed the river on a narrow steel truss bridge.

Now on the eastern side of the river, they passed by open farmland in the fertile Vovvitlet Valley, arriving at the junction to the Great Eastern Highway ten kilometers later.

Chispo took a right, and he and Chameur headed to the east on the straight and narrow highway. They were now north of the eastern side of the Urlachia Mountains, and the scenery to the east appeared to be mostly flat as far as they could see. For the straightness of the highway, Chispo drove at 120 km/h, whizzing by opposing traffic with ease and passing slower vehicles where necessary.

He and Chameur listened to more music from Chispo's on-board holodisk player. It was an enjoyable morning's drive, and they talked and swapped stories, pleased to be in each other's company. Chispo's hair raising stories also gave Chameur plenty of laughs along the way.

A range of mountains came into view in the distant eastern horizon. They passed a small sign on the side of the highway, verifying that they were now in eastern Caloma.

After another half hour, they reached the foot of the mountains, known to those of eastern Caloma as the Talequa Mountains. Their slopes were well forested.

"Oh, wow!" Chispo commented, noticing the Southern Beech trees in the forest. "Nortralakt Trees . . . up here in Caloma."

"They really have become well established here on this world," Chameur stated.

"That's right," he agreed. Chispo now turned and spoke out the car's window. "And you didn't think Caloma had any *Nortralakt Trees*, Rinto and Fraxino!" and he laughed.

The highway left the green plains behind, rather abruptly entered the forested mountain slopes, and immediately began the climb to the plateau 1,000 meters above them. Chispo whizzed up the mountainous road, taking the hairpin curves with ease. There were plenty of other curves, as well, and half an hour later, they crested and entered the outstretching plateau, forested with Southern Beeches and various Pine trees. Every so often, they passed by beautiful grassy meadows, some of them with small lakes. Other meadows had springs and wetlands. Deer-like animals could sometimes be seen grazing.

Now the highway was a lot straighter, and Chispo resumed his cruising speed of 120 km/h. Thirty kilometers later, they entered the town of Echelosa, population 2,600. It looked much like a resort town. Most of the buildings were made of stone blocks, and some appeared like lodges.

"Cliss said he lives half a kilometer off the main highway on the right," Chispo said to Chameur. He slowed down as he drove into town and was looking for the appropriate street. "There it is!" he suddenly announced when he recognized the name of the street that Cliss had told him. He turned right, drove by several houses, and arrived at Cliss' residence, marked by a big Southern Beech tree in the front yard.

"This has gotta be it," said Chispo as he pulled into the driveway. "He said to be on the lookout for a big tree."

Beep-Beep. Chispo blew his horn.

It was now straight up noon, the middle of the day.

The side door to the house soon opened. "*There* he is," Chispo said with a smile as Cliss walked out of the house. Chispo and Chameur both stepped out of the car.

"How's it going, Chispo?" Cliss greeted him.

"What's going on, Cliss?"

"You guys made awesome time!" Cliss told him.

"120 kilometers per hour, man!"

"Wow! You *did* do some serious cruising."

They shook hands, glad to see each other.

"So, this is your friend from Atlantis?" Cliss asked Chispo as he looked at Chameur.

"Sure is. This is my friend, Chameur."

Cliss and Chameur greeted each other.

Cliss now looked at Chispo and smiled. "Really made a good *catch*, didn't you?"

Chispo returned a smile and simply commented, "Seriously."

Cliss showed Chispo a surprised and playful look, and then they both laughed.

"Come on inside," Cliss offered. "Bring your things in. I was just preparing some lunch."

Chispo and Chameur both took their bags out of the car, and they followed Cliss into the house. They continued following him into the kitchen area.

"So, you say your research work is going well?" Chispo asked Cliss.

"Oh yeah. It's going great, man! And you say you and Chameur are looking for some Quanac?"

"That's right."

"Well, as it turns out, I've got the afternoon off. After we eat some lunch, I'll take you to a place where some of it is growing."

"Excellent!" Chispo responded.

"Here, you and Chameur help yourselves to some lunch. Make yourselves some sandwiches, and help yourselves to whatever you find in the cupboard."

"Thanks, Cliss."

Chispo and Chameur helped themselves accordingly, and they sat down to eat lunch with Cliss in the adjoining room. They looked out the back window at the forest across the backyard. While they were eating, the three of them talked and visited. Chameur told Cliss some stories from Atlantis, most of which she had already told Chispo, Rinto and Fraxino, soon after their revival from their time frozen status. Cliss was very intrigued and was glad to find out about some of Atlantis' heritage.

"Have you got daypacks with you?" Cliss asked Chispo and Chameur, after they had finished lunch.

"Yeah, they're still out in my car," Chispo replied.

"You'll need them. The walk's going to take around five hours round trip. I'll get my daypack out of my room and meet you outside in a few minutes."

"All right, man."

Chispo and Chameur walked outside to the car and got their daypacks out of the trunk. They threw in some water, food, and extra clothing. When Cliss came outside a few minutes later, they started walking. They continued down the same street until it stopped nearly a kilometer later at a trailhead.

"This trail is called the Matilanga Way," Cliss informed Chispo and Chameur. "This whole region is called the Matilanga Plateau because of its relative flatness, Southern Beech and Pine forests, grassy meadows, wetlands, springs, water holes, and lakes."

They entered the trail and were now in the forest. Cliss continued talking. "We have a decent amount of rain here in eastern Caloma. Mosquitos were rampant when I arrived a few weeks ago, but now they've pretty much died out for the season. For the wetlands in this region, there are a variety of rare and exotic plants not found anywhere else on this planet of Artenia. One of them is the Quanac flower. The group I research with just took me and showed me a group of them last week. There's a sense of peace and strangeness to the plant, very rare to say the least."

"They only grew in selected areas in the forested sections of Atlantis," Chameur said to Cliss. "My friends and I don't know if any of it survived on Earth, but its main use was to calm upset stomachs."

"That's what one of our research leaders told us," said Cliss. "Where he knew that from, I don't know, but he's an eccentric man who studies ancient ways."

"People who are like that know *more* valuable information than they are given credit for," said Chameur.

"That's very true," Cliss agreed.

They walked for two hours through the beautiful forest. Some of the Southern Beech trees were very large, with trunks up to three meters in diameter. In some places, the forest was so thick that Al Nitak's rays hardly reached the ground. They passed grassy meadows from time to time and stopped to rest a couple of times at water holes.

Finally, they arrived at a partially forested, yellowish-green, grassy meadow with a calm and peaceful spring right at the meadow's edge. A few Southern Beech trees grew around the spring with the meadow being more open beyond. The water was nearly still as it emerged and gently flowed into the meadow, beginning its journey downstream.

As they left the trail and walked over to the spring, Cliss said, "This is where they grow."

The three of them soon reached the water's edge.

"Oh, how exquisite!" Chameur exclaimed as she saw the plants.

Along the water's edge grew an abundance of Quanac plants, between 30 and 40 of them. Each one was a stem with the dull, brownish-grey flower on it. None of them had blades or leaves.

"This is the most I have ever seen in one group," Chameur informed them, smiling. "Such an abundance here."

"Yes, we're glad our world has some," said Cliss.

"These are identical to the ones that used to grow in the forests of Atlantis," said Chameur. "Do you think these are of Earthly origin?"

"The research group leans heavily toward that idea," Cliss answered, "especially the eccentric man I was telling you about earlier."

Chameur and Chispo looked at the plants with interest. The view of the meadow from this vantage point was a magnificent scene of grandeur and peacefulness . . . so pristine and removed from civilization.

"The Quanac has intelligence properties that are very helpful for the stomach," Chameur informed Cliss and Chispo. "They are known for helping the nerves of the stomach lining to communicate better, easing tension and stress. People of Atlantis used the herb in that respect."

"I was telling Chameur I don't doubt it," Chispo now said to Cliss, "with all their mood control experiments and other problems going on."

Chameur continued observing the Quanac plants.

"You know," Chispo suggested, "we might want to include the intelligent properties of the Quanac in the project your friends and Rinto and Fraxino are working on."

"Yes, indeed," she responded. "That's just what I was thinking about." She paused. "We need to take a few of these back to Rinto and Fraxino and my friends right away."

Both Cliss and Chispo showed some surprise.

"How many of them are you thinking?" Cliss wanted to know.

"Four," Chameur answered. "Two of them for the project and two more to take back to Earth to restart the species there."

"Sure," said Cliss. "I don't think anybody will mind."

Chameur located a piece of tree bark lying on the ground and used it to carefully remove four Quanac plants from the cool, moist soil of the bank at the water's edge. Next, she carefully placed them in the daypack she was carrying so they would stay well protected.

"You know," Chispo said to Cliss, "by normal means it takes a day and a half to drive back to Zantaayer from here."

"Why don't we telephone your friends?" Cliss suggested.

"Good idea," said Chispo. "I wish we'd brought Robert or Morris or one of their friends with us. They can transport themselves by thought. They'd be able to take these plants and arrive at Rinto and Fraxino's cave research room in *seconds*, man!"

"Too bad they didn't come," said Chameur.

"I know. They stayed back on Earth," said Chispo, lamenting.

"You said their cruiser craft flies, doesn't it?" Cliss asked Chispo.

"That's right."

"Then let's head back to my house and phone them."

"All right, man. Let's go," Chispo agreed.

The three of them left the meadow and took the Matilanga Way back to Echelosa. They walked at a fast pace, arriving in just under two hours.

Cliss went straight to the phone once they entered his house. "What's Rinto and Fraxino's phone number," he asked Chispo.

"65732. Put 24 in front of that for Zantaayer."

Cliss dialled the number.

"Hello?" It was Glecko who answered in Artenian.

"Hi, this is Cliss. I'm Chispo's cousin from Zwever, Caloma," he told Glecko in Artenian.

"Yes, what can I do for you?"

"We need Rinto and Fraxino to come right away. It's important for the project they're working on with their Atlantean friends."

"Well, they're not here right now. They're up in their cave in the mountains working on the project right now."

"Uh . . . can you send for them?"

"Yes, I'll see what I can do. It's going to take me several hours." About that time a vehicle pulled into the Zapatero's driveway. Glecko saw it. "Oh wait! They're just arriving now . . . haven't seen them since yesterday morning. Hold on just a minute." Glecko put down the handset and walked outside to intercept Rinto and Fraxino as they were stepping down from their vehicle-craft. "Rinto, Fraxino, it's Chispo and his cousin on the phone. They're calling from Caloma."

"Oh really? What timing!" Fraxino responded. He dashed inside and went straight to the telephone. "Hello?" he said as he picked up the handset.

Meanwhile, Cliss had passed the phone over to Chispo.

"What's going on, Fraxino?" Chispo greeted him.

"Hey! What's going on, dude?"

"Adventures as always, man," Chispo answered. "Listen, Chameur and I have located some Quanac flowers."

"Oh, cool!" Fraxino remarked.

"She tells me the plant's intelligent properties need to be included in your project. It's very important. We need to get these plants to you right away. It would take me a day and a half to drive back to Zantaayer, and since Chameur and I still want to do some more things here in Caloma, could you guys fly up here?"

"Yeah sure, Chispo. Just a minute." Fraxino talked to Rinto, now standing by him, and he explained what Chispo just requested. Then he put Rinto on the line.

"Hey, Chispo."

"What's going on, Rinto?"

"Where exactly are you?"

Chispo gave directions and explained the route as it would be seen from the air.

"We'll put our craft in high gear and be there in two hours," Rinto assured him.

"Excellent!" said Chispo.

"We're going to load and unload some supplies, and we'll leave in just a few minutes," Rinto told him.

"Cool! We'll see you around," said Chispo.

"Okay, bye."

They both hung up.

"Man, they're going to be here in two hours," Chispo told Cliss and Chameur.

"Wow! Their cruiser craft can fly pretty fast!" Cliss commented. "Want to see a little bit of Echelosa while we wait for them to arrive?"

"Sure, man," Chispo agreed.

The three of them walked out of the house. It was now late afternoon. The sky was clear and sunny, and a cool breeze was blowing from the northwest. They climbed into Chispo's car, and he drove them around town under Cliss' direction. They cruised the main street by the highway and stopped at several stores. Cliss stocked up on groceries from the local market.

In the remaining time, Cliss took them to the research facilities where he worked, and he showed them around. He introduced Chispo and Chameur to some of his co-workers.

Then they returned to Cliss' house to wait for Rinto and Fraxino to arrive. An hour and a half had passed by, and they expected it wouldn't be much longer.

Meanwhile, back in Zantaayer, Rinto and Fraxino made preparations to leave. Fraxino dashed up to the attic for some more rock, mineral, and crystal supplies while Rinto unloaded some other items they had brought down from the mountains. They hurriedly stocked up on some food from the kitchen pantry. In five minutes they had everything ready, and they were back inside the vehicle-craft.

Rinto backed them out of the driveway, and they headed straight for the mountains. Tecoloteh and Latorna had stayed in the cave up in the mountains, as they were right in the middle of crystal growing and telepathic intelligence installation operations.

The street's pavement ended, and then Rinto whizzed up the mountain on the winding gravel road, hurriedly negotiating the hairpin curves. They reached the ridge top in just over 20 minutes. He drove along the ridge and parked on the side road near their cave.

"Fraxino, go to our cave and fetch Latorna and Tecoloteh," Rinto directed. "Tell them to come with us or at least let them know what we're doing. I'll wait here."

"Right on, brother!"

"Here, take this food to them." Rinto handed Fraxino a bag of food from the kitchen pantry.

He grabbed the bag and took off jogging down the forested gully to their cave below.

Meanwhile, Rinto pulled out the map of Zotola and Caloma and studied the layout of roads and highways, including cities and towns. In a few minutes, he figured out the shortest route and telepathically programmed the Ulexite main controls crystal and crystal array under it.

It was 30 minutes later when Fraxino finally returned, exhausted and nearly out of breath.

"Wow! Back already?!" Rinto declared.

"Record timing," Fraxino managed to say, and he immediately climbed aboard.

"And Latorna and Tecoloteh?" Rinto asked.

"Whew!" Fraxino sighed, catching his breath. "They're staying behind."

"You advised them of what we're doing?"

"Oh yeah," Fraxino assured his brother.

"Good. Let's be off to Caloma!" Rinto stated with enthusiasm. He started the engine and quickly accelerated as he drove back to the ridge road. He then pulled back the lever, and the craft left the road and ascended, passing by trees and then clearing the mountainous ridge in short order.

He sent a telepathic command to the crystal array, and the craft accelerated at full force, laying them back in their seats, and quickly attaining a high altitude with a cruising speed of 2,500 km/h.

They followed, with the help of their on-board controls crystal, the terrain, layout of the mountains, and highway routes as they quickly approached Caloma. In less than an hour, they were passing by Zwever, way down and to their left, and they made a gradual turn to the east as they approached the Talequa Mountains and the Matilanga Plateau where the town of Echelosa was. Rinto slowed the speed of the craft and lowered their altitude upon recognizing the plateau.

"Do you see Echelosa yet?" Rinto asked his brother.

Fraxino looked out the windows on both sides of their craft as he scanned the plateau below them. "There! There it is," he called out upon seeing the town off to the left.

Rinto lowered the altitude even more as he brought the craft in for a landing. He cruised at treetop level, just out of sight of the highway and checking it for the right opportunity. He waited till the right moment when there was no traffic in sight, and then he casually moved over to the left and guided the craft in alignment with the highway. He touched down at a speed of 80 km/h.

"Whew! We made it!" Rinto declared. He started the engine, put the transmission in 4th gear, engaged the clutch, and proceeded down the highway. They were just a few kilometers west of Echelosa. "How much time has gone by?"

Fraxino checked the time. "Just under two hours."

"Perfect!"

"Chispo said Cliss lives in a house off on a side street, right?" Fraxino asked.

"Right," Rinto answered.

He drove them into the town. Rinto instinctively sensed the moment when they reached the appropriate street, and he turned right and drove the half kilometer to Cliss' house.

As they were pulling into the driveway, Chispo, Cliss, and Chameur emerged from the house to greet them.

"Wow, dudes!" Chispo said, somewhat laughing. "You made it."

"Right on time!" said Rinto with a smile.

"How do you two always time it so well?" Chispo wanted to know.

"Timing and destiny programming," Rinto jokingly answered.

Rinto and Fraxino now got out of the vehicle-craft.

"This is my cousin Cliss, from Zwever, Caloma," Chispo said as he introduced him.

They greeted each other, and Rinto and Fraxino said hi to Chameur, as well.

"Come on inside a few minutes," Cliss offered.

"The Quanac plants are inside waiting for you," Chameur told Rinto and Fraxino.

"Excellent!" said Fraxino.

They walked inside the house.

"So, how's the project coming along?" Chispo asked Rinto and Fraxino.

"At this moment," Rinto answered, "Latorna and Tecoloteh are very busy attending the complicated crystal growing operations."

"They were super impressed with our cave facilities," Fraxino added.

By now they made their way into the kitchen.

"Oh, cool!" Rinto suddenly exclaimed when he saw the four Quanac plants on the counter.

"Radical, unique looking plants," Fraxino remarked, "and no leaves, just a flower for each."

"Let's go ahead and take them to our craft," Rinto directed.

"We'll be right back, guys," Fraxino assured them.

They carried the four plants out to the vehicle-craft and then returned inside to visit for a few more minutes.

"So, how many more days do you think?" Chispo asked Rinto and Fraxino.

"I'd say three or four, maybe a week at the most," Rinto answered.

"And what about you guys?" Fraxino wanted to know.

"Chameur and I are going to cruise Eastern Caloma a few days," Chispo answered, "see the mountains, go camp, and then drive back to Zantaayer."

Fraxino gave Chispo a look that suggested more, and Chispo jokingly returned a smirk for that.

Rinto and Fraxino talked a few minutes with Cliss. They brought Chameur up to date on what Latorna and Tecoloteh were doing, and they talked over the project plans briefly.

"Right, we better get these plants back to Zantaayer," Rinto announced.

"Nice meeting you, Cliss," Fraxino said to him.

"Yeah, it's great to finally meet the two gurus Chispo's talked about so much."

Both Rinto and Fraxino laughed.

"See you guys in a few days," Rinto told them.

"See you around, *gurus*," Chispo jokingly responded.

"And remember, two plants are for the project, and the other two go to planet Earth with us," Chameur reminded them.

"We got it," Rinto assured her.

Rinto and Fraxino walked out to their vehicle-craft, and they drove away. Cliss, Chispo and Chameur walked outside and waved at them as they saw them off.

"How wonderful that they came so quickly for the plants," Chameur commented. "I could sense that Latorna and Tecoloteh needed them to continue their project."

"Yeah, Rinto and Fraxino are really with it," Chispo told her. "They get things accomplished."

They walked back into the house with Cliss.

"You guys are certainly welcome to stay overnight," Cliss offered Chispo and Chameur.

"Thanks, Cliss," said Chispo. "We'll be glad to."

"Excellent! I was hoping you would. Want to go do something?"

"Let's take another cruise through Echelosa," Chispo requested.

They walked back outside, got into Chispo's Velva Dibe, and Chispo drove them around town.

"Man, have you seen the new movie, *Vision from the Ciruclar*?" Chispo asked Cliss.

"No, I haven't. What's it about?"

"It's about this man named Quinoteh who leads an expedition team up in the mountains surrounding Zantaayer, and they uncover some Atlantean artifacts."

"Cool!" Cliss responded.

"They find a bronze crate full of rocks and crystals, a sacred story stone, and Quinoteh has this vision of Atlantean settlers, and . . ."

They cruised the town, visiting several places, and Cliss introduced Chispo and Chameur to several of his friends. Chispo told plenty of hair raising stories about their recent adventures in Mexico, his time in Tennessee the year before, and Chameur told several stories from Atlantis, all very interesting to Cliss. He was really enjoying their visit.

Several hours later, they finally returned home. Cliss showed Chispo and Chameur where to sleep, and they all turned in for the night.

When morning arrived, it was partly cloudy. Birds were making their calls outside in the backyard. The three of them got up not long after the crack of dawn. Cliss had his work to go back to this morning. He offered Chispo and Chameur to help themselves to some breakfast and some cereals, which they did.

After they finished breakfast, Chispo and Chameur took their things to the car. Cliss walked out with them, closed the door to the house, and was on his way to work.

"Chispo, it's been really great having you and Chameur come and visit."

"My pleasure, too," said Chispo. "Come see us in Zantaayer."

"Guaranteed. I'd like to see the gurus' cave research room, as well."

Chispo laughed. "I don't know. Their crystallized *protection* might not let you," and he said it with a twinkle in his eye.

Cliss laughed, knowing that he was kidding. He said goodbye to both of them, walked across the street, and across the next lawn on his way to work.

Chispo and Chameur got into the car, and he drove them back to the main highway.

"You know, I wonder what's east of here," Chispo said to Chameur.

"Let's go find out," she suggested.

He turned right and drove to the eastern side of town, where he stopped at the Exxoll station by the highway. "Fuel tank's empty," Chispo announced. "They'll have maps here, as well. Do you want anything?"

"No, I'm fine."

"Okay." He stepped out of his car and walked inside.

A few minutes later, he emerged from the store, and he was looking at his just purchased, unfolded map as he walked back to his car, where Chameur was waiting for him. He got inside and backed his car over to the hydrogen fuel pumps, where a woman attendant filled his car's hydrogen tank. Chispo paid her 8 zúbolas and then drove away.

"There are some really neat mountains east and south of here, according to the map," Chispo informed her.

"Really? What are they like?"

"I don't know. I've never been there myself," Chispo admitted. "There's a town called Davino at the base of what they call the Tarima Mountains. We can spend a day or two cruising that area and then head back to Zantaayer. Rinto and Fraxino and your friends are going to be a few more days on their project, anyway."

"How far away are those mountains?"

"About three hours on the road, and we're there," Chispo answered.

"Excellent! Let's go," Chameur eagerly requested.

By now, they were just leaving the edge of town. Chispo shifted his transmission to fourth gear, and he accelerated to highway speed. As they headed east, they continued across the forested Matilanga Plateau. They listened to more Zotolan pop music, and they talked along the way.

Some 50 kilometers east of Echelosa, they reached the abrupt edge of the plateau. The highway began the descent with some very sharp hairpin curves, followed by more curves during the descent into what was called the Cedrela Valley.

At the foot of the descent, they arrived at a highway intersection. Chispo turned right, now heading south, sometimes along the banks of the medium-sized Cedrela River. The highway was narrow and scenic as it wound its way through forests and woods. Plenty of Sycamores along with other trees grew along the banks of the river, and some of the trees were very large.

Chispo pulled the car over at the middle of the day, and he and Chameur enjoyed a picnic by the river. They talked and laughed about things. They even took a swim in the river, splashed each other, and played like children, all which gave them more laughs. They were really enjoying each other. After half an hour of swimming, they walked back up onto the bank and dried off.

"That swim was great!" Chispo told her.

"I thoroughly enjoyed it," Chameur agreed. "With you, I feel like a playful teenager again," and she laughed. She gave Chispo another inviting look.

Chispo responded by wrapping his arms around her, and they kissed several times. They continued to stay by the riverside a few more minutes to enjoy the scenery. Then they walked back to the roadside.

Once back in Chispo's car, they travelled further south, eventually crossing the river and entering the town of Davino, Caloma. It was a town of 5,000 residents and was a central location for many farmers up and down the valley to bring their produce in for trading. In addition to that, it supported river tourists and also those who came to see the Tarima Mountains.

"Let's go on up in the mountains and camp for the night," Chameur proposed.

"Right, I'll just check with somebody here in town and find out where's the best place to go." As Chispo drove through town, he was looking for an information center. Then he saw a place just ahead. "There's an Exxoll station. They'll know something. I'll pull over there." He entered the station's parking area and parked in front of the store. "Wait up a minute. I'll be right back," he told Chameur, and he got out of the car and walked inside.

A few minutes later, he came back to the car smiling, and he got inside. "They told me about a perfect sensational place up in the Tarima Mountains, up and away from everybody. It's half an hour from here and two hours in on the trail . . . beautiful lakes and streams surrounded by peaks and mountains.

"Sounds marvelous," said Chameur.

"I believe it," Chispo agreed. "I've got the directions right here. We'll be there and set up three hours before it gets dark." He started his car, and they took the highway east as it began its climb up into the Tarima district, as they called it.

Scenery was magnificent as the highway wound its way, climbing up the canyon gorge. There were Pines and Cypress-like trees throughout the terrain. Sheep were grazing the pastures and grassy slopes. The gorge became narrower as Chispo continued driving, and the upper part of the gorge was totally forested as the highway finished the climb, hugging the edge of the small creek on the right and hugging the rock faces and cliffs on the left. There were plenty of curves in this section.

"This really is a scenic area," Chameur commented.

"Even more so where we're going to walk in and camp."

"I can imagine," she agreed.

Once the highway reached the top of the gorge, they were at the narrow crest of the mountains. Chispo pulled his car over to the right and parked in a small gravel parking lot used by trail hikers. There was one other vehicle parked there, and he pulled up beside it.

"Okay, let's make tracks for the mountains!" Chispo declared as he parked his Velva Dibe.

"These mountains really charm me," Chameur sincerely told him.

"I'm excited, too," said Chispo.

They stepped out of the car, took some camping gear out of the trunk, along with their daypacks. They gathered together some food and water. Chispo closed the car's doors and trunk lid, and they began the two hour walk toward the south.

The trail followed the ridge of the somewhat jagged mountain range for the first hour and a half, after which it entered a gentler area of alpine meadows with copses of Fir, Spruce, and Larch trees growing in places. The trail meandered its way along, passing by peaceful lakes and streams. There were small waterfalls in places.

They veered away from the trail and walked cross country, searching for the ideal spot to pitch their tent. Chameur spotted a beautiful grove of Fir trees next to a rock ledge.

"Let's set up the tent within that grove of trees," Chispo suggested.

"That's just where I was thinking," she agreed.

"Excellent."

They both walked under the trees and set up their tent and equipment on the ground, which was nice and soft with plenty of Fir needles. Their sweet smell made the spot ideal indeed.

Al Nitak was exactly three hours from setting. So, Chispo and Chameur enjoyed the afternoon together and explored the area. They also enjoyed a good swim in the nearby lake a few hundred meters away from where they set up camp.

Afterwards, they prepared some supper. It was so peaceful here. The colors displayed by Al Nitak as it set in the northwest sky were exquisite, and their reflection off the nearby lake amplified the effect.

"Chispo, this is such a beautiful world you live on," Chameur told him.

"Yeah, I love it here. We people here on Artenia have a lot to be thankful for."

"You do indeed," Chameur carried on, "and the energies feel so peaceful and calm, so much better than the tension and stress nearly everyone telepathically felt back on Earth's Atlantis."

"I hear you on that one, Chameur," Chispo agreed. "Tell me some more stories from Atlantis, something about the trees."

"Well, let's see," she began. "Oh, I know a good one. You're familiar with the Ginkgo tree, aren't you?"

"Yes, that's a very ancient Earth tree, isn't it?"

"That's right," and Chameur began to relate the story. "Back in Atlantis, we called it the *Viepto*, and it had become totally extinct on planet Earth some 100,000 years ago during a glacial ice age. Ancient legends throughout Atlantis had related and told stories about its qualities for causing mental clarity. Well, as you know, our Atlantean scientists had a need, of course, for anything helpful along those lines. With their knowledge of the past extinct Ginkgo tree, one of Earth's ancient trees, they wanted it for their experiments in mind control, telepathy, and telekinesis. They brainstormed and figured out a way to bring that tree back into existence. They researched ancient records, realized some knowledge of an ancient art, grew some appropriate crystals, and they set out on an expedition to what is now southeast China. Way up in a mountain gully, some 60 of them meditated, using the crystals to intelligently amplify their thoughts and wishes, and they literally thought into existence a whole forest of those trees, plucked from their reality of their past and bridged with ours to begin their lives as the new Ginkgo, a living fossil on planet Earth."

"Wow! So, some of the stuff those scientists did was actually good," Chispo realized.

"Exactly," Chameur agreed. "There is good to nearly everything. I wonder how well the Ginkgo has flourished on planet Earth, since 12,500 years ago?"

"I've seen literally thousands planted in yards and gardens in Tennessee alone. Even here on Artenia, there are a few, as well."

"That's wonderful," she responded. "Another tree of interest is the Sycamore tree."

"Oh, yeah, the Buttonball Tree," Chispo broke in with enthusiasm. "We found a clear quartz egg-shaped crystal with an image of its seed ball cluster down at that galactic dump site south of Zantaayer."

"Really? That tree has sacred qualities, valuable to the human race, and it is representative of other intelligent races, as well, including the dolphins. It's a very important tree for what it represents to us, a reminder of our ancient heritage, for those who realize it."

"Far out!" Chispo exclaimed. "Chameur, we have an old legend here on Artenia that the Sycamore or Buttonball Tree is definitely of extraterrestrial origin, being of sacred value to several intelligent races. Legend has it that it comes from the planet Alíonux, way off in another star system. I believe the star is called Saidd."

"Yes, that is true for its original place of origin," Chameur agreed, "but legends also have it that the tree arrived on Earth via the dolphins, who brought it from their past home world, 35 million years ago."

"Morris told us that, too," said Chispo. "According to what he said, that would be Delikadove. He told us the Eucalypts arrived with them, too. He said the tree has ancient origins and whatever civilization grew those egg-shaped crystals were very aware of the trees."

"That's definitely true," Chameur agreed. "That's part of the knowledge and legacy they left behind for us in Atlantis."

"You know," Chispo brought up, "there's an ancient word, *Nothgierc*, meaning global cluster of seeds, and the seed ball cluster has importance for keeping peace and harmony among the races, the way the seeds are all bunched together. If there were ever a mascot tree for the all-one-race symbol, the Buttonball Tree would be it."

Chameur suddenly stared into Chispo's eyes with surprise, the realization ringing true. She was impressed with his explanation.

"Wh . . . What?" Chispo hesitatingly asked her.

"Chispo . . . That's brilliant!" she praised him. "That last point I had never considered."

"Well, you know. It just seemed the right thing to . . ."

"Chispo, what you said about the Sycamore tree being a mascot tree for the all-one-race symbol is *so true*. For several different intelligent races living on Earth, that tree is sacred to them for various reasons."

"Far out!" Chispo remarked again. "What did you guys call the Sycamore back in Atlantis?"

"It didn't grow naturally in Atlantis, being a northern tree on Earth, but we referred to it as *Ligwiixplaa*. Also, some of our local dialects referred to it as *Wipartuo*."

"Ligwiixplaa," said Chispo, and he laughed. "Now that name *does* sound unique."

"Oh, it is," Chameur agreed. "It has to do with the unique pointed leaf buds and the soft, almost furry leaves."

"Wow! So, any more stories?" Chispo asked her with an irresistible look on his face.

She thought a few seconds and then smiled. "Yes, there is one. There was an ancient legend that families throughout Atlantis used to tell their children at bedtime. It was a story about a man from a different dimension of reality. His name was Alquzoque, a man from the sea who used to live in a cave under the ocean off the west coast of the continent north of us. He was guardian of the sea and was regarded with high respect by the people throughout the regions."

"How different!"

"Yes, it was definitely a thought provoking story," Chameur went on. "He was known to be able to change himself and come onto land, and he passed on many sacred and valuable stories of his race to the ancestors of our people. Some said he came from the *other side*. Others in Atlantis thought they still saw him by the shores of the seas, his ghostly apparition materializing above the water for a brief moment. His legends and stories live on among us."

"I love it!" Chispo told her with all interest. "And you said his name was Alquzoque?"

"That's right. Alquzoque."

They turned toward each other and gazed into each other's eyes.

"Chameur, I want to tell you, I feel so comfortable and at ease in your company." She placed her hand on his shoulder. "Chispo, I've never known anybody who's surpassed your strong sense of being tuned in with me as we talk and visit. I feel like I came here to my future for the rewards and pleasures of knowing *you*."

"There's no other way to say it than I just simply *love* you, and that's how it is."

"Oh, Chispo," she sincerely responded. "You're irresistible! I love you, too." She gazed into his green-brown eyes, *so peaceful* and soothing they were.

Chispo also gazed into Chameur's beautiful brown eyes, and she gave him another one of those inviting expressions. His hormones were caused to flare within him, and his burning desire for her took on a new level of stronghold. He wrapped his arms around her and kissed her madly. She responded accordingly, rewarding him with more kisses.

"Let's ..." *kiss* "... make for our ..." *kiss ... kiss* "... tent," Chispo managed to say.

They both slid over to the tent, crawled inside, and resumed their kissing. As the burning desires and excitement increased within Chispo and Chameur, they could stand the temptation no longer. So, they unclothed and made love, bringing their bodies into one, kissing incessantly, and they achieved that special sensational level of ecstasy that comes with such a pleasurable joining of arms wrapped around each other, legs intertwined, in addition to the feelings of genuine love and energies they felt for each other. They carried on for some time. Eventually they finished their performance, having satisfied their strongest desires. They felt so content as they disentangled, rolled over, and slept together peacefully and soundly through the night.

Morning arrived. Never had Chispo slept so peacefully in all his life. It had been one of Chameur's best nights, as well. Both of them now felt a new level of soothing peace and friendship within them.

They both got up and ate breakfast, enjoying the sunrise of Al Nitak.

"Chameur ... last night ..." Chispo smiled and told her. "That was *incredible!*"

"I *thoroughly* enjoyed it," Chameur responded.

"Whew! You're not kidding," Chispo totally agreed. He paused, thought for a moment and then looked at her. "Want to stay here for the day and explore the area some more?"

"That sounds marvelous."

"Great! Let's do that. I kind of want to explore the mountains and meadows around here."

Chameur readily agreed. She knew that she was all his, and Chispo also knew that he was all hers. They'd go anywhere with each other now. Their love was like a circle of white light of the purest and cleanest form imaginable. They felt such a soothing and peaceful connection of friendship and love that they knew they were truly meant for each other. They had achieved their goals, having found each other by the means of destiny across different time periods and star systems. They were truly happy with each other, and they knew they wanted to spend the rest of their lives together as partners.

They left their tent and camping equipment under the grove of Fir trees, and they took off walking for several hours, enjoying the meadows and beautiful scenery, flanked by the mountains and jagged peaks, the highest ones having some snow and glaciers. They walked to the peaks of two different mountains and were afforded spectacular views of eastern Caloma and the Cedrela Valley below.

The day remained clear and sunny. A cool and steady westerly breeze was blowing. From time to time, they stopped and wrapped their arms around each other, sharing their closeness of friendship as they gazed at the scenery. Chispo was truly happy, and Chameur equally so. What satisfied them more than anything was the knowledge that here on Artenia, there were no bad energy systems to contaminate them, to break up their perfect friendship. Even if that were so, they had created such a strong bond of love and friendship that nothing was ever going to break their plans of being lifelong partners.

They returned for lunch and took an afternoon swim in the nearby lake. They splashed around and played with each other like children, laughing all the while. There were no other campers in the entire meadow, and they had the place to themselves to enjoy their perfect peace and harmony.

When evening arrived, they enjoyed another exquisite sunset as some high clouds eased in from the west, causing the colors to surpass the previous evening's. As night arrived, they looked up at the stars, talked about various topics, and told each other more stories. Later that night, they crawled into their tent and slept under the same grove of Fir trees.

They awoke to an overcast day. Chispo was the first one out of the tent, and he looked off to the western sky. A moderate breeze was blowing in from the southwest.

"We've got somewhat of a south wind," Chispo announced. "Looks like rain may be coming in by afternoon."

"The timing might be right to return to our friends in Zantaayer," Chameur suggested.

Chispo paused a moment and thought. "Yeah, you're right. We need to head on back."

"I wanted to stay in this charming meadow longer."

"Me too, but then everything has its timing, right?"

They both prepared and ate some breakfast, packed their equipment and daypacks, and they walked the several hours back to the highway crossing where Chispo had parked his car. They arrived by late morning, and the rain was just beginning.

"Let's throw our things in the car and cruise out of here," Chispo cheerfully said.

As they climbed into his car, Chameur looked at Chispo and sincerely said, "Thank you . . . for such a wonderful camping and hiking trip."

"With pleasure, Chameur."

They kissed each other.

"So, how are we getting back to Zantaayer?" Chameur wanted to know.

"We're going to return to Davino down in the valley and then take a more southerly route." He paused a moment. "Right, let's be *cruising!*"

Chameur laughed at Chispo's enthusiastic way of saying it. He started the car, and they headed back down the gorge along the narrow winding highway. The rain picked up as they made the descent, and by the time they reached Davino half an hour later, it had turned into a steady downpour.

"I hope we get through this drenching rain sooner than later," said Chispo as he negotiated the turns through the town.

On the western edge of town, they crossed the Cedrela River, and Chispo made a left turn, heading south. The route they took missed Zwever, Caloma by several hundred kilometers. Most of the terrain was flat and mostly forested, with some farmland. The rain finally ceased when they were 100 kilometers south of Davino.

It was a two day drive back to Zantaayer, and they camped the one night on the way at a beautiful forest park.

On the evening of the second day, they were entering the eastern edge of Zantaayer. Al Nitak was just setting behind the partially cloud covered western range of the Ciruclar Mountains across the city, an attractive welcoming scene indeed.

"Chispo, when I look at your city of Zantaayer, I can't help but think about Taltipocheh, back in Atlantis," Chameur told him as she looked at the colorful sunset.

"Yeah, Zantaayer's a really neat city. We'll be back at Rinto and Fraxino's in 20 minutes."

Still on the eastern edge of the city, Chispo pulled over at the Exxoll station, and the attendant filled his car's hydrogen tank. He paid him 8 zúbolas, and then they entered Zantaayer. They crossed the central district and reached his house a short while later.

"Back home again!" Chispo joyfully declared as he parked his Velva Dibe in the driveway.

"How many days were we away travelling?" Chameur asked him.

He thought a few seconds. "Six days. Yeah, those two gurus have had *plenty* of time by now. Let's go ahead and get the car unloaded." He opened the door and stepped outside. Chameur did likewise. Chispo stretched and yawned. "Oh, it's great to be back!" he declared.

"I'm looking forward to seeing my friends," said Chameur.

"Let's take these things back in the house, and then we'll go find them over at the Zapateros or up in the . . . Oh, wow! There's Mom."

Chispo's mother, Vironga Colancha, had just stepped out of the house. "Chispo, how have you been?" She looked at Chameur and then gave Chispo an inquisitive look.

"Hi Mom . . ." Chispo began, and he looked at her curious stare. "Oh, yeah! The clothing. Mom, I can explain . . ."

"Yes . . . I'm missing several slacks and *blouses*, as well as some shirts, out of my closet and wardrobe," she mentioned, smiling.

"Mom, this is my new friend, Chameur," as he introduced her, conveniently changing the subject at hand.

"Hi, my name's Vironga. I'm Chispo's mother." She and Chameur shook hands.

"My name is Chameur. Chispo and I have been up to Caloma for six days."

"Yes, so the Zapateros said. How was it?"

"We thoroughly enjoyed our time together."

"That's wonderful. They say you're one of several from Atlantis?"

"Indeed I am."

"How exotic that must be!" Vironga commented. "My son's really had some adventures with those two friends of his across the bushes. Come on inside and visit."

"If you need your clothing back . . ." Chameur began.

"No, that's okay. You can keep them," Vironga assured her. "I've got more than enough, and I certainly understand."

"Thank you."

"So, how do you like it here on our world?" Vironga asked Chameur.

"It's so wonderful and peaceful."

"Mom, this Chameur is a whiz about the trees," Chispo told her. "She's told me all kinds of really neat stories about them and about Atlantis and . . ."

The three of them walked into the house, and Chispo and Chameur continued telling Mrs. Colancha all about their trip to Caloma.

Later that night, Chispo and Chameur went over to the Zapateros to inquire about the others. Glecko and Sosta informed them that Rinto, Fraxino and the two Atlanteans were still up at the cave in the mountains. They were nearing completion, but they were still very busy, performing the final touches on growing the various crystals and instilling the intelligence within them. They were hoping to be finished by morning.

CHAPTER 11

STRANGE DISCOVERY AT THE STATION

During the course of the six days that Chispo and Chameur had been travelling, and while Rinto, Fraxino, Latorna and Tecoloteh had been very busy with their project at hand, Tom and Caymar's crew back on Earth had been making serious progress on the excavating of the big room inside Mt. Isto in northern Alaska.

It had been two days since Rinto and Fraxino had left Alaska to return to Al Nitak. Robert and Steven had briefly visited Chris and Richard Bell on the Planet of the Islands around the Garnet Star, and when the four of them arrived to Alaska, Tom had hired them to help assemble the numerous frames and racks, including soldering the numerous switches and contacts into place. At the moment, the four of them were doing the work inside one of the huge underground warehouses on Sirius B. Other Sirian crew members had joined them and were busy with the work, as well.

In Alaska, it was mid day, July 31, 1985. Without ever having notified the Galactic Federation of the major design change, Tom had directed his crew to excavate the big room in the shape of a giant, 4-sided pyramid instead of the original cubical rectangular design. The pyramidal design, suggested by the five Atlanteans, was far superior and would eliminate the need for vertical supports, which would have proved cumbersome, anyway. The excavating crew was nearing completion. Only a few more sections of ceiling had to be laser cut away and carried way outside to the glacier. The floor of the room would measure 50 by 50 meters, and the apex some 42 meters in height upon completion.

In two days, Quicho and Seglima had finished the data tablets programming of their device-craft. They had also very carefully loaded the energy systems, recorded in their crystals from that special compartment in the crate.

Meanwhile Steven and Robert, along with Chris and Richard Bell, were inside one of the Galactic Federation super warehouses situated underneath one of the many deserts of planet Sirius B. They were busy soldering the many wires to the numerous metal contacts of the main central device, a huge cube that measured 25 meters on each side. It was full of racks and frames throughout. Several Sirian crew members were also assisting, as the contacts numbered in the millions.

"Boy, I never saw such a contraption of wires and contacts!" Steven declared.

"At least the Galactic Federation is paying us well enough," said Robert.

"Yeah, that's for sure," Steven agreed. "Thanks to our good fortune and rewards Tom has given us, I'll be able to pay for my whole college career in the future."

"Chris," his brother Richard called out to him, "after this soldering project, let's take the money we earn and travel to Australia and New Zealand again."

"Good idea," Chris responded. "While we're at it, let's get some more trees from there for our arboretum and Earth museum."

"Indeed."

"Wonder how Tom and Caymar are going to get this contraption into their pyramidal room?" Steven asked.

"Teleportation, no doubt," Richard responded.

"It would be the only way," Steven agreed.

"Certainly won't fit through that narrow tunnel entrance," said Robert.

"You got *that* right!" Steven declared.

"So, how much longer do you think till they have it all up and running?" Robert asked them.

Suddenly, all of the Sirians cried out a gesture as if they were in pain, and they stopped their work immediately. Chris and Richard telepathically received a sharp pain of a loss of lives somewhere. Both Robert and Steven picked up on the fact that something was very wrong, seeing how everyone had stopped working, and the room was *so quiet*. Richard was the first one to realize what the problem was.

"I think something's the matter with Tom and his crew," he said.

"Oh my goodness!" Steven responded.

All of the crew members climbed down to the floor of the cubical device, and some of them were seen to immediately teleport away.

"Let's go to the galactic station and see if everything's all right," Robert suggested.

"Good idea," said Steven.

Robert, Steven, Chris and Richard climbed down to the floor, and the four of them immediately transported themselves to the glacier on Mt. Isto in Alaska. Upon arriving, they felt a sudden sinking feeling to their stomachs, and they could sense that something was very wrong.

"Guys, I don't feel good at all, now that we're here," Richard told the others.

The four of them walked into the ice tunnel with apprehension. Several Sirian crew members were seen to be hurriedly running out of the tunnel, seemingly in fear. One of them stopped and walked over to Robert and gestured to him and his friends to follow him to the big pyramid room.

"Something is very wrong indeed," Chris commented.

They followed the Sirian fellow, and before they entered the pyramid room, Tom was seen to walk out into the tunnel hallway. He intercepted them by reaching out with both his hands and saying, "Fellows, there's just been a terrible accident. Three Sirian crew members have just lost their lives."

"Ohh . . ." was all Richard could say.

". . . How?" Steven came around to ask.

"A shaft of rock dislodged near the apex as we laser cut one of the last sections," Tom explained.

"Oh no!" said Robert sadly.

"Rock came tumbling down," Tom continued. "We've lost three members . . . C' . . . Come on in and see for yourselves."

Tom was under a considerable amount of shock and grief as he led them into the giant pyramid room. Sure enough, there were three crew members pinned under a pile of rock and rubble, a sorry sight indeed! A few other Sirian crew members, who had not run in fear, were making efforts to remove the rubble and pull the bodies free, all in fear and trepidation that more rock might suddenly fall from the suddenly revealed shaft some 40 meters above them.

Tom, and now Caymar, stood more toward the edge of the room in grief. Tears came to their eyes in recognition of the fact that they had just lost three of their friends: Denchulo, Huante, and Llacudo.

"If we had just followed federation mandate and kept the room rectangular cubical," Tom lamented.

Some more crew members who had just teleported in from Sirius B entered the room with another excavator and first aid kits and crystals in hopes of reviving them. They hurried over to the casualties and began working to move the pile of rocks to one side. After some ten minutes, they finally freed up the bodies and pulled them to the side of the room.

Both Tom and Caymar went to work using crystals in efforts to restore the damage, but the three bodies were crushed beyond recovery. Tom laid the crystals down on the floor and said, "They're beyond repair. They've long since departed. In respect of our loss, work will cease here immediately for 30 hours. We must make funeral arrangements right away."

"I'm sorry, Tom," said Steven.

"We don't know why this happened," Caymar said to them, "but we hope there's a good reason why."

As Robert, Steven, Chris and Richard stood and watched, Sirian crew members loaded the three bodies onto the bed of one of their vehicles, and they drove out to the glacier. The remainig rock and rubble lay on the floor, to be sifted through more carefully 30 hours later.

"Come with us," Caymar offered Robert, Steven, Chris and Richard. "We're taking the three casualties by spacecraft straight to the sacred burial site."

They walked out of the tunnel, locked the double doors to the entrance, and boarded the spacecraft parked out on the glacier.

*   *   *

It was nearly a day later. Sirian relatives of the casualties: Denchulo, Huante, and Llacudo, had been contacted. Funeral services were being conducted by Wasser, leader of the Sirian Council.

The location was latitude 75° south in a beautiful cove situated in the high Guaitecoh Mountains, whose slopes were forested with tall and graceful Kanofleh trees, very similar to Incense Cedars, except for the needles being more of a silver hue. High rock walls and cliffs surrounded the cove, and other coniferous shrubs and trees dotted the landscape.

The Guaitecoh Mountains were known for their spiritual inclinations, and many Sirians came on retreat to these high mountains from time to time, to relax and enjoy a moderately warm climate, as compared to the hot, desertlike weather throughout most of the planet.

"We are gathered here today to express our remorse for the loss of three of our kind," Wasser began. "Their lives were sacrificed at the expense of galactic communication, an accident of sorrow that will be regreted by friends and relatives for years to come. These three: Denchulo, Huante, and Llacudo, served their planet well, helping Tom and Caymar carry out their important mission on planet Earth's Alaska. In our highest respect for the Kanofleh, a sacred tree brought from Vega to remind us of our previous planetary homeland, we wish these three to go well on their return journey home."

The 700 or so Sirians attending the funeral chanted approval of Wasser's wise words, and they sang an ancient song, which was all part of Sirian ritual to help the spirits of the three casualities return to their place of soul origin. Three white ghostly lights were seen to rise up and float off toward the highest reaches of the mountains where they were seen to disappear. The 700 attendees watched, now in silence, while they telepathically gave their best wishes.

Next, the three bodies were placed in their graves, and several Sirians shoveled dirt on top of them. The service was over. Numerous relatives visited with each other. Some went walking in the mountains, and others simply teleported themselves back home.

Robert, Steven, Chris and Richard had stood and watched. The funeral had not been entirely different from how one would have been conducted back on planet Earth. The four of them decided to go into the mountains and camp among the Kanofleh trees. They would return to the underground warehouse in the morning to begin work again.

*   *   *

At the end of the 30-hour mourning period, Tom and Caymar and their crew returned to Alaska to finish the last bit of excavating. They parked the spacecraft on the glacier, stepped down, opened the entrance doors and walked to the giant pyramid room. The pile of fallen rubble still lay on the floor.

Dotsero led his crew as they started up the machines to collect the last bit of rock to carry outside to the glacier. Another crew member started up a laser cutter to cut away the remaining rock near the apex. He made sure and kept himself to the side of the operation for fear of another accident. Before he could get the laser cutter positioned, one of the crew members sorting through the fallen rock called out to the others. They stopped what they were doing and watched as he pulled a decent size bronze tablet out of the rubble. It measured 30 by 40 centimeters in size.

"What have you found there, Cahueno?" Dotsero asked with curiosity.

"It appears to be some sort of tablet document," he answered, as he began to examine it. Evidently, it had fallen from the recently revealed shaft above. It had survived the fall with hardly any scratches at all.

Dotsero and the others now reached Cahueno, and they examined what appeared to be foreign script casted on the tablet. There were small pieces of orange

Calcite stones carefully placed throughout the script, as well.

"Glory be!" Dotsero exclaimed. "It's a bronze tablet from Lyra . . . written in Lyran script!"

Tom and Caymar picked up on the excitement and walked over to the others. Dotsero placed the tablet in Tom's hands, and he stared at it in amazement and wonder.

"An extraordinary find indeed!" Tom declared. "This will definitely be placed along the wall of this room." He examined the Lyran script which read:

translation:
From the star Vega of Lyra we came, to start a new race, a new beginning, a beautiful world to found our new colony Oautlaam (Atlantis). We designate this sacred mountain as the centrálle for galactic communication and connection. May peace and harmony prevail for always.

"What a nice dedication tablet!" Caymar remarked.

"And to think they knew . . . about this project?" Tom asked the others.

"Or do you think there's an ancient central above us?" Dotsero asked Tom and Caymar.

"I really don't know," Tom admitted. "Crew, we need to do a thorough investigation of that revealed shaft above us. Cahueno, continue with the others searching through that rock rubble to see if any more artifacts fell down with this tablet. This has really got my curiosity up."

Carefully, they sifted through the rest of the rock and rubble and loaded piece by piece aboard one of the Sirian vehicles, after which they carried the load outside to the glacier and dumped it. No more artifacts had fallen.

Then Tom arranged an investigation. He, Caymar, and several crew members hoisted themselves up to the shaft with one of their machines, and they entered the vertical shaft. It was 1 meter in diameter and was 2 meters long, and as they climbed up it with considerable difficulty, they came into a small room 7 by 9 meters in size. It seemingly had no other entrances nor exits, not on any side nor above, and since the shaft below had not seemingly gone anywhere before, it remained a mystery just how this chamber or room was created and ever accessed before.

The room had various crystals, some of them very large, interspersed around the walls with some of the larger ones on the floor. Most of them were colored orange, and there were some green ones, as well. Some were geometrical and others were round and smooth. The main feature of the room was a 1 by 1 by 1.5 meter block of orange Calcite situated at the far end.

Tom was the first one to reach the perfectly rectangular block of Calcite, and he and the others were quite surprised to see a 3D holographic movie seemingly project itself on top of the block. The scene presented was of an old man standing on the shoreline of a sea on an alien world. Both the sea and sky were purplish in color, and the old man began to speak.

```
"Greetings to those who enter. I give this telepathic
response holographic movie to all who find their way into my
secret and by normal means inaccessible requiem. Through my
ways, means, and travels throughout galactic stars and time,
I created this chamber as a requiem to give high regard to
the all-one-race of beings throughout the universe, with
special regard to the dolphins, whales, and also the humans,
in high hopes that the humans achieve their quest, make
amends, and succeed in re-establishing galactic contact and
communication via this galactic station directly below. From
my time of birth on this planet, I travelled to the 200,000
year ago past and created this room, among other projects I
had achieved before."
                                        - Maalkarrai -
```

"Caymar, he looks so familiar," said Tom, "and who is Maalkarrai?"

"For some reason. I'm caused to think of Morris."

"No, you're kidding!" said Tom with disbelief. "Let's see if we can view the movie clip again."

Automatically, the 35-second 3D holographic movie reset itself and played again. Tom and Caymar examined the face of the old man speaking.

"Caymar, that *is* Morris, but much later in his time!"

"Amazing what he's created here," Caymar commented.

"An unexpected surprise indeed!" Tom declared.

"Maybe it was already said by destiny that we would be caused to make the room pyramidal instead of cubical rectangular," Caymar suggested.

"So that we would find this," Dotsero added.

"Besides, I also believe we were meant to find this room," said Caymar.

Tom thought a few moments. "What a baffling situation! Let's get back to work and proceed with lining the entire pyramidal room before any more rocks mysteriously fall on us."

They climbed back down the shaft, and their hoist machine carried them back to the floor. Tom proceeded to give instructions to the crew members to begin the lining procedure. They cancelled the last remaining rock laser cutting that would have been done near the apex. It wasn't necessary, especially with the shaft and requiem room above them. Instead a special staircase and ladder would be installed to provide future tourists access to the room.

As Tom thought about it, he was somewhat disturbed at Morris. Even though it had never been Morris' intentional fault, the fact remained that the mysterious creation of his requiem room caused a shaftload of rocks to tumble down on three of his Sirian crew, who lost their lives as a result.

The crew under Dotsero's direction unloaded the Titanium-Vanadium expansion reinforcing kit from the spacecraft and took it and the special hoses into the tunnel with them. Tom and Caymar had accompanied them to the spacecraft, and they were now re-entering the big pyramidal room, when suddenly they stopped with quite a look of surprise on their faces.

There stood Morris in the middle of the room directly below the shaft, accompanied by Denchulo, Huante, and Llacudo, alive and perfectly intact!

"Morris?" was all Tom could say. His mouth dropped open in total surprise.

"Are these our three crew members?" Caymar asked Morris in disbelief.

"They are indeed," Morris replied calmly and smiling. "I rescued them from the dead, performed a time jump, and revived them."

"Well done! Excellent going, Morris!" Tom happily declared.

"I'm glad I could do it. I sensed and was aware of the casualties, and the dolphins soon pointed out the accident that was unintentionally my fault. I couldn't have *that* hanging over me, so I took appropriate actions and erased the repercussions."

Tom, Caymar, Dotsero, and the other crew members walked over to the three revived Sirians, unsure whether or not to believe if they were really real.

"Don't be timid. They're perfectly there," Morris reassured them. "They have no memory of the accident, by the way. I snatched away a duplicate of each one of them right before the accident occurred. So, they're perfectly intact."

All of them happily greeted each other, glad to see each other again. There were shouts of joy.

"Morris, you're brilliant indeed!" Tom commended him.

"And to think we had the funeral for these three," said Dotsero.

"Oh, the funeral was still appropriate," Morris stated. "Those three bodies definitely died, but their families are *really* going to get a shocker when they see their revived duplicates ... well, now originals, complete with their original minds and personalities installed."

"In other words, they have their bodies back," said Tom.

"Exactly," Morris answered.

"Morris, thank you ever so much for making that right," said Tom. "I didn't know how I was *ever* going to get out of that one with the Galactic Federation."

"My pleasure. So, it looks like you got the room all finished, except for lining it, and you found my requiem room, no doubt."

"That's an understatement," Tom responded.

"Hope that room makes a nice addition to the collection of machines and equipment," said Morris, "a nice novelty for tourists and visitors. Right then, I'll return to the dolphins back on Delikadove and let you fellows get to work with the reinforcement lining."

"Morris, we found a bronze tablet that fell out of that shaft with the rocks," Tom mentioned.

"Oh yes, that's an original Lyran artifact, and it was brought by a very wise and knowledgeable colonist at that time."

"You mean 200,000 years ago?" Tom asked.

"That's right. That will make the tourists think a little bit."

"It will do that all right," Caymar agreed.

"Oh, and who is Maalkarrai?" Tom wanted to know.

"That's my galactic name, assigned me by the dolphins."

"Very original name," said Tom.

Denchulo, Huante, and Llacudo expressed sincere appreciation to Morris for his having revived them, and they shook hands with him. With that, Morris placed his hands on either side of his body, brought on the energy of the pink glow and whirring wind, and disappeared over a period of several seconds.

Tom looked at Caymar and then at the three revived Sirians. "Yahoo! We've got our crew members back alive!"

"We no longer have to go before the Galactic Federation to explain," Caymar said with relief.

"That's right. We don't," Tom agreed, "and thank goodness and thanks to Morris. That was going to be a very big and sticky problem. They wouldn't have pardoned it, because I made that design change without federation approval."

"We do have a lot to be thankful for now," said Dotsero.

"Indeed we do," Tom agreed. "All right, let's get this pyramidal room lined and reinforced right away. Denchulo, Huante, Llacudo, let's go straight to Sirius B and notify Wasser, the Sirian Council, and your relatives that you're miraculously returned from the dead." The four of them teleported away.

Caymar stayed with Dotsero and the crew as they lined the pyramid room with their special Titanium-Vanadium resin. In a period of four hours, its application would be nearly half a meter thick and stronger than steel.

By the time the lining process was finished, Tom and the three crew members had returned from Sirius B.

"Excellent! Excellent work!" Tom commended as he inspected the entire pyramid room. "No more falling rocks. That's for certain."

"Thank you, Tomarius," Dotsero responded. "We do our best."

"That you do indeed," Tom agreed. "We have a lot to do yet. It's time to teleport the equipment pieces into here, connect the cables, then install the special Ulexite slab in the cradle, bring in what Rinto, Fraxino, Tecoloteh and Latorna are building . . ."

"Then we have the towers to install on the ridge," Caymar added. "We've got to bury a massive fiberoptic trunk cable to the west to access the Alaska pipeline."

"Along with the stone lodge to accommodate guests and government officials," said Tom.

"Who I'm sure we'll have plenty of," said Caymar.

"Let's see if the equipment is ready in the warehouses," Tom directed.

Tom, Caymar, and Dotsero disappeared, teleporting themselves to Sirius B, while the other crew members remained in the pyramid room, prepared to receive the equipment.

At the moment they arrived on Sirius B, Robert, Steven, and the others, as it turned out, were just finishing up the soldering of wire contacts on the big cube, perfect timing indeed. Tom notified them that it was time to teleport them to the big room, that it had just been lined and reinforced.

"You guys really get down to business," Steven declared.

"We've got something to tell you about that shaft we discovered," Tom announced.

"You're really going to be surprised on how it got there," Caymar added.

"What? What is it?" Robert wanted to know.

"We'll show you when we get there," Tom answered.

"It has to do with Morris," Caymar informed them.

"With Morris?!" Steven reacted.

Tom and the crew in the warehouse began to place a forcefield over the large cube, followed later by other equipment and devices. Over a period of 30 seconds, the large cube was enveloped by the energy of a pink glow and whirring wind, and it disappeared.

CHAPTER 12

PROJECT CRYSTALS FROM ZOTOLA

While Tom and Caymar and their crew successfully teleported all of their equipment into the pyramidal room and connected all the cables accordingly, Rinto, Fraxino, Latorna and Tecoloteh had been very busy growing crystals for use in the galactic station and also in their device-craft.

Chispo and Chameur had stayed out of the others' hair by vacationing and joy riding up in Caloma for six days, visiting cousin Cliss, going hiking and camping, and enjoying each other's company. They had just returned to Zantaayer at sunset, and when they went over to the Zapateros to inquire about the others, Glecko and Sosta informed them that Rinto, Fraxino, Latorna and Tecoloteh were performing the final touches on the project. Chispo and Chameur returned to Chispo's house for the night, and they visited with Mrs. Colancha.

It was now the next morning, a crisp sunny morning with a cool breeze. Al Nitak shined clearly in the turquoise blue eastern sky. Chispo and Chameur got up and walked over to the Zapateros.

Just as they walked under the row of tall bushes, Rinto and Fraxino's Velosa cruiser craft was seen to pull into the driveway and park. The four of them stepped down from the vehicle-craft and soon saw Chispo and Chameur walking toward them.

"Chispo and *Chameur*," Fraxino spoke their names and smiled. "How was your *honeymoon*?"

"Dude, now don't you start," Chispo responded, returning a smile.

"Where did you go after the Quanac flower findings?" Rinto asked.

"We went further east to the Tarima District and went hiking and camping up in the mountains," Chispo answered.

"Whoowee!" Fraxino declared, suggesting something more.

"Fraxino, you genius guru you," Chispo responded, changing the subject.

"Did you four finish growing the project crystals?" Chameur now asked the others.

"Oh yeah," Rinto answered. "All perfectly done while you two went *joy riding* for the past six days."

"That's what you dudes wanted, wasn't it?" Chispo asked.

"Yeah, we're only joking with you," Rinto assured Chispo. "Come and see our setup. We've got part of it here in our craft."

"There are three more large pieces still up in our cave," Fraxino informed them.

"Tom's crew will have to teleport those," Latorna told them. "They were too big to carry out of the cave up to the craft."

"Wow, you gurus *have* been busy!" Chispo remarked.

"That's for sure," said Rinto.

Chispo and Chameur walked over to the back of the vehicle-craft. Rinto now opened the back door, revealing what they had grown.

". . . Far out!" Chispo came around to say.

"Impressive work!" Chameur complimented.

"This one's going directly underneath the large Ulexite slab that was quarried from that mine south of here," Fraxino told them.

The crystal was impressive indeed, measuring nearly 1 meter in diameter. The base was made of green Fluorite with gold specks, and there were 7 Ulexite cubes evenly spaced in different directions around the main Fluorite base. Each Ulexite cube measured 7 centimeters on each side.

"This device will help channel the sending and receiving signals to the different parts of the galaxy," Fraxino explained.

"All part of of the soul travel section of the galactic station," Rinto added.

"The Fluorite with gold specks adds value to the peace and friendship aspect of galactic communication," Tecoloteh mentioned.

"Of the other three arrays up in the cave, one is for time travel use in our device-craft," Latorna informed them. "Another one is for their main frame central."

"And the third one is for blocking intelligence suppression," Tecoloteh added.

"Anyway, we're going to get some supplies together and take this first piece down there this morning," Rinto announced.

"Ready to come with us?" Fraxino asked.

"Oh yeah, man. We've been waiting on you gurus for *six days*," Chispo answered in a joking manner.

Both Rinto and Fraxino laughed. The six of them walked into the Zapatero's house. Rinto carried some empty chemistry flasks and bottles with him from the craft, and they rounded up a few more supplies, including some food from the kitchen. Chispo and Chameur briefly went back over to his house to get their supplies and then returned to the Zapateros. Glecko and Sosta were just getting up when Rinto and Fraxino were stocking up with food in the kitchen.

"Well, good morning, sons," Glecko greeted them. "Are you all finished?"

"Just finished this morning, Dad," Fraxino replied.

"Nice going, sons! Let's see your setup."

Rinto and Fraxino briefly took their parents to the vehicle-craft where they opened the back door.

"Triumph again, sons!" Glecko complimented them. "I knew you could pull it off."

"I'm proud of you," their mother told them.

"Thanks, Mom," both Rinto and Fraxino responded.

"So, explain to me, how does this work?" Glecko wanted to know.

"The green Flourite base has gold specks and other minute impurities grown within it for the instilled intelligence of achieving soul travel and astral connections with different regions of the galaxy, and the 7 Ulexite cubes . . ." and they explained the whole process.

"We've got more grown arrays still up in the cave," Fraxino explained.

"Tom and his crew will have them teleported there," Rinto added. "We're leaving here shortly to have that arranged."

"Fine work. Excellent work, sons," their father complimented again. "Were your Atlantean friends of help?"

"Oh yeah," Rinto answered. "They've got a better handle on this than we do."

"Really?" Glecko asked with surprise.

"They really are whizzes when it comes to growing crystals," Fraxino stated.

"Well, I suppose that would make sense," Glecko admitted. "After all, they are original Atlanteans, who certainly know the art."

After looking over the array, they walked back in the house again. They ate some breakfast, and Glecko read Zantaayer's morning newspaper.

"Land sakes! Another scandal from planet Earth!" he declared.

"What's it about this time?" Rinto asked his father.

"This report has to do with Earth's use of MSG, known as Monosodium Glutamate, another byproduct of manufacturing. Instead of disposing of it properly by sending it to the Sun, food and drug companies across planet Earth have been paid under the table to approve the nasty chemical to enhance food flavor, to the point that they don't even list it on the ingredients of food products that contain it."

"How can they get away with that?" Fraxino wanted to know.

"They use clever cover-up names like: Natural Flavoring, Autolyzed Yeast, and Hydrolyzed Vegetable Protein, of which MSG is a considerable part of each one of those."

"Dad, how scandalous do they get, down there on planet Earth?!" Rinto declared.

"I'm telling you!" Glecko agreed. "The report goes on to say that the use of MSG is at an all-time high, as a result."

"How awful!" Fraxino exclaimed.

"The main driving force behind it is intelligence suppression. MSG is a nasty chemical and has no business ever being added to food products. It causes headaches, and for those more allergic to it, it causes paralysis for up to hours and disarms certain people of their senses and mental capacity."

"Golly! Why don't they ban the stupid chemical?" Fraxino asked his father.

"Because chief administrations have been paid under the table," Glecko simply stated. "It's just one more part of the intelligence suppression study driven by unscrupulous factions that need to be halted. Let's just hope the arrays you four have built and grown do the trick."

"Thanks, Dad. We'll hope for the best," said Rinto.

"Of course, here on Artenia, as you know," Glecko pointed out, "nasty chemical byproducts like MSG are flown *straight* to Al Nitak, a far superior incinerator than what this world has to offer."

"Right on, Dad!" said Fraxino.

"And why can't Earth capture that bright idea?" Rinto asked his father.

"I wish they would, sons."

After breakfast, they loaded their supplies into the vehicle-craft, and they were all, including Chispo and Chameur, ready to go.

"Fellows, best of luck taking the cargo to Alaska," Glecko kindly said. "I hope it all works."

"Thanks, Dad," said Fraxino.

Their mother wished them well.

They boarded the vehicle-craft. Rinto did the driving and backed them out of the driveway. Glecko and Sosta waved at them as they left. Once on the street, Rinto proceeded to drive them toward the mountains.

"How much fuel have we got?" Fraxino asked his brother.

Rinto looked at the gauge. "About half a tank. That will do us."

"Okay, let's be off to Alaska, dudes!" Chispo shouted with enthusiasm.

"Right on, Chispo!" Fraxino responded.

"Have you all got the four Quanac flowers on board?" Chameur asked them.

"Indeed we do," Latorna answered.

"They were a great help in programming appeasement qualities into the appropriate crystals grown," Tecoloteh informed them.

"Excellent," said Chameur. "We need to plant them in an appropriate place on planet Earth. Their ecological balance needs some maintenance."

Shortly after they reached the edge of the residential section where the pavement ended and the gravel road began, Rinto pulled back the lever, once out of sight of any houses.

"Already, man?" Chispo asked with surprise.

"Yeah, we've decided to be a little more casual about it," Rinto explained. "After all, no one's going to see us disappear with the camouflage of the trees."

"Besides, the way hydrogen fuel costs have been increasing nearly every week," Fraxino added, "and all the trips we've been making up and down this mountain, we've got to save a little bit somewhere."

"I hear you on that one," Chispo responded.

The craft left the road's surface and once barely above the trees, Rinto caused the craft to swiftly accelerate up the mountain slope, pressing everyone back in their seats. The Fluorite-Ulexite crystal array was carefully secured and cushioned in a shallow box so as not to suffer any damage during transport. Rinto maneuvered the craft just above treetop level to minimize the chances of city residents possibly seeing their flying craft. Once they crested the ridge of the mountain, the familiar forcefield accompanied by a faint green glow overtook them.

In seconds they found themselves flying south toward Alaska's Mt. Isto. Earth time, it was 10 AM, August 5, 1985.

"Tom and Caymar will be glad to receive this piece, I'm sure," Rinto told his brother.

They cruised in toward the glacier and came in for a soft landing, touching down right by the large spacecraft around 100 meters from the tunnel entrance.

"Oh wow, dudes!" Chispo remarked. "They've installed the doors."

"And look up at the ridge," Fraxino indicated. "They've already put up the receiving/sending towers.

"Down there in the cove, they're already breaking ground for the government accommodation lodge," said Rinto as he noticed.

"Okay, let's get this crystal array unloaded," Fraxino directed.

All of them stepped down from the vehicle-craft. Chispo went to the back door and opened it while Rinto, Fraxino, and Tecoloteh each grabbed a side of the box and took it out of the vehicle-craft. They carried the assembly through the tunnel doors. Chameur carried the four Quanac plants into the tunnel with them, and she placed them by their device-craft. They walked through the tunnel and into the project room. Quicho and Seglima were not there, as they found out. They were in the big pyramid room helping Tom and Caymar and their crew. They continued carrying the assembly further, finally entering the pyramid room. Tom was the first one to see them, followed by Quicho and Seglima.

"Fellows, would you look at that!" Tom declared, marvelling at the Fluorite-Ulexite crystal array.

Quicho and Seglima, who were with Tom at the moment, came over to greet them.

"How did the growing operation go?" Seglima asked Tecoloteh and Latorna.

"Excellent," Latorna answered. "There are three more arrays, grown and yet to be brought."

"You've been *busy*!" Seglima remarked.

"What about you two?" Tecoloteh asked.

"We finished our programming in two days," Quicho replied, "and we've been helping Tom, Caymar, and their crew with the equipment installation since then."

"Where are Robert and Steven?" Fraxino thought to ask Tom.

"At the present moment, they're in one of our warehouses on Sirius B, working on more racks and frames to be brought."

Chispo was looking around the big room. "Wow! You dudes do fast work!"

"Already excavated and reinforced with your special lining," Rinto commented.

Most of the equipment was already installed and firmly bolted into place, including the big cube which would serve as the main frame central. The framework and cradle for the main Ulexite slab was already installed to its left, and there were a couple of other unknown machines to the right of the main cubical frame, evidently intended for use by government officials and special visitors.

"And you have most of the equipment already in place?" Fraxino asked.

"We do, fellows," Caymar replied. "In just a short while, we're going to levitate the Ulexite slab and maneuver it into its special cradle."

"Then we can position your fabulously grown crystal array underneath it," Tom added. "Oh, here it comes now."

The others watched as several Sirian crew members carefully guided the 4 by 5 meter slab into the room from where it was temporarily stored by the Atlanteans' device-craft. It was hovering in the air, and they watched it, seemingly by magic, float over to the specially designed and built cradle and ease itself right into place.

Next, another piece of special framework containing a large inverted receiving cup was caused to float upwards and position itself on top of the cradle. Several crew members climbed the cradle tower and bolted the inverted cup frame to the four corners of the special cradle, thereby firmly securing the Ulexite slab in place.

Excellently done, Tom telepathically commended the crew.

Next, Rinto, Fraxino, Tecoloteh and Latorna moved the Fluorite-Ulexite crystal array into the lower section of the cradle tower and placed it on a shelf, already made and waiting for it. It slid into place perfectly.

"All right! Ready to go!" Rinto declared.

"Tom, we've got three more pieces up in our cave that were too big to bring," Fraxino told him.

"Can you maneuver them out of the cave out into the open?" Tom asked.

"Yes, but with a minimum of six of us," said Fraxino.

"Have them waiting outside the cave, and we'll collect them with our spacecraft," Tom offered.

"Why don't you come with us in our cruiser craft and teleport them here?" Rinto suggested.

Tom thought about it a few moments. "Yes, good idea. Let's go. The spacecraft would be cumbersome, anyway."

"Yeah, and it's so big you might get noticed by some of Zantaayer's residents," Chispo added.

"Good point," Tom agreed. *Dotsero, man the crew. We're going for the other crystal arrays.* "Caymar come with us."

Four of the five Atlanteans stayed so they could integrate the intelligence properties from the Quanac flower into their device-craft. Meanwhile, Rinto, Fraxino, Chispo and Chameur, Tom, and Caymar walked out through the tunnel to the glacier outside. They boarded Rinto and Fraxino's vehicle-craft. Fraxino did the driving. He pulled back the lever, and the craft silently left the glacier. At Fraxino's telepathic command, the main controls crystal caused the craft to swiftly accelerate over the ridge of Mt. Isto to the north.

"Impressive flying craft of yours!" Caymar stated.

"Thank you. It serves us well," said Rinto.

"Fraxino's going to put this cruiser craft in high gear," Chispo boasted, "and we're going to be flying over the Ciruclar Mountains of Zotola in seconds, dudes!"

Fraxino gave another telepathic command, and the forcefield accompanied by the green glow overtook them for a brief moment. Then they were flying over the southern range of the Ciruclar Mountains.

"Our cave is just a few kilometers north of here," Fraxino announced.

"We'll be there in just a few minutes," Rinto added.

Fraxino cruised the treetops of the mountainous ridge, lined up the craft with the gravel road, and when the first sufficient opening between trees was seen, he brought it down to the road, whizzing by trees and landing at approximately 80 km/h. Immediately, he slowed down.

"Wow! You fellows are somewhat wreckless!" Caymar declared.

"Oh, don't worry," Chispo assured Tom and Caymar. "Fraxino and Rinto got it all figured out, man. They've got correction crystals on this craft to guide them in for exact and perfect landings every time."

"Except that one time in Mexico," Rinto reminded.

"Oh, yeah," Chispo recalled.

Fraxino placed the transmission in second gear, engaged the clutch, and he drove them along the gravel road that wound its way through the forest of dominant Southern Beech trees. He pulled over on the side road, parked, and the six of them walked the 20 minutes down the gully to the cave below.

"We haven't yet told you fellows what happened to three of our crew members," Caymar brought up.

"No, what?" Fraxino asked with interest.

Caymar proceeded to tell them the whole story about the surprise of the mysterious shaft, the death of three of their Sirian crew, the bronze Vegan tablet, the discovery of Morris' requiem, and most of all, the real surprise of the three Sirians' miraculous resurrection. All of this Caymar related to them as they walked down the gully. Next, they entered the cave.

Tom and Caymar had never visited their cave before, and neither had Chameur. After walking down several corridors and climbing the rope to reach their cave research and growing room, they were impressed with how out of the way and secure Rinto and Fraxino's facilities were.

Two of the three crystal arrays had been moved out of the room and were sitting in the corridor. The final piece was still in the room, and it was to be used to aid the device-craft in time travel.

"Here they are," Fraxino announced. "We need them teleported to Alaska."

"Of these two here," Rinto indicated, "the one on the left goes inside your main frame central cube." It was big, measuring 2 meters across, being somewhat rectangular, and consisting of a decent amount of Ulexite as the basis with thin vertical lines of gold, iridium, and Rutilated Quartz lines to aid in achieving better etherical connections throughout the main frame central. "The one on the right is for installation in one of your machines in the further end of your pyramid room," Rinto further indicated. This piece was smaller, around 1.2 meters across, more rounded in shape, and colored mostly black, consisting of mostly black Obsidian, grown with a secret Atlantean formula of impurities specifically designed to block intelligence suppression maneuvers without anyone ever realizing it.

They walked inside the cave research room and marvelled at the crystal array for use in time travel assistance for the device-craft. Its colors were mostly green with some orange Calcite, and within its basic colors were grown more secret Atlantean formulas of elemental impurities to achieve perfection in time travel assistance.

"Fellows, you really pulled it off well this time," Tom commended.

"Thank Tecoloteh and Latorna more than us," Rinto admitted. "Those two whizzes knew *exactly* what to do."

"Their being from Atlantis, I'm not surprised," said Tom.

"We have a lot to be grateful for that they are helping us on this project," Caymar told them, "along with being grateful for your help, as well."

"Thanks, Caymar," said Rinto.

"If everyone's ready," Tom announced, "I'll go ahead and teleport these three pieces back to our station." The others gestured approval. "I'm going to do them one at a time. As the third one disappears, I'll be accompanying it to the station. We'll place that third one next to your device-craft, post arrival."

"Excellent," Fraxino approved.

"Caymar will be accompanying the rest of you all as you return in your craft," Tom added.

"That will be fine," said Rinto. "We'll see you there in around an hour."

Tom waved his walking staff over each piece, bringing on a pink glow of energy accompanied by the sound of whirring wind. At the same time, he telepathically communicated with Dotsero and his crew to position themselves accordingly and be ready to receive each piece. One piece disappeared, and Tom waved his walking staff over the second assembly, causing it to disappear. "Okay, now for the final piece," and he walked into their cave research room where he performed the same procedure. Once it disappeared, Tom instantly and silently teleported away. He and his crew in Alaska were now already attending to the placing of each of the three assemblies in their appropriate places in the station.

"Amazing, dudes!" Fraxino exclaimed. "They're out of here."

"Wonder why we struggled getting that Fluorite-Ulexite crystal array out of this cave the hard way?" Rinto asked his brother.

"Yeah, now that's what I want to know," Fraxino agreed.

"Hope they got there all right," said Rinto.

"Don't worry," Chispo reassured them. "Knowing Tom, they did."

"This is certainly an impressive research room," Chameur complimented. "So, this is where Tecoloteh and Latorna spent the last six days with you?"

"This is it," Rinto verified.

They spent several minutes looking around. Then they walked back through the corridors and out of the cave back outside. Twenty minutes later, they were back at the vehicle-craft, and Rinto drove down the gravel road.

Once in an appropriate place on the road, Rinto pulled back the lever.

"Yet another trip to Earth!" he enthusiastically declared as they became airborne. The scenery changed, and in seconds, they were flying toward Alaska's Mt. Isto, and they came in for a landing on the glacier again.

As they were stepping down from the craft, they suddenly heard the sound of whirring wind. They quickly looked in that direction and saw four pink glows which soon faded away.

"Robert, Steven!" Chispo declared. "What's going on, dudes?"

"Hey, how's it going?" Rinto called out.

The others greeted them, as well.

"Who are the other two with you?" Fraxino wanted to know.

"These are Chris and Richard Bell," said Steven, "who we met while hiking in

Tasmania back in April. They're extraterrestrials from the Planet of the Islands."

"They have an arboretum with trees from all over the galaxy," Robert told them.

"And we helped them install a thousand-line step office a couple of months ago," Steven added.

They introduced each other and shook hands.

"So, how have things gone for you all this past week?" Robert asked Rinto, Fraxino, and Chispo.

"Busy, busy," Rinto answered.

"Except for Chispo and Chameur," Fraxino remarked with a smile. "They went off *joy riding* to Caloma for six days?"

"Is that right?" Robert responded.

"Did you get everything grown and made okay?" Steven asked.

"Sure did, man," Fraxino answered. "Tom just teleported the grown assemblies to the station. They're supposed to be installing them right now. Come on in and let's take a look."

They started walking toward the tunnel.

"I guess you noticed they put the security doors up?" Steven said and indicated as they walked by them.

"Oh yeah," Rinto acknowledged.

"Man these gurus grew a total of four separate masterpieces," Chispo boasted as they walked through the ice tunnel.

"Complete with secret Atlantean formulas of impurities for added clarity and instilled intelligence," Fraxino added proudly.

"No kidding!" Steven responded.

They soon reached the device-craft where Quicho, Seglima, Latorna and Tecoloteh were busy positioning the greenish-orange time travel crystal array into place. There was just enough room for it in a reserved compartment at the tail end of the device-craft. After installation, they would make proper connections and integrate the array with their main on-board central crystal, to finally achieve the long awaited and desired feat of time travel.

They observed the four Atlanteans a few moments and then continued walking, soon entering the pyramid room. Tom and the crew were busy securing the big array within the cubical main frame central. The black Obsidian array had yet to be installed.

Caymar walked over to that piece, and Rinto, Fraxino, and the others helped them install it into one of the top secret government-use soul travel devices, after which Caymar closed the door to the secret compartment and reinstalled the metal panel in front of it.

"Ready to go!" Caymar declared triumphantly, and he smiled.

Chispo looked up toward the apex of the room. A small spiral stairway and passageway had been installed with a ladder that went up through the mysterious shaft.

"Oh, yeah, the shaft," said Rinto when he looked up there also.

"Let's go check it out, dudes," Chispo requested.

"Follow me to Morris' mysterious requiem," Caymar offered.

Chispo, Chameur, Rinto and Fraxino followed Caymar over to the spiral staircase. Robert, Steven, Chris and Richard had seen the requiem the other day, so they stayed down in the pyramid room. Before climbing up to the apex, Caymar showed them the bronze tablet written in Lyran script.

"Wow!" Rinto declared. "That's pre-Atlantean sure enough."

As they looked at it, they could decipher some of the script, as it had some similarities to Atlantean. They climbed the narrow staircase, reached the shaft, and climbed up the ladder into the room.

"Far out!" Fraxino stated, upon seeing the different crystals in the room.

They walked over to the large Calcite rectangular cubical slab.

"And you said this thing plays a holographic movie clip?" Rinto asked Caymar.

Before another word was said, the 35-second movie proceeded to play for them, with an image of an older version of Morris.

"Oh, wow!" Chispo reacted. "It *is* Morris!"

"I'm surprised he doesn't show himself as a dolphin," said Rinto.

"But the scenery looks like the dolphin world," Fraxino pointed out.

They finished watching the clip, had another look around the room, marvelled over the crystals, and then descended the shaft and staircase back into the main pyramid room.

"Rinto, we need to take those Quanac flowers and plant them," Chameur brought up.

"Okay, let's go ahead and take them now," he answered.

Caymar, and also Chris and Richard, stayed with Tom and the crew as they connected and interfaced the crystal arrays.

Rinto, Fraxino, Robert, Chispo, Chameur, and Steven walked out of the pyramid room, briefly stopping at the project room to talk to the four other Atlanteans, who were busy integrating the time travel crystal array with their device-craft's main controls crystal.

"I believe we're going to make it work," Seglima told them.

"It's installing very well," said Quicho.

"Excellent," Fraxino responded.

"Listen, we're going to go ahead and plant those Quanac flowers," Chispo told the others.

Tecoloteh reached for them and handed them to Chispo and Chameur. Then the six of them walked out the tunnel out onto the glacier where they boarded the vehicle-craft.

Rinto drove, and once they were inside, he pulled back the lever, and the craft silently left the glacier's surface. With a telepathic command, the craft quickly accelerated toward the south and gained altitude. In seconds, they were clearing Mt. Isto's southern ridge and crossing Alaska's icy tundra terrain.

"Where's a good place to plant the Quanac?" Rinto asked Chameur.

"Somewhere in a deep, moist virgin forest."

Chispo translated Chameur's answer to English.

"There's a lot of that along the west coasts of British Columbia and Washington," Robert informed them.

"Where do you think the best place is?" Fraxino asked.

Robert thought a moment. "For some reason, Vancouver Island in British Columbia comes to me."

"Then let's go there," said Fraxino.

"All right, dude," Chispo directed Rinto. "Let's put this craft in high gear and zoom on down there."

"Right on, Chispo!" Rinto shouted.

With another telepathic command, the craft accelerated at full force, pressing them back in their seats. Of course, Chispo and Chameur were sitting by each other, and they enjoyed another experience of being pressed closer together by the force of acceleration.

For the next hour, they flew at very high altitude, reaching Alaska's southern coast, veering to the left and following the west coast of Alaska, passing by Juneau, and eventually entering British Columbia further southeast.

"How much further is it to Vancouver Island?" Rinto asked Robert.

"Some ways yet," Robert answered.

"It's almost to Washington," Steven also answered.

After another 20 minutes of fast flying, they saw the big, oval shaped island come into view. Rinto slowed the craft accordingly and lowered its altitude.

"Wow, that island's got some mountains!" Fraxino remarked.

As they began to fly over the large island, Chameur used her expert senses to choose the best location.

"There's a large park in the central region of the island called Strathcona Provincial Park," Robert informed the others. "It's supposed to have plenty of virgin temperate rain forest."

There were several roads along the way. Some crossed the island. Others didn't.

"Fraxino, pull out our atlas," Rinto said to him. "Let's see if we can find this park."

A minute later, they had their atlas open to the appropriate page. Fraxino and Chispo showed the atlas to Chameur, and they chose one of the lakes in that park. Rinto lowered the craft's altitude to cruise the treetops, to avoid being seen by any possible authorities and rangers.

"There's a mountain called Golden Hinde," Chispo pointed out.

"That's it straight ahead of us, isn't it?" Fraxino asked.

"Exactly," Chispo verified. "According to the map, there's a decent size lake south of there. Let's touch down on the shore of the lake."

Rinto flew the craft around the west side of the snow-covered mountain, which stood more than 2,000 meters high. A few kilometers further south, they located the lake, crossed it, and landed on its southern shore. No one else was in sight.

It was around 7 PM. The day was August 5, 1985.

As they stepped down from the craft, Chameur said, "Let's take those Quanac flowers up the tributaries to this lake, to plant two each in two separate springs."

The scenery was magnificent. The air was clear with blue sky. Sure enough, the terrain around the lake was thickly forested with plenty of Firs, Spruces, Western Red Cedars, Alaska Yellow Cedars, Bigleaf Maples, and the forest floor had plenty of moss and ferns.

Rinto and Fraxino attended the craft while Robert, Steven, Chispo and Chameur explored the forest, looking for small streams and springs feeding the lake. They spent several hours searching, finally finding two appropriate places. Chameur planted the Quanac with Chispo's help, after which they turned toward each other, wrapped their arms around each other, and kissed. Robert and Steven certainly noticed how Chispo and Chameur were in love with each other.

Meanwhile, Rinto and Fraxino talked over further plans, what they were going to do next.

"Boy we're *really* going to have a smashing success of a report to hand to our Ancient Atlantean History class this next year," Fraxino told his brother.

"Complete with five live Atlanteans to tell us all we need to know," said Rinto.

"The history class is only going to get a small percentage of all we really know about it."

"That's for sure. The rest will go into the book we can write about it."

It was just getting dark when the others arrived.

"We found some ideal springs and planted them," Chispo told them with a smile.

"Indeed an ideal location," Chameur stated. "Perfect for transmitting positive vibrations for peace and also for maintaining the ecological balance."

"Hmm . . . the ecological balance," Rinto repeated.

They talked about the Quanac flower a while longer, and they pitched their tents and camped for the night by the lakeshore. There were some mosquitos, but inside their tents, they were safely away from their annoyance.

The next day, Rinto and Fraxino flew them back to Alaska's Mt. Isto. They arrived near noon. As they stepped down from the vehicle-craft just outside the tunnel entrance, Tom and Caymar happened to emerge from the tunnel.

"How's it going?" Robert called over to Tom and Caymar.

"We're fine," Tom answered. "Good timing."

"Did you find a good location for those Quanac flowers?" Caymar asked.

"Oh yeah. We did," Chispo replied.

"You fellows and the Atlanteans have done a superb job," Tom commended them. "The station is in good running order, the best we can tell."

"Once we teleport in our Sirian power generator and give the station power," said Caymar, "we'll know for sure."

"Excellent!" Rinto declared.

"We've got to dig a trench to connect to the Alaska pipeline," Tom mentioned.

"Oh, yeah," Chispo responded, smiling, "for the secret fiberoptic cable buried parallel to the pipeline."

"Exactly," said Tom, also with a smile.

"Tomorrow, we're going to begin work on the stone lodge down in the cove," Caymar announced.

"Our laser cutter tools, levitation skills, and special cements will make that job feasible in a day," Tom added.

"That's all?" Rinto asked in a surprised manner.

"I'll say that's quick," Robert declared.

"With you Sirians, nothing surprises me anymore," Steven remarked.

"Right, fellows," Tom now spoke in a business-like manner, "your work has been successfully accomplished, a job well done. Come aboard our spacecraft in regards to the 100,000 zúbola reward."

"Oh wow!" Fraxino responded.

"I forgot all about the monetary reward," Chispo admitted.

"Me too," Rinto also admitted.

Meanwhile Quicho, Seglima, Latorna and Tecoloteh were inside the mountain with their device-craft. Chris and Richard were inside the big room working with the Sirian crew. The others: Rinto, Fraxino, Chispo and Chameur, Robert, and Steven, stepped aboard the spacecraft with Tom and Caymar. Once inside, Tom opened a cabinet and took out a silver metal container. He opened its lid and took out a stack of notes.

"I don't know how you fellows want to divide up the money," Tom said to everyone, "but here is the reward. Thank you for a job well done for this galactic station in Alaska." He handed the bundle of notes to Fraxino. "Robert, Steven, I'll be paying you fellows, along with Chris and Richard, separately as you know."

"Yes, that's fine," Steven acknowledged.

"Wow! Thanks, Tom," Fraxino told him. He divided the money equally among the three of them.

"Thank you," said Rinto.

"I really appreciate this," Chispo acknowledged. "Dudes, we'll be able to travel all over Artenia now. Yahoo! We no longer have to depend on work to make a living!"

"And we can do even more projects . . ."

They continued talking about it as they stepped down from the spacecraft with Tom and Caymar and re-entered the ice tunnel.

"You know, what percentage do we need to give to our Atlantean friends?" Rinto asked Fraxino and Chispo.

"I don't know," Fraxino answered. He thought a moment. "What about 40% of it? After all, Latorna and Tecoloteh did most of the work. As we know, two of them stayed here with their device-craft."

"And Chameur was joy riding for 6 days and . . ." Rinto commented. He stopped, thought, and then said, "Chispo, what are you doing with part of this money?"

"I stayed out of you hair, like you wanted."

"Rinto, Chispo and Chameur did find those Quanac flowers, remember," Fraxino pointed out.

"Yeah, that's true," said Rinto. He paused. "Yes, that will be fine, Chispo. Stay with that money. Consider it a wedding present."

"Rinto," Chispo responded, giving him a smirk.

"Yeah, we know," Rinto told him. "Besides, we want you to help us with our next project, to help us compile our book. I want you to buy a computer setup and crystal array, so we can keep a copy of all our data at your house."

"Sure, guys. I'll be glad to," Chispo consented, "and Chameur can help for sure."

They reached the project room and device-craft, where the other four Atlanteans were.

"Fellows, thanks again for growing these excellent crystal arrays," Tom said to them. "Caymar and I are going to return to the big room and continue making connections. We've got other star systems to bring into the picture."

"Thanks for hiring us," said Fraxino.

"Our pleasure," said Tom.

"Come back next week," Caymar invited them. "By then we'll have everything up and running. You can experience different machines, soul travel, and the rest of it."

"Thanks, we will," said Rinto.

"Want to come with us to Zotola?" Rinto offered Robert and Steven.

"Yeah, sure. Thanks," Robert replied.

"No, that's okay," said Steven. "I'll stay here with Tom and the crew."

"We didn't mean to brush you off last week," Rinto reassured him. "It's just our project at hand . . ."

"Oh, I know," said Steven. "Don't worry about it."

"Okay."

"You going to be around here?" Robert asked Steven.

"Yep, sure will."

"I'll see you here in a few days."

"Okay, see you later," said Steven.

They all wished each other well. Tom, Caymar, and Steven then continued walking to the big room. Rinto, Fraxino, and Chispo started talking to the other Atlanteans. Of the 100,000 zúbolas, they handed them 40,000 of it.

"Thank you very much," Seglima said to them.

"We're not sure where we're going to live the rest of our lives," said Latorna, "but we're likely going to choose Zantaayer. If so, this Zotolan currency will serve us well."

All of them were grateful for the money.

"So, do the four of you want to return to Artenia with us?" Chameur offered them.

Seglima looked at Chameur, then said, "You really have taken up with Chispo, haven't you?"

Chameur gave an admitting gesture.

"I knew you had," said Seglima, smiling.

"How nice that you've found such an excellent replacement for Qwintelo," Latorna told Chameur.

"Yes, that was a sad loss," Chameur responded, recalling her lost romance.

"We still need to do a little more interfacing with the time travel array," Quicho informed everyone.

"Like how much more time do you think it will take?" Rinto asked.

"Two more hours, and we'll have it all programmed," Seglima answered.

"Then we can time travel," said Quicho.

"Go visit Atlantis," said Tecoloteh.

"Yes, but the bad energies?" Seglima reminded them.

"True," said Tecoloteh. "We don't want to get tangled up in *that* again."

"Can you wait two hours, and we'll all come with you?" Seglima requested.

"No problem," said Rinto.

For the next two hours, Rinto, Fraxino, Chispo and Chameur looked over the device-craft with the other Atlanteans. Meanwhile, Robert took a walk outside to the glacier and walked down to the cove. Sirian crew vehicles were beginning to laser cut a trench for the fiberoptic cable. The trench would cross the tundra laden valley way down below, west of Mt. Isto, and connect with the northern end of the Alaska pipeline.

Another crew was already beginning work on the stone lodge. Robert walked over to the site and observed them. The first laser cut rocks were being installed around the foundation.

Robert noticed that this galactic station was being built in an incredibly short period of time. Why it would require 15 years until its grand opening at the turn of the millennium, Robert didn't know. It seemed like everything was nearly ready, certainly no later than 1986. Perhaps it would indeed be up and running by the next year but not officially recognized until that time much later. Besides, it might take that long to establish connections with the numerous star systems throughout the galaxy, and maybe some from other galaxies, as well. In addition to that, lots of area codes would need to be added to Canada, the USA, and Great Britain, and time would be required to free up those blocks of millions of phone numbers without the public becoming suspicious.

Robert walked back up the glacier to the tunnel entrance, and walked to the big pyramid room, where he talked with Chris, Richard, and Steven.

"How much longer are you guys going to work for Tom and Caymar?" Robert asked them.

"Probably another week," Richard answered, "until that stone lodge is finished."

"You all haven't mentioned a thing about Mr. Mayfield," Robert brought up. "How does he like your planet?"

"Oh yeah. He's doing fine," Chris answered.

"He comes over and visits us from time to time," Richard also answered.

"He likes our arboretum, and he likes fishing, as well," Chris added.

Back at the beginning of the summer, after school was out, Robert and his friends had transported their high school science teacher, Mr. Mayfield, to Chris and Richard Bell's home planet, the Planet of the Islands. He had been enjoying a peaceful summer vacation away from the daily stress and rituals of planet Earth.

"Let's not forget to bring him back home to Earth by the end of this month," said Robert.

"Oh no, we won't forget," Chris reassured him.

"I'll bet he'd like to see this galactic station," said Robert.

"Good idea," said Richard. "I'd say he would be impressed."

"We'll bring him here next week when it's all finished," said Chris.

They walked around the place, looking at the large equipment, marvelling at the huge cubical main frame central, and the other special use machines, as well.

"This would make quite a tourist attraction," said Robert.

"If the general public were to know about it," Steven added comment.

They walked up the spiral staircase to Morris' requiem and marvelled at the crystals, the large orange Calcite slab, and of course the 35-second 3D holographic movie clip.

When they came down into the pyramid room again, Tom walked over to them.

"Robert," said Tom, "I understand you're going to Artenia with Rinto, Fraxino, and the Atlanteans."

"Right, and Steven, Chris and Richard are going to stay here to do more work."

"Here, let me pay you for your past week's work," Tom offered. He took out of one of his pockets several $100 notes. "Here's $500."

"Thank you, Tom," said Robert.

"No problem. Thanks for your work. Come back and visit next week."

"I sure will," said Robert.

"Oh, and remind your friends," Tom offered, "they're certainly welcome to look through our Galactic Federation historical records, if they need to."

"Thanks. I'll tell them."

"Steven, Chris and Richard, I'm also going to pay each of you for your work so far." Tom handed each of them $500.

They all thanked him.

"I'd say I'll need you fellows for another week . . ." Tom began.

Robert walked back to the device-craft in the project room. The Atlanteans were just about to finish with interfacing the time travel crystal array. Rinto, Fraxino, and Chispo were observing, impressed by all they could do.

"Okay, ready to run!" Quicho declared in triumph.

"It's totally interfaced and time travel ready," Seglima announced.

"Right, let's go visit Zantaayer for a while," said Tecoloteh.

All of them stepped out of the device-craft. Chameur did the honors of telepathically locking the door. Then they walked down the tunnel to the glacier outside, where they boarded the vehicle-craft.

There were a total of nine of them: the five Atlanteans, Rinto, Fraxino, Chispo, and Robert.

"Robert, from the time we met you and your Earth friends," Chispo brought up, "you've all gone your separate ways."

"Yes, that's the way things go sometimes. Thanks for inviting me back again."

"No problem," Rinto assured him. "The crystal arrays project is finished. We can all relax and enjoy, now." He got into the driver's seat.

"Dudes, sit back," Chispo boasted to the Atlanteans. "Rinto's going to put this craft in high gear, and we'll be in Zantaayer in a matter of seconds, man!"

Rinto pulled back the lever. The craft left the ground and swiftly accelerated to the north, clearing Mt. Isto's ridge in seconds. The green glow briefly enveloped them, and then they were suddenly flying over the desert valley south of Zantaayer's Ciruclar Mountains. It was right at mid day, and Al Nitak was high in the sky.

"Want to hear *The Hydragyros*?" Chispo offered, speaking to Robert.

"Yeah, sure."

Chispo took out the holodisk and inserted it in their on-board player. In seconds, the first song on the album was playing, so impressive and original, such a moving piece that Robert was still impressed each time he heard it play. It really did make its listeners want to take charge of their life and live it to the fullest.

"Dudes, I tell you that group's done excellent," Fraxino informed them. "In a month's time, they've already achieved number 5 on Zotola's top 12 pop charts."

"They're predicted to soar to number 1 in the next few weeks," Chispo added.

"With that impressive song, they will," Seglima predicted.

Rinto brought the craft in for a landing, touching down on the highway just before crossing the southern ridge of the Ciruclar Mountains. Zantaayer, and the Elizabeth Ocean beyond, came into view, and the Atlanteans were impressed by the scenic forested highway as they descended the hairpin curves into Zantaayer.

"These mountains are truly filled with Noirtrel Alaktt trees, aren't they?" Chameur commented.

"That's right," Chispo answered. "Nortralakt trees along with other trees, as well."

"I didn't tell you this but those trees are specially known for adding humidity to the mountain climate."

"In addition to maintaining the subterranean balance of water," Tecoloteh added.

"Yeah, that would make sense," said Chispo, "now that I think about it, seeing how we've got mostly desert valleys to the south of us."

"I have a feeling," said Chameur. "The valley where Zantaayer now is, was a lot drier before Cresma and his people came here, all those years ago."

"I'd say you're right," said Chispo, "seeing what it looked like in that holographic movie of yours."

Rinto finished the last hairpin curve on the narrow forested highway. The road straightened, and they entered the city of Zantaayer. They passed industries and manufacturers until they got nearer the city center.

"Oh wow!" Chispo suddenly called out when he saw an advertisement sign on the side of the highway. "They're playing tonight."

"Who, *The Hydragyros*?" Seglima asked.

"Exactly," Chispo verified. "They're performing at the outdoor arena on the grounds of Zantaayer's University of Zotola."

"Excellent!" Fraxino remarked.

Chispo next told Robert in English.

"Yeah, I'd like to see them . . . such an impressive group."

"We'll have to check that out," said Rinto.

"Looks like it will be a good night for it," said Fraxino.

Twenty minutes later, they were pulling into the Zapatero's driveway. By chance, Glecko was just arriving home from doing errands. He pulled up behind them in his immaculate Tolejo sedan. Once they parked, they all stepped outside.

"Hi guys," Glecko greeted them. "How was it?"

"The station's built, Dad," Rinto answered.

"The four crystal arrays arrived perfectly with Tom's teleportation skills," Fraxino answered.

"And they are a grand success," Rinto added.

"Success again, sons," their father praised them. "I knew you and your Atlantean friends could pull it off."

All of them walked inside and visited. They told Glecko and Sosta more stories. The Atlanteans told an earful as well, including plenty of stories from Chispo and Chameur, not to mention, their adventures in Caloma.

That night, Rinto, Fraxino, and Chispo took Robert and the five Atlanteans to Zantaayer's outdoor arena, where the young pop artists of *The Hydragyros* gave their complete performance, a thrilling success indeed. Their songs promoted peace, love and forgiveness, as well as taking charge of your life and living it to the fullest. Seeing their performance personally was even better than hearing it over a holodisk player, and the acoustics were perfect, not too loud, not too soft. After the concert, they went up on stage and met the group, shook hands with them, and talked a few minutes. The group was really surprised to find out that five of them were from Atlantis.

As Rinto drove them home later that night, Chispo remarked, "I really am impressed by that group." He repeated the same comment in English to Robert.

"Never before have I heard so many good sounding songs on the same album," Robert declared.

"A masterpiece indeed," Tecoloteh stated.

"I have a feeling about that group," Chameur brought up.

"Really, what?" Chispo asked.

"On Earth, exactly 12 years from now, the equivalent to that album of songs by *The Hydragyros* will be conceived, written, and performed by a group of young pop artists. They won't realize it, but they will be capturing those same songs and reproducing them almost identically and in all their quality, on Earth."

"Excellent! What year will that be, then?" Rinto asked his brother.

"Either 1997 or 1998."

"Good, that will serve Earth well, for those who can realize it," Rinto stated.

"Robert," Chispo told him, translating to English what Chameur predicted, "you're going to be surprised by an album that's going to be released on Earth 12 years from . . ." and he explained the prediction.

"That'll be interesting," said Robert. "I'll be on the lookout for it."

They arrived home, pulling into the Zapatero's driveway. They entered the house and went to sleep. Chispo and Chameur went across the bushes and slept at Chispo's house.

For the next week, while all the Atlanteans were visiting, Rinto and Fraxino took them all around Zantaayer. They visited the beach, the city center, the University of Zotola, and of course, the library, with all its ancient documents. They went up in the Ciruclar Mountains and enjoyed the serene beauty of the forest with its dominant Southern Beech trees. They took them to the ancient galactic dump site 100 kilometers south of Zantaayer, and they enjoyed a really good scavenge.

They camped there one night and Chispo pointed out the stars to everyone, showing them where Earth's star the Sun was, with Sirius A near it in the sky. He also pointed out the stars, Al Nilam and Mintaka, their two nearby neighbors.

Over the course of the week, Rinto and Fraxino made serious progress on their heritage compilation on Atlantis. Of course, their five friends were of immense help. Chispo bought a computer setup, and with help from the others, they installed a specially designed crystal array oriented toward compiling the data with ease. Chameur, having been the compiler of the holographic plates, was excellent at typesetting the whole document.

Both computer setups automatically produced the text in Artenian, and at Robert's request, a version was also produced in English text so he could show it to his good friends back in Tennessee. Robert also gave it a good reading, and he edited the entire text.

Rinto and Fraxino went to an office supply store and bought a fine, top-of-the-line laser printer, and they printed the thousand-page document in both Artenian and English. Then they went to a printing company and paid 2,000 zúbolas to have 1,000 hardback book copies produced in Artenian, and an additional 250 copies in English, those to be taken to Earth and anonymously delivered to certain government officials, and also to Robert's friends and interested people. Of the Artenian copies, half of them were stored at Rinto and Fraxino's house, and the other half at Chispo's house.

"Man your history class professor is *really* going to raise his eyebrows when he sees this!" Chispo told Rinto and Fraxino.

"I'll say," Fraxino agreed.

"We were thinking of only submitting a summary," said Rinto, "but now that we have this book, we'll just submit this."

"Yeah, I believe it will get him out of his chair, to put it mildly," Fraxino stated.

"More like going through the roof in surprise," Chispo clarified in a joking manner.

They laughed.

"There, that stores them," Fraxino declared, as they stacked the last of the books.

"Whew! What a triumph!" Chispo stated.

"I believe we're ready to go back to Alaska," Rinto suggested. "Guys, thanks a lot for all your help."

"It's our pleasure," Quicho replied.

"Information is very important, especially the truth," said Latorna.

"Since we've lived here beyond our era by 10,130 of your years," Chameur pointed out, "for what happened to us, there were no historians to intervene and corrupt the data."

"That's for sure," Fraxino agreed.

"We have the most accurate document on Atlantis' heritage in existence," said Rinto.

"Right on, brother!" Fraxino exclaimed.

They brought their hands together in triumph. Chispo joined in, and the Atlanteans did, as well. They were very proud of the work they had just done: *The Heritage of Atlantis*. Rinto, Fraxino, Chispo, and the five Atlanteans listed themselves as the authors on the front page of the book.

"And when we get back from Alaska, not before," Rinto said to everyone, "we'll drop an anonymous copy over at Zotola's news media."

Chispo laughed, along with the others.

"Man, that will get them out of their chairs for sure!" Chispo declared.

They all laughed heartily.

"Just remember to cut the front page out before delivering it," Fraxino reminded his brother.

"Yes, of course."

An hour later, they had their vehicle-craft loaded and ready to go. All 250 English version copies of *The Heritage of Atlantis*, along with a few Artenian versions, were also loaded. They occupied 10 boxes. It was a tight fit with all the books, but they all managed. Glecko and Sosta wished them all well, and Fraxino backed them out of the driveway.

"Let's see if Tom and their crew have the station finished," Fraxino said to everyone.

He drove them toward the mountains, and when the road entered the forest at the base of the mountain slopes, he pulled back the lever. They became airborne and swiftly picked up speed. The green glow enveloped them, and before they totally realized it, they were flying toward Alaska's Mt. Isto, soon making their landing on the glacier. Tom and Caymar's Sirian spacecraft was still there.

The date was Friday, August 16, 1985.

As they all stepped down from the craft, they noticed that the stone lodge down in the cove was all finished. A grand mansion it was indeed! There were also two helicopters parked beside it.

"Wow, dudes!" Chispo declared. "Take a look at that stone lodge. We'll have to check that out."

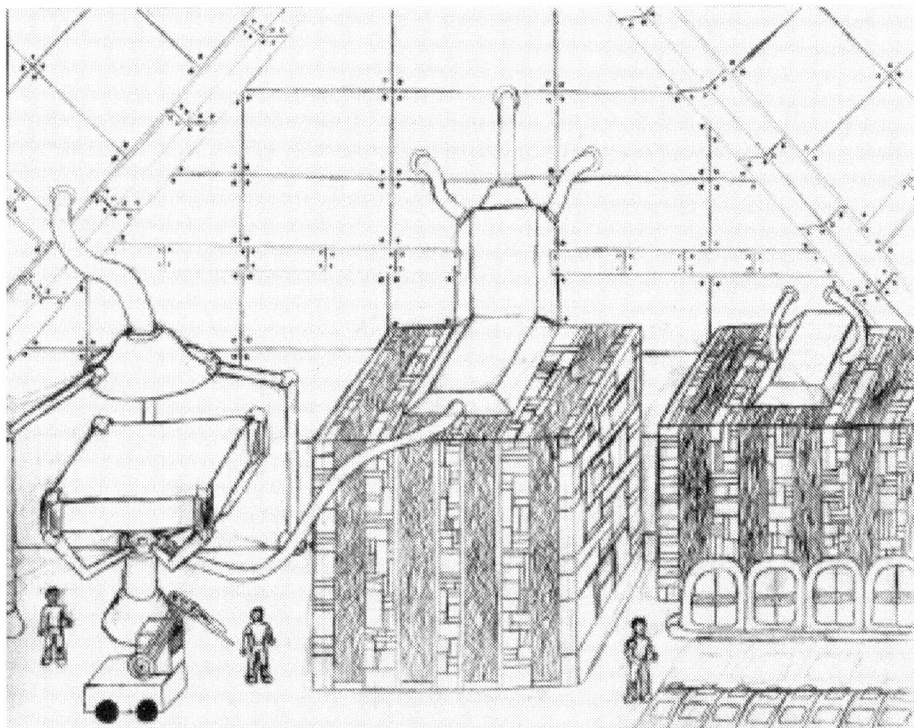

They walked inside the ice tunnel. The Atlanteans stopped at their device-craft, telepathically unlocked the door, and entered. Each of them carried a copy of their recently printed book, to add to their collection of other artifacts.

With that done, they walked further down the corridor to the big pyramid room. Tom, Caymar, and their crew, along with Steven, Chris and Richard, were there. Tom appeared to be lifting up a lever. Lights turned on simultaneously on all pieces of equipment, both big and small. A few seconds went by.

"Yahoo!" they declared simultaneously.

"It all works!" Tom declared triumphantly. At that moment, he noticed that Robert, Rinto, Fraxino, Chispo, and their friends had just entered. He walked over to them.

"Rinto, Fraxino," Chispo quietly told them, "how do you two always manage to time it just right?"

"Just crystallized common sense," Fraxino replied.

"Fellows, you're perfectly on time," Tom declared. "Welcome to our station. We just got it turned on this very moment."

"Yes, we saw," Rinto responded.

"Be our first guests to use our equipment," Caymar offered.

"I see you got your lodge all finished down in the cove," Robert told Tom.

"Oh, yes," Tom answered. "The president is down there right now, along with

Britain's prime minister."

"Really?" Robert reacted.

"Yes, indeed," Tom confirmed.

"As it turns out," Caymar explained, "there are some secret summit talks taking place among top government officials and leaders down in Fairbanks, behind the public's eye, of course. Our galactic station was part of the reason they chose Fairbanks for the talks."

"They're walking up here right now," Tom informed them, "but you fellows will have first use of the equipment. You're the ones who helped us make it all possible."

"Thanks," Fraxino said.

All of them walked over to one of the special use machines to experience soul travel.

Steven, Chris and Richard, and Mr. Mayfield were present.

"How's it going, Robert?" Mr. Mayfield greeted him.

"Hey, Mr. Mayfield. How are you?"

"Oh, pretty good. What have you all been doing?"

"You won't believe what all we've done. We met these guys from Al Nitak. We've been to their world, to Mexico, and now here. We just finished compiling a book about Atlantis, too."

"Sounds very interesting. You seem like you've been pretty busy then," said Mr. Mayfield. "An impressive setup they've installed here, isn't it?"

"Yes, it is," Robert agreed.

"Looks like they're using some spiritual ether, along with gravity waves."

"Probably are," said Robert. "They tell me this here is a soul travel device. So, how was Planet of the Islands?"

As Robert and Mr. Mayfield talked about their adventures, Chispo and Chameur stepped inside the soul travel device. They were the first users.

Once inside, Chispo looked into her eyes and said, "Where do you wish to go?"

"Let's see . . . How about Atlantis?"

Next they lay down next to each other and pressed a button.

Lights turned on, and a whole virtual reality experience was granted them for the next twelve minutes. They felt totally relaxed as they felt themselves pop over to Atlantis and view it as Chameur knew it in her time. The beautiful mountains around Taltipocheh could be seen. Then they floated inland to the town of Atenkor, after which they entered the high mountains above the town and viewed the forests of Noirtrel Alaktt trees and Coldtog trees, as well. It was a sensational experience, perfectly controlled telepathically, which left both Chispo and Chameur spellbound and seriously impressed at the end of the twelve minutes.

They both stepped out of the device in somewhat of a daze, feeling totally satisfied.

"How was it?" Robert asked Chispo and Chameur.

"Far out!" Chispo replied, and smiled.

"Such an authentic experience," Chameur declared, "as if we really went there."

While others looked at some other equipment, Tecoloteh and Latorna both entered the special soul travel device. They lay down next to each other, and as they pressed the button, they thought about the Southern Beech forest of Atlantis.

In short order, they saw an image of a star in the night sky, a star called Sintecsi, 60 light years away and in position just above the Ursa Major constellation. They zoomed in on the star system, arriving at a planet by the name of Sxintleeni, the 2nd planet out from that star. A world very similar to Earth, they realized as they zoomed in on it, a world full of temperate rain forests, mountains, and humidity. The dominant tree was the Southern Beech (*Nothofagus*), 25 varieties of them, also known as the Noirtrel Alaktt, an ancient tree dating back 180 million years to its origin. Other trees resembled Celery Top Pines (*Phyllocladus*), Ginkgoes, Cedars, and some fruit trees.

There existed a race of humans called the Ellevec Ultlaplac. 72 million years ago, the Nothofagus was brought to Earth's southern hemisphere to regulate and maintain the balance of subterranean water reserves, in addition to other detoxifying properties the tree possesses. The Fagus and Castanea of the north were later evolved varieties originating from the Nothofagus of Earth's southern hemisphere.

Latorna and Tecoloteh observed more breathtaking scenery from this home planet of the Nothofagus, after which they were returned to their bodies. They stepped out of the device, also dazed. Quicho and Seglima were waiting to enter next.

"Wow!" Tecoloteh commented to Quicho and Seglima. "That machine is incredible!"

"We just found out the origin of the Noirtrel Alaktt," Latorna informed them.

"Really?!" Seglima reacted.

They entered the device next, to experience another revelation.

Immediately, Quicho and Seglima were whisked away through the stars, passing through a strange dimensional door between the Ursa Major and Ursa Minor constellation. They felt themselves pick up speed as they accelerated and zoomed across the heavens, passing by stars and galaxies, until they came in on one of them. Soon, a star came into view, a star called Sikrahk, 25 million light years away from Earth. A planet called Centón Etihelf, the 12th in their solar system, came into view, and they soon saw a beautiful world full of temperate rain forests of literally thousands of varieties of Ficus trees along with orchid flowers, as well. On that world lived a special race of beings called the Centurions.

Next, a particular version of a tree came into view, the *Ficus sycomorus*. They saw a historical summary portraying the revelation of that tree, that it was taken to planet Earth some 55 million years ago, and that it made its home in the Holy Land. Over the course of time, it came to be adopted by the Hebrews and Jews as the tree of reconciliation and forgiveness. In the old days, it was known as the *Yom Kipor*, later being given the Latin name *Ficus sycomorus*.

The old name, however, stayed with the Hebrew and Jewish culture, and it became a sacred yearly ritual to set aside one day each September to close all places of business, to stop and think, to repent, to throw away all grudges, and most importantly to forgive. The day became known as Yom Kippur, the day of atonement, and various sacred rituals would be carried out on that day each year. A very special day it became and very important to their culture, for thousands of years to come.

Quicho and Seglima next found themselves returned to the device. They got up, spellbound, and stepped out into the pyramidal room.

"How was it?" Latorna asked them. "Incredible wasn't it?"

"Eeuusyn sxcorr . . ." said Quicho, and he proceeded to relate the experience they just had.

By this time, the president and Britain's prime minister, both accompanied by armed body guards, walked into the big room. Tom saw them enter and walked over to greet them.

"Welcome to our galactic station," Tom greeted them and quickly continued by saying, "Look, we must have your guards remove their arms and ammunition from this facility immediately."

They looked at Tom with immediate defense and a look of confrontation.

"That's *strict* Galactic Federation mandate!" Tom firmly stated. "Set those weapons outside the tunnel on the glacier immediately! This area is protected. Weapons of all types are prohibited. No one's going to harm any of you here."

The president and the prime minister simultaneously looked at their armed guards and said, "Do as Tom says. The Galactic Federation is above our rank." The guards were seen to immediately leave the premises.

"Excellent!" Tom said. "Now we can begin our tour."

Tom was generally a peaceful man, but since he came from Sirius B, a world where weapons did not exist, the sight of armed guards was enough to rightfully irritate him. He knew that it was long overdue time for planet Earth to advance and do away with paranoia, arms and weapons, locks of all types, and most of all, to do away with hatred and wars.

Caymar and Dotsero joined Tom, and they gave the president and prime minister a grand tour of all the facilities, including Morris' mysterious requiem above the apex. They were very impressed with that, along with the functioning of all the equipment in the main room. Tom and Caymar explained the reasoning behind the whole project and that the purpose of the whole galactic station was to achieve galactic communication, no doubt, in addition to peaceful friendly interaction among different galactic races. The requiem above was a sign that dolphins would be a major link to this station, helping to provide a telepathic mindset designed at achieving peace and dispelling bad energy systems throughout.

"So fellows," Tom concluded, "I think you can understand why we strongly and quickly object to weapons in our facility."

"Yes sir!" the president quickly acknowledged. "We do request your pardon."

They escorted the president and prime minister to the project room where the

Atlanteans' device-craft was located. A brief explanation, omitting details, was given them, basically explaining that it was a major help to the project.

With that done, the president and prime minister left. They walked out of the tunnel onto the glacier, rejoined their armed guards, and returned to the stone lodge where they were staying.

After the important tour, the rest of them took experiences in the soul travel device.

The first block of Earth's telephone numbers had been freed up. A new area code, 718, had just been added to New York City. The now available 212 prefixes and lines were beamed up to Alaska, partially by satellite and also by the buried fiberoptic cable in Alaska. Caymar moved a big lever upwards and brought the new block of numbers to life.

"Rinto, Fraxino, and Chispo," Tom said to them, "in honor of your planet Artenia around your star, Al Nitak, and in recognition of the fact that Earth was blocked from your star system for over 12,000 years, we have done your people an honor by connecting Artenia's phone system to Earth, first and foremost before the others. Honor us by being the first to use our phone system here in our galactic station."

"Wow!" Chispo commented, being the first to respond.

"First and before the president!" Fraxino happily stated.

"Chispo, you be first," Rinto urged him. "Why don't you call your cousin Cliss?"

"Yeah, good idea, man." Chispo walked up to the phone instrument hanging on a rack at the base of the main frame central. "Wow! It's a dial phone with twelve holes." He picked up the handset and heard a strange dial tone. "So, what do I dial?"

"763 is the star system code for Al Nitak," Tom explained. "Then dial the local code and number."

Chispo dialled the number and soon heard the ringing on the line. It sounded a little distant, but that was still pretty good, since Echelosa, Caloma was 76.3 light years away. He laughed in amazement as he heard the ringing on the line. Suddenly, the call was answered, and a voice spoke.

"Cliss?" Chispo spoke, immediately recognizing his cousin's voice.

"Chispo, is that you?"

"It is, dude."

"You sound so distant. Where are you?"

"Man, you're not going to believe where I'm calling from."

"No, where?"

"I'm here at the galactic station on Earth's Alaska, man."

"You *what*?! Really?!" Cliss reacted, no doubt surprised. "On Earth's Alaska?"

"That's right, man. This call is history," Chispo boasted. "This is the first intergalactic call to be placed over this new station."

"The first one?!"

"That's right," Chispo verified.

"Wow! What an honor, Chispo."

"So how are things up there in Echelosa?"

"They're going great, man," Cliss answered. "Did you and Chameur enjoy the rest of your trip?"

"Oh yeah, man. We went over to the Tarima District and . . ."

Chispo and Cliss talked a few more minutes. Then they wished each other well and hung up.

History was made. The first phone call had been completed. The time was 2:30 PM, Friday, August 16, 1985. It was just the beginning. Plenty more phone calls would be placed in the future.

Tom and Caymar telephoned Manta at the telephone station on Sirius B.

The others looked on. Robert told Steven, Chris and Richard about the book they had just compiled: *The Heritage of Atlantis.*

"You've got 250 of them in Rinto and Fraxino's craft?" Steven asked in a surprised manner.

"Sure do."

"Yeah, I'll be glad to have one," said Steven.

Chris and Richard expressed the same interest, as well.

Rinto and Fraxino called their parents, and they called a few friends of theirs in Zantaayer, also. Their friends were quite surprised, needless to say.

"Is the Pleiades connected yet?" Steven asked.

"Not yet," Caymar replied. "We hope to have them connected by the weekend."

"Their star system code will be 363," Tom informed them.

"What about our world?" Richard asked.

"It may getting connected as we speak," Tom answered.

"Let's see if it works," said Caymar. "What's the code for the Planet of the Islands?"

"567," Tom answered. "Chris and Richard, what's the number for your family?"

"3649."

Caymar dialed 567-3649, and the call went through. "Here, Richard. It's ringing."

The line answered.

"Mom?" Richard spoke.

"Oh hi, son. How are you?"

"Fine. You're going to be amazed where I'm calling from . . ."

They talked a few minutes. Chris came on the line after Richard, and they spoke a few more minutes.

When the call was finished, Tom declared, "The station works perfectly!"

"Amazing what utilizing gravity waves makes possible," Caymar commented.

"The miracle carrier wave," said Tom.

"Anyway, fellows," Caymar announced, "that completes our major work here."

"Of course, over the next 15 years," Tom explained, "many more blocks of phone numbers will be made available to this station, and my crew and I will be coming from time to time for maintenance and addition of lines. We'll also be rather busy teleporting ourselves to different star systems, connecting telephone exchanges, connecting telepathic imagery machines, soul travel, and of course connecting a special type of experience apparatus from the world, Delikadove, where Morris presently is."

"Wonder what that will be?" Steven asked.

"Morris has yet to tell us," Tom answered, "but he says he and the dolphins are working on it now."

"Huh! Interesting," said Steven.

Tom paid Steven, Chris and Richard for the rest of their work. The Sirian crew silently teleported away. Dotsero and a few remained. They would later walk outside and take the spacecraft home to Sirius B.

"So, let's see how the Atlantean time travel device works," Caymar requested.

All of them walked out of the pyramid room and into the project room. Latorna and Tecoloteh were already there, inside the device-craft.

"Where do you suggest we time travel first?" Latorna asked Chameur and Chispo.

"I'd really love to visit Zantaayer in their 10,130 year ago past."

"I would, too," said Latorna. "I want Cresma to know all the things that happened to us and that we still live."

"That would appease him very much," said Chameur.

"You know," Fraxino brought up, "you all never told us how you move this thing. Going back in time right here will lock you in place, the ice of the glacier being . . ."

"That's right, we never told you," Seglima answered. "Want to break the news to them?" she now asked Latorna.

"Yes, go ahead. Now's the time."

"We instilled in our main controls crystal," Seglima explained, "very similarly to how you fellows did it, the intelligence to make this device-craft levitate, fly, and teleport to other worlds."

"That's how we moved our device-craft from Atlantis up here to Alaska all that time ago," Latorna explained.

"Wow!" Rinto exclaimed. "So, *that's* how it worked."

"What we lacked was the time travel intelligence, which we now have," Seglima continued to explain.

"Once we contact Cresma," Quicho informed them, "were going to design and grow appeasement crystals, using information and data we've collected from, for one the Quanac flowers, and perform a mission to dispel and neutralize the bad energies of planet Earth."

"Excellent plans!" Fraxino praised them.

"A lot of it is already programmed," Quicho replied. "We just need to grow the crystals."

"Want to come back with us to Zantaayer?" Rinto invited.

"Yes, definitely," Seglima answered.

"We'll follow you," said Tecoloteh.

Latorna and Tecoloteh went over to the five bronze crates in which they had been time frozen. They were sitting out in the project room. One by one, they carried them inside the device-craft and stacked them on top of each other, to take them to their friend, Cresma.

Robert walked over to them. "Rinto, Fraxino, and Chispo, It's been great knowing you and becoming friends with you and the Atlanteans."

"Man, we've really had some adventures this past month and a half," said Chispo.

"Steven and I are going to visit the Planet of the Islands some more with Chris and Richard."

"Take care, Robert, Steven, the rest of you, and the others when you see them," said Rinto.

"Oh yeah, my books," said Robert suddenly. "I need to unload them and have them taken to the step office building in the corner of my woods."

"I can teleport those books to Tennessee with you, right now," Tom offered.

Tom, Caymar, and Robert walked out the tunnel to the glacier. Rinto, Fraxino, and Chispo came with them.

"Hey, Robert!" Steven called out.

"Yeah?"

"Chris and Richard and I and Mr. Mayfield are going to transport to the Planet of the Islands. We'll see you there shortly."

"That's fine. I'll see you there."

They transported away, using the energy of the pink glow and whirring wind.

The others reached the glacier. Rinto opened the door to the cruiser-craft, and Robert and Tom unloaded the ten boxes of books along with Robert's backpack and supplies.

"Robert, I'll see you at the step office," Tom said. He used his walking staff and created an energy around the boxes, which soon teleported away, along with Tom and Caymar.

Robert looked at Rinto, Fraxino, and Chispo.

"See you around, Robert," said Chispo. "Good luck distributing those 250 books."

"Thanks, Chispo."

They shook hands.

"Later on, Robert," said Fraxino. "Come visit us anytime."

"You know how to find us," said Rinto. They shook hands.

"Thanks for everything," Robert told them.

Robert placed his hands on either side of himself, brought on the energy of the pink glow and whirring wind, and transported himself home. Tom and Caymar were there waiting for him with the ten boxes of books, having safely arrived. They stored them near the back corner of the building, away from the racks, frames, and Strowger switches.

"Thanks so much, Tom," said Robert. "Here take a copy each with you." Robert opened one of the boxes, took out two books, and handed them to Tom and Caymar.

"Thank you," said Caymar. "This will make for very interesting reading."

Tom also thanked him.

"Well, Robert," Tom stated, "this galactic communications device is now obsolete."

"It was our practice run," said Caymar.

"But in honor of what it is, it will remain open indefinitely," Tom added.

"That's good to hear," said Robert.

"Robert, good luck to you and all your friends," Tom sincerely told him.

"Come see us on Sirius B," said Caymar.

"And at the galactic station in Alaska," Tom also said.

They both said goodbye to Robert and teleported away to Sirius B. Robert went into the barn and freed up his Ford LTD station wagon that he and his friends had hidden within stacks of hay bales in one of the barn halls. He moved all the hay bales aside, started it, and drove it down to his house. He would visit with his parents, spend a night at home, and transport to the Planet of the Islands tomorrow. He used the phone, and through the galactic communications step office there in the corner of the woods, he called Chris and Richard to let them know.

Meanwhile, back on Mt. Isto in Alaska, Rinto, Fraxino, and Chispo were somewhat startled to suddenly see the Atlantean device-craft emerge from the ice tunnel and float over to hesitate beside their cruiser craft.

"Oh wow!" Fraxino declared.

Chispo laughed in amazement. They had not been aware of the device-craft's having any visual window, but now they realized it did have a small round window on the left end, which was now the front end of the craft. The door on the right opened, and Chameur stepped down.

"We're ready to follow you to Zantaayer," she told them. "Once we're there, we'll make the trip back in time. For now, I'm riding with you."

Chispo felt really good about that, and Chameur boarded Rinto and Fraxino's craft with Chispo. Rinto got in the driver's seat, pulled back the lever, and in seconds they swiftly accelerated over Mt. Isto's ridge. The other four Atlanteans in the device-craft followed them likewise, and both crafts disappeared in a green flash.

The spacecraft remained on the glacier. Dotsero and his crew would soon close up the tunnel and fly the large craft home to Sirius B.

EPILOGUE

Over the next 15 years, the galactic station grew. Tom and Caymar, with some of their crew, made periodic visits to add blocks of phone lines and other equipment and to add star systems from throughout the galaxy. Government officials came from all over the world from time to time, and they stayed in the stone lodge. Tom and Caymar left their hut standing in the cove permantly, as they used it during their periodic visits. Besides, it gave them privacy from other government beings.

Spacecrafts and navess from other star systems and galactic civilizations made frequent visits to the galactic station. They could be seen landing in the cove. Some of them also used the lodge as accommodation, as it was open to all visitors. These galactic officials often came to oversee the connecting of their world to the galactic station. Being representatives from their star systems, they were the authorized ones to give approval and report back to their appropriate governments on their worlds.

The galactic station also became a place of data storage, to be accessible by the public via computer modems and the *Internet*. Several blocks of phone numbers moved to Alaska were set aside specifically for special use server lines to give the general public access to the data bases. Eventually, soul travel and even time travel experiences telepathically accessible, via computer modems and the *Internet*, became available through the galactic station. These experiences were even dialable from other star systems.

Long distance carriers began levying a "Universal Service Fund," including a "Carrier Line Charge," for beaming the numbers to Alaska, and a "Universal Connectivity Charge," to fund the connecting of the lines to the galactic station and to other star systems.

Near the turn of the millennium, federation mandate placed several satellites in appropriate orbits to send and receive calls, signals, and various other telepathic transferences. Some of the satellites even accommodated galactic visitors and officials from various star systems. A masterpiece of its time, Earth's galactic station in Alaska would become a central pivot of communication and peace throughout.

*   *   *

Rinto, Fraxino, Chispo and Chameur, and the other four Atlanteans safely arrived to Zantaayer. They made their appearance over the Ciruclar Mountains and came in for a landing on the rim road. Rinto and Fraxino parked their vehicle-craft on the roadside at the top of the gully, after which they boarded the Atlanteans' device-craft. They became airborne, and cruising the treetops, they carefully made their way down the steep and treacherous gully to the cave entrance below.

From that point, while inside the device-craft, they travelled back in time 10,130 Artenian years. They floated over the now grassy Ciruclar Mountains and descended into a much smaller Zantaayer, a city of buildings and houses with hovercrafts and flying vessels.

They recognized some of their friends who were overjoyed to see them, and they guided them to Cresma Atenkor's residence on the eastern side of the city nearest the sea. When they arrived at his residence and Cresma came to the door, a look of absolute surprise crossed his face. Tears came to his eyes, and he cried with joy to see his lost friends. He happily greeted them, and he immediately welcomed them inside where they introduced Rinto, Fraxino, and Chispo from the future Zantaayer.

Cresma had just returned home after inspecting the two bronze crates of tablets, and he had just sent out a mandate for collecting all questionable crystals, scheduled for a mass dumping at the galactic dump site next week.

They told Cresma the whole story, how they had been time frozen, found in Alaska 10,130 Artenian years in the future, and revived from their time frozen sleep. They explained to him about the 3D holographic movie their device-craft had recorded and shown to them when they rediscovered their device-craft inside Mt. Isto, and they really surprised Cresma when they played the movie for him, showing the senseless mass dumping, that from their future, really took place.

Cresma saw reason and was now shocked at what he was about to have done.

"Thank you, my good friends, for your fortunate forewarning," Cresma sincerely told them. "I will instead set up a museum to safeguard the crystals, that would have been dumped, as a national treasure, a heritage collection from our Atlantis."

"Excellent!" Chameur told Cresma. "I'm glad we reached you in time."

They went on to explain to Cresma about the two bronze crates of data tablets and holographic plates, and that they would need to be specifically buried exactly as shown in the 3D movie to fulfill the destiny time loop, so that Rinto, Fraxino, and his friends would find them.

Physical copies would need to be made of the originals, pertaining to various egg-shaped crystals and a certain Calcite sacred story stone from Vega, also to fulfill the destiny time loop. They were to be carefully placed at the galactic dump site. In fact the final decision was made to proceed with the mass dumping operation, the only difference being to make physical copies of the original crystals and safeguard all originals in a museum . . . which would later become a part of Zantaayer's central library.

Arrangements were made, and with Rinto, Fraxino, Chispo, and the five Atlanteans overseeing it, the mass dumping of the physical copies was carried out successfully.

Rinto felt the most relieved of all, that this important error and turning point in Artenian history had been corrected. They presented Cresma a copy of their book: *The Heritage of Atlantis*, which he was very glad to receive.

The eight of them ended up staying for two weeks. There were so many friends for the five Atlanteans to visit with, and they were so intrigued by their exotic story and also by their mission to neutralize Earth's bad energy systems.

As a sidenote, a decision was made for a wedding to take place, for Chispo and Chameur to become married. They would have the wedding among Zantaayer's original residents with Cresma conducting the ceremony, after which Chispo and Chameur would travel forward in time and live in Zantaayer's 10,130 year future. Of course Rinto and Fraxino attended the wedding and were Chispo's best men. Chameur's four friends were her best men and maids of honor, and a grand wedding it was, with festivities following the ceremony. This was truly a joining across time and destiny between two worlds and star systems.

The decision was made by Latorna and Tecoloteh to grow the appropriate crystals in old Zantaayer, then take them forward through time to Earth's year 2000 AD, and place the crystals on one of the high mountain tops of Antarctica, to transmit peace giving qualities, love, and forgiveness to all of planet Earth. Rinto, Fraxino, Chispo and Chameur accompanied them on the mission.

Latorna, Tecoloteh, Quicho and Seglima, after their mission to Earth's future, made the decision to stay in old Zantaayer. Cresma was glad to have them reunited with him and his friends again.

Chameur continued living with Chispo at his house in Zantaayer. The Colanchas were very glad to have her for a daughter-in-law. They attended the University of Zotola together, and Chameur became well renowned throughout Zantaayer for her uniqueness and her knowledge and expertise about Atlantis. Her friends, Quicho, Seglima, Latorna and Tecoloteh sometimes came forward in time and visited them, sometimes bringing Cresma to visit, as well. At times, Chispo and Chameur went back with them to old Zantaayer so Chameur could visit her friends and relatives. Sometimes, Rinto and Fraxino joined in as well, and they went travelling together, enjoying the pleasures of life.

Zotola's news media was spellbound with mouths dropped open upon the arrival of an anonymous copy of *The Heritage of Atlantis*. The chief editor of Zantaayer's newspaper got out of his chair, the book in hand, and walked into the press room immediately! Soon newspapers throughout the region wrote a major 10-page story about the mysterious arrival of the book, a document of their heritage from the past, and the major points discussed in the book were printed in the 10-page story, along with copies of some of the illustrations that came with it.

The story was the talk of the town, actually the whole planet, for months to come. Who had written and compiled that excellent historical document: *The Heritage of Atlantis*? For several months, Rinto, Fraxino, Chispo and Chameur managed to keep a lid on it, by not yet releasing the nearly thousand copies they had in stock. However, on the day of Cresma at the beginning of the year 10131, they performed a launch of the book and caused its release to numerous bookstores throughout Zotola, Caloma, and eventually the whole of planet Artenia. The launching ceremony took place in Zantaayer's largest bookstore. Cresma Atenkor travelled forward in time for the event, and he did the honors by giving the opening speech.

The four of them became world renowned historians, and well respected they were. *The Heritage of Atlantis* was the first of several documents that they wrote and produced.

For years to come, Chispo and Chameur travelled across the whole of Artenia, gathering information about archaeological artifacts, coming across various ancient legends, including finding origins of anomalies, myths and beliefs. Throughout their travels, they were lucky enough to come across a few sacred story stones, as well. They continued to know Rinto and Fraxino, and when they were at home in Zantaayer, they frequently crossed the row of bushes between their backyards, doing different projects with each other.

Rinto became a part-time professor of ancient history at Zantaayer's University of Zotola. Fraxino became a geologist, studying rocks, crystals, and minerals. He excelled and became an authority in his field. He frequently led student groups to different sites outside Zantaayer to go rock hunting. Both of them were highly admired for their uniqueness and accomplishments.

A few students were fortunate enough to become good friends with Rinto and Fraxino, and they helped them with some of their future projects. Rinto and Fraxino rewarded them by taking them on exotic trips in their Velosa cruiser craft, to visit Earth, and also other worlds.

*　　*　　*

For the most part, Robert and his friends went back to their normal lives. They returned to Tennessee at the end of the summer in September and attended their senior year of high school.

Mr. Mayfield had enjoyed his summer on the Planet of the Islands, and during Physics classes, he was known to frequently tell some tall tales including, needless to say, stories from the Planet of the Islands, along with other far-fetched concepts and speculation pertaining to future galactic communication with other star systems. His stories were very entertaining, especially to Robert and his friends, who kept quiet about what they really knew.

Robert became a writer and made his career writing science fiction, along with other historical documents. He continued to live on the family farm.

Andrew had spent the rest of the summer in Bustamante, enjoying his relationship with Perlona and her family. He really felt at home with the Mexicans, visiting at times with Roel, Rudy, Alvaro and Pegaso. Orolizo and Lumela had become great friends with Pegaso and his two sisters. They had enjoyed their trip to Puerto Vallarta. Before Andrew returned to Tennessee, he transported Orolizo and Lumela back to their homeland in the mountains of southern Zotola.

Morris ended up spending the rest of his life with the dolphins on Delikadove. Though the others never knew it, he sent a holographic copy of himself back to Earth to go through the motions of attending his senior year of high school and living his lifetime on Earth. Once he graduated, his copy, being in telepathic contact with his original on Delikadove, started writing a book about dolphins and their origins. It was finished the next year, and the book became a grand success with world renowned status.

Chris eventually became a philosophy professor at the local university. He obtained his Ph.D. from Nebraska.

Steven studied engineering, and he became a well respected consultant for the government, in addition to his continuance in helping Tom and Caymar with their maintenance and upgrading of the galactic station from time to time.

James forgot to come home from planet Aleyone in the Pleiades, where he spent the rest of the summer with Suzanne. When three days of school had gone by, his parents became very concerned that he was lost. Robert's friends had to explain that James had separated from the group and had decided to travel on his own. Meanwhile, Robert transported himself to Aleyone to fetch him. Upon Robert's arrival, James reacted with surprise. He admitted that he had simply lost track of the time, not realizing that it was already September.

Paul made his career in the cabinet manufacturing business with his father, and William went to work with the telephone company.

Throughout their lifetimes, the eight of them would have reunions and meet out at Robert's farm to go camping in the woods. Sometimes, they transported themselves to other worlds for a weekend adventure, enjoying their permanent gift of transport from Tom.

From time to time, Rinto, Fraxino, Chispo and Chameur would come and visit Robert and his friends in Tennessee, and they would sometimes take them travelling to Artenia, as well. Chispo also visited several friends of his he had made during the previous year when he had stayed in Tennessee.

Over the course of time, Earth became a more peaceful planet. Positive energies prevailed more and more, thanks to the Fluorite peace keeping crystal being returned to Earth and being placed on Mt. Timpanogos, the Quanac flowers being planted at Vancouver Island, and of course, the peace giving crystals the Atlanteans had placed way up high in the mountains of Antarctica.

Appendix: Technical Description of Characters

10 Main Characters:

Chameur:
species: human being, Atlantean type
height: 5' 7"
hair: black, long and straight
eyes: brown
appearance: very beautiful, tall and slender, appearing to be in her early 20's,

Colancha, Chispo:
species: human being, Zotolan type, descendant from Atlantis
height: 6 feet
hair: dark brown, straight, medium length
eyes: green-brown (more green than brown)
appearance: tall and slender, appearing to be in his 20's, somewhat longer face,

Joslin, Robert:
species: human being, Earth type
height: 5' 10"
hair: medium brown, slightly curly, shorter length
eyes: green-brown (more green than brown)
appearance: slender and strong with somewhat long, narrow face, age 18,

Latorna:
species: human being, Atlantean type
height: 5' 8"
hair: black, long and straight
eyes: brown
appearance: slender and beautiful but with an imposing stature, appearing to be in her mid 20's,

Price, Steven:
species: human being, Earth type
height: 5' 10"
hair: light brown, straight, medium length
eyes: blue
appearance: slender and strong with somewhat rounded face, age 17,

Quicho:
species: human being, Atlantean type
height: 5' 9"
hair: dark brown, straight, medium length
eyes: dark brown
appearance: slender with rounded face, appearing to be in his early 20's,

Seglima:
species: human being, Atlantean type
height: 5' 6"
hair: black, curly, medium length
eyes: dark brown
appearance: slender with somewhat rounded face, appearing to be in her early 20's,

Tecoloteh:
species: human being, Atlantean type
height: 5' 9"
hair: black, medium length, straight
eyes: dark brown
appearance: slender and strong with somewhat longer face, appearing to be in his mid 20's,

Zapatero, Fraxino:
species: human being, Zotolan type, descendant from Atlantis
height: 6 feet
hair: reddish-blond, straight, shorter length
eyes: green brown (more brown than green)
appearance: slender and strong, appearing to be in his 20's, more of a squarish face,

Zapatero, Rinto:
species: human being, Zotolan type, descendant from Atlantis
height: 5' 11"
hair: dark brown, mostly straight, longer length
eyes: green-brown
appearance: tall and slender, appearing to be in his 20's, somewhat rounded face.

Other Characters:

Bell, Chris:
species: human being, from Garnet Star
height: 6' 1"
hair: brown, fairly short
eyes: green-brown
appearance: tall and slender, squarish face, dressed in Earth-type clothing,

Bell, Richard:
species: human being, from Garnet Star
height: 6' 2"
hair: brown, medium length
eyes: green-brown
appearance: tall and slender, squarish face, dressed in Earth-type clothing,

Caymar:
species: human being, Sirian type
height: 6 feet
hair: dark brown, medium length
eyes: brown
appearance: tall and slender, appearing to be in his 20's, somewhat longer face,

Chanford, Chris:
species: human being, Earth type
height: 5' 10"
hair: brown, straight, medium length
eyes: brown
appearance: slender and strong with somewhat rounded face, age 17,

Cliss:
species: human being, Zotolan type, descendant from Atlantis
height: 5' 11"
hair: very light brown, straight, medium length
eyes: green-brown
appearance: slender, rounded face, appearing to be in his early 20's,

Crate of holographic plates:
species: irrelevant
size: the same as a footlocker
appearance: crate made of tarnished bronze
description: crate contains 144 bronze metal tablets with holographic material containing data,

2nd crate of bronze data tablets:
species: irrelevant size: 1 meter by 50 cm by 30 cm, a little smaller than the crate of holographic plates
appearance: crate made of tarnished bronze
description: crate contains numerous bronze data tablets with hieroglyphs casted into them; small crystals and holographic segments also fastened to most of the tablets,

Crystal Base Computer:
Rinto and Fraxino's computer operates by the use of a Ulexite cube and a crystal array serving as an information processor, instead of operating by programs, disks, and hard drives. It is also interfaced with a monitor and a keyboard as an adaptation to accommodate more Earthly related matters. They use it to read the holographic plates and also to analyze other crystals.

England, Morris:
species: human being, Earth type
height: 5' 8"
hair: dark brown, mostly straight, shorter length
eyes: brown
appearance: strong and stocky with long, rounded face, age 18,

Egg shaped crystals:
species: crystal, silicon type,
origin: artificially grown on Earth over 100,000 years ago
race or color: Quartz, clear
length: 10 centimeters from end to end
appearance: egg-shaped, known for containing ghostly image of a tree cone within,

Esalina:
species: human being, Zotolan type, descendant from Atlantis
height: 5' 7"
hair: light brown, straight, longer length
eyes: brown
appearance: slender, medium height, appearing to be in her 50's, somewhat long but also rounded face,

Exotic Crystal, (Fluorite peace keeping crystal of Atlantis)

species: crystal, silicon type

origin: artificially grown on Earth over 100,000 years ago, stolen from Atlantis over 15,000 years ago, recovered from Aleyone in the Pleiades, returned to Earth, and left on slopes of Mt. Timpanogos in Utah in first novel,

race or color: Green Fluorite and Citrine (orange)

length (end to end): 25 centimeters

appearance: egg-shaped, greenish-blue appearing in various shades or bands throughout, contains orange colored pyramid within,

Lumela:

species: human being, Zotolan type

race or color: Atascosan, a beautiful olive green complexion, native of planet Artenia

height: 5' 6"

hair: brown, straight, longer length

eyes: green-brown (more green than brown)

appearance: exquisitely beautiful and attractive, appearing to be in her late teens,

Orolizo:

species: human being, Zotolan type

race or color: Atascosan, slightly green, native of planet Artenia

height: 5' 11"

hair: dark brown, straight, medium length

eyes: brown

appearance: slender, medium build, appearing to be in his 20's, rounded, almost squarish face,

Orolizo, Pegaso:

species: human being, Earth type, Mexican

height: 5' 11"

hair: black, curly, very short

eyes: dark brown

appearance: tall and stocky, imposing stature, somewhat squarish face, age 18,

Roel:

species: human being, Earth type, Mexican

height: 5' 10"

hair: black, straight, medium length

eyes: dark brown

appearance: slender and strong with somewhat rounded face, age 16,

Rudy:

species: human being, Earth type, Mexican

height: 5' 9"

hair: black, straight, shorter length

eyes: brown

appearance: slender and strong with somewhat squarish face, age 15,

Sacred Story Stone:

species: crystal, silicon type

race or color: Calcite, orange

origin: Vega, known for relating a sacred story

length or size: 15 centimeters from end to end

appearance: orange rock with holographic filmstrip pasted onto it, from 150,000 to 200,000 years old,

Tomarius (Tom), the galactic salesman:

species: human being, Sirian type

height: 6' 4"

hair: nearly black, mostly straight, longer length

eyes: brown

appearance: tall and slender, almost boyish with somewhat longer face; wears a white robe,

Tremain, Andrew:

species: human being, Earth type

height: 5' 9"

hair: black, straight, medium length

eyes: brown

appearance: slender and strong with somewhat narrow but rounded face, age 17,

Zapatero, Glecko

species: human being, Zotolan type, descendant from Atlantis

height: 5' 9"

hair: mostly grey, straight, medium length

eyes: brown

appearance: stocky build, appearing to be in his 60's, rounded face,

Zapatero, Sosta:

species: human being, Zotolan type, descendant from Atlantis

height: 5' 7"

hair: brownish-grey, straight, longer length

eyes: brown

appearance: somewhat tall and mostly slender, appearing to be in her 50's, somewhat long, narrow face.

Acknowledgments

It was in January 1995 that I began writing my first novel: MISSION OF THE GALACTIC SALESMAN. I remember one day that a friend of mine told me how interesting it would be to write a novel about a human civilization on another star system on the same level of technological advancement as we are here on Earth. He is the real Fraxino of this story. I am grateful to him for giving me the seed from which I wrote this novel's prequel (published 1999): MISSION BEYOND THE ICE CAVE: *Atlantis-Mexico-Zotola*.

It was in October, 1998 that I began to write my third novel, this novel: HERITAGE FINDINGS FROM ATLANTIS. I wasn't sure where to carry the theme from book two. I had written some more holographic plates that I knew my characters were going to examine on their crystal base computer, back in Zantaayer, Zotola on Al Nitak's planet Artenia.

As I was in regular communication with Martin A. Enticknap, he came forth and volunteered an offer one morning by phone. He told me he had been thinking a lot about my third novel recently and that he saw a vision and had some good ideas for it. Since I was somewhat at a loss for ideas at the time, I accepted Martin's offer, his ideas and suggestions with eagerness, and good ideas they were indeed! He suggested that I have my characters go to northern Alaska to assist in the building of a secret galactic station, and while they are there, they can find several frozen crates with Atlantean bodies. They revive them, and they become a major part of the project, including telling my characters where their hidden equipment exists, deep within a mountain. I took two pages of handwritten notes, and I stand amazed at Martin's ability to tune into a story's energy systems and capture the plot and theme of the story better than I could do it myself. He also receives credit for helping me figure out the title, especially pertaining to the words *Heritage* and *Atlantis*. That was in March 2000 when I was already writing chapter 10.

It was in June 1994 that I met Martin when I walked into a remote mountain refuge hut. He related to me some exotic stories and various experiences, some of which I found very interesting. I appreciate the time he has spent talking with me since that fateful day. Over many conversations, he has told me his views on human philosophy, and he was very helpful with reading, reviewing, and giving me suggestions for my novels, along with ideas and concepts he requested I include in my story. It was Martin who had initially related to me a story about a galactic salesman offering him a crystal ball in a dream.

I am grateful to Martin for all the help and ideas he has supplied me, and in addition to that, the fabulous wrap around cover image he surprised me with when he emailed it to me in May 2000. He definitely receives a 100% for that fine piece of artwork, which he did on his computer paint program.

Martin A. Enticknap is the author of EXODUS: the Dolph/in Saga, published 1999, ISBN 1-928798-35-7. I acknowledge the use of the words and concepts of: *Danetar*, *Delikadove*, and *Dolph*, which came from his novel, a very interesting story about the dolphins on their old home world of Delikadove, their way of life and culture, and why they came to Earth 35 million years ago.

I am very grateful to Jesús Lucio of Bustamante, Nuevo León for five times (from January 1999 through July 2000) letting me stay at his remote ranch house in a desert valley some 18 kilometers out of town, a place where I was able to be by myself so I could concentrate and write this novel without the daily distractions and interruptions back home in Tennessee. I also appreciate the two times in 1997 that Sr. Lucio took me and some friends to see Chiquihuitillos, the ancient paintings on the mesa sidewalls in the same desert valley of northern Mexico.

Finding an artist was not easily done. David M. Dubois, the artist for my sequel, though I made several efforts, just could not be talked into doing the artwork for this novel, partly because he was preoccupied that he would not have the time. Whatever mysterious reasoning was behind that, I met with some success when I met Mark J. Volzer at a Sci-Fi convention in Memphis, Tennessee in March, 2000. Mark, a smart, competent fellow, successfully completed the drawings for me, and I'm grateful to him for having gone to the trouble of doing the drawings, making it possible for this novel to have illustrations, something I deem as important.

It was in March, 2000 that I had really given up on ever receiving a decent answer to my *Query for the Reader* at the back of my novels. Then the very next month, I met with blessing sure enough when a recent friend of mine stepped forth and surprised me by admitting that he knew a lot of information *mas allá*, including data about trees, their origins, and star systems. He is known as Yalí Peré Grinanón-N, and he has literally answered my *Query for the Reader*. I stand amazed at the voluminous knowledge he has within his mind, and I'm very grateful to him for answering that subject of interest that I'm still researching: trees of extraterrestrial origin. It's incredible how well destiny worked on that one, that someone actually came out of the woodwork and answered my query.

I thank Roberto Ipinza of the country of Chile for kindly answering a query of mine by phone and email pertaining to the indigenous names of various Southern Beech (*Nothofagus*) tree species that grow in Chile. He also referred me to a book called: *Botanica Indígena de Chile*.

I am thankful to Paul Wulfsberg for reading, editing, and reviewing this novel in June, 2000.

I am grateful to Patrick E. Parris and April Stevens at Parris Graphics & Printing in Murfreesboro, Tennessee for producing the book cover design and for typesetting the entire text, including the illustrations, by converting my Lotus Ami Pro files to Adobe Page Maker so that they could be readable by the equipment at Lightning Source, Inc.

I thank Janet Young and Olivia Tackett at Lightning Source, Inc. in LaVergne, Tennessee for the publishing, printing, and distribution of this novel and its prequel.

I also thank the Kearney family of Murfreesboro, Tennessee for having referred me to Lightning Source, Inc. in November, 1998 and also for their advice and consultation.

I am grateful to have met and known certain people over the past several years from whom I have derived takeoffs for this novel and its prequel: especially the real Chispo, Rinto, Fraxino, Roel, Rudy, and Morris. Some of them remain my true friends.

I am grateful to my family and parents for their support as I wrote this novel, and I am grateful to all of those who have supported me and have bought a copy of this novel for their reading enjoyment. Most of all, I sincerely appreciate all of those who are my *true* friends and *will remain* my true friends through life.

A QUERY FOR THE READER

If you are someone who astral travels to other star systems and are also very interested in trees and shrubs, knowing and having paid special attention to details, such as specific species types, and also knowing which specific star systems you've travelled to, I would like to talk to you about which trees grow where and how they compare to Earth's trees and shrubs, whether the same or different. This is an ongoing subject of interest I am researching. Please contact me.

Robert S. Sanders, Jr.
Armstrong Valley Publishing Company
P.O. Box 1275
Murfreesboro, TN 37133 USA
office: 1-615-895-5445
Fax: 1-615-893-2688

Robert S. Sanders, Jr.

Copies of
1)*Mission of the Galactic Salesman*
2)*Mission Beyond the Ice Cave: Atlantis-Mexico-Zotola*
3)*Heritage Findings from Atlantis*
are available directly from the author at the above listed Armstrong Valley Publishing Company. They may also be ordered at retail price directly from Ingram Book Company of LaVergne, Tennessee.

ORDER FORM

Please send me: quantity amount

Mission of the Galactic Salesman

special reduced price @$12.00 _____ $ _____

Mission Beyond the Ice Cave: Atlantis-Mexico-Zotola

@$15.95 _____ $ _____

Heritage Findings from Atlantis

@$15.95 _____ $ _____

subtotal $ _____

Tennessee residents add 8.75% sales tax to subtotal $ _____

Plus shipping and handling for one book
  (surface rates: $3.00 within USA, $5.00 foreign) $ _____

Plus shipping and handling for each additional book
  (surface rates: $2.00 within USA, $3.00 foreign) $ _____

Please remit funds in US dollars.
Total enclosed $ _____

Make checks or money orders payable to the author: **Robert S. Sanders, Jr.**
Discounts:
10 to 99 books: 10% off
100 or more books: 20% off

Books make great gifts for your friends and relatives.

Name _____

Address _____

City _____ State_____Postal Code_____

Phone number (optional) _____

Send order to:

Robert S. Sanders, Jr.
Armstrong Valley Publishing Company
P.O. Box 1275
Murfreesboro, TN 37133 USA
office: 1-615-895-5445
Fax: 1-615-893-2688

www.ingramcontent.com/pod-product-compliance
Lightning Source LLC
Chambersburg PA
CBHW031829090426
42741CB00005B/184

Section 3: Personal Development

FORWARD

My Message To All Daughters

My sincere hope is that you read this book not just as an intellectual, but as a daughter. If possible, I ask you to set aside the name of the author and approach this book for what it is, as a letter. While fathers may come in all shapes and sizes, the heart of true fathers are all one alike. We fathers all fear the same, hurt the same, hope the same, and love the same. We share all the same thoughts, feelings, and intentions in our efforts to be good fathers, even if those efforts fall short of their objective. So, as you read these letters, it makes little to no difference whether they come from your father, because the sentiments herein emanates from that same heart, we all possess.

Through the love I have for my daughter, how could I not love you? Therefore, as I address my daughter in this book, I am also addressing all daughters. With that said, I begin by apologizing to you for the imperfections of us fathers. I acknowledge you deserve so much more than we can give you. In fact, you deserve much more than anything we could ever give you. As fathers, we are responsible for providing something much more valuable than material gifts. As your father, it was my responsibly to partake in this journey of life and ultimately secure the jewels necessary for the sustainment of your personal wellbeing. These jewels being life lessons you would need in your journey. But as we fathers set out to acquire these jewels of life, what if we ourselves are ill-equipped to complete this task? What if the father lacks the necessary life lessons to navigate his own journey? My daughter, I ask you to empathize as this is exactly what is occurring every single day with us imperfect fathers. We partake in life's journey without the lessons we need for our own well-being and find ourselves lost, and thus unable to see you off on your journey. This leads to so many daughters partaking on their life journey unprepared.

Now having acquired these jewels of life for both you and I, even after being absent for most of your life, my desire is to give you what little I have in hopes you can derive some type of benefit for the remainder of your journey. There is so much a father provides by his physical presence, yet there is nothing you will need more from me than a guiding perspective. In the time of your development, when you